Communicating
the Law

Communicating the Law

Lessons from Landmark Legal Cases

Janice Schuetz
The University of New Mexico

WAVELAND

PRESS, INC.

Long Grove, Illinois

For information about this book, contact:
    Waveland Press, Inc.
    4180 IL Route 83, Suite 101
    Long Grove, IL 60047-9580
    (847) 634-0081
    info@waveland.com
    www.waveland.com

My dedication is to the scores of students
to whom I have taught legal communication in the past
who have developed distinguished careers as
mediators, attorneys, judges, and court officials
and for future students who aspire to work in these careers.

Contents

Preface

This book joins together the two different theoretical traditions of communication and legal advocacy using the title *Communicating the Law*. This approach draws on a long and rich tradition that began with Greek theories of rhetorical genres and has evolved to include a variety of contemporary theories of communication and legal practice. Studies of legal advocacy originated in the rhetorical works of Cicero and have expanded into complicated studies enunciating the relevance of the principles, procedures, and protocols of law to successful legal practice. The book is especially designed for advanced undergraduate students with interests in legal communication, argumentation, rhetoric, and persuasion. Although many students seek careers in the legal profession, few teaching and learning resources bring together the theories of communication with legal advocacy. *Communicating the Law* is an attempt to fill this gap.

The book takes a perspectivist point of view; that is, it examines several different communication perspectives that aid in understanding contemporary legal processes and practices. The first two chapters outline the dominant communication and legal perspectives. Chapter 1 introduces the communication perspectives that will be applied in the subsequent chapters. These perspectives emphasize theories of discourse, language, argumentation, narrative, dramatism, and games. Choosing any one of these perspectives can illuminate the central role communication plays in legal practices and processes. Chapter 2 provides theoretical grounding about the U.S. common law system by explaining key legal principles, procedural rules, and protocols that enable and constrain communication in legal contexts and forums.

The nine chapters that follow are case studies about landmark legal cases that illuminate connections between theories and practices of communication and law. Chapter 3 examines the role of investigative journalism in the Boston priest sex abuse civil settlements. The chapter stresses the dramatic evolution of the *Boston Globe*'s serial news coverage and its effect on producing civil settlements with the victims of priest sex abuse. Chapter 4 analyzes the use of evidence in the discovery process of lawsuits against the Big Tobacco companies from the perspective of the moral drama attorneys created and the gaming strategies and tactics that they used. Chapter 5 investigates the norms for opening statements in the Timothy McVeigh trial using theories of narrative, persuasion, and language. Chapter 6 emphasizes the processes and practices of direct examination in the Lindbergh kidnapping trial, using traditional rhetorical theories as well as contemporary theories about narrative social constructions. Chapter 7 concentrates on the gaming strategies and tactics of refutation used by the attorneys in the cross-examination processes of the Sacco-Vanzetti trial. Chapter 8 focuses on how the theories of narrative and performance illuminate the prosecution and defense attorneys' summations in the O. J. Simpson murder trial. Chapter 9 uses the trial of the Chicago Eight to examine how trial participants can subvert legal processes by converting the trial into a stage for a burlesque drama. This chapter emphasizes violations of the legal norms for professional and judicial conduct. Chapter 10 examines how attorneys hired by the National Association for the Advancement of Colored People (NAACP) conducted a persuasive legal campaign focusing on compelling narrative evidence about the harms of segregation that resulted in the Supreme Court decision of *Brown v. Board of Education* (1954). Chapter 11 concentrates on the role of practical argumentation and its use of fictions in the appeal briefs and the Supreme Court decision in *Roe v. Wade* (1973). My hope is that all of these chapters will teach students important lessons about how law is communicated.

1

---◆---

Communication Perspectives

When we read a daily newspaper or turn on the national news, we frequently gain some information about a particular trial in progress, such as that of Martha Stewart or Michael Jackson, or we learn about controversial appellate decisions. Some of us might be regular viewers of the evening talk shows that deal with stories about a missing person, a child molester, a prison break, an execution, a Supreme Court decision, or a congressional hearing to confirm a federal or a Supreme Court judge. Others of us follow the business corruption trials of corporate leaders. We are attracted to legal stories because they are about human foibles, the contest between "good and evil," the redemption of victims, the punishment of perpetrators of crime, the resolution of difficult social issues, and the rights and responsibilities of individuals. As spectators, we often rely on information from the media to create our knowledge of the law. Legal processes, however, are more complicated than most spectators view them to be.

This book focuses on how the law is communicated by media, attorneys, judges, and laypersons. This chapter identifies the communication theories that dominate legal practice; chapter 2 examines how principles, procedures, and protocols enable and constrain the communication that takes place in trial and appellate courts; the subsequent chapters present case studies that elaborate different connections between theories of communication and legal practices and processes.

The authority of a government establishes laws for the good of its citizens and the judiciary understands and enforces these laws. The "law" is "a comprehensive and definitive text" that "consists of a code systematically organized by subject matter" with a common goal of maintaining social order. The law "consists of mutually binding rules pronounced collectively by the people, through representatives who give voice to the people's will" (Hazard & Taruffo, 1993, pp. 75–77). Law is "a pragmatic activity" with three different guises (Posner, 1990, p. 225). First, law is "a distinctive social institution," consisting of legal actors—lawyers and judges, "a collection of propositions," rules and principles that help lawyers and judges make predictions, and "a source of rights, duties, and powers" that indicate how parties to the law should act (pp.

220–221). Second, legal practitioners use complicated communication processes to resolve disputes between people and institutions. Third, law is a set of discourses, consisting of written codes, rules, and appellate decisions connected together through language and propositional statements, which regulate interactions between people and serve a common goal. One kind of discourse differs from another according to the legal goals it serves and the level of complexity in the language and propositional statements it contains.

A variety of communication perspectives serve as lenses for observing and interpreting legal processes and practices. A perspective is a viewpoint, "a strategy of emphasis" that permits spectators to look at a phenomenon from one point of view and highlight some features that appear in the foreground of understanding and permit other features to recede into the background (Brockriede, 1985; Wenzel, 2006). Using a variety of perspectives for studying communication and law offers several advantages. First, this approach acknowledges that many legitimate perspectives are available for those interested in the study of communication and law. The approaches that interpreters use differ, but one perspective can be just as valuable or illuminating as others are. All of the different perspectives recognize that communication is a significant part of legal practices and processes. Second, different theoretical lenses reveal different ways of observing and interpreting how communication influences legal practice. Since legal practice involves a complex process of verbal and nonverbal communication within adversarial legal settings, all of the communication relies on language, produces legal discourse, and involves dialectical argumentation.

The following sections identify key perspectives, summarize research relevant to each, and foreshadow how the perspectives apply to legal practices. The first three perspectives concentrate on (1) discourse, (2) language, and (3) argumentation, theories that can be used as lenses for micro analysis of legal practices and processes. Then I examine the theoretical analogues of (4) narratives, (5) dramas, and (6) games that configure discourses, language, and arguments.

I use one or more of the perspectives to explain how the law is communicated in each of the case studies included in this volume. Additionally, each chapter includes relevant features of the legal and social situation, explains a particular part of the trial or appeal, and identifies the relevant legal rules. The explanations of the different communicative perspectives should enable readers to understand the interdependent relationship between communication and law. The communication perspectives help to answer the question: How does communication affect legal practices and processes?

DISCOURSE AND LAW

Law-related discourses consist of units of speech and verbal exchanges placed together to create meaning and to serve an explicit legal purpose. A unit of discourse can be a statute, a legal decision, the question-and-answer sequence in witness examination, a series of news reports about legal processes, or social conversations about law. This kind of discourse consists of a set of texts that connect together various fragments of language, propositional statements, speech acts, and arguments into messages that serve both legal and communication purposes. Some discourses are relatively short, as is the opinion about desegregation in *Brown v. Board of Education* (1954), or the discourses can be of immense length, such as the transcript of the O. J. Simpson murder trial. For this reason, the subsequent case studies concentrate on the parts of trials and appeals that give insight into the whole process.

The professional, the representational, and the prosaic are three different faces of discourse. Many law journal articles are professional discourses that comment on statutes and appellate decisions. Professional legal discourse serves as attorneys' and judges' starting points for resolving disputes brought before the courts. Articles in communication journals emphasize media representations and prosaic discourses concerning the law. Everyday discourse about the law often evolves from meanings and interpretations supplied by others.

Professional Discourse

The professional discourse is the first face of the law. It uses technical language to define what the law is and to explain rules and procedures for understanding and practicing the law. This kind of discourse appears most often in statutes, decisions of appellate courts, and scholarly commentaries found in law journals. It is an elite discourse in that legal practitioners and consultants, who have been trained to understand and use it, apply it on behalf of ordinary people who lack this knowledge. Although the professional discourse exists to serve the needs of the people involved in legal disputes, it usually is accessed with the assistance of legal consultants and legal professionals (Conley & O'Barr, 1990).

Despite the fact that the law exists to solve human problems and regulate human conduct, the professional discourse typically presents abstract principles, such as rights, justice, and fairness, using technical words and phrases that most of us cannot understand. Even the language of the Miranda warning, "you have a right to remain silent, you have a right to have an attorney present . . . ," may be unclear to those being arrested (*Miranda v. Arizona*, 1966). Legislators, judges, and law school professors create discourses that have specialized meaning for their professions, but this discourse can be incomprehensible to many of the people affected by it.

In most trials and appeals, attorneys translate the professional discourse so that laypersons can understand the way it applies to them. Some attorneys provide better translations than others. The attorneys for McVeigh and Simpson as well as advocates representing the children in segregated schools and pregnant women seeking abortions translated the legal discourse so their clients could use it to achieve specific personal and social goals. Sacco and Vanzetti and the tobacco companies received competent legal counsel, but the trial judges impeded their full access to the professional discourse because they did not apply legal rules in an equitable fashion. For example, judges in the Sacco-Vanzetti trial and the Minnesota tobacco case treated prosecutors and plaintiffs differently than they did the defense.

In rare instances, a defendant waives his or her right to legal counsel as some of the Chicago Eight defendants did. These defendants tried to cope with the professional discourse by mocking the language, the legal procedures, and courtroom protocols. As a result, the defendants created a subversive and refutational discourse that challenged the power of the legal system.

The professional discourse attempts to control legal processes and practices by limiting the impact of representational and prosaic discourses. Professional discourse can never completely suppress what the media and the public say about a particular legal dispute.

Representational Discourse

A second face of the law consists of representational discourses found in novels, films, television dramas, news media reports, theatrical performances, and music. These discourses mix fact with fiction, confuse information with entertainment, and sometimes create public misconceptions about the professional discourse. Nonetheless, representations are the most prominent face of the law because they permeate popular culture. The *Boston Globe*'s news reports about the priest scandals created a pseudo civil trial. John Grisham (1996) fictionalized the Mississippi tobacco litigation in his best-selling novel, *The Runaway Jury*. Michael Mann's (1999) film, *The Insider*, told the story of a whistle-blower, Jeffrey Wigand, who exposed the sins of the tobacco companies. Newspapers, magazines, Court TV, and biographies reconstructed the life and motivations of Timothy McVeigh even before the case came to trial. Film newsreels and books written about the Hauptmann trial provided media evidence that attempted to show that the kidnapper of the Lindbergh baby was innocent. Live media coverage of the O. J. Simpson trial featured guest commentators giving their interpretations of the trial as it took place. Newspapers and television stations used the daily depictions of the Chicago Eight trial as visual evidence for their explanations of what was happening inside of the trial. In 1990, some of the original trial participants re-enacted the Chicago Eight trial for a television documentary. After the decisions in *Brown* and *Roe*, participants in the appeals wrote about their roles. Representations of some trials and appeals are so abundant that the public finds it difficult to ignore the cases. The representations of the trials and appeals discussed in subsequent chapters exerted significant influence on public understanding of the cases.

Representations contain some factual information, but they also can create fictional ideas that serve the self-interests of interpreters and distort the facts. Although my interpretations rely on court transcripts, even the transcripts contain interpretations of court stenographers about what was said and done in legal proceedings. The representations in the court record, however, resemble the proceedings more closely than most media representations do. Representations are not duplications; instead they are interpreters' attributions of meaning to actions, persons, and events. Representations can reflect, mask, and/or distort "the real" (Hutcheon, 2000, p. 31). Grisham's (1996) narrative about jury tampering in a Mississippi lawsuit against Big Tobacco depicted fictional legal practitioners and real issues that surfaced in the tobacco cases. This novel made the attorneys appear more flawed and less responsible than they really were and distorted the processes jurors use in rendering a verdict in a civil case. The books written by attorneys who were involved in the various criminal trials represent rather than replicate the trials. The dozens of nonfiction books about the Simpson trial, for example, present factual events from a self-serving perspective that illuminates certain aspects of the trial and excludes others. For example, both the prosecutors who lost the case (Clark, 1997; Darden, 1996; Goldberg, 1996) and the defense attorneys who won (Cochran, 1996; Dershowitz, 1996; Uelman, 1996) defended their strategies and criticized their adversaries in books published after the trial.

The Internet provides a limitless forum for representational discourses. Internet sites have the potential to contain large amounts and varieties of information, including facts about historical and contemporary cases as well as daily updates about investigations, case theories, evidence, and interviews with people involved in ongoing legal disputes.

Legal Web sites, such as Court TV, are excellent sources for research about trials and appeals. These sources relate facts and provide links to issues and evidence in a variety of different cases (www.courttv.com). The Internet also permits those with a self-interest to present evidence even before a case goes to trial. Since 1995, defendants, victims, and attorneys have used the Internet to present their case theories and evidence at the time legal disputes unfold. For example, the Big Tobacco companies and the attorney generals of the states who sued them presented some of their arguments and evidence on Internet sites. During her arrest, trial, and incarceration, Martha Stewart used a Web site to present her side of an insider trading case. This site not only provided evidence to show the domestic diva's innocence, it also encouraged her supporters to remain loyal to her products. Prior to and during the trial of Scott Peterson, his family defended his innocence and the family of Laci Peterson (the wife jurors later convicted him of murdering) provided evidence that he was guilty.

Since 1998, legal blogs have expanded the ways that users of the Internet construct representational discourses about the law. Internet blogs can privilege the everyday discourse of those involved in a dispute over the professional discourse; blogs are a way for those with little information to present their opinions on a legal process or practice and offer some persuasive reasoning about the evidence and potential theories for a case. Schuetz (2005) examined two different Internet blogs that dealt with the right to die controversy involving Terry Schiavo, a brain-dead woman. Schiavo's parents wanted to prolong her life, and her husband wanted her to "die with dignity." In this case, one sophisticated legal Web site explained the statutes and legal maneuvers, and other popular Web sites discussed the religious position and the gut feelings of bloggers posting their opinions (Schuetz, 2005).

Some media representations appear to be objective reports of the trials when in fact they are subjective interpretations that entertain audiences, make a profit for the producers of the representations, promote the self-interests of the sources, and give voice to those outside the legal forums. Most representational discourses are one-sided reconstructions of legal events that bring together verbal, visual, and oral texts to represent legal processes and practices. This type of discourse removes legal information from the control of legal practitioners and empowers nonprofit and for-profit media to control the sources and the content of the messages. The media discourses often supply visual evidence to stress the importance of some part of the trial discourse. The pictures of victims of the Oklahoma City bombing or of the police beating demonstrators in Chicago framed the trials in terms of the personal consequences suffered by victims. The effect of media representations can favor one side of the case over another, or it can devalue, distort, or debunk the professional discourse. Media representations impact the legal processes directly through pretrial news coverage that can affect jurors, trial coverage that emphasizes some evidence and strategies and ignores others, and posttrial commentaries that explain the social and legal consequences of verdicts and/or the appeals. Representations surface during the trial through the courtroom artists and television, radio, and newspaper reporters permitted inside the courtroom.

The subsequent chapters examine the impact representational discourses have on the public's understanding of legal processes. Film newsreels created a huge impact on the Hauptmann trial. Courtroom artists influenced public knowledge about the Chicago Eight trial. Live television coverage transformed the O. J. Simpson trial. The reports of print media impacted the Sacco-Vanzetti trial and appeal and emphasized the role of the civil rights' movements in the *Brown* and the *Roe* appeals. The print media, some television coverage, and the Internet strongly influenced the proceedings in the pedophile priest cases, the McVeigh trial, and the Minnesota tobacco trial.

Prosaic Discourse

A third face, the prosaic discourse, consists of people's everyday and vernacular expressions and conversations concerning their beliefs, opinions, interpretations, and analyses with regard to legal processes and practices (Conley & O'Barr, 1990). This talk provides personal meanings, establishes social relevance, presents critiques of the law and legal practice, and speculates about the social importance of legal processes. Prosaic communication depends more on the content of the representational discourse than it does on the professional discourse. When Lela Hunt (2003) and I (Schuetz, 2003) asked college students to tell us what they knew and understood about the law, few identified direct experiences with either trials or appeals. Nonetheless, students had formed strong beliefs about law and legal practices. Many acknowledged they formed their opinions of the legal practices and processes from television and film representations. Student responses generally noted that legal processes and practices are flawed.

COMMON BELIEFS ABOUT LEGAL PRACTICE

- Those with financial means can buy justice.
- Minority defendants do not get as fair of a trial as Anglo defendants do.
- Police are sometimes racist.
- Attorneys can win cases with the rhetorical skills that emphasize style rather than substance.
- Civil litigation is out of control; people file hundreds of frivolous lawsuits.
- Media are not as critical of legal processes as they should be.
- Media take sides and distort the law.
- Jurors commonly award outrageous million-dollar settlements.
- Trial lawyers are wealthy.
- Trials provide compelling social dramas that attract spectators.
- The legal system in the U.S. is the same as in other democracies in the world.

Our survey of participants' beliefs and attitudes resemble those presented in Internet blogs, television news reports, and television talk shows. These prosaic discourses about the law contain many incomplete and incorrect understandings of the professional discourse, and they demonstrate the nature of the influence of the representational discourses on public perceptions about law.

In addition to being laypersons' interpretations of the law, prosaic discourse surfaces as part of the trial process. During witness examination, for example, the rules of legal procedure permit attorneys and judges to shape how witnesses communicate their observations and experiences. Attorneys cannot tell witnesses what to say, but they can make recommendations about how they say it. To a large extent, legal procedures control the witnesses' stories and limit the way their testimony uses everyday expressions, presents observations, or conveys beliefs.

Determining the impact of the prosaic discourse on potential jurors is a major function of the process of *voir dire,* the questioning of potential jurors by judges and attorneys. Judges and attorneys question prospective jurors in order to discern the salience of representational and prosaic sources with regard to their assumptions and knowledge about the impending trial. Attorneys' questions typically include some of the following: Have you read or heard any media coverage about this trial? Have you formed an opinion about the case from the media? Do you understand that a defendant is innocent until proven guilty? Do you believe that persons from racial minorities are profiled by the police? Do you think that large corporations should pay damages if their products are defective? When potential jurors express beliefs or understandings that might affect how they decide a verdict, attorneys and judges exercise their challenges for cause that enable the judge to remove a person from the jury pool. Legal rules governing jury selection recognize that common beliefs and everyday talk provide clues to prejudices that might impede a potential juror from fair consideration of the evidence.

Judges' instructions to jurors during the trial also recognize the persuasiveness of representational and prosaic discourses in juror deliberations. Judges warn jurors not to read or talk about the trial with anyone before the deliberations, forbid jurors from speculating about what occurred and from re-enacting crime scenes, and ask them to consider only the evidence presented at trial.

Critical theorists from the disciplines of critical legal studies and communication recommend that courts pay more attention than they have in the past to the prosaic discourse of trial participants, including listening to the voices of racial minorities, women, children, and the poor. According to this view, professional discourse should relinquish its hold on what participants say and allow them to express their reasons and their perceptions and opinions in their everyday vernacular (Conley & O'Barr, 1990). Ball (1993) suggested that law should be "a means of giving expression to grievances and hopes of people whose voices have not been heard" (p. 158). Herbeck (1995) and Bruschke (1995) advocated that communication scholars investigate ways that professional discourses marginalize the powerless and empower the professional elites, and rhetorical scholars (e.g., Hasain, 1994, 1995, 1997) have identified how sources of power and ideology marginalize the voices of the people. Theorists have raised consciousness about the ways in which professional discourse silences voices that should be heard in legal processes. For example, Matsuda (1989) urged the courts to give more voice to victims of crime. She recommended that the courts "look to the bottom," to the views of the common person for solutions to crimes (pp. 323–324). In some cases, the critique of the absence of the voices of victims has expanded the professional discourse so that now victims can testify in civil and criminal sentencing processes (Schuetz, 2004).

LANGUAGE AND LAW

Language is the substance of the discourses of the law. Since language is part of all laws and legal practices, the perspective of language is central to the study of legal disputes. For example, law consists of authoritatively written statutes and decisions communicated through language. Legal principles, procedures, and protocols usually appear as written codes that seek compliance from those participating in legal forums. Law is a "language, a set of resources for expression and social action" (White, 1985, p. 77). The language of law constitutes the institution of law and leads to "a way of thinking and a mode of organizing life and living together" (Ball, 1997, p. 159). Laws are discursive statements about the principles and conduct that people in a social community should follow. Laws may be simple statements, such as regulations about fines for parking illegally or regulations for serving alcohol in a bar. Laws also can be complex and technical statements about conduct, specifying the conditions of a contractual agreement; the procedures for conducting an election campaign; the safety standards for a product; or the conditions that create a felony crime such as arson, statutory rape, or first-degree murder.

The language of the law constructs its meaning. In ways similar to all language, the language of the law does not provide a direct correspondence between the words, events, and actions it purports to describe. Legal language is polysemic; it has multiple meanings that depend on language users for interpretation. Legal language is multivocal; that is, many voices present and interpret the law. For example, practitioners in a criminal trial interpret a criminal statute through the actions and events connected to an alleged crime; attorneys in a civil trial determine how complaints fit with the stipulations of laws; and appellate judges decide how the language of the statutes and precedents fits with a particular set of facts. The language of the law informs the case theories of trial attorneys, the decisions of jurors and judges, and the approaches of attorneys. Before practitioners conduct a legal case, they pay attention to the language, attribute meaning, and make interpretations based on that language.

Just as there are different types of discourse, the language has more than one guise—the legal and the rhetorical. The professional discourse may stress the formal legal language and shortchange the persuasive rhetorical language, even though both types of language reside in most discourses. The representational and prosaic discourses present, reconfigure, and reword the legal language so it can be understood by adjudicators in a trial or appeal and by the public.

Legal Language

Legal language translates the everyday words, phrases, sentences, and personal reasons involved in a dispute into a technical language that connects it to the professional discourse. The law is a specialized and technical language bound by rules about content and structure and infused with legal labels, clichés, and abstractions that make the law authoritative and impersonal. Law specifies conditions for legally righteous behavior, and people are expected to comply with its prescriptive stipulations about personal and interpersonal and social and moral behavior. The stipulations include threats of punishment and promises about enforcing these threats. The law claims, asserts, alleges, dictates, produces a record, renders judgments, summons, subpoenas, stipulates, overrules, sustains, enforces, remands, nullifies, and punishes. Legal language can be a vehicle for power; it exerts control and forces compliance. In no place is the controlling language more explicit than in indictments, complaints, and sentencing guidelines. In another sense, though, legal language dresses up the law and gives it emotional connotations that relate the law to the experiences and values of laypersons. Legal rules, for the most part, seek to reduce the impact of the rhetorical language that advocates use in litigation and appeals. Witnesses express the language according to their differing language competencies, and judges use rhetorical language to persuade audiences of the righteousness and reasonableness of their decisions.

A perspective on legal language considers words, phrases, and propositions as expressions of social action, but legal language is more than "a set of propositions"; it is "a repertoire of forms of actions and life." For this reason, legal practitioners should give as much attention to language as they give to logic and reason (White, 1990, p. xi). White claims that the failures of practitioners and laypersons to pay attention to language result in legal proceedings that are bureaucratic and devoid of feeling. Law is "a set of activities by which minds use language to make meaning and establish relationships with others" (p. 17).

Rhetorical Language

Taking a rhetorical perspective toward language facilitates understanding about how legal practitioners construct and interpret legal words, phrases, and statements. In his provocative analysis of judicial opinions, Haig Bosmajian (1992) pointed to what he calls the "tropology" of judicial opinions, emphasizing how appellate court reasoning has relied on metaphors, synecdoche, metonymy, and personification. His work explained the persuasive impact of tropes, such as the "marketplace of ideas," "wall of separation," "chilling effect," and "schoolhouse gate." These tropes condense and simplify the meaning of an opinion in evocative terms that are easy for the public to understand. Other communication scholars (Birdsell, 1993; Fritch & Leeper, 1993; Voth, 1998) examined how tropes are important to processes of legal argumentation and often are features of judicial decisions and trial discourse.

Courts are venues for adversarial persuasion that establish facts through evidence, inferences, and justifications. Legal scholars should pay attention to the language used to express those arguments. Attending to the meaning and relevance of legal language is also an important task for jurors and judges. The persuasiveness of courtroom speeches, appellate arguments, and judicial decisions often depends on tropes and imagery and other rhetorical devices, such as direct address, irony, satire, ideographs, allegory, and rhetorical questions. The rhetorical choices of legal practitioners enable participants and observers to envision the conditions in which the evidence was gathered and understand what the facts and issues in a dispute mean in relation to complaints or indictments. Carefully chosen rhetorical language helps jurors to see as well as hear the facts, evidence, and arguments.

The opening statements in the McVeigh trial and the summations in the O. J. Simpson trial illuminate the importance of tropes, imagery, and rhetorical devises in courtroom speeches. The satirical language and burlesque performances of the Chicago Eight illuminate how ridicule and exaggeration can reduce the persuasive potency of professional discourse and enhance the power of prosaic discourse. The chapters on *Brown* and *Roe* show that the rhetorical language of the appellate arguments and decisions support socially and politically charged ideological positions.

The theories of language developed by Kenneth Burke (1964, 1969a, 1969b, 1970) can enhance understanding of legal practices just as they do other kinds of social influence. Burke claims that the words we use to identify a person, situation, or event give rise to particular attitudes; words are clues to motives; and language provides terministic screens that permit audiences to make some interpretations and eliminate other possible interpretations. Devil terms tend to be linked with repulsion and evil; they are the "thou shalt nots" of society that portray evil people and evil acts (1970, p. 20). God terms point to goodness and subsume all other positive terms; they carry the blessing of the people and reveal motives for social action (1969). Devil terms are common to the language of statutes, indictments, complaints, and to the trial and appeal arguments. God terms enter into the language of those testifying at trial, especially that of character witnesses. This type of language enters into appellate briefs, the formal written arguments presented to judges to initiate an appeal, and the judicial decisions that decide the appeal. Burke (1966, 1969b) asserts that the terministic screens of language permit sources of messages to circumscribe what the interpreters of a message will see and hear and what they will ignore. From Burke's perspective, language has a magical power that can transform how audiences interpret evidence, arguments, and adversarial rhetoric.

Consider the potent language found in the complaints, indictments, precedents, and statutes associated with the cases presented in this text. The *Boston Globe* complained that Cardinal Bernard Law was "negligent," engaged in "secrecy and cover-up" of sexual abuse by clergy under his supervision, and therefore the Boston Roman Catholic Archdiocese was "liable" for the pain and suffering of the victims. The Minnesota tobacco trial dealt with complaints of "misrepresenting and hiding of evidence," "product liability," "consumer fraud," and "smoking-related illness." The 11 indictments against Timothy McVeigh featured the language of "conspiracy," "weapons of mass destruction," "substantial planning and premeditation," "capital homicide," "grave risk to death," "aggravating and mitigating circumstances," "firearms," and "bombs." The Hauptmann trial grappled with the meaning of "murder in the process of kidnapping," "ransom," and "revenge." The trial of Sacco and Vanzetti centered on both the statutory language of the indictments, "robbery" and "murder," and the political language of "anarchy, "consciousness of guilt," "political loyalty," and "treason." The Simpson trial dwelt on the language of the case theories, that is, "domestic abuse," "institutional and social racism," "racial epithets" and "police malfeasance." The appeal in *Brown* centered on "equal protection," "racial discrimination," "space and place," "segregated schools," and "sociological harms." The *Roe* decision stressed constitutional language, including "states rights," "privacy rights," "equal protection," the "rights of the fetus," and the "reproductive rights of the women."

Legal language is technical and denotative as well as rhetorical, connotative, and even magical. Although communication scholars typically focus on the rhetorical and ignore the legal language, a perspective on legal language should consider the influences of the words and phrases on legal processes and practices.

ARGUMENTS AND LAW

An argument perspective examines traditional theories, practical and theoretical approaches, contemporary legal argumentation, and critical legal approaches to reasoning. In ways similar to the lenses that emphasize discourse and language, the argument perspective resides in both legal and communication scholarship. This perspective considers analytic and formal procedures and logical forms, such as deduction and induction. It also includes parts of the argument, types of arguments, kinds of fallacies, and patterns of inference and justification. This perspective incorporates Balthrop's definition of argumentation as "a particularized form of language use which serves the function of 'reason-giving' and 'providing justifications.'" An argument perspective need not emphasize rationality but should emphasize reasonableness (1980, p. 187). Stephen Toulmin (2001) explains that reasonableness involves three elements: the way that arguers situate their reasoning in a context, the intellectual force of the content, and way the arguer adopts a style that is appropriate to the content and context. Reasonableness applies to the arguments presented by advocates at the trial and appellate levels, and those found in judicial decisions.

Legal argumentation consists of informal reasoning about facts, issues, character, feelings, and human relationships. Informal reasoning seeks to persuade without using explicit logical forms such as syllogisms. This type of reasoning draws inferences from evidence in ways appropriate to a legal process. The term "argumentation" brings to mind a variety of faces. An argument can be a logical product, an utterance that involves a claim and support for that claim (Brockriede, 1977, 1985; O'Keefe, 1977). In legal discourse, a logical product centers on reasoned interpretations of evidence in relation to specific indictments. For example, an attorney can claim that a defendant is guilty of driving while intoxicated based on blood alcohol evidence, witnesses to erratic driving, and visible manifestations of inebriated behavior, such as slurred speech and inability to walk a straight line.

Another face of argumentation is its dialectical and adversarial reasoning process—advocating, defending, modifying, or refuting claims in order to persuade adjudicators that one side of the case is more believable than another. The trial is a lengthy dialectical and adversarial process with the goal of persuading judges and/or jurors beyond a reasonable doubt or persuading them that the preponderance of evidence justifies a civil verdict. In another sense, each part of a trial or an appeal is a distinctive process conducted with different strategies under a unique set of rules.

A third face of argumentation concentrates on the procedures that arguers use to achieve a legal goal. Statutory interpretations used in appellate decisions, for example, usually follow a set of procedures. The rules of discovery identify procedures that affect the acquisition and use of evidence in the arguments of a trial or settlement.

The tradition of studying practical reasoning and its argumentation products and processes began with the early Greeks and continues in some contemporary scholarship in legal communication. Practical reasoning refers to arguments used in social interactions, rather than in formal logic. For example, some prominent European scholars (Alexy, 1989; Feteris, 1999, 2003; Peczenik, 1995; Soetman, 1995) concentrate on formal logical principles and the rules that permit rigid and precise reason to dominate over rhetorical and critical interpretation. As a result, their research relegates rhetorical processes to the background, emphasizes the foreground of logical products and legal rules, and concentrates on reasoned decision making as the goal of legal interpretation. Many theorists that follow this perspective study argumentation practices in a civil rather than common law system. They privilege specific forms and patterns of logical inference over rhetorical reasoning that accounts for influences from contexts, sources, and audiences.

Traditional Legal Argumentation

In the *Rhetoric*, written in the fourth century BC, Aristotle presented argumentation as logical products and rhetorical processes. He enunciated the connections between argumentation and law as they applied to forensic speaking in ancient Greece (1954). Aristotle equated legal speaking within the forensic, a genre that involves accusing and defending a person on trial for a crime. He noted that a crime consists of a voluntary harm to another that is contrary to law. To convince citizens of the guilt or innocence of a defendant, advocates need to define the crime, know the motives behind it, ascertain the states of mind of criminals, and discern the character of the perpetrators and victims of crimes.

Aristotle identified *topoi*, topics that legal speakers use to construct a well-argued case. He listed a number of topics: those that establish motives, explain a criminal's state of mind, describe the situation in which the crime occurred, stipulate the conditions under which an act violates a law, and explain the seriousness of a crime. In addition to his taxonomy of topics, Aristotle differentiated the type of proof by defining nonartistic proof as the evidence that advocates gather from others, such as eyewitness testimony; the stipulations and conditions of contracts; and real evidence pertaining to the crime, such as weapons or forged documents. In contrast, artistic proof centers on *ethos*, that is, honesty, trustworthiness, and knowledge that attest to the character of attorneys, defendants, and witnesses; on *pathos* or emotions about a crime aroused in the minds of citizen audiences (those deciding the verdict); and on *logos*, the evidence, patterns of inference, types of reasoning, and means of justification advocates use to support their approaches to issues.

Aristotle also described argumentation products as forms. He identified types of reasoning: induction, which begins with particular observations and leads to general conclusions, and deduction, which starts with a probable premise, associates a person or act with that premise, and then draws a universal conclusion from the premise. An example of an inductive argument in a trial would be the common facts of five different witnesses that lead to the same conclusion. A formal deductive argument is a syllogism that starts with a legal rule in the first premise, such as first-degree murder involves intention, premeditation, and malice of forethought in the killing of another person. The second premise establishes facts through evidence that the acts of a particular defendant (e.g., Timothy McVeigh) were premeditated and were intended with malice to kill the occupants of the federal building in Oklahoma City. The conclusion that follows from these premises is that McVeigh's actions prove that he is guilty of first-degree murder.

Aristotle characterized enthymemes as incomplete syllogisms in which the information presented by advocates is completed by audiences. Legal rhetoric consists of many enthymemes, including precedents in which appellate arguers contend that the issues in an appeal are situationally similar to previous decisions, and therefore the findings of the previous decision should apply to the case currently being appealed. According to the principle of *star decisis,* precedents stand unless challenged; judges understand the principle and expect audiences to be persuaded by it. In accepting this principle, audiences must rely on the judges' knowledge of previous cases and their ability to apply those decisions to current cases. Some of Aristotle's principles of argument apply to contemporary practices of appellate law. These principles, however, may limit public understanding of the full range of communication that affects different parts of the legal processes.

Aristotle classified the logical practices that pertained to Greek legal proceedings, and Roman rhetorical theorists emphasized the practical and performative features of legal advocacy in the Roman courts. Marcus Tulius Cicero (1949), a Roman procurator (prosecutor) and author of books on forensic rhetoric from the first century BC, explicated the works of Aristotle and applied them to the Roman Code, called Twelve Tables. He modified theories borrowed from Aristotle and added rhetorical theories that stressed the character (*ethos*) of the advocates, defendants, and witnesses; the role of dynamic performance, evocative language, and impassioned delivery (*pathos* and elocution); and the role of the emotions and experiences of the adjudicators, the people deciding the verdict (Kennedy, 1994; Murphy & Katula, 1994). Cicero recognized that the style and delivery of legal arguments added persuasiveness to their logical content. Although Cicero made many contributions to the study of rhetoric and law, he relegated logical forms to a secondary position and elevated rhetorical and dialectical reasoning to a primary position (Fisher, 1987).

Additionally, Cicero developed the concept of *stasis*, legal issues presented through the dialectical reasoning of adversaries. He claimed that legal advocates clash over several types of issues: conjectural issues describe what happened, definitional issues explain whether or not a crime was committed, general issues address the nature of the criminal act, objectional issues inquire whether the evidence is relevant to an issue, and translation issues decide the appropriate jurisdiction for a legal case. In contemporary legal practices, attorneys base their arguments on similar issues. For example, in criminal trials advocates use conjectural issues from the indictments to inquire about whether a terrorist act, burglary, rape, or murder was committed by the defendant. In a civil trial, conjectural issues evolve from the complaints alleged against the defendants that inquire about whether a person or an organization committed fraud or engaged in negligence. Definitional issues stipulate how an action fits with the specifications of a statute, indictment, complaint, or precedent. General issues concern whether the quality of an act was intentional or involved self-defense, deception, negligence, or conspiracy. Objectional issues contest the evidence presented by adversaries at a trial. Translation issues deal with the appropriate jurisdiction of courts or tribunals—a metropolitan, state, federal, or specialized court such as a juvenile, family, or drug court.

The subsequent case studies identify issues like those described by Cicero as well as other specific issues related to the complicated statutes and codes of the jurisdiction in which cases are tried. As a general rule, trial courts consider issues of fact and appellate courts stress issues of law. Issues of law were not of as great a concern to Cicero as they are to contemporary legal practitioners because the Roman courts had relatively few procedural rules for legal practice. Contemporary appellate cases consider whether or not the trial attorneys, judge, and the jury acted according to the provisions of the principles, procedure, and protocols during legal proceedings. If any of these practitioners violated the official and binding rules, then appellate courts can overturn the trial verdicts.

Any legal case contains disputed issues. Legal practitioners use argumentation to persuade adjudicators that their respective analyses of issues are more probable than that of their legal adversaries. It is difficult to ignore issues in legal disputes because these issues provide the basis for attorneys to build a case and construct evidence and justifications for trials and appellate proceedings.

Contemporary Legal Argumentation

Classical theories of argumentation emphasize products and processes of reasoning in specific legal forums. In the 1960s, argumentation theorists expanded the classical concepts to make them apply to the diversity of contemporary legal practices. Chaim Perelman's (1963, 1967, 1980; Perelman & Olbrechts-Tyteca, 1969) research about justice and practical argumentation provided communication scholars with a rich theoretical background for studying law through the lens of argument. Some U.S. scholarship has relied on Perelman's (1980) principle of formal justice; that is, every similar legal action must be treated similarly, and judges who violate this principle are said to be unjust. The disparate treatment of prosecution and defense witnesses by judges in the Sacco-Vanzetti, Chicago Eight, and Minnesota tobacco trials qualify as unjust under this definition. Perelman emphasized that practical reasoning involves value judgments about the quality of both acts and persons and theoretical reasoning concentrates on attempts to establish a probable truth. In theory, the goal of legal argumentation is to discover the probable truth of an action. Perelman's work emphasized how practical and theoretical reasoning converge in legal practice. The subsequent case studies emphasize the practical over the theoretical and identify how attorneys and judges transform theoretical argumentation into practical reasoning using narratives, dramas, or games.

The work of Stephen Toulmin (1960, 2001) explained how fields or jurisdictions of argument have different goals, rules, and standards for evidence. The strength or weakness of the argument depends on how it meets the general standards of that field. Legal argumentation is a specific field with its own peculiar standards and rules. The reasoning in the legal field is subject to standards that are different from reasoning in science and religion, and the different legal processes (witness examination, summation, appellate arguments, and appellate decisions) also are subject to even more specialized rules, procedures, and protocols than processes in most fields are (Toulmin, Rieke, & Janik, 1979). The subsequent case studies rely on standards that apply to the legal field generally as well as to specific rules for a particular part of a legal process.

Studies of legal communication should not ignore the centrality of argumentation to legal practice and processes. The fact that certain legal practices are named closing arguments, testimonial arguments, appellate arguments, and judicial arguments enunciate the role of arguments in legal forums. Many contemporary scholars (Birdsell, 1993; Fritch & Leeper, 1993; Madsen, 1993; Voth, 1998) have focused on the rhetorical or persuasive elements of the language of legal argumentation. Other theorists (Matlon, 1988; Rieke & Stutman, 1990; Schuetz & Snedaker, 1988) stress the impact of rhetorical argumentation on legal outcomes; they analyze the effectiveness of arguments according to the findings of social science research about credibility, emotion, and logic; message order such as primacy and recency; message effects; and attitude change in relation to jurors. Matlon (1988) examined argumentative content and persuasive strategies in the different stages of the trial, starting with jury selection and moving to judges' instruction to jurors. Some legal communication research (Scallen, 1995; Schuetz, 1994) concentrates on narrative, inductive forms of reasoning, evidence, and the persuasive impact of value arguments.

Contemporary approaches acknowledge the existence of different traditional bases of legal argumentation, such as presumption and burden of proof, fact and value arguments, and types of reasoning—arguments from cause to effect or effect to cause, arguments from sign, arguments from analogy, arguments from authority, and arguments by definition. Scholars who use a more contemporary approach emphasize the rhetorical force of reasoning emanating from language, patterns of inference, speech acts, narratives, dramas, and games.

Critical Theories and Argumentation

Critical theorists examine legal argumentation, not as logical products, processes, or procedures, but as ideological discourses that empower some people and organizations and disempower others. Critical approaches rely on assumptions from critical theories of rhetoric (McKerrow, 1989, 1991) and imply that rhetorical argumentation should "unmask or demystify the discourse of power" and show how power "invites or inhibits" social change (1989, p. 91). Although McKerrow does not deal directly with rhetorical argumentation or legal practice, he urges researchers to emphasize the power of professional and representational legal discourses. He claims that the dominant social or political class creates discourses of power in order to keep others without power "in their place" (1989, p. 96). Legal practice can be a tool of the government, lawyers, and the judiciary, and these bureaucratic forces strive to keep others under their control.

McKerrow recommends that scholars examine discourses, presumably including law, by focusing on the naming of others, examining multiple processes of influence rather than causality, paying attention to what is absent as well as what is present, examining the polysemic meanings of a discourse, and addressing the ideology that underlies the discourse. Several legal communication scholars (Bruschke, 1995; Hasain, 1994; Herbeck, 1995) follow McKerrow's approach by emphasizing the rhetorical properties of the law.

Critical theorists also direct their attention to the social impact of legal practices rather than examining the underlying reasoning process. They stress the hidden meanings of the rhetoric, the political posturing and power moves of legal practitioners, the public memory and social effects of law, and the ideological perspectives of legal practitioners. Critical approaches enable researchers to point out the limitations of traditional argumentation and concentrate on social consequences of legal processes and practices. Some of the principles articulated by McKerrow and his followers provide insights about how the law influences those subject to it. The purpose of my analysis is not to critique conventional approaches to reasoning as much as it is to understand and apply both traditional and contemporary theories of argumentation to legal processes and practices.

The argumentation perspective recognizes the importance of traditional components of legal reasoning, such as finding facts, using evidence, employing patterns of inference, and drawing conclusions, as important to the study of legal practice (Carter, 1984; Levin, 1992; Savellos & Galvin, 2001). Contemporary rhetorical theorists tend to relegate types and forms of deductive reasoning to secondary positions and elevate the inductive reasoning constructed through language, narratives, dramatic sequences, and gaming strategies to a primary position.

NARRATIVE AND LAW

One of the rhetorical analogues that encapsulates discourse, language, and argument is narrative. Readers know from experience that disputes consist of competing and contested narratives about how people and groups should relate to each other. Narratives are constituted through language. The processes of legal counseling, legal interviews, mediation, arbitration, and formal legal trials rely on witnesses' and victims' narratives. People present their interpretations of events through narratives that feature a scene or setting; actors engaging in actions that breach rights and responsibilities; sequences of action that imply causes, effects, motives, and purposes; expressions about ethical issues; characterizations of people and groups; and emotional responses to legal disputes.

The Narrative Paradigm

Scholars in communication and in law agree that narratives are important to legal practice. Walter R. Fisher's (1984, 1987, 1989) narrative paradigm as an alternative approach to traditional argumentation enunciates the role of value justifications. He recognizes that stories feature characters, actions, plots, settings, and themes. The storyteller relates the value-laden narratives, and the audience evaluates the stories according to their coherence, probability, and fidelity. Audiences conclude that stories are probable to the extent they possess coherence and consistency. Audiences attribute fidelity to a narrative if it fits with other stories they know and with the ones that "ring true" with their own experiences. Fisher admits that some clever and unethical narratives may seduce audiences into believing false information.

Attorneys and witnesses use narratives to convince jurors and/or judges of the probability and fidelity of their stories in relation to the disputed facts in civil and criminal trials. Some of the stories attorneys tell are factual, and others are fictional. Stories presented by one side of the case may be untrue, but they persuade jurors and judges because they seem more probable and resonate with jurors' experiences more than the stories presented by the other side of a case. The prosecutors' stories in the McVeigh, Hauptmann, and Sacco-Vanzetti trials seemed more probable to jurors than the defense's narratives, because they were coherent and cohesive. Appellant attorneys representing Jane Roe created fictions to complete their stories about violations of legal rights. Judges consider the character, scene, and evidence of the actions embedded in narrative constellations indirectly when they summarize the trial stories on which the appeal is based. However, judges construct opinions based on what they claim are issues of law and evaluations of attorneys' reasoning.

Models of Legal Storytelling

Bennett (1978, 1979) constructed models to explain how stories are told in criminal trials. Bennett (1978) noted the stories in criminal trials structure information in ways that help listeners interpret that information. Specifically, he claimed that stories enable jurors to connect the information to a story theme, make inferences that fit the various parts of the story with a theme, and decipher whether the story is consistent and complete. Bennett characterized trial narratives as a kind of everyday logic, rather than formal logic, that enable jurors to make social judgments about excusable and inexcusable behavior, using symbols that evoke emotions and feelings. In a subsequent article, Bennett (1979) noted that attorneys' rhetorical strategies determine whether the jurors will connect the evidence to the story and whether they will understand how large amounts of trial information fit together. Bennett's collaborations with Feldman (1981) enunciated how stories affect the social judgments of jurors and how attorneys and witnesses construct and reconstruct definitions and embed those definitions within a comprehensive trial story. My use of the narrative perspective in analyzing the direct examination in Hauptmann's trial expands Bennett's theories of storytelling.

Some legal scholars (Brooks & Gewirtz, 1996) have concentrated their research on theories of legal narrative. Gewirtz (1996) explained that legal storytelling occurs "within a culture of argument." He concluded that "everyone in legal culture" tells stories, including the trial lawyer, the trial judge, the appellate judge, and the law professor (p. 5). Each segment of a trial or an appeal consists of multiple stories that attorneys collate and reframe from story fragments presented by witnesses. The attorneys frame witnesses' stories so they fit a common theme, but legal rules and procedures regulate how stories are told. Brooks (1996) acknowledged that law "formalizes" the conditions for telling stories to assure they are presented according to the rules of the court (p. 19). He further asserted that judicial decisions interweave arguments with the narratives derived from precedents to make legal appeals conform to the rules of statutory interpretation. Additionally, legal storytelling fits with the traditions of common law reasoning because it remolds particular facts from past actions into a present story (Minow, 1996). The subsequent chapters show how the narrative features of opening statements, direct examination, and summations follow, modify, dismiss, or circumvent legal principles, procedures, and protocols.

Attorneys' constructions of the narratives of opening statements, direct examination, and summations follow a predictable sequence. When a dispute enters the legal system and becomes a "case," the legal procedures for that type of professional discourse help attorneys decide how to mold their civil or criminal story into narrative constellations that contain both legal and rhetorical language and argumentation. First, attorneys elicit story fragments from the information that witnesses provide about the evidence. This process begins when attorneys take depositions from witnesses prior to the time a trial begins; attorneys ask potential witnesses to tell their story about a legal dispute as they perceive it. Second, court reporters transcribe the oral depositions and attorneys decide if and how the testimony of witnesses fits within their theory of a case. Third, when witnesses testify at trial, attorneys elicit evidence from them that supports or refutes the prosecution's, plaintiffs', or defense's stories. Rules about evidence limit the form and content of the stories that witnesses can tell. Legal procedures give attorneys the authority to alter witnesses' stories in ways that may differ significantly from their original narratives given at the deposition. Finally, attorneys construct their stories from the narrative fragments provided by the witnesses and emphasize the segments of the testimony that fit with their case theory and story theme.

The witnesses supply parts of the narrative content by reporting their versions of the dispute using familiar characters and story lines. Narratives of witnesses typically are sincere interpretations of the dispute rendered from their personal standpoints. Through open-ended questions in direct examination, witnesses collaborate with attorneys in telling a consistent story. The purpose of cross-examination may be to challenge the coherence, consistency, and facticity of the stories witnesses tell during direct examination. In parts of the trial, attorneys participate directly in the construction of witnesses' narratives. Some witnesses, however, knowingly contrive insincere and distorted narratives that violate their oaths "to tell the truth and nothing but the truth." They do so for a variety of reasons, such as to mock the legal system, support a particular side of the case, or help the victims or the perpetrators. Other witnesses unintentionally provide incoherent narratives because they lack the necessary cognitive and language skills for telling believable stories.

The narrative evolves through several segments of the trial. Attorneys reconstitute witnesses' story fragments in order to develop a preface to their theory of a case in opening statements, elaborate their story during direct examination, refute the story of the opposition during cross-examination, and defend the story told in opening statements and during summations. The various discourses, the legal and rhetorical language, and the various kinds of arguments constitute the narrative constellations found in trials and appeals. The chapters featuring opening statements (McVeigh), direct examination (Hauptmann), and summations (Simpson) identify the role of narrative in criminal trials. Narratives about teachers and students and inferior schools were important to the facts used for the decision in *Brown v. Board of Education* (1954).

DRAMA AND LAW

The dramatic perspective examines legal actions situated in specific social contexts that often feature dramatic performances. It also helps explain the stages in the evolution of a drama. This second kind of rhetorical constellation relies on discourse, language, arguments, and some narrative as well. An observer can view legal performances through the lens of dramatic form (Berger, 1997; Burke, 1973; Wright, 1972), as social and cultural theater (Goffman, 1959; Turner, 1982, 1988), and as carefully orchestrated communication performances (Ball, 1997; Harbinger, 1971). A theatrical drama evolves in phases that encourage the involvement of audiences with the characters, their actions, their motives, and the meaning of their actions.

Dramatic Form

Just as in theatrical dramas, the dramatic action of trials and appeals unfolds through a prologue, rising action, complication, climax, denouement/resolution, and epilogue (Berger, 1997; Wright, 1972). The stages in the evolution of a drama can explain the stages in the media coverage of a legal proceeding or the sequence of a legal process.

STAGES IN A DRAMA

- *Prologue* refers to the preface or introduction that precedes the drama.
- *Rising action* is the exposition of the characters, the scene, the relationships, and the targeted audience. Rising action informs audiences about the character of the actors and how their actions likely will proceed.
- *Complications* occur as the result of oppositions between characters, actions, and events. These complications constitute the conflict.
- *Climax* (sometimes called crisis) is the turning point in a drama when the disputed actions of the characters create consequences.
- *Resolution* (denouement) explains to the audience how the story turns out.
- *Epilogue* is a commentary or explanation of the point of a drama and its consequences.

STAGES IN A TRIAL DRAMA

- The media present the *prologue* to a trial through their news reports about a case or about social and cultural factors that led to a trial. The attorneys add a prologue to jury trials when they introduce the issues of the trial through the questions they ask jurors during *voir dire*.
- Trial attorneys explain the *rising action* in their opening statements. The themes and/or case theories identify what events ignited the legal dispute.
- The depositions acquired through the discovery process and stipulations agreed to by both sides of the case constitute the *complications* prior to the trial. During the trial, the testimony and evidence presented through attorneys' direct examination of their own witnesses and their cross-examination of adversarial witnesses reveal details about the complications.
- The summations of the attorneys often are the *climax* of the trial because they explain the legal consequences that plaintiffs and prosecutors believe should evolve from the actions of defendants.

• The jurors' verdict or the judge's ruling can create the *resolution* of a legal dispute. The settlement hearings in a civil case or the victim impact statements in a criminal case are other ways of resolving a trial drama.

• The *epilogue* consists of interviews with jurors and legal experts that explain why the trial turned out as it did.

The stages of a drama can be applied to a longer legal proceeding that culminates in a Supreme Court decision or to stages of media coverage. This analogue is useful for analyzing structural and sequential development of media and legal processes.

Social Performances

In addition to the dramatic form, the dramatic perspective focuses on social performances (Goffman, 1959) and theatrical courtroom enactments (Schuetz, 1983; Schuetz & Lilley, 1999; Schuetz & Snedaker, 1988). Goffman explains that when performers play parts, they convey an impression to an audience. Performers can present a sincere impression of genuineness, or they can foster an insincere impression leading the audience to doubt the authenticity of their performances. Attorneys, witnesses, perpetrators, and victims jointly stage their performances for jurors and/or judges. When performers "incorporate and exemplify" the values of their audience, they are believable. In a similar way, courtroom performers impress jurors and judges about their character, truthfulness, and authenticity. If a witness or an attorney uses "an unmeant gesture," acts "out of character," or commits a "faux pax," these performers likely will produce a flawed or an unbelievable performance for jurors and judges (Goffman, 1959, pp. 210, 216). If the performances of key prosecution witnesses are out of character, as they were in the O. J. Simpson trial, then the impression of the entire case may be spoiled.

Performances, Goffman (1959) asserted, are given by teams. Team performers "cooperate in staging a single routine" (p. 79). The plaintiffs, the prosecutors, the defendants, the defense attorneys, the jurors, and the appellate judges constitute different performance teams. For example, the plaintiffs' team consists of those people or entities bringing the complaints, along with their witnesses. Similarly, the defense team includes witnesses and attorneys who work together to maintain "a particular definition of a situation" (p. 105), such as a team-constructed theory of a case. Team members engage in cooperative interaction that conveys a joint purpose and creates a unified impression. If successful, team cooperation fosters the impression of close interplay, dialogue, and interdependent interaction between team members. In another sense, teams resemble "secret societies" because they are held "together by a bond that the audience does not share" (p. 104).

Goffman claimed that success of a team performance depends on "dramaturgical loyalty and discipline," that is, team members' ability to maintain their moral obligations, keep secrets, and conform to the plan for the performance (p. 212). Dramaturgical discipline among the members of a litigation team helps to foster a favorable impression and persuade jurors of the "reasonableness" and "facticity" of their side of case. The Chicago Eight trial illustrates the failure of the prosecution and defense teams and their clients to maintain believable legal dramaturgical performances; at the same time, it shows a believable burlesque performance created by the defense team.

Performance Strategies

The surface (easily seen and heard) level of the drama in a legal process can conceal some of the elaborate substructure of trial participants' strategic and tactical moves. Several theatrical techniques, according to Ball (1997), can help attorneys communicate with jurors. An awareness and understanding of these techniques may be useful to students who analyze representational legal discourses or observe live courtroom proceedings. Understanding this kind of perspective may also aid spectators' analyses of Court TV documentaries of trials, videotapes or film reels, or audio recordings of the oral arguments presented to the Supreme Court. Ball recommends the following performance strategies, including viscerals, props, point of view, forward analysis, backward analysis, and stage directions. Some of these techniques (such as viscerals and props) might not be allowed by the procedures and protocols of the courts during particular segments of the trial.

THEATRICAL TECHNIQUES

- *Viscerals* affect jurors at "a gut level." Viscerals "bypass the intellect" and produce immediate physical and emotional responses. Viscerals can be actions, such as child abuse, lying, illicit sex, conspiracy, fraud, and violating trust, or emotions, such as love, hate, revenge, and jealousy. Viscerals make jurors take notice of the actions of a legal dispute (pp. 94–100). Attorneys can interject viscerals in the broader themes and stories they tell or in the specific words and phrases they use in their opening and closing statements to the jurors as well as in the questions they ask witnesses.

- *Props* are visuals that enable jurors to clarify and attribute meaning to the evidence. What jurors hear *and* see is more persuasive than what they just hear. Props are ways of visualizing evidence. Visuals are "logos" for evidence in a trial (pp. 83–92). Pictures of a crime scene, hard copies of e-mails, and weapons used to commit a crime are props. Blood-stained garments, a video of a victim who became a paraplegic because of the defective tires on his SUV, pictures of handwriting samples, pictures of cigarette ads, or visual profiles of a defendant's DNA all qualify as props.

- *Point of view* is the position attorneys take in relation to "events, behavior, and opinions" of witnesses, the judge/s, jurors, and other attorneys. In other words, the attorney's point of view affects how he or she conceives of evidence and testimony (p. 136).

- *Forward analysis* compels jurors to listen to the evidence and testimony. Attorneys create the forward analysis through the presentation of their theme, the placement of witnesses, and the phrasing of questions for examination. Attorneys should construct a case that has tension, suspense, and mystery.

- *Backward analysis* is a retrospective understanding of how a piece of evidence or a fragment of testimony makes sense in relation to what preceded it. Backward analysis begins after discovery and continues through the design of opening statements and summations.

- *Stage directions* are advice that attorneys give to their clients and their witnesses about how they should dress; how they should act toward attorneys, witnesses, and jurors; and their personal demeanor, such as eye contact, appropriate emotional responses, and posture.

When attorneys conceive of a trial as having social or political significance, they tend to pay more attention to the performance details than if they are in a routine one- or two-day trial or hearing with few public and media spectators. Since the subsequent case studies examine trials and appeals for which there were social and political consequences, the performances of some trial participants loom large in the outcome of a case.

GAMES AND LAW

Games are a third kind of theoretical analogue that encapsulates discourse, language, and argument. Many legal practices fit with the analogue of games that explain how rules, roles, and goals influence the strategical and tactical interactions of persons involved in contests (Davis, 1983; Rapoport, 1970; Schelling, 1960). Hugh D. Duncan (1968) views games as rule-governed interactions in which "the honor of winning" depends on how the contestants are matched. Litigation games, in ways similar to other games, are contests in which adversaries struggle to gain strategic advantage in order to win a verdict or an appeal.

Anatol Rapoport (1970) explains that games are based on "agreement of opponents" who "strive for incompatible goals within the constraint of certain rules" (p. viii). In a game, the "strong opponent" is of greater value than "a weak one," and the players assume their opponents will "try to do their best, speak a similar language, and act rationally" (p. 9). Games involve calculated choices, and each choice in a given situation creates different consequences. Each player in a game makes "choices or moves" on the basis of consequential reasoning, that is, how the moves he or she makes will affect the moves of the opponent.

These choices are motivated by what is lost or gained, and they result in different types of payoffs. For example, an attorney may choose not to allow the defendant to testify, believing that the opposing attorney will impeach the defendant's character and thereby reduce the probability the testimony will benefit the case. Or defendants may choose to testify in order to promote a specific agenda, such as one that involves a political rather than a legal payoff. Defendants may get a political payoff by calling attention to a particular ideology, even though this may nullify the payoff of a favorable verdict or settlement. Attorneys in a legal game make choices (moves) based on the choices (moves) of their opponents and the legal situation. A trial and an appeal both have an outcome or an endpoint. The payoffs of a civil legal outcome may be sympathy for the defense, a costly settlement, or a finding of not guilty or no financial remuneration. The payoffs for prosecutors in a criminal case can be public praise of the attorneys or legal system, a belief that justice was done, or a deserved conviction resulting in a suitable penalty for defendants. The payoffs for the defendant are avoiding paying damages or avoiding incarceration. If a defendant engages in a plea bargain, the payoff may be no jail time in return for testimony against others or fines and community service rather than incarceration. The choices of attorneys are reasonable, rather than rational, because before they make moves, they consider the constraints of a particular legal situation. Game theory has heuristic application especially for the strategy and tactics of pretrial discovery and settlement talks and for the conduct of cross-examination. This theory can explain the impact of attorneys' strategical and tactical moves on outcomes, such as those produced in the discovery process of the Minnesota tobacco trial and in the cross-examination conducted in the Sacco-Vanzetti trial.

Legal proceedings are contests that feature adversaries with competing goals. These contests begin with an analysis of the evidence and arguments of a case. The attorneys act as game players; they adopt strategies and tactics that navigate the rules and try to outwit each other in their effort to win a verdict. Rules and procedures enable cooperative interactions that promote reasoning, competitive interactions that outmaneuver one's adversaries, and controlled interactions that limit the moves of others under the rules of the game. In games as well as legal proceedings, the utilities (resources) and the moves of the players are intertwined.

Social and legal games similarly use calculated strategies and tactics to produce outcomes. Michel de Certeau (1988) shows more interest in the strategic and tactical options of game players than in outcomes. He notes that the strategies are ways of "navigating the rules"; that is, players choose rules and adopt strategies that lead to a personal competitive advantage in a social game. For him, strategies are "calculated uses of power" that establish a sense of the player's authority in a situation (pp. 35, 54). In legal proceedings, attorneys strategically assert a power advantage by controlling what witnesses say. Tactics, on the other hand, are timely procedural maneuvers that allow players to intervene and transform a situation to achieve a personal advantage. When attorneys find themselves in a position of low power, they resort to tactics that permit them to get around the rules.

Legal game players rely on some modicum of chance. Although the different players in any game exert some control over the outcome, their strategies and tactics depend on and are affected by the moves and countermoves of the other players as well as on rules of interaction that are enforced by judges. Each side uses strategic and tactical actions and calculated reasoned choices in order to achieve desirable outcomes that impede the opposing side from achieving the outcomes they desire—outcomes that are decided by adjudicators, judges, or jurors. Specifically, attorneys engage in a number of moves that resemble games of chance (Rapoport, 2001):

GAMING MOVES

- Attorneys can "roll the dice," take chances with limited evidence in a jury trial.
- Attorneys can "force the other side to show their hand," make demands for evidence in the discovery process.
- Attorneys can "take a trick," make a plea bargain that gives a deal to the defendants, enabling them to convert a legal move into a personal advantage.
- Attorneys can "play a trump card" that limits the planned moves the opposition can take.
- Attorneys can "call a bluff," ask the opposing side to call the witnesses and present the evidence they have promised in opening statements.
- Attorneys "keep a poker face," a metaphor for concealing one's personal attitudes and feelings when a witness testifies.
- Attorneys "call a spade a spade," draw reasonable inferences from the evidence presented at trial.
- Attorneys engage in "a high stakes game," taking their chances with a favorable settlement, verdict, or risky legal move.
- Attorneys "win and lose" legal games; they succeed or fail to achieve a desirable settlement, verdict, or appeal.

Some legal practices resemble strategic games conducted within a framework of rules that constrain what players can do and say. In his discussion of legal rules, legal scholar Richard Posner (1990) explains that legal rules are contestable: "The rules do not determine the game's outcome," nor do they "force compliance." Instead rules are guides for how to win a game that can be changed if the rules do not serve legal goals (pp. 49–51). Players can choose to subvert or manipulate the legal rules for their own advantage in trying a case, negotiating a settlement, or arguing an appeal. Both games and legal processes involve power, money, and credibility that affect the persuasiveness of players' calculated strategic and tactical moves. Legal practitioners cannot make any move they want to. The rules of the court define and limit the communication moves of plaintiffs, prosecutors, defendants, petitioners, respondents, judges, and jurors. The goal of most adversarial proceedings is to win a settlement, verdict, or appeal. Legal rules about reasonable doubt guide decisions of jurors in criminal trials and rules about a preponderance of evidence govern the verdicts in civil cases. Rules of statutory interpretation impact appellate arguments and the decisions that follow from them.

All of the case studies featured in this text to some extent contain reasonable moves based on calculated choices designed to win cases. Since laws are tested in adversarial proceedings under rules of procedures and guidelines for professional conduct, each of the case studies contains some strategic communication characteristic of games. Some parts of the trials, such as the pretrial motions, the discovery process, the presentation of evidence, and the trying of test cases, illuminate how specific legal rules promote interactions that assert power and control over adversaries. The Minnesota tobacco trial features extensive game-like moves during discovery and the settlement. The cross-examination of the Sacco-Vanzetti trial consists of numerous strategic and tactical moves. The Chicago Eight trial exemplifies how trial participants can subvert and mock the legal rules and procedures in order to gain personal advantage or to change the power relations within the courts.

LESSONS

A variety of perspectives are available for observing and analyzing the communication of trials and appeals. Each perspective offers a different lens that permits the researcher to place some communication theories in the foreground and place others in the background. The perspectives explained in this chapter illuminate the communication practices used in the nine case studies examined in this book. One theoretical perspective focuses on three faces of discourse—professional, representational, and prosaic. Another perspective emphasizes legal and rhetorical language. The third theoretical perspective examines practical reasoning and rhetorical argumentation. In addition to these micro-theoretical approaches, the chapter identifies three broadly configured analogues of narrative, drama, and games. These perspectives should help students understand how communication resides at the core of legal processes and practices. These perspectives provide lenses for students to use when they observe a live trial, read or see a media representation of a legal proceeding, or engage in critical analysis of a legal practice or process.

2

Legal Rules
Principles, Procedures, and Protocols

The United States' legal system evolved from principles and practices originating in the British common law. As a result, this system has strong parallels with the trial and appellate practices of England, Ireland, Canada, Australia, and New Zealand and has significant differences with the civil law systems of Mexico, South and Central America, and most of Eastern and Western Europe. When first adopted, the British common law focused upon the resolution of conflicts involving personal property, contracts, fraud, and personal injury. The British legal commentaries of Sir William Blackstone enunciate key principles, such as the sources of common law, the use of citizen jurors, and the reliance on adversarial argumentation for finding facts (Hazard & Taruffo, 1993). The term "common law" refers both to customs, the way things have traditionally been done, and to precedents, the accumulated legal interpretations of judges. In the United States, the common law consists of a body of precedents, which interpret laws created by the Constitution and by legislation. The U.S. common law derives from the judgments of previous cases and from changes in response to new legal issues, and it "aids in the systematic development of a richer and presumably more just law" (Abraham, 1980, p. 13). In common law systems, judges typically decide issues of law and act as the voice of the official government, and jurors decide issues of fact based on community standards of justice found in statutes (Hazard & Taruffo, 1993).

The purpose of this chapter is to explain how rules influence different legal and communication processes and practices. Rules consist of principles, procedures, and protocols. These rules have several purposes, including: (1) to connect the law to specific processes of legal reasoning, (2) to equalize the power relations among the practitioners, and (3) to ensure the authority and decorum of the courts. Legal rules try to protect the official discourse from being devalued by prescribing the meaning of legal language, limiting the impact of emotions and feelings, enforcing interjurisdictional standards for attorneys and judges, and privileging the discourse of the trained legal professionals over that of the ordinary person. Chapter 1 explained how professional, representational, and prosaic discourses, technical and rhetorical language, and practical argumentation communicate the law. The analogues of narratives, dramas, and games bring together these features into complex theoretical constellations that permit macro analysis of legal practices and processes. Although some legal communication research ignores legal rules, this chapter emphasizes how these rules affect communication processes and practices in legal settings.

Legal rules influence trial practices through (1) general principles—the Constitution, statutory law, and trial and appellate jurisdictions, (2) specific principles about case origin and standard of proof, (3) procedures related to media coverage, jury selection and decision making, opening statements, direct examination, cross-examination, summations, and appellate procedures, (4) professional conduct of legal practitioners, and (5) courtroom protocols.

GENERAL LEGAL PRINCIPLES

A legal principle is a fundamental doctrine from which other tenets evolve. These principles outline the relationships between the government and the people. The Constitution; statutory law; and local, state, regional, and federal jurisdictions establish broad principles that guide how the U.S. legal system functions.

The Constitution

The most fundamental legal principles appear in the U.S. Constitution. Seven of the ten amendments, located in the Bill of Rights and fully ratified by Congress in 1791, laid the groundwork for the rights of the accused as well as for protections of the freedoms of individual citizens.

LEGAL PRINCIPLES IN THE CONSTITUTION

- The First Amendment provides for freedom of religion, speech, press, and assembly and permits citizens to petition the government for grievances.
- The Second Amendment permits citizens "to keep and bear arms."
- The Fourth Amendment prohibits "unreasonable search and seizure" unless law enforcement has "probable cause."
- The Fifth Amendment establishes the grand jury indictment for capital crimes and provides due process for all citizens. Additionally, this amendment prohibits the courts from trying a person twice for the same crime (double jeopardy), from forcing persons to testify against themselves (self-incrimination), and from the government taking private property without just compensation.

- The Sixth Amendment provides for a speedy and public trial by an impartial jury in the location where the crime was committed. This amendment states that the accused should be informed of accusations against them, be able to confront witnesses who testify against them, provide the court with witnesses in their favor, and have the right to the assistance of counsel in a criminal proceeding. The Sixth Amendment also provides a trial by jury for a civil case that involves more than $20 in damages.
- The Seventh Amendment forbids excessive bail, fines, and cruel and unusual punishment for those accused and convicted of crimes.
- The Fourteenth Amendment, ratified in 1868, guarantees due process and equal protection for all citizens.

The meaning of these different legal rights has evolved in the years since they were ratified through numerous appellate opinions, but these amendments remain foundational principles for the judicial system. Subsequent chapters illuminate how these rights have been clarified, extended, and applied in specific cases.

Statutory Law

A statute is an enactment by a legislative body that is expressed in a formal document, such as a federal or state legal code. The common law and the Constitution provide principles that legislative bodies use as the basis for statutes and jurisdictions. The primary task of the U.S. Congress or of any lawmaking body is to enact legislation, creating new statutes that build upon or replace existing laws. For example, Congress created the "No Child Left Behind Act" that stipulates how public schools should assess student progress. The "PATRIOT Act" identifies what constitutes terrorist acts, legal methods of surveillance, and punishments for engaging in terrorist acts. States enact a variety of statutes that govern specific jurisdictions. For example, guidelines about the legality, the standards, and the processes for running charter schools and the laws that require sex offenders to register are state statutes. City ordinances about where people can smoke are statutes that establish laws for a particular local community. Legal forums decide whether or not someone has violated a statute and provide penalties for the failure of individuals to comply with the laws. The federal, state, and local courts enforce the laws in their jurisdictions.

The federal courts hold jurisdiction over matters specified in the Constitution and federal legislation, including working conditions for employees; equal treatment of citizens in regard to their age, gender, and race; securities and bonding; and federal transportation and commerce. States have jurisdiction over public education, contracts, state transportation, and taxation as well as felony and misdemeanor crimes committed within their boundaries. These cases are tried in state district courts. Cities and other small governments establish laws concerning zoning, graffiti, parking, and public conduct, and magistrate or metropolitan courts hear cases that violate city laws. The statutes of most jurisdictions differentiate between civil and criminal laws.

Civil laws differ from criminal laws. A party filing a civil suit pursues private interests, such as disputes about contracts, divorce or child custody, defamation of character, civil rights, negligence, personal injury, or product liability. In contrast, the government conducts criminal cases against individuals and/or organizations that have committed misdemeanors, such as traffic violations, trespassing on others' property, and petty theft. City magistrate/metropolitan courts usually decide misdemeanor cases by levying fines, creating court orders, or mandating community service as punishments. Felony crimes involve a different level of gravity with significant negative consequences for victims. Felonies include manslaughter, murder, espionage, sabotage, rape, burglary, bank robbery, perjury, and securities fraud.

Two separate and parallel court systems exist for civil and criminal proceedings. Each of the states has its own court system that coexists with the federal court system. Each system typically has three tiers of courts (Nebraska is an exception to this generalization): trial, appellate, and supreme.

Trial Courts

The first level is the trial court. Trials may be conducted as a bench trial before a judge or with jurors who decide a verdict. State trial courts deal with violations of state constitutions and statutes according to common law. In jurisdictions with high caseloads and large populations, judicial forums often are subdivided into family, drug, probate, and traffic courts. Judges and jurors serving criminal courts decide whether a crime has been committed according to the statutes of the state. In civil cases, judges or jurors decide whether or not the plaintiff is entitled to some kind of monetary settlement or relief resulting from the negligence or harm created by defendants. The federal trial courts determine issues of fact regarding federal crimes and civil matters, including "all crimes against the United States; all civil actions arising under the Constitution, laws, and treaties of the U.S., wherein the matter in controversy exceeds $10,000" (Abraham, 1980, p. 167).

The cases discussed in subsequent chapters represent a small sample of all possible legal violations, jurisdictions, complaints, and indictments. The cases of Hauptmann, Sacco-Vanzetti, and O. J. Simpson occurred in the criminal state trial courts since the defendants had been indicted for felony crimes that violated state statutes—extortion, robbery, and murder. The trials of Timothy McVeigh and the Chicago Eight took place in federal courts. State civil courts heard the tobacco cases. Federal courts heard the constitutional cases that preceded the appeals in *Brown v. Board of Education* (1954) and *Roe v. Wade* (1973). Although the trial of pedophile priest Geoghan occurred in a state criminal court, most of the settlements from the *Boston Globe*'s pseudo cases took place in state civil courts.

Appellate Courts

When parties receive an adverse ruling or verdict in a trial court, they can appeal the verdict to a second instance court, often called the court of appeals. The purpose of the appeals courts is to review the decisions of a lower court. Some appellate courts, such as a state court of appeals, consider the merits of all appeals in that jurisdiction.

Just as in the state system, the federal jurisdiction has a court of appeals. This appellate system contains twelve circuits, with official names that represent the First Circuit Court of Appeals, the Second, and so on. The decisions rendered by these circuit courts are recorded according to the name of the case, the number of the circuit court, the page number where the case appears in the reports, and the date of the case. A sample federal court appeal citation is *Roe v. Alabama,* 43 F. 3d 574, 1996.

The defense has an automatic appeal if the verdict involves a death penalty and can appeal other verdicts if the trial process abridged the law. For example, the defense can appeal a trial verdict based on perjury of witnesses, juror misconduct, failure of the prosecutor to report evidence critical to the verdict, or failure of one party to turn over documents during the discovery process. If the appellate court agrees that a defendant's right to a fair trial has been compromised, then the appeals court overturns the verdict, and the government then has to decide whether or not to retry the case. Extensive appeals followed the Sacco-Vanzetti trials, but McVeigh recommended that his attorneys limit their appeal process after he received the death penalty.

In civil cases, both the plaintiffs and the defense can appeal the case. The plaintiff can appeal if violations of legal procedures occurred during the trial when attorneys believe their clients were not treated according to the law or if the settlement their clients received was unsatisfactory. For example, judges determine if civil awards are reasonable by deciphering if the amount of the award "shocks the court's conscience or is manifestly unreasonable" (Jonakait, 2003, p. 276). Before appealing a case, parties to a lawsuit can request corrective action from the trial court judge in order to address procedural errors or insufficiency of evidence in support of the verdict or findings. The appeal for corrective action takes the form of a posttrial motion in which the trial judge decides the appeal and determines if a new trial should be ordered. The defense makes an appeal based on procedural errors or insufficiency of proof. If the appeals are denied, then the court attempts to enforce the conditions of the award to the plaintiffs.

If appellate attorneys contest the decision of an appellate court of first instance, then a higher level court, typically called the supreme court, may agree to hear the case and overturn the decision made in the first level of appeal. In state supreme courts as well as in the U.S. Supreme Court, judges have the discretion to accept some cases and to refuse to hear others (Abraham, 1980; Stern, Gressman, & Shapiro, 1986). The decisions of the state supreme courts are printed as formal written texts in the books published annually called *State*

Court Reports. A typical citation appears in this form: *Roberts v. City of Boston,* 59 Mass. 198, 1850. The first number identifies the volume number, the abbreviation indicates the state appellate jurisdiction (in this example the state is Massachusetts), the next number refers to the page where a reader can locate the opinion, and the final entry is the year of the decision.

The U.S. Supreme Court, the so-called court of last resort, establishes legal precedents that supersede the decisions of state and federal courts of appeals. For example, the precedents in the *Brown* decision overturned state school statutes permitting segregation, and the *Roe* decision superseded restrictive state abortion laws. The Constitution; federal, state, and local statutes; and jurisdictional forums establish broad legal principles influencing how law should be practiced. Specific principles regarding the origin of cases and the standard of proof directly affect the conduct of the trial processes.

SPECIFIC LEGAL PRINCIPLES

The public is more familiar with criminal than with the civil trials or appellate decisions because significant media coverage results from the dramatic elements of compelling crime stories. In reality, however, the civil courts hear many more cases than criminal jurisdictions do. Jonakait (2003) claims that more than 50,000 civil jury trials take place each year. These civil cases involve plaintiffs suing businesses or independent parties for damages, liability, or infringements of their rights. The media and the public pay little attention to civil trials unless they involve a celebrity defendant, such as Martha Stewart, or a large American company, such as Microsoft. Although reports about civil cases likely will not appear on the front page, the media usually report the amount of financial settlements and summarize the content of appellate decisions.

Specific legal principles determine how cases originate, how attorneys reach settlements, and what constitutes an appropriate standard of proof.

Case Origin

Criminal trials start with an arrest filed by law enforcement officers. After the arrest, the state takes the defendant/s into custody and brings those arrested before a judge in an arraignment proceeding (a formal and official reading of the indictment) to enter a plea. On the advice of attorneys, a trial judge determines whether the accused should be set free or held to answer the charges. If the court decides to hold the accused in custody, then the judge sets the amount of bail, the conditions for the release of the accused, and details about whether the case will proceed to the grand jury or a preliminary hearing. Prior to bringing charges for serious crimes, a prosecuting attorney of the jurisdiction in which the crime took place presents the case to a grand jury, a group of 23 citizens of the community, who meet in a secret proceeding to decide if the government has sufficient evidence to proceed with a criminal trial. Only the prosecuting attorney and the witnesses supporting the government present evidence, and the court excludes the defendants and their legal counsel from the grand jury proceedings. Grand jury indictments preceded the trials of McVeigh, Hauptmann, and the Chicago Eight. An alternative to a grand jury indictment is a preliminary hearing, a proceeding used for high-publicity trials. Preliminary hearings are minitrials since they feature a two-sided adversarial public presentation of evidence by prosecutors and defense attorneys and their witnesses. Prior to the high-publicity criminal trial of O. J. Simpson, the state of California held a preliminary hearing.

A civil trial begins with a complaint filed by plaintiffs and their legal representatives. The plaintiffs' complaint seeks a remedy for some harmful action—breach of a contract, personal injury, discrimination, and so forth—that resulted from negligence by the parties named as defendants. The claim is a "short and plain statement" arguing that the plaintiff is entitled to some monetary relief for harm or damages (Kane, 1996, p. 93). After receiving a copy of the complaint, the defendant/s usually file their response or answer to the complaint and make counterclaims. The defendant can respond to a complaint by denial, introducing an affirmative defense, seeking awards from the plaintiffs, or admitting the allegations (Kane, 1996). The defense's response results in pleadings about factual issues in dispute. Because civil actions are not initiated by the government, this type of proceeding has no grand jury or preliminary hearing. Additionally civil litigants lack the protections afforded the accused in a criminal trial, such as probable cause, immunity from self-incrimination, presumption of innocence, and a guarantee of counsel.

Plea Bargains and Settlements

After formal charges are filed in a criminal case, the accused then enters into an arraignment and makes a formal plea before a judge. Following the process of evidence gathering called discovery, attorneys may recommend that the accused make a plea bargain, that is, plead guilty in exchange for a lighter sentence than likely would result from a conviction at a trial. As many as 90 percent of all criminal cases result in plea bargains. Even after plea bargains become final, as many as 40,000 cases per year still end up in trial courts. If the case goes to trial, jurors typically will decide whether defendants are guilty or not guilty (Jonakait, 2003).

Prior to a civil trial, parties to the suit try to resolve their conflict by using methods of alternative dispute resolution—arbitration, negotiation, or mediation. If the conflict is resolved through alternative dispute settlement processes, the civil action does not go to trial. Settlement talks also can occur during the different stages of the trial. Sometimes attorneys reach a settlement prior to a trial, other times after the plaintiffs have presented their evidence, and still other times after the evidence for both sides has been presented but before the case goes to a jury. Most of the cases against Boston pedophile priests settled prior to a trial. The settlement in the Minnesota tobacco case took place after the presentation of evidence but before the case went to the jury.

In criminal trials, defendants often do not testify because of their vulnerabilities as witnesses and the Fifth Amendment provision protects them against self-incrimination. O. J. Simpson did not testify at his criminal trial nor did Timothy McVeigh at his. However, Sacco, Vanzetti, Hauptmann, and the Chicago Eight defendants did testify. In civil cases, defendants testify without the benefit of Fifth Amendment protection. State and federal laws required institutional representatives from tobacco companies, Catholic officials and clergy, and officials of segregated schools to give testimony.

Standard of Proof

Both civil and criminal trials hear and see evidence to establish case facts, and judges and/or jurors then decide whether or not those facts support the charges or complaints. The standard of proof in a criminal case is "beyond a reasonable doubt," a standard that has different meanings to different jurors. Jurors must determine what the standard is and how their interpretations of trial evidence fit with the standard. Johnnie Cochran's oft-quoted line from his summation in the O. J. Simpson murder trial was "if the glove does not fit, you must acquit." His rhetorically clever phrases created reasonable doubt in the minds of jurors. Rhetorical tricks of this type usually are insufficient for meeting the standard of reasonable doubt resulting in a unanimous verdict. After deliberations are complete, jurors appear before the judge and give their verdict as "guilty" or "not guilty." Although media representations of trials frequently claim that "the defendant was found innocent," these are not the words used in most criminal courtrooms.

In civil cases, the standard is "preponderance and sufficiency of evidence." In other words, the civil jury decides if the injury or harm alleged by the plaintiff occurred because of the negligent actions of the defendants. Through a majority vote, jurors decide civil verdicts. If the case is tried before a six-person jury, five of six must agree. In a twelve-person jury, nine of twelve must agree. In many civil cases, unanimous verdicts occur even though this degree of consensus is not required. If the plaintiff wins a case, the civil jury "finds for the plaintiff" and recommends a financial award. The civil trial judge then decides what that award is and what enforcement procedures will be used to gain the compliance of the civil defendant with the conditions of the verdict. The jurors in the famous McDonald's hot coffee case, for example, came to a unanimous verdict in favor of plaintiff Stella Liebeck who had suffered severe burns from the hot coffee she spilled in her lap. In this case, jurors recommended that McDonald's pay Liebeck an award of $2.7 million, but the trial judge reduced the award to $600,000 ("McDonald's Settles," 1994). In both civil trials, just as in criminal cases, judges may hear victim impact statements prior to making the final award or issuing the sentence.

PROCEDURAL RULES

General legal principles supply foundations that guide the communication processes of the legal system; specific principles predict the general content and structure of legal processes; and procedural rules establish guidelines for the communication of legal practitioners in litigation and appellate proceedings. Procedural rules (1) try to ensure the rights of the litigants and (2) provide for orderly conduct of legal processes. The overview that follows in this section establishes procedural guidelines for media coverage, jury selection and deliberation, opening statements, witness examination, and summations.

Media Coverage

Media coverage of trials informs the public about legal processes and practices and creates interest in legal proceedings. In many high-publicity cases, the public participates vicariously as spectator-jurors deliberating about the facts and evidence they glean from the media representations of the trials. Civil cases and appellate decisions typically attract less media interest than criminal trials do because criminal proceedings involve intense interpersonal conflicts, irreconcilable differences between parties, complex social issues, and life and death decisions. Throughout American history high-profile criminal trials have captured media attention because they provide live public entertainment. Sensational trials in the eighteenth and nineteenth centuries received extensive coverage from newspapers and handbills (Goldfarb, 1998). Because of their involvement of the international labor movement, the Sacco-Vanzetti trial gained notoriety through the international press (Young & Kaiser, 1985). The advent of radio in the 1920s, combined with the celebrity status of the Lindbergh family, resulted in live radio reenactments of the Hauptmann trial. In the Hauptmann trial, defense attorney Edward J. Reilly received his salary from the Hearst publishers in exchange for newsreel and newspaper access to the proceedings (Kennedy, 1985; Scaduto, 1976). By the 1950s the press coverage of trials had become so excessive that new restraints on the media needed to be added.

Nine years after the trial and guilty verdict for prominent Cleveland physician Sam Sheppard for the murder of his wife, F. Lee Bailey appealed Sheppard's conviction. The U.S. Supreme Court heard the appeal, and then the justices reversed the trial verdict, based on adverse pretrial publicity. As a result, the Court released Sheppard from prison, and jurors in a second state trial acquitted him of the murder charges. The appeal produced *Sheppard v. Maxwell* (1966), a landmark decision that developed laws regarding trial coverage and attempted to prevent the press from interfering with the rights of defendants. This decision mandated that judges take specific precautions in high-publicity trials to protect the constitutional rights of the accused (Schuetz & Snedaker, 1988).

PROVISIONS OF *SHEPPARD V. MAXWELL*

- Attorneys and judges can conduct extensive *voir dire* (questioning of potential jurors) to prevent pretrial publicity from influencing seated jurors' attitudes toward the accused.
- Judges can change the venue, that is, move the trial to another location to prevent potential jurors from exposure to the high levels of prejudicial pretrial publicity in the jurisdiction where the crimes took place.
- Judges can grant a motion of continuance to delay the trial until the emotional reactions of the community settle down.
- Judges can issue gag orders to limit the media from reporting details of the crime or the trial proceedings.
- Judges can issue silence orders to prohibit the participants in the trial from talking with the media.
- Judges can sequester jurors and prohibit them from communicating with their families and friends during a trial.

The *Sheppard* decision altered the way that judges balance the free press provisions of the First Amendment with the provisions for an impartial jury in the Sixth Amendment and the due process safeguards for defendants found in the Fifth Amendment. The provisions of *Sheppard* apply to newspapers, radio, television, and film producers. At this time, judges have not yet applied these provisions to Internet communication about legal actions.

Tensions still exist between the media's desire to cover the trial and the court's demand to protect the defendants. Denniston (1980) explains this tension:

> The journalist tells the story moving from the most significant to least, the lawyer moves in an opposite direction; the journalist wants immediate impact, the lawyer wants contemplated decisions; the journalist looks for the novel, the attorney for the familiar; the journalist is fascinated with the illogical; the attorney tries to establish a logic. (p. 6)

The positive impact of representational discourses about legal proceedings is that they have the potential to create positive social outcomes, expose legal injustices, identify procedural violations at trial, monitor police and the judiciary, and provide legal information to the public. In contrast to the positive consequences, this same coverage can negatively affect defendants' rights to fair trial, distort the conditions and amount of civil settlements, and confuse the public about the effects appeal court decisions may have on them.

The tensions between free press and a fair trial have produced many appellate rulings about media access to the court proceedings, the due process rights of defendants, the rights to an impartial jury, protections against adverse pretrial publicity, and judicial discretion in allowing cameras in the courtroom (Schuetz, 2001). The protections for the criminal defendant do not apply to civil defendants who often are maligned by the media prior to, during, and after a trial as Boston church leaders and the tobacco companies were. The media tend to report civil jury awards and pretrial settlements that involve large financial awards to plaintiffs. In a similar way, civil cases that originated as federal bench trials involving civil rights complaints, such as the trials that initiated *Brown v. Board of Education* and *Roe v. Wade,* received less media coverage before and during the legal process than they did after the Court published its decision. In contrast to these landmark decisions, however, the typical appellate decision attracts little media attention.

At the end of the twentieth century, all but three states permitted cameras in state trial courts under the discretion of the judge (Goldfarb, 1998; Graham, 1998). After the circus atmosphere of the O. J. Simpson murder trial, judges in state courts limited the use of cameras in their courtrooms. Some state appellate courts permit cameras in their appellate proceedings. Cameras were not allowed in the federal trials of McVeigh or the Chicago Eight, although victims of the Oklahoma City bombing observed the McVeigh trial through closed circuit television. Cameras typically are not permitted in federal courts or in federal appellate actions, although a few exceptions have occurred. Decisions about allowing cameras in courtrooms continue to fuel debates about the rights of the press to cover the courts, the public's right to know about legal matters affecting them, and the defendants' rights to a fair trial.

The Trial Jury

The Sixth Amendment provides for the criminal jury and the Seventh Amendment allows, but does not require, juries for civil cases. Those who support the jury system argue that jurors apply community standards, permit citizen participation in the justice system, guard against arbitrariness of judges, and provide a collective consciousness about the meaning of justice and fairness (Jonakait, 2003). The specific rules about jury size, composition, and decision making have undergone significant changes in the last twenty-five years. The norm for criminal juries is to have 12 persons representing a cross-section of the community who come to a unanimous verdict after being instructed by a judge. But, in 34 states (Starr & McCormick, 1993), criminal juries of 6 rather than 12 persons can decide cases. Civil trials typically have 6 or 12 persons. Jonakait (2003) emphasizes that over half of the states allow for nonunanimous civil verdicts, but the federal courts "may permit parties to agree to a nonunanimous verdict, otherwise [they] still require unanimity" and only 14 states require unanimous verdicts in civil cases (p. 96).

Complex jury selection procedures are a rather recent innovation. Until the late 1960s, some courts picked juries by the "call man" system that designated outstanding citizens of the community to select jurors. This method was used in both the Sacco-Vanzetti and the Hauptmann cases. Since the implementation of the *Uniform Jury Selection and Service Act* (1980), each state uses a jury commission to devise a plan for random selection of jurors for both criminal and civil juries. In 1995, Congress initiated new rules for jury selection, mandating that courts choose jurors from among vehicle registration lists, called motor-voter registration, a procedure devised to increase the diversity of persons in the jury pools. After choosing the jury venire (pool), typically 48 to 60 people, a judge or judicial clerk subpoenas a random sample of that population to report for jury service. In some high-profile criminal cases and high-stakes civil cases, attorneys hire jury consultants to design and evaluate juror profiles. In routine cases, the attorneys create juror profiles based on standard court surveys that elicit information about jurors' suitability for service in a particular case. The judge brings groups of potential jurors to the courtroom before the trial, and these potential jurors then undergo a process called *voir dire*, permitting the court to qualify citizens for service after they have been questioned and attorneys and judges have selected or challenged them. Judges conduct the *voir dire* questioning in some states, attorneys conduct questioning in other states, and both judges and attorneys jointly question jury pools in other states. Criminal cases require *voir dire,* but judges exercise considerable discretion in deciding what processes can be used in questioning potential jurors.

During this selection process, attorneys and judges can exercise cause and peremptory challenges resulting in the dismissal of a person from the jury venire.

PROCEDURES FOR JURY SELECTION

- The challenge for cause occurs when a judge or attorney believes the prospective juror is biased or incompetent.
- Peremptory challenges result in jurors being dismissed without reasons being given (*Swain v. Alabama*, 1965).
- The number of peremptory challenges allowed by judges depends on the potential punishment for defendants.
- In the majority of federal courts, the judge does all of the questioning, but attorneys issue most of the challenges.

Juror Decision Making

Once jurors and alternates are seated at a trial, they are expected to review the facts and discern the guilt or innocence of the defendant based on the criminal charges and decide the preponderance of evidence related to civil complaints. After the judge instructs jurors on how to proceed, they deliberate in secret. Although a number of myths claim that jurors make decisions based on their dislike or like for the attorneys, their sympathy for victims, or racial or gender justifications, most of the social science research shows that jurors make their decisions based on the evidence and in accordance with the law (Jonakait, 2003). In civil cases, judges tend to agree with the jurors' verdicts 84 percent of the time (Hannaford, Dann, & Munsterman, 1998).

To resolve the question about how jurors make decisions, Hastie, Penrod, and Pennington (1983) concluded that jurors engage in the following steps during their deliberations. They (1) establish "judgment categories based on judges' instructions," (2) exclude "irrelevant facts," and (3) apply a story model that condenses and connects evidence to characters, actions, and causal sequences (pp. 20–23). During deliberation, jurors initially vote with the majority, few individuals control the discussion, and jurors select verdicts according to the "internalized standard" they hold for "proper conduct" (pp. 23–29). Recent studies show that jurors use their own life experiences to organize the facts they receive from trial narratives and then draw plausible inferences about the story based on what scenarios fit best with their life experiences (Bennett & Feldman, 1981; Finkel, 1995).

Some of the recent innovations implemented by states to improve their jury systems are the training of jurors after they have been selected (Dann, 1993), taking steps to enhance the clarity of the judge's instructions to juries (Hannaford, Dann, & Munsterman, 1998), experimenting with mid-trial deliberations (Myers & Griller, 1997), and permitting jurors to ask questions of witnesses through written inquiries presented to the presiding judge (Heuer & Penrod, 1990). Advocates of jury reform claim that the lack of judge–juror communication is a major problem in the jury system. To improve the quality of communication between judges and jurors, Smith (1996) recommended judges simplify their instructions, provide commentary on the evidence, and permit some of the routinely excluded evidence to be heard by jurors. Myers and Griller (1997) advised courts to try to enhance jurors' decision making by allowing them to discuss evidence among themselves prior to deliberations, submit written questions directly to witnesses, and address oral questions directly to the judge. A 1993 Arizona law that included most of the aforementioned court reforms shows a record of success in implementing changes.

Opening Statements

The importance of opening statements to trial outcomes is the subject of much debate. For example, some trial lawyers believe that a cogent opening statement leads jurors to make up their minds about a verdict early in the trial process (Murray, 1995). Other research (Burke, Poulson, & Brondino, 1992; Jonakait, 2003) claims that jurors hear all of the evidence before they make their decisions. Procedural rules permit attorneys to introduce a case theory by describing the key characters (defendants) and their relationships to witnesses, identifying the scene where the alleged illegal acts occurred, and offering causal explanations of the alleged action (Murray, 1995; Spangenberg, 1982). A primary function of the opening statement is to condense the theory of the case into a believable story with a theme or slogan that encapsulates the case theory (Matlon, 1993; Schuetz & Snedaker, 1988). Some of the themes that subsequent chapters identify are: The defendants committed evil acts because of mental illness (the pedophile priests). The defendants concealed health information from smokers and enhanced the addictive potency of cigarettes to make money (Minnesota tobacco). The defendant sought revenge against the government because he distrusted government policies (McVeigh). The crime was committed by someone other than the defendant (Hauptmann). The defendants confessed under duress caused by physical or psychological abuse (Sacco-Vanzetti). The defendant was framed by the police (Simpson). The attorneys argued that state laws violated the constitutional rights of Brown and Roe.

The procedural rules allow judges to impose time limits on opening statements, usually 30 minutes to one hour. Opening statements in complex trials, however, may consume as much as three or four hours of time. The following rules restrict the content of the communication in opening statements:

PROCEDURES FOR OPENING STATEMENTS

- The rules prohibit attorneys from arguing in this phase of the trial and from presenting a two-sided explanation of the facts.
- The rules prohibit attorneys from asking jurors to decide evidence and inferences about the meaning of the evidence.
- The rules prohibit attorneys from using emotional appeals that play on the prejudices of jurors, making remarks about the character of opposing attorneys, and referring to the attorney's personal experiences and beliefs (Tanford, 1983).
- The rules ask attorneys to preview only the evidence that will be presented in the trial for their side of the case.
- The rules ask attorneys to refrain from discussing the case of their opponents.
- The rules ask attorneys to eliminate references to legal principles that do not apply to their case.
- The rules permit attorneys to use visual aids and evocative language.
- The rules permit attorneys to identify objects that will be used as an exhibit in the case (Haydock & Sonsteng, 1991; Julien, 1980; Murray, 1995).

The purpose of these rules is to restrict the content to one-sided persuasion and to limit the emotional content so that the opening statement is a condensed explanation of the whole case.

Witness Examination

The attorneys use the testimony of their own witnesses to elaborate the stories they tell in opening statements. The specific purpose of direct examination is to get the witnesses to elaborate a piece of the whole story that has been forecast in opening statements by introducing evidence and connecting it to the story of the case advanced by the attorneys examining them (*Federal Rules of Evidence*, 1995).

Although attorneys have more latitude in conducting direct examination than they do in cross-examination, the following procedural rules place limits on how attorneys examine their own witnesses:

PROCEDURES FOR DIRECT EXAMINATION

- Attorneys should "ascertain truth," avoid "needless consumption of time," and "protect witnesses from harassment."

- Attorneys should control "the manner, order, and scope" of the witnesses' testimony through open-ended questions.
- Attorneys should ask questions to frame and limit the stories of witnesses.
- Attorneys should ask open-ended questions that enable witnesses to elaborate on their observations.
- Attorneys should present their witnesses in a coherent order so that they report facts and verify themes related to the story presented in opening statements.
- Attorneys can introduce demonstrative evidence, such as documents, objects, and visual materials with witnesses.
- Attorneys can use direct examination to introduce physical objects or real evidence, such as weapons, bomb fragments, clothing from the crime scene, fingerprints, shoe prints, and DNA blood evidence (Haydock & Sonsteng, 1994a).

The rules for direct examination enable witnesses to tell their stories in everyday language as long as they refrain from talking about matters that do not pertain to the disputed issues of the case. In contrast, the rules for cross-examination tend to impede prosaic storytelling, refute the facts witnesses have stated under direct examination, and establish the credibility of witnesses.

Cross-examination

To accomplish the goal of impeaching witnesses' testimony, cross-examination rules permit attorneys to elicit testimony favorable to their side of the case and discredit the witnesses of the opposition (Bailey & Rothblatt, 1971; Haydock & Sonsteng, 1994a; Iannuzzi, 1982). The rules for cross-examination are more restrictive than they are for direct examination.

PROCEDURES FOR CROSS-EXAMINATION

- Attorneys should reshape "adversaries' evidence into pieces, which, by the end of the trial, will fit together with the advocate's own evidence," forming a "mosaic of fact" that supports the case (Iannuzzi, 1982, p. 8).
- Attorneys should cross-examine witnesses that have a central role in the case because of their proximity to the crime, their eyewitness accounts, their victimage, or their unique information about the circumstances of the crime (Schuetz & Snedaker, 1988).
- Rules prohibit cross-examiners from asking questions that go beyond the scope of direct examination.
- Rules forbid cross-examiners from asking questions that argue, confuse, intimidate and/or assume facts not in evidence (Lubet, 1993).
- Rules enable attorneys to change the order of the testimony presented during direct examination. Instead of eliciting stories of the witnesses in a chronological order, rules permit cross-examiners to elicit testimony in a different order from the direct examination.

In addition to specific guidelines for the content of direct and cross-examination, rules of evidence apply both to direct and cross-examination. These rules of evidence permit attorneys to object to the lines of questioning adopted by the opposition during witnesses' testimony under the following conditions:

PROCEDURES FOR USING EVIDENCE

- The question is incompetent because the witness lacks the knowledge or personal observations to answer the question.
- The question is irrelevant if no relationship exists between one item of evidence and facts that pertain to the case.
- The question is immaterial when it does not pertain to issues of an indictment or a pleading.
- The question calls for a conclusion because the witness must interpret rather than report information.
- The question calls for hearsay evidence based on reports of others rather than on the witness's own knowledge.
- The question lacks a foundation because the assumptions behind the question are not presented by the questioner.
- The question is unclear, complex, compound, or in some way unintelligible.
- The questioner argues with a witness by challenging what the witness says.
- The witness provides information beyond the scope of the question.

The process of examining witnesses is so important to fact-finding in trials that courts have established a broad range of procedural rules to facilitate fairness in questioning and to ensure that the quality of the evidence meets judicial standards. These rules may appear overly stringent, but the subsequent case studies indicate that these kinds of rules do not inhibit attorneys' rhetorical efforts to develop and refute narratives, engage in believable performances, or create clever game strategies to outmaneuver their opponents.

Summations

The summations of the prosecution and defense attempt to solidify the facts and evidence presented by their witnesses during direct and cross-examination as well as refute the testimony given by the witnesses of opposing attorneys. Effective and ethical direct and cross-examinations pave the way for a strong summation. The success of summations depends to some extent on the preceding content. Although sources disagree about the importance of summations (Ball, 1997; Mauet, 1992; Schuetz & Lilley, 1999; Stein, 1985), most sources acknowledge that this final speech creates a dramatic apex for a trial. This part of the trial should contrast the quality of evidence and credibility of witnesses for one side of a case with that of the opposing side. The rules for a summation focus on argumentation and refutation. The summation consists of two parts: closing arguments and rebuttal. The law typically defines the scope and content of summations as "an organized presentation of your case in its best possible light: a theory of what happened supported by evidence and common sense" (Tanford, 1983, p. 133).

PROCEDURES FOR SUMMATION

- Rules permit attorneys to reiterate and emphasize the theme of the case, organize and emphasize favorable evidence, present the position they want the jury to adopt, refute the allegations of the opposition, suggest ways the jury should resolve conflicting testimony, explain the law, and demonstrate how the evidence mandates a verdict favorable to one's own side of the case.
- Rules prohibit attorneys from appealing directly to jurors' sympathies or playing on their emotions or prejudices.
- Rules prohibit attorneys from putting themselves in the victim's or the defendant's position, asking jurors to base their decisions on broad social issues, and addressing a single juror by name.
- In the rebuttal phase of the summation, rules allow attorneys to emphasize the issues presented in their summation but prohibit them from introducing new lines of argument and new exhibits.

The aforementioned rules attempt to elevate the importance of the argumentation and reduce the importance of emotion. Such rules, however, do not foreclose the probability that attorneys will configure their summations into persuasive narratives and performances. The legal issues embedded in the attorneys' narratives create cognitive frameworks for jurors to use to interpret the law and decide facts according to their coherence, probability, and believability.

Appellate Procedures

The procedures emphasize the stages of the appeal process more than the conduct of the appellate practitioners. The first stage is to file a notice of appeal, usually within 10 to 30 days, with a clerk of the court in which the trial took place. After receiving the notice of appeal and the appeal briefs, the clerk mails copies of the appeal to the other parties and to the court where the appeal will be decided. The clerk then places the appeal on a docket of an appellate court and lists the names of the parties involved. Second, the petitioners (those representing the people initiating the appeal) pay a fee for the appeal. The size of the fee varies according to the statutes of the jurisdiction. Third, the respondents (those contesting the appeal) file briefs along with a written record of the trial court proceeding with the appeals court. The appeals court usually limits attorneys' briefs to 50 pages. The briefed arguments and evidence follow an explicit structure; the briefs begin with the statement of the legal questions to be decided, identify the relevant statutes, note the factual basis of legal questions, argue about what legal precedents apply, and ask for a reversal or affirmation of the arguments presented to the court. Appellate judges can refuse to hear cases because the arguments submitted in the briefs lack merit. Some courts decide cases based only on the content of the briefs without giving an opportunity for attorneys to make oral arguments. Fourth, after the appeals court agrees to hear a case, attorneys can present oral arguments, using summaries of the issues followed with questions from the judges about the issues, the meaning of the statutes and precedents, the content of the briefed arguments, and the implications of those arguments. The appeals court usually limits the length of the oral arguments to 30 minutes for each side. Clerks reread and evaluate the content of the briefs, and judges discuss the case prior to issuing a written opinion. The written opinion becomes part of the common law of a jurisdiction and serves as a precedent for future decisions on similar issues and becomes part of the official legal discourse (Abraham, 1980; Schwartz, 1996; Stern, Gressman, & Shapiro, 1986; Weiner, 1967).

Each of the above procedural rules attempts to increase the fairness and orderliness of legal proceedings. Some of these procedural rules, for example, those specified in the *Sheppard v. Maxwell* (1966) decision, create guidelines that are subject to the judge's discretion in relation to the media publicity of a particular case. Other rules establish limits on the power of attorneys over witnesses, such as the procedures for direct and cross-examination. Still others, such as the rules for summations, attempt to constrain the passions of courtroom participants and retain the focus of the trial on adversarial argumentation and fact-finding. The procedural rules specify the conditions under which the communication in legal proceedings should take place. Although legal practitioners often violate procedural rules, one role of the judiciary is to apply these rules equally to the different sides of the case. Some research on legal communication ignores the procedural rules and focuses instead only on rhetorical practices and social outcomes. Because legal principles and procedural rules constrain the communication of legal practitioners, these important restraints should not be ignored. For this reason, the subsequent interpretations of types and features of discourses, language, arguments, narratives, dramas, and games take into account how principles, procedures, and protocols constrain and frame trial and appellate communication.

PROFESSIONAL CONDUCT

Professional codes specify the responsibilities that legal professionals should uphold, and they supply ideals for ethical legal practice. The Model Code of Professional Responsibility (adopted by the American Bar Association in 1969 and amended over the years since then) and the Model Code of Professional Conduct (adopted by the American Bar Association in 1983 and amended over the years since then) provide different, but overlapping, guidelines for ethical conduct. These sources provide specific guidelines for legal and communication practices and processes.

CODES OF CONDUCT AND PROFESSIONAL RESPONSIBILITY

- Conflicts of interest should preclude attorneys from conducting a case.
- Attorneys should uphold their duties to clients, including attorney–client confidentiality and privilege.
- Attorneys should share trial evidence with opposing attorneys according to the rules of discovery.
- Attorneys and judges should take seriously their responsibility for protecting the fairness of the judicial process.
- Attorneys should honor financial agreements, such as charges for services and free service to indigent clients.
- Attorneys should avoid needless delays of the court proceedings.
- Attorneys should be truthful and honest in their dealings with the courts and with their clients.

Since the codes are not laws per se, attorneys and judges may violate these standards without suffering adverse consequences. Violations of conduct that abridge laws, however, can result in contempt-of-court charges and lead to fines or other court-ordered restraints or punishments. Egregious violations, such as bribery of witnesses or soliciting perjured testimony, are also under the sanction of criminal statutes and can result in the removal of attorneys and judges from legal practice. Although these codes were not in the same form as they are today, they still affected the professional conduct of trial attorneys, defendants, and judges in the Hauptmann, Sacco-Vanzetti, and Chicago Eight cases.

When they established their Model Code of Professional Conduct, the American Bar Association (1983) prohibited attorneys from engaging in the following conduct:

PROHIBITED CONDUCT

- Attorneys may not state or allude to any matter that they have no reasonable basis to believe is relevant to the case or that will not be supported by admissible evidence.
- Attorneys may not ask any question that they have no reasonable basis to believe is relevant to the case and that is intended to degrade a witness or other person.
- Attorneys may not assert their personal knowledge of the facts in issue, except when testifying as a witness.
- Attorneys may not assert their personal opinion as to the justness of a cause, as to the credibility of a witness . . . the culpability of civil litigants, or . . . the guilt or innocence of the accused.
- Attorneys may not fail to comply with known local customs of courtesy or practice of the bar of a particular tribunal without giving to opposing counsel a timely notice of their intent not to comply.

- Attorneys may not engage in undignified or discourteous conduct that is degrading to a tribunal.
- Attorneys may not intentionally or habitually violate any established rule of procedure or evidence.

The guidelines provide the basis for what constitutes professional conduct. Explanations of procedural rules for trial advocacy (Fontham, 1995; Mauet, 1992; Tanford, 1983) often incorporate some of these provisions into their training manuals. And some of the rules for criminal and civil procedure incorporate provisions from the Model Code of Professional Conduct. In addition to these kinds of general rules, trial lawyers have identified pertinent ethical consideration for those who conduct jury trials. These standards offer guidelines for attorney relationships with jurors and the judiciary, communication to the media, the content of trial speeches, the treatment of one's own and adversarial witnesses, and the relationships between attorneys and their clients. Subsequent chapters identify specific rules that pertain to the ethical practices of trial participants in selected case studies.

PROTOCOLS

Protocols may be more important to judges than codes of conduct are. Protocols refer to the communication associated with routines, rituals, and formalized practices of the courts. In some cases, protocols take the form of written and codified rules; at other times, they are statements about behavior that are orally transmitted by the bailiffs and judges to the trial participants and spectators. The lower the court, the less explicit the protocols are. City courts permit less formality and fewer protocols than state courts, and federal courts and courts of appeals require more formality that the lower courts do. All courts abide by some formal and ritualistic practices about addressing the judge, the use of courtroom space, and acceptable language and demeanor. A person unfamiliar with these protocols learns about them from the clerk of the judge who is hearing a case or from the courtroom bailiff who transmits this information through written and oral statements to participants and spectators before the trial. When citizens participate as witnesses, attorneys ordinarily inform them about the protocols they should follow. During the trial, judges and attorneys are expected to follow the protocols of the jurisdiction where they are practicing.

The architecture of the courtroom reinforces protocols that give authority and respect to judges and emphasize the formal communication expected from trial court participants. For example, "the judge's bench dominates the courtroom" and is located opposite the public entrance. The judge is seated above the proceedings in a place of power and the trial practitioners address judges as "Your Honor." Trial judges dress in ecclesiastical robes and speak with authority about the meaning of the rules and procedures. Trial judges also ask attorneys to seek their permission to move away from the lectern or approach the judge when they speak.

The witness chair usually is located to one side of the bench, with the witnesses "facing the same direction as the judge, but seated at a lower level." The bailiff administers the oath asking witnesses to swear "to tell the truth and the whole truth." The judge reprimands witnesses if they violate the norms for respectfulness to the court. "The jury box is located against the side wall on the same side of the bench as the witness chair" so that judge, jurors, attorneys, and court reporters can hear and see the witness and the exhibits introduced with the testimony. Jurors wear badges with numbers on them and stand to show their respect when the judge enters the courtroom.

Counsel tables are provided for the attorneys and their clients. This table usually faces the judge and the witnesses, enabling the defendants and their attorneys to see the faces of those who have accused them. The counsel tables hold notebooks and stacks of documents that add visual evidence about the amount of proof attorneys have accumulated to support their side of the case. The attorneys for each side can whisper to each other when witnesses are testifying. Clients, however, usually communicate using notes and/or nonverbal acknowledgments (Jeans, 1993, pp. 254–266).

The bailiff often is the stage director for the trial court proceeding; he or she explains the process as well as the roles and demeanor appropriate for the legal proceeding. The bailiff signals the opening of the court session by a rap of a gavel or some type of hand signal that directs all those present in the courtroom to stand. While everyone is standing, the judge and jurors enter the courtroom. Then the bailiff likely reads or speaks an official proclamation similar to the following: "Everyone please rise. The District Court of the _____ judicial district in the County of _____ is now open. Judge _____ is presiding. Please be seated." The bailiff maintains order as attorneys, witnesses, and the public assemble in the courtroom, during the trial, and even during recesses in the proceeding. Bailiffs admit witnesses to the courtroom, direct spectators to their seats, monitor the admission of spectators to the court, and assess the seating capacities of the courtroom. Court clerks (bailiffs may also serve this role) swear in witnesses, ask each witness to state his or her full name for the court, and invite witnesses to be seated while they testify. Bailiffs assemble jurors in the jury room, warn them about a recess, provide tools for taking notes, and ensure jurors can hear and see the proceedings.

Attorneys uphold the decorum of the court by advising their clients and witnesses about appropriate behavior. Attorneys, as officers of the court, are expected to uphold the honor and maintain the dignity of the profession by rising and remaining standing while addressing the court and jurors and by asking the judge's permission to approach the bench or to introduce evidence. Attorneys maintain the decorum of the court by referring to the judge as "Your Honor" or "The Court," asking permission to talk with the judge or to circulate documents, and making explicit requests: "Your honor, may I approach the bench?" The court expects attorneys to be polite, respectful, and refrain from interrupting the communication of other court participants.

Judges' responsibilities resemble those of the officials at a sporting event. Presiding judges are also dignified representatives of justice and fairness in the legal system whom the public expects will, in an impartial manner, show respect to attorneys and witnesses and show interest in the evidence and arguments presented during the trial. Some of the trappings of the courts reify the power and prestige of judges by requiring them to wear a robe, sit above the proceeding in a place that enables them to have surveillance over the courtroom, give orders to participants, reprimand bad behavior, and compliment good behavior of trial participants. Judges typically refrain from examining witnesses. The judge holds responsibility for order and decorum of the court and for enabling court reporters to produce a clear and accurate record of the court. The judge also keeps order. If attorneys or witnesses overstep the boundaries established by procedural rules, then the judge interrupts them and restores order. Judges have discretion over the behavior, demeanor, dress, and talk permitted in their court. Some judges are strict, and others are permissive. Through the legal grapevine and through personal experiences, attorneys learn what protocols a particular judge will enforce in his or her court. When participants violate protocols, the judge has the power to dismiss the court or to issue a contempt order because some judges view protocols as important legal rules that enable dignified communication practices in courtrooms.

The protocols for the courts of appeals are even more extensive than those of the trial courts. The architecture of the Supreme Court gives the courtroom the look and feel of a royal palace in which thick red velvet drapes line the walls and ushers dressed like royal guards seat the spectators. The chamber's 24 marble columns reach to the 44-foot ceilings. The portraits of lawgivers from history line the high walls. "The room is dominated by the Justices' long raised bench"; they are dressed in black robes with white collars (Schwartz, 1996, p. 15). Tables for the appellate attorneys located beneath the justices direct them to face upward to the justices when they speak. The attorneys can use the goose quill pens placed on their desks while they await their chance to present oral arguments. Schwartz (1996) described the scene for the 1989 arguments of the *Webster* case in this way. He recalled:

> At the sound of the gavel, all in the packed courtroom rose and remained standing while the court crier intoned the time-honored cry, "Oyez! Oyez! Oyez! All persons having business before the Honorable, The Supreme Court of the United States, are admonished to draw near and give their attention, for the Court is now sitting. God save the United States and the Honorable Court." (p. 14)

Attorneys address the judges as "Justice Breyer" or "Justice Kennedy." The court addresses the attorneys as "Mr. Oliva" or "Ms. Murray." The justices interrupt the appellate attorneys' oral arguments soon after they begin to speak by asking them to provide detailed evidence for the arguments they make or to explain what precedents mean in terms of the case that is being argued. At times, they reprimand the attorneys for speaking too fast or for making unclear arguments. When I personally visited the Court, I was struck by the fact that during the oral arguments, the ushers enforced silence on all of the spectators. When some law students seated near me created barely audible sounds by rustling through some papers, the ushers told them to remain quiet or they would have to leave the courtroom. Protocols of respect for authority, formal dress, polite demeanor, and communication rituals also apply to many of the state and federal appellate courts. These protocols emphasize the importance of the communication, the authority of the decision makers, and the potency of the professional legal discourse.

LESSONS

The Constitution and statutes provide the foundational principles for legal practices and processes. Procedural rules try to create fair and balanced legal processes. Rules for professional conduct identify standards for ethical practices, and protocols ensure the decorum of the practitioners in court and enforce formal demeanor. The principles of the Constitution and statutes are the grounds for legal proceedings. What makes legal disputes unpredictable is that the general principles and the statutes are open to more than one interpretation. The role of interpreter is shared between judges, trial attorneys, trial witnesses, jurors, and appellate attorneys and judges. The specific principles regarding case origins, settlements, and standards of proof are not principles about human conduct but about legal processes and, as such, do not create much controversy.

The procedural rules attempt to ensure the rights of those on trial; at the same time, they try to provide for fair and orderly processes. These procedural rules usually are part of the professional discourse that regulates the impact of representational and prosaic discourses. In conducting cross-examination, for example, the rules of procedure place significant constraints on what attorneys can say and do. In other phases of the legal process, the rules guide rather than proscribe attorneys' communication. Rules of professional conduct offer ethical guidelines for the communication presented in legal proceedings. These rules of conduct provide ideals, such as respectful relationships, truthful messages, and fair use of strategies and tactics. The rules of conduct privilege reasoning over passion, efficiency over redundancy, and judicial authority over attorney autonomy.

The protocols embellish the narratives, performances, and games that occur in courtrooms. Protocols attempt to impress courtroom spectators and participants that the court is a powerful social authority that demands dignity and decorum. The protocols differ in intensity from the court of one judge to that of another, from one legal jurisdiction to another, and from one type of legal proceeding to another. Protocols make it clear that the court has the power to make citizens comply with the law. Bailiffs and clerks are stage directors, holding the responsibility to communicate what the protocols are to those who participate in or observe the proceedings. Transgressions of protocols result in reprimands, such as a nonverbal sign to quit talking or to move to a different location, or more severe sanctions including removal from the court. Protocols affect the communication of the law in significant ways that will be elaborated in subsequent chapters.

Trial attorneys learn from their own experiences and those of others that some judges are lenient, and others enforce strict compliance with all rules. Judges in the Hauptmann, Sacco-Vanzetti, Simpson, and Chicago Eight trials contravened some of the expectations for orderly conduct of the trial because they failed to enforce some of the rules of procedure, conduct, and protocols of the courts where they presided. In combination with the general and specific principles, the procedural and conduct rules and protocols shape what trial participants can say and do in legal forums and provide semblances of uniformity across different jurisdictions. These rules may differ slightly from one jurisdiction to another, and some courts and judges may be more rigorous in enforcing the rules than others. Collectively the principles, procedures, and protocols influence the language, arguments, discourses, narratives, dramas, and games that occur as part of legal processes and practices.

3

The Pseudo Civil Case of the *Boston Globe* v. Archdiocese of Boston

The *Boston Globe*'s coverage of priest sex abuse created a crisis for the church that Thomas Groome claimed was the church's September 11 (Dokecki, 2004). The *Globe*'s coverage of the pedophile priest abuse cases had immense consequences for the Catholic Church as an institution. Moreover, the case revealed how systematic and thorough investigative reporting can produce institutional change. Powers (2002) explains the impact of the reporting in this way:

> The Catholic Church's pedophilia crisis, which began in Boston last year with one monstrous priest, has quickly become an international news story of the first magnitude. . . . Here is a tale of corruption at the highest levels of an immensely important global institution; of the powerful exploiting of the powerless; of lying to the public, private cover-up, and high-grade hypocrisy. In short, it has all the elements of a truly epic news story, the sort of thing that comes along once or twice in a generation and winds up changing society in fundamental ways. (p. 4)

In most sensational cases, media coverage influences the conduct of the trial, but the *Boston Globe*'s reporting about priest sex abuse had far greater consequences than influencing a trial. The *Globe*'s extensive coverage influenced international church policies, changed the ways seminaries train men for the priesthood, gave voice to victims, attacked the church's hierarchy, and even got the attention of Pope John Paul II in Rome. The content and the consequences of the coverage are significant. This chapter does not analyze how the reporters conducted their investigation. Rather it explains how they reported their investigation in ways that resemble a pseudo civil case. This chapter (1) explains the relationship between the press and crime; (2) identifies the goals that guide investigative reporters; (3) analyzes the content of the news reports created by the investigative reporters of the *Boston*

Globe as they evolved through (a) a prologue, (b) rising action, (c) crisis, (d) falling action, and (e) an epilogue; (4) shows how each of these dramatic stages create a pseudo civil lawsuit; and (5) describes lessons learned from this example of investigative reporting of crime.

NEWS COVERAGE AND LAW

Newspapers have a long history of covering crime, starting in the early days of the nation and continuing in the present time. For example, Graber (1980) found the three major newspapers in Chicago gave 25 percent of their coverage to crime and related issues. A content analysis of the front pages of major newspapers in Chicago, Los Angeles, and Philadelphia showed that 30 percent of front-page coverage dealt with crime and justice (Lotz, 1991). After the advent of Court TV and extensive cable coverage of crime and justice issues, newspapers continued to feature front-page stories on crime (Goldfarb, 1998). Frequently, the day-to-day reporting about crime and criminals attract audiences' attention by emphasizing the character traits of the perpetrators and the accusers, dramatizing the motives and effects of criminal actions, and commenting about the performances of the attorneys.

Some of the coverage of crime and corporate malfeasance results from investigative reporting, but most media coverage does not. Instead, media coverage concentrates on the police's search for perpetrators of the crime and, later, on how the courts help bring the perpetrators to justice through plea bargains, settlements, and/or trials. In general, the media get involved with criminal trials because these legal proceedings attract more public interest then civil cases do. The media tend to pay attention to civil cases only when they involve celebrity defendants, such as Martha Stewart; the products of companies that are so negligent that people die, such as lethal pharmaceutical products; or flawed institutional polices that produce extensive financial repercussions, such as those of Enron executives. In a few high-profile civil actions, such as negligence of automobile manufacturers, reporters added evidence from their investigation to show the effects of the defective products. However, investigative reporting that aids the settlement of a civil case is rare, and the systematic and committed reporting that mirrors the procedures of a civil action is exceptional.

INVESTIGATIVE REPORTING

Infrequently, newspaper reporters take on the role of investigators who serve as "custodians of public conscience" (Ettema & Glasser, 1998, p. 3). The Spotlight Team of the *Boston Globe* took on this role when they covered the priest sex abuse cases in the Archdiocese of Boston. Investigative reporting differs from the typical approaches to covering crimes or reporting institutional malfeasance. This kind of reporting, according to Ettema and Glasser (1998), produces "stories that are carefully verified and skillfully narrated accounts of specific injury and injustice . . . with a meaning that always transcends the facts of a particular case" (p. 3). The *Globe*'s investigative reporters uncovered hidden meanings and exposed detrimental policies from their research of one criminal trial involving one priest in Boston. Through their sophisticated reporting, they showed the consequences of this one trial for the policies of a powerful international private institution, the Roman Catholic Church.

Several features distinguish investigative reporters from typical news gatherers (Ettema & Glasser, 1998):

GOALS OF INVESTIGATIVE REPORTERS

- Reporters "call attention to the breakdown of social systems and the disorder within public institutions that cause injury and injustice." (p. 3)
- Reporters "implicitly demand the response of public officials—and the public itself—to the breakdown and disorder." (p. 3)
- Reporters ask "us as a society to decide what is and what is not, an outrage to our sense of moral order, and to consider our expectations for our officials, our institutions, and ultimately ourselves." (p. 3)
- Reporters address immoral actions, "civic vice," and show "the possibility of enhanced virtue in the conduct of public affairs." (p. 7)

The explanations noted above indicate that investigative reporters focus their attention on vices of public officials and moral problems of public institutions. The *Boston Globe*'s investigative reporters, the Spotlight Team, dealt with the moral breakdown in the Catholic Church, a private institution. The reporters emphasized that priests committed sex abuse and church leaders disregarded the needs of victims of that abuse. Moreover, these reporters demanded an accounting of the church's immoral behavior, used their news stories to create a sense of public outrage about priest sex abuse, proposed a response for the church to take with sex abuse victims, and attempted to restore virtue to the church leadership.

Investigative reporters begin with public information, and then they seek out suppressed information, secrets, unknown facts, and sources that know what is behind a story. The *Globe*'s investigative team first reported information that was available from the criminal trial of retired Boston priest John Geoghan, a defendant that jurors later convicted of molesting young boys. The information the reporters gathered from the documents and proceedings of that criminal trial convinced them that the incidents of abuse were a symptom of a much deeper problem in the Catholic Church. The trial sparked their interest about the breadth of the problem of clergy sex abuse and involvement of church leaders in dealing with pedophile priests and their victims. The *Globe* reporters then interviewed and published news stories about dozens of other victims of Geoghan and of other priests in the Boston area. Eventually, with the assistance of the attorneys representing the newspaper, the reporters gained access to the church's personnel files of priests accused of sex crimes. As the process continued, reporters eventually targeted the person in charge of the priests in Boston, Cardinal Bernard Law. Hundreds of stories written by the investigative reporters of the *Boston Globe* about the vices of the church created moral outrage, especially with Boston Catholics and also with other citizens throughout the country.

This chapter emphasizes the positive role that investigative reporters can play in informing the public about crime and injustice and promoting institutional change. The traditional role of investigative reporters is to find and report facts about wrongdoing of public officials and institutions. In recent years, the press's role has expanded to include surveillance of questionable practices of private and religious institutions and their leaders. When investigative reporters determine that either public or private entities have obviated their responsibilities or failed to live up to public moral standards, they try to force the institutions to account for their actions. The investigative reporting of the *Boston Globe* resembled coverage of political scandals. For more than a year, *Globe* reporters mounted a vigorous and relentless set of complaints against Cardinal Bernard Law, asked him to apologize and resign, and exposed the long history of the Archdiocese of Boston's negligence in dealing with pedophile priests and their victims. In particular, the investigative reporters claimed Cardinal Law knew about priest abuse of children, but he failed to take appropriate actions against the perpetrators.

In a long, dramatic news serial, extending from January 2002 through January 2003, the *Globe*'s investigative reporters created a pseudo civil case against the church on behalf of the sex abuse victims. By pseudo case, I mean a legal proceeding that is not real but has the appearance and creates the illusion of a real civil proceeding. This pseudo case followed many of the processes and procedures of conventional legal actions. If the *Globe* acted as a plaintiff in a real trial, the reporters would file a complaint against the Boston archdiocese, ask the church to give an accounting of its actions to the public, and seek relief for the victims of priest abusers.

The investigative reporters (the Spotlight Team) did not intend to conduct a pseudo case, but they lodged substantive and damaging complaints, brought forth witnesses and evidence, conducted complex adversarial negotiations, impeached church leaders, and demanded monetary settlements and institutional change in ways that mimic the processes of real civil legal proceedings. Editorial and legal support from the owners and operators of the *Boston Globe* enabled the reporters to pursue the case and to produce extensive and potent coverage that resulted in constructive changes in Catholic Church policies and practices. In contrast to the common practice of blaming the press for interfering with the courts, this chapter emphasizes how committed and persistent reporters covered the story and acted as custodians of the public's moral conscience.

The *Globe*'s serial coverage produced thousands of column inches and hundreds of different stories that related to this drama. These stories were transformed into a book by the investigative reporters (Investigative Staff, 2002). Other journalists praised the efforts of the investigative reporters. For example, Bill Keller of the *New York Times* credited the Spotlight Team with making the church accountable. He said, "Every detail of the sordid story has had to be dragged from the reluctant archdiocese, mostly by the dogged investigative reporting of the *Boston Globe*" (quoted in Cannon, 2002). Tom Fox, publisher of the *National Catholic Reporter,* wrote that "getting the secret deliberations of a Cardinal out in the open was a revelation . . . [that the church] was not pastoral, it was defensive and legalistic" (quoted in Cannon, 2002, p. 24). Columnist Ellen Goodman compared the scandal in the Boston Catholic Church to that of Enron because both involved a cover-up, a near bankruptcy, and a CEO scrambling to save his reputation (Goodman, 2002). The coverage produced a "national mega story" that persuaded Catholics that priests and their superiors (bishops, archbishops, and cardinals) should be immediately removed when they engage in sex abuse or fail to report or remove known abusers (Jurkowitz, 2002).

ANALYSIS OF THE COVERAGE

The subsequent analysis connects stages of an emerging newspaper drama with features of civil proceedings: (1) the prologue situates the dispute in an historical and legal context; (2) the rising action identifies church leaders' actions and reactions regarding clergy sexual abuse; (3) the complications explain how the press initiated the pseudotrial by issuing complaints, seeking church responses, and engaging in the discovery of evidence; (4) the climax features the impending settlements, disseminating new evidence, and the impeaching of Cardinal Law; (5) the resolution centers on the expansion of complaints and contentious negotiations; and (6) the epilogue speculates about the investigative reporters, pseudo civil trials, and institutional policy.

Prologue

The prologue for this coverage is unusually long because the issues are situated in a complex legal and historical context. My purpose here is not to claim that the reporters researched the legal and historical background as I have done. Rather this section explains the legal and institutional history that likely influenced the actions of church leaders and motivated the investigative reporters to cover the sex abuse story. This explanation of the legal principles, church policies, and circumventions of law provides grounding for the issues of the dispute addressed by investigative reporters.

Legal Principles.   The legal principle of separation of church and state was at issue in the *Globe v. Archdiocese of Boston.* Conflicts between church and state law are well documented in First Amendment Supreme Court decisions. One of the church–state issues is the right of citizens to the free exercise of religion. The Court has defined "free exercise" in several cases involving the right of Jehovah Witnesses to engage in door-to-door soliciting, the rights of members of some religious groups to refuse military service, the suspension of education requirements for Amish children, and the legitimacy of government aid for church-affiliated schools (Miller & Flowers, 1977). The courts, however, have not dealt with jurisdictional issues involving church and state law in any systematic way. In fact, the appellate courts have permitted churches to retain separate policies and practices that protect them from government intrusion into private institutional matters. This legal tradition enabled the Catholic Church to have its own policies and rules regarding personnel, a separate code called canon law for defining standards of clergy conduct, a separate set of procedures for resolving disputes using a church tribunal, and an unstated policy of protecting clergy sex abusers from criminal charges in the public courts. The church hid clergy sex abuse behind "the wall of separation," an interpretation of the First Amendment that guarantees a separation of religious organizations from state control. When the pedophile priest scandals became public, *Globe* reporters started to tear down the wall that had allowed Catholic Church officials to avoid the provisions of Massachusetts laws regarding sex abuse of children.

Every state, including Massachusetts, has statutes that prohibit adults from having sexual contact with minors. Legal authorities mistakenly assumed that Massachusetts's Catholic leaders had an effective policy written in canon law for dealing with sexual abusers, and therefore the state decided not to intervene in the personnel matters of this private institution. According to canon law, a clergy member against whom criminal allegations have been made and supported, or even suspected of being supported, can be suspended from duties without a trial by means of a church-ordered decree. Those charged can also face a tribunal and have the matter decided by rules of canon law and church-appointed lawyers (Della Rocha & Fitzgerald, 1980; Niehoff, 2004). Until the 1990s, few priests had their priestly duties suspended, and church officials usually avoided the tribunal altogether. It turns out that the usual procedure was that Boston church officials wrote letters to suspected child sex abusers and then moved them out of the locale in which they had been charged and placed them in another church location where their reputation was unknown to church members. When victims filed civil charges claiming damages from clergy sex abusers, church lawyers, representing the Boston archdiocese, quietly settled these cases out of court with secret settlements and sealed records preventing public access and prohibiting the victims from talking about the abuse.

Church Policy.   For decades, church leaders assumed that state laws did not apply to them or to those they supervised. Cardinals, archbishops, and bishops did not report allegations of sex abuse. They used their discretion to deal with priests by private channels of communication. Donald Cozzens (2002b) claimed church leaders followed this policy because they believed the hierarchical system of the church would protect them from the secular legal system. He explained that in this system "the priest is accountable to his bishop, the bishop is accountable to the pope, and the pope is accountable to God" (p. 29). Rarely do church leaders emphasize accountability of priests to fellow clergy, church members, children, and women. Cozzens offered a second reason for the failure of the church to address the problem, a factor he called "institutional denial" (p. 32); that is, the church leaders just refused to believe the civil legal system could challenge their power and authority. Another reason for the church's denial of the abuse, Richard Sipe (1995) noted, was that many bishops wanted to protect their "privileges and prerogatives as well as the church's property" (p. 43). He correctly predicted that settlements from civil suits eventually would force the church to sell much of their property, the main source of their financial wealth, to pay the damages for church negligence involving sex abuse by priests.

Circumventing the Law.   Boston church leaders made executive decisions to protect the priest abusers and to dismiss the allegations of victims. In many cases, church leaders also ignored the pain and suffering of the victims of the abuse. Clearly Cardinal Bernard Law failed to obey canon law, use the church tribunal, or offer financial and psychological support to victims. He did, however, protect the abusers by sending them for psychological testing, giving them time off, and reassigning them to other church congregations.

The issue of pedophile priests was neither a public nor a church secret. Long before the *Globe*'s investigative reporters addressed the issue, some church leaders worried about how they would keep the issue out of public view. In the mid-1980s, Tom Doyle, a Catholic priest, published numerous magazine and journal articles in church forums on pedophilia, lectured to the clergy in New Zealand and Australia, and prepared a report on the extent of the problem for the National Conference of Catholic Bishops (NCCB) in 1987 (Burkett & Bruni, 1993). Doyle warned church leaders to keep detailed personnel records because they could be subpoenaed by the courts. He also admonished leaders against purging files of potentially damaging material about abusive clergy, saying this could result in charges of contempt of court or obstruction of justice. After church leaders failed to create a workable policy, Mark Chopko, general legal counsel for the NCCB, reported that the council had no jurisdiction over bishops, but he promised that church leaders would suspend some priests from an active ministry (if they were known sex abusers) and try to promote healing of the victims and rehabilitation of the offenders (Berry, 1994). Church leaders ignored Chopko's promise and continued to cover up incidents of priest sex abuse.

In fact, some church leaders actively tried to circumvent the state law. In 1990, Bishop James Quinn, a canon lawyer for the church from the Cleveland archdiocese, suggested that the Catholic Church protect itself against lawsuits by sending its personnel records to the Vatican embassy. His reasoning was that diplomatic immunity would keep church personnel documents secure so they could not be subpoenaed by state courts (Berry, 1994). That same year Montana Judge Thomas M. McKittrick ruled that bishops from Great Falls and Helena dioceses were not obligated to surrender files on accused priest sex abusers because this action violated the privacy provisions of canon law (Berry, 1994). The Catholic Church understood what the state law was, but tried its best to avoid the law's sanctions.

As a result, neither the legal system nor church law had much impact on the conduct of church leaders. After investigative reporters in various parts of the United States started to expose the problem, the public became aware of the extent of the church cover-up of priest sex abuse. The cover-up first came to public attention through the extensive investigative reporting of Jason Berry (1994), who chronicled the history of Louisiana priest Gilbert Gauthe's sexual abuse of children from 1984–87. Berry exposed the horrific nature of Gauthe's abuse of children and the secretiveness and ineptness of church superiors in dealing with him. Berry's reporting produced legal results. Eventually, the criminal courts charged, convicted, and sentenced Gauthe to 250 years in prison for several counts of felony sexual abuse of children. The success of this investigative reporter, and other reporters in New Mexico, Minnesota, and Tennessee in the 1990s who exposed priest sex abusers, surely influenced *Globe* reporters to follow their path.

The investigative reporters built their case on issues that were already prominent in the public discourse. Legal commentators, scholars in the Catholic Church, and other investigative reporters identified these issues. The rising action of the *Globe*'s coverage detailed how these issues related to priest sex abusers in the Boston area.

Rising Action

During the rising action, investigative reporters elaborated the issues, constructed depictions of the leading characters, offered descriptions of the setting, and gave explanations of the actions and reactions of leading characters. The Spotlight Team constructed the rising action in their newspaper drama beginning with their critical coverage of the criminal trial against Boston priest John Geoghan. This defendant was a tragic and despicable character who had molested dozens of children while he was a priest in Boston. He never acknowledged his guilt or apologized to his victims. The other leading character was a defiant and power-driven church official, Cardinal Bernard Law. The Spotlight Team added a list of characters who played supporting roles to Geoghan, priests who continued to serve long after victims complained that these men had sexually abused them. The reporters also named other supporting characters, former bishops and archbishops, who had committed the same transgressions as Cardinal Law because they knew that some priests were sex abusers and did nothing to stop them. The reporters found Law's character especially flawed because men with the title of "cardinal" fill the highest position of power and honor in the Roman Catholic Church, except for the pope. The other leading characters were the victims of the sex abuse. They called the investigative reporters and told them the circumstances of their abuse by Geoghan and some other Boston priests. As a result of this information, investigative reporters became advocates for the victims.

Although Geoghan was tried and convicted of criminal sexual abuse of a child, the investigative reporters did not concentrate on the verdict but instead emphasized the underlying actions and lack of actions from church leaders that permitted Geoghan to remain a priest for so many years. The reporters explained that during his 30 years in the Boston archdiocese, church leaders moved Geoghan from one parish to another in order to conceal his long record of child sexual abuse. According to the *Globe*'s Spotlight Team (2002, January 6), "Since the mid-1990s, more than 130 people have come forward with childhood tales about how former priest John J. Geoghan allegedly fondled or raped them during a three-decade spree through a half-dozen Greater Boston parishes" (p. A1). The news story asserted that even after Cardinal Law knew about "Geoghan's predatory sexual habits," he "approved his transfer to St. Julia's parish in Weston" where he was placed "in charge of three youth groups" (p. A1). The Spotlight Team asked, "Why did it take a succession of three cardinals and many bishops 34 years to place children out of Geoghan's reach?" (p. A1). This article noted further that Boston's church leaders concealed Geoghan's egregious record of abuse and also failed to take advantage of canon law or state law to stop the abuse.

According to the rising action in this coverage, church leaders failed to supervise their personnel and as a result their incompetence created hundreds of victims. According to the investigative reporters, priest sex abuse continued because church leaders were negligent. The Spotlight Team (2002, January 6) claimed that "since 1997, the archdiocese has settled about 50 lawsuits against Geoghan for more than $10 million—but with no confidential documents ever made public." In fact, when Cardinal Law was named as "a defendant in 25 of the lawsuits, a church attorney asked a judge to impound any reference to the cardinal, arguing that his reputation might be harmed. The judge refused" (p. A1). This part of the coverage faulted church leaders and institutional policies as the real cause of the extensive sex abuse in the Boston archdiocese.

The investigative reporters tried to figure out why the church was so negligent in their dealings with clergy sex abusers. They concluded that the state was partly at fault. Most professionals have a legal obligation when they hear about sex abuse allegations to report them to the State Department of Social Services. This agency in turn reports the allegations to law enforcement. Until the Geoghan case, however, the church was not included in the list of professionals who had this kind of obligation (Investigative Staff, 2002). Since many members of the state legislature and the judiciary in Massachusetts are Catholic, the reporters explained, the political system allowed the church to hide allegations, and the state courts made it easy for this institution to engage in secret settlements with victims. One way this was done in Massachusetts and elsewhere was to keep the filings and the settlements with victims sealed in confidentiality agreements. The agreements stated that a victim could receive financial settlements only if he or she agreed to keep silent about the abuser and about the church practices regarding abusive priests. The church's idea was that victims would be spared public embarrassment and be protected from public ridicule and shame. Another way that the Boston church could protect itself was through the doctrine of charitable immunity; this law limited the church's liability to $20,000 per victim (Investigative Staff, 2002). This part of the coverage implicated state legislators and legal officials as sharing a part of the blame for the church's secrecy and cover-up.

For several weeks, the Spotlight Team concentrated on the priest abusers and their victims as the most important characters in their newspaper drama. Instead of the victims suffering in silence, they told their stories, and these stories made their way onto the front page of the *Boston Globe*. In turn, the stories of some victims gave other victims the courage to tell their stories of abuse to the investigative reporters. This part of the coverage did not yet have the features of a pseudo civil trial, but the Spotlight Team continued to gather evidence that would turn their moral outrage about church leaders into coverage that resembled some civil proceedings.

During the rising action the number of characters in the drama expanded. Eventually, the main perpetrator was not Geoghan but dozens of other past and present Massachusetts priests. Cardinal Law remained a main character, but other past church leaders were named as his coconspirators. At first Geoghan's victims were the main focus, but later hundreds of people claimed that as children they had suffered sexual abuse from priests. The drama eventually moved from the offices of the Boston archdiocese, where Cardinal Law was at the seat of power, to the Vatican in Rome, where Pope John Paul II was in charge.

Complications

In the complication stage of the coverage, investigative reporters adopted the role of advocates who made complaints against the Boston archdiocese. In dramatic theory, complications result from oppositions between characters over disputed actions and disparate standpoints. This part of the coverage identified the oppositions between the press, the state, the institution of the church, the leaders of the church, and the victims. The reporters' complaints against church leaders demanded a response. Additionally, the reporters were conducting their own discovery process by publishing large amounts of evidence to prove the negligence of church leaders.

Complaints. Typically a civil action begins when a plaintiff files a complaint with a court in the jurisdiction in which the plaintiff seeks a settlement. The complaint states a specific grievance and alleges certain facts, that if established by evidence, constitute grounds for a financial settlement or other compensation. Typically, a legal complaint has five parts: (1) identification of the plaintiffs and the defendants, (2) descriptions of the interactions that took place between the parties to the dispute, (3) "descriptions of the conduct of the defendant that produced injury to the plaintiff[s]," (4) statements of the damages or injuries, and (5) a request for judgment from the court (Hazard & Taruffo, 1993, p. 105).

The complaint made by the *Globe*'s reporters was not a single formal document presented to a particular court jurisdiction. Instead this complaint took the form of a set of detailed allegations that evolved over several weeks in various news stories. The *Globe* assumed the role of a team of plaintiffs' attorneys representing past and present victims of clergy abuse. The defendants were Cardinal Bernard Law and his predecessors who had hidden allegations of sex abuse. The Spotlight Team (2002, January 6) first presented its complaint in an explosive multiple-article edition that blamed church leaders for protecting pedophile priests. The first argument of these articles made allegations in this way:

> For decades, within the U.S. Catholic Church, sexual misbehavior by priests was shrouded in secrecy—at every level. Abusive priests—Geoghan among them—often instructed traumatized youngsters to say nothing about what had been done to them. Parents who learned of the abuse, often wracked by shame, guilt, and denial, tried to forget what the church had done. The few who complained were invariably urged to keep silent. And pastors and bishops, meanwhile, viewed the abuse as a sin for which priests could repent rather than as a compulsion they were unable to control. (p. A1)

The *Globe*'s complaint further charged that the Boston clergy and their supervisors committed two types of grievous offenses. The newspaper identified one offense as permitting clergy sexual abuse of children and another offense as aiding and abetting priests' violations of their religious vows of sexual purity and obedience. In his complaint, Carroll (2002, January 6) cited some evidence supporting one of these offenses from Joanne Mueller whose four sons suffered abuse from Geoghan. When she reported the abuse, church officials did not take the allegations seriously. Maryetta Dussourd also reported Geoghan's abuse of her seven boys to the pastor of a parish near the location where Geoghan served; the pastor confronted Geoghan about the allegations, and the perpetrator admitted to the abuse. Instead of reporting the abuse to church officials, however, this pastor told Dussourd to keep the matter private to protect Geoghan and the church.

Other reporters identified a third offense—church leaders hid the sexual abuse from legal authorities and protected the perpetrators rather than helping the victims. To support this accusation, the Spotlight Team (2002, January 6) noted that a former priest, Anthony Benzevich, "alerted church higher-ups that Geoghan frequently took young boys to his rectory bedroom." Instead of taking action against Geoghan, church leaders "threatened to reassign him [Benzevich] as a missionary in South America" to silence him (p. A1). At first the complaint centered on the more than 130 victims of Geoghan that "he fondled . . . as children over three decades" (Burge, 2002, January 17, p. A1). Later, the *Globe*'s complaint implicated other abusers and identified the consequences of the abuse as producing profound and long-lasting effects on the victims, including suicide, social withdrawal, psychological dysfunction, and inability to hold a job. In numerous versions of this serial complaint, the *Globe* asked for the following kinds of relief: apologies from the church, the resignation of Cardinal Law, monetary damages for the sex abuse victims, and changes in church and state policy regarding clergy sex abuse.

At the same time that the *Globe* issued its complaint against the archdiocese, attorneys for victims started to file real civil suits on behalf of Massachusetts's abuse victims. The news reports, for example, quoted one attorney who represented 25 victims. This attorney said that "it is the plaintiffs' position that the cardinal did not act reasonably given what he knew at the time" (Rezendes & Carroll, 2002, January 16, p. A1). Before real civil attorneys made official legal allegations against Law, the *Globe* already had implicated him as the person who could have stopped the abuse but did not. The reporters' complaint took place without the approval of a state or federal court jurisdiction. Instead, the newspapers' attorneys and editors permitted the issuance of the complaint. The Spotlight Team did not present the complaint to a judge, but it made the complaint to a court of public opinion represented by readers. The newspaper condensed many complaints of victims; some were part of ongoing civil actions and others were new allegations that appeared for the first time in stories of the Spotlight Team. The complaints led to other complications in the drama by magnifying the extent of the problem, demonstrating the urgent need for a solution, and attempting to force the church to conform to the state laws that governed all other professions. The *Globe*'s complaint challenged the power of the church leaders and exposed the moral failings of institutional governance. In effect, the reporters invoked the power of the press to subvert the power of the church.

One emphatic part of the Spotlight Team's complaints concerned the magnitude of suffering of the sex abuse victims. The *Globe* mimicked the provisions of a real legal complaint by avoiding allegations that could not be proven, impressing church defendants and the public (judge) about the significance of the allegations, and publishing specific and detailed testimony from victims. In an official complaint, plaintiffs give defendants a specified time period for their response, usually 30 or 60 days. In this pseudotrial, the church took nearly nine months to make a complete and official reply.

Responses.   After issuing public complaints, the investigative reporters demanded a formal response from the church defendants. Cardinal Law's failure to provide the desired response added more complications to the press drama. The response sought by the newspaper reporters resembled a formal legal response; that is, the church leaders would

> state in short and plain terms the defendant's responses to each claim
> and "admit or deny" the allegations made in the complaint. When

> defendants fail to respond in an appropriate manner to a complaint, the
> plaintiffs consider the defendants have admitted to the alleged wrongdo-
> ing stipulated in the complaint. (Dessem, 1998, pp. 113–114)

The reporters envisioned the conditions of a real complaint, but church officials, at first, viewed the complaint as frivolous and failed to give a substantive response.

A defendant in a civil action has several lines of defense, including
admitting the allegations, claiming lack of information or knowledge about
the allegations, denying the allegations in total, and making counterclaims
refuting the allegations (Dessem, 1998). In ways similar to the Spotlight
Team's serialized complaint, the Boston archdiocese response evolved in
installments printed as separate stories or as parts of stories over a period of
time. In his first partial response to the conviction of Geoghan and the
Globe's allegations of other priest abuse, Cardinal Law "publicly apologized
to Geoghan's victims and ordered clergy and volunteers to report allegations
of abuse against minors." The Spotlight Team (2002, January 24) took credit
for Law's response when reporters noted that "Law's apology followed pub-
lication of a two-part Spotlight Team series reporting that Law and other
church officials had shuttled Geoghan from one parish to another although
they knew of his sexual abuse of children" (p. A1). Law promised that in the
future, the archdiocese would have a "zero tolerance" policy for sexual
abuse (Lavoie, 2002). Later, the reporters acknowledged that Law's admission was conciliatory even though he refused to resign. Cardinal Law said, "I
wish it were possible to go back in time and to undo some of the decisions
that I made. I now see that these were wrong decisions. . . . My resignation is
not part of the solution as I see it" (Paulson, 2002, July, 27, p. A1).

The failure of this church leader to admit the extent of his negligence
provoked more detailed complaints from *Globe* reporters. Pfeiffer (2002,
January 24) faulted Cardinal Law for failing to acknowledge the extent of
Geoghan's problems. As evidence for this charge, the reporter quoted a letter Law had written to Geoghan, in which the cardinal said "it is most heart-
ening to know that things have gone well for you and that you plan to resume
your efforts with a renewed zeal and enthusiasm. . . . With my warmest personal greeting and my blessing upon you and all whom you serve" (p. A1). In
addition to questioning Law's sincerity and veracity, the reporters also questioned his judgment. For example, Pfeiffer (2002, January 24) claimed that
psychiatrists whom Law selected to examine Geoghan and other pedophile
priests lacked proper knowledge and credentials.

Finally, after a month of complaints, the *Globe* published this response
from Law (Spotlight Team, 2002, January, 29):

> In the terrible instances of sexual abuse, the Archdiocese of Boston has
> failed to protect one of our most precious gifts, our children. As Arch-
> bishop, it was and is my responsibility to ensure that our parishes be safe
> havens for our children. . . . I acknowledge that, albeit unintentionally, I

> have failed in that responsibility. The judgments which I made, while
> made in good faith, were tragically wrong. . . . Some of these tragedies
> occurred on my watch, and I cannot and will not avoid my responsibility
> to ensure the prevention of such tragedies in the future. (p. B4)

Law's response emphasized that he would prevent future clergy sex abuse, demand mandatory reporting of allegations, create an education program, and establish a review board to strengthen current policies. In this same statement, however, Law reiterated that he would not resign (Ranalli, 2002).

At the time that the *Globe* was faulting Law for failing to fully acknowledge his own negligence, negotiators were trying to reach out-of-court civil settlements of $30 million with the victims of Geoghan. Perhaps the most important development in this phase of the drama was the legal victory won by the attorneys representing the *Globe*. The newspaper won a court order that forced the church leaders to make public the names of 100 Massachusetts priests whose personnel files showed accusations of child abuse (Robinson, 2002, March 12). The Spotlight Team eagerly welcomed this stash of evidence since it would bolster their case against the church in general and Law in particular and enable their news drama to continue. This windfall of evidence motivated reporters to participate more extensively in the discovery process, a crucial part of a successful civil lawsuit.

Discovery.   In a real civil action the process of discovery requires plaintiffs and defendants to disclose to each other relevant, unprivileged evidence. The initial disclosure for a civil case calls for the plaintiffs and defendants to provide names and phone numbers of persons possessing information relevant to the dispute, a description of the location of relevant documents, a computation of the monetary damages provided to injured parties, and a record of insurance agreements with the defendants that would offset the damages (Dessem, 1998). When church leaders, the pseudo defendants, failed to provide the information requested by the investigative reporters, further complications developed in the *Globe*'s serial drama.

Parties to a civil action discover evidence through the use of depositions, interrogatories, admissions, and pretrial motions. Depositions are formal statements taken by lawyers in which witnesses under an oath are subject to cross-examination from opposing attorneys (Matlon, 1988). The depositions give evidence about facts relevant to a lawsuit. In the *Globe*'s pseudotrial, reporters took statements from victims and other relevant parties about priest sexual abuse and church negligence without benefit of oaths or adversarial cross-examination. In addition to depositions, attorneys can use interrogatories, written questions that supplement the information provided through depositions. Attorneys submit written questions about relevant facts and then request written answers to these interrogatories. Attorneys can use pretrial motions to expand or limit the evidence and testimony that can be heard at a trial. The reporters attempted to expand the evidence the public could consider in their pseudotrial. Throughout this serial drama, the investigative reporters asked questions similar to interrogatories in their news stories about church policy and received formal written defenses of church policy from the public relations office of the Boston archdiocese.

Another way to secure evidence is through admissions, stipulations to which parties in a dispute agree (Hazard & Taruffo, 1993). After the reporters presented statements from victims and published the personnel records of abuse priests, Cardinal Law admitted abuse had occurred. He claimed that, at the time, he lacked sufficient knowledge to handle the abuse in an effective way. Law never explained why he failed to use the church tribunals, canon law, or refer the cases to civil authorities.

The *Globe* reporters continued making complaints about Law and his predecessors, and they also published new evidence that added to the complications of their serial drama. The *Globe*'s discovery process relied on the court orders filed by the newspaper's attorneys that had granted access of the Spotlight Team to church personnel files and statements of attorneys representing victims in ongoing civil actions. These sources permitted the *Globe* to continue gathering evidence against the church between January and March of 2002.

The newspaper's discovery process evolved in several phases. First, after the Spotlight Team (2002, January 24) gained access to personnel records, they reported that church leaders had failed to heed warnings about some priests' illicit sexual behaviors. The files included evidence that church leaders had removed Geoghan from four parishes, reassigned him to different church positions, kept silent about the nature and extent of the abuse, failed to notify other priest superiors about Geoghan's pedophilia, and remained sympathetic to Geoghan after repeated allegations had been made against him.

Second, the reporters identified new evidence from victims—Francis Leary, Leonard Muzzi Jr., Peter Menendez, and Leona Scott (Rezendes & Carroll, 2002, January 26). The Spotlight Team also named other priest sex abusers, including Bernard Lane (Pfeiffer & Kurkjian, 2002, January 28), Paul R. Shanley, Robert Burns, Ronald H. Paquin, Jay M. Mullin, and C. Melvin Surrette (Spotlight Team, 2002, January 31). By the end of January, the Spotlight Team (2002, January 31) had convinced readers that the priest sexual abuse of children in the Boston area was extensive and church officials had not interceded to stop it. In fact, the church had "quietly settled child molestation claims against at least 70 priests," and placed "102 priests . . . on sick leave or otherwise removed [them] from parish assignments in the early to mid-1990s." Although Cardinal Law had removed a few pedophiles after the 1992 conviction of James Porter, he continued to assign other priest abusers "back in parishes" because he believed they had received "appropriate treatment" and "proper monitoring" (p. A1).

After the church's personnel records became available to the Spotlight Team, the floodgates opened, supplying the reporters with massive amounts of evidence that led to more intensive coverage of priest abusers and church malfeasance than had gone on before they had the evidence. After allegations drawn from the evidence were published, the coverage resulted in the resignations of some clergy and the identification of many additional victims. Several priests voluntarily removed themselves from the archdiocese because they knew their personnel records contained sex abuse claims (Rezendes & Carroll, 2002, February 8). In other instances, victims identified priests, such as Joseph L. Welch, who had molested them in the past but were still active in the priesthood (Robinson & Pfeiffer, 2002). As many as 100 new victims said that they had been abused, and 10 active priests resigned. These actions proved that Cardinal Law had erred when he had claimed a month earlier that "no priest with a record of abusing children remained in any assignment in the archdiocese" (Robinson, 2002, February 24, p. A1). The reports of victims served as depositions, inquiries about Cardinal Law's role in the reassignment of priests resembled interrogatories, and interviews with psychiatrists corroborated evidence about what Law knew and when he knew it (Barry, 2002). The *Globe*'s successful court order was a major breakthrough for the Spotlight Team that provided a substantial amount of damaging evidence against church officials.

When testimony and documentary evidence in real civil actions support the allegations of the plaintiffs, then the case usually proceeds to a settlement rather than a trial. In the discovery process of this pseudo case, the evidence created a similar effect. Robinson (2002, February 24) summed up the effects of the *Globe*'s discovery process in this way:

> Lawyers and victims' advocates said that the extent of the problem that has been disclosed in Boston, and the admission of errors in handling priest sex-abuse cases by Cardinal Bernard F. Law, have created a climate that encourages victims to come forward. "What is encouraging is that we are seeing in Boston, in a much more concerted way than ever before, that average Catholics, as well as prosecutors, judges, and elected officials, are treating the Catholic Church like any other institution"—with no special favors or blind trust or tremendous deference, said David Clohessy, the national director of the Survivors Network of those Abused by Priests. (p. A1)

Through the evidence generated during the discovery process, the *Globe* convinced readers about the moral failures of the church and its leaders. The *Globe* reporters took credit for their role in adding complications to their serial drama, and they then attempted to create a climax for their news drama.

Climax

The climax or crisis in a drama refers to the turning points when the disputed actions of the protagonists and antagonists lead to specific consequences (Berger, 1997). In contrast to a real drama where the crisis has a definable turning point, the climax in the Spotlight Team's serial drama materialized, evaporated, and then resurfaced again. The climax started with stalled settlements, developed into distinctive adversarial case theories, promoted the idea that a preponderance of evidence existed against the church, continued with reporters' demands for Cardinal Law to testify, and finally culminated in successful settlement talks.

Settlement Negotiations.   In this pseudo case of *Globe v. Archdiocese of Boston,* settlement talks followed the extensive process of discovery. The *Globe* reported problems with the terms of the settlement offers made by the church to victims, the shortcomings in the willingness of church officials to make equitable offers, and the lack of good faith involvement from the attorneys for the church. For example, Robinson (2002, March 5) reported that the church was about to pay $20 million to John Geoghan's victims, an amount added onto the $15 million already paid in prior secret settlements. Robinson projected that church settlements with victims would eventually "reach $100 million or more" (p. A1).

Beginning in May and extending through July, the *Globe* reporters described the barriers church officials had constructed that impeded settlements with victims. The reporters faulted church leaders for announcing a settlement had been reached in March, but in May denying that the settlement had ever taken place after the archdiocese finance council had voted down the deal. According to reporters, several factors made the settlements difficult. Although the lawyers for the victims had established acceptable terms for a general settlement with multiple victims, the church pulled out of the deal when it discovered that its insurance companies would "not say how many of the claims they would honor" (Kurkjian & Burge, 2002, p. A1). For this reason, the settlement stalled until August of 2002 when the attorneys representing the church and the victims presented the conditions of the proposed settlement to a panel of judges at the Massachusetts Superior Court. The court ruled these settlements were legal.

Case Theories.   In a civil case, the testimony and documents gathered during the discovery process enable the attorneys to develop a case theory, a condensed story with themes about what the issues of the dispute mean. The Spotlight Team's theory of the case was that Cardinal Law reassigned known child sex abusers to other parishes. His actions were motivated by a desire to protect his own power and that of the institution he served (Burge, 2002, July 13, July 17, July 27, August 3). The *Globe* reporters faulted church leaders for permitting the sexual abuse, keeping it secret, ignoring the advice of well-known psychiatric professionals, sympathizing with the abusers, and discounting the harm suffered by victims (Weber, 2002). The defense's case theory denied any negligence on the part of Cardinal Law or other church leaders. Specifically, the defense maintained that the church leaders acted reasonably because they sent sex abusers to counseling, received information from psychiatrists that the abusers were cured, and assigned the problem priests to other parishes only after they believed treatment had been successful. Selected statements from Cardinal Law and his public relations director related this theory through the newspaper to the readers. The *Globe,* however, claimed the church officials did not own up to their negligence, did not settle in good faith, and committed fraud "by publicly embracing the agreement and then walking away" (Burge, 2002, August 7, p. A4).

Presentation of Evidence.   The *Globe* aggressively pursued the defendants by publishing more and more evidence about the church's negligence. Civil courts expect the plaintiffs and the defense to use relevant, competent, unprivileged, and unprejudiced evidence. Evidence in civil suits typically consists of testimony and documents—financial and employment records, letters, conversations, policy statements, safety reports, and warranties, etc. According to the *Federal Rules of Evidence* (1991), evidence is relevant to the extent that it applies to the issues in dispute (IV: 402). For example, in real civil court cases involving the negligence of the church and demands for financial compensation from sex abuse victims, the evidence should show direct negligence on the part of the church and Cardinal Law that resulted in harm to the victims. *Globe* reporters implicated Law specifically in Geoghan's case in February and linked him to other cases later on.

Law did not respond until July when he wrote a letter to the archdiocese newspaper, the *Pilot.* In his letter, Law denied the allegations made against him. He said that

> [n]ever was there an effort on my part to shift a problem from one place to another. . . . The sexual abuse of minors by priests is one of the most painful problems facing the contemporary Church. . . . Not only is the trust that should exist between a priest and child broken, but families and friends are also shaken in their own trust. . . . I only wish that the knowledge that we have today had been available to us earlier. (Paulson, 2002, July 27, p. A1)

Additionally, Law defended himself by claiming that he had followed 1993 guidelines for suspending all clergy sex abusers. In light of the evidence the investigative team published, the veracity of Law's response was in doubt. In a rebuttal to Law, the Spotlight Team faulted this church leader for failing to provide a timely and complete response and for failing to acknowledge the pain and suffering of the abuse victims. The reporters' refutation sought a response from Law to other specific complaints.

Evidence is competent to the extent that it comes from firsthand observers with personal knowledge, rather than from secondhand hearsay information based on what others say (*Federal Rules of Evidence*, 1991). When witnesses authenticate records or documents using firsthand knowledge, they supply competent evidence. In this pseudotrial, two major sources of firsthand evidence came from the victims themselves. One example of victims' testimony came from Margaret Gallant; she reported that Geoghan abused her children, Law knew of the abuse, and yet he transferred the priest to another parish. The *Globe* authenticated her testimony by quoting from copies of Gallant's letters to Law and from copies of letters she had received from the archdiocese (Pfeiffer, 2002, January 25). Other newspaper articles cited court documents from the ongoing civil suits against the church that quoted the victims' lurid details about the context and nature of the sexual abuse they suffered. For example, the newspaper reported that "Greg

Ford, a 24-year-old Newton man, charged that priest Paul Shanley had repeatedly raped him during the 1980s and much of that abuse occurred after Law knew Shanley was a danger to children" (Pfeiffer, 2002, February 13, p. B1). In these instances, the *Globe* presented relevant evidence, authenticated by witnesses and documents.

Evidence should not breach the rule of privilege, including legal deference to confidentiality (*Federal Rules of Evidence*, 1991). In civil cases, the court grants privilege to communication between employer–employee, physician–client, and clergy–parishioner. The *Globe*'s access to Geoghan's employment records provided damning evidence against the archdiocese. The Spotlight Team (2002, January 24) quoted personal notes from Bishop Robert J. Banks claiming that a psychiatrist had told him that:

> "You had better clip his [Geoghan's] wings before there is an explosion. . . . You can't afford to have him in a parish." Other notes showed that Bishop Daily had "urged relatives of seven sexual abuse victims to keep quiet [about their abuse from Geoghan] to protect the church." A response letter from this family to the archdiocese said that telling us to "keep silent to protect the boys is absurd. . . . It is an insult to our intelligence." (p. A1)

After the *Globe* published additional information from the personnel files of Geoghan, attorneys representing the church won a court order from Judge James McHugh to keep other documents from previous settlements sealed because church law required confidentiality and "prohibited lawyers from discussing them. Even the parties in the cases could not view them [the documents] without first signing written statements swearing not to disclose anything they saw." In November Judge Constance M. Sweeney reversed this decision, noting that the victims wanted their "psychological and counseling records" made public to show they had been adversely affected by the abuse. Sweeney wrote that a "delicate balance" exists between freedom of religion and the right of the public to know. Her opinion stated that the public needed to know that "members of society knowingly or carelessly allow appreciable harm to be visited upon children who have allegedly been entrusted to their care or oversight" (Burge, 2002, November 30, p. A1). Throughout the *Globe*'s coverage of the sex abuse scandal, attorneys representing the newspaper tried to overturn the judicial rulings that protected confidentiality because these rulings impeded reporters' efforts to publish evidence about the negligence of church leaders.

Finally, courts exclude prejudicial evidence based on illegitimate inferences. Prejudicial evidence means that "the probative value is substantially outweighed by the danger of prejudice" (*Federal Rules of Evidence*, 1991, IV: 403). Evidence about the past wrongs and the amount of insurance that a defendant carries are both considered prejudicial. Civil cases, however, can use character evidence based on legitimate inferences about the conduct of plaintiffs, defendants, and/or victims (*Federal Rules of Evidence*, 1991). Although the *Globe*'s evidence was relevant and competent, it also was prejudicial. Since the evidence evolved in the discovery process of a pseudo case rather than in real proceeding, no code prohibited the Spotlight Team from using prejudicial evidence. In fact, the prejudicial evidence served an important function for the investigative reporters because it helped to force the church to admit negligence and engage in settlement negotiations. The Spotlight Team published such an extensive record of the church negligence that their own attorneys attempted to contest this prejudicial evidence because they feared it would lead the church into financial bankruptcy. The prejudicial evidence also placed the church in a weak negotiating position.

Witness Impeachment. Part of the process of challenging the competence, relevance, confidentiality, and prejudice of evidence occurs during the impeachment of key witnesses. Since the defendants must testify in civil cases, the *Globe*'s impeachment of Cardinal Law in its pseudo case resembled what would occur in real civil proceedings. The word "impeachment" means to accuse someone of misconduct and to ask that person to give an accounting of his or her actions. Impeachment refers to the adversarial process that trial attorneys use to impugn the character of witnesses and cast doubt on the evidence they give. The *Globe*'s approach to the impeachment of Cardinal Law resembled the two senses of the word *impeachment*. The newspaper made accusations against the church leader, and then when he tried to defend himself, the investigative reporters mounted additional attacks by alleging his testimony lacked veracity, served his self-interests, and was inconsistent.

The attempts of the investigative reporters to impeach Cardinal Law escalated during the summer months of 2002. The *Globe*'s allegations shifted from Law's neglect of responsibility to charges that he reneged on promised monetary settlements for victims (Burge, 2002, July 13, August 3). Other stories focused on Law's court deposition and his maneuvering to get the church's insurance companies to pay the victims (Kurkjian & Burge, 2002). Reporters concentrated on the court's issuance of a subpoena for Law to appear as a witness in a hearing about the sex abuse settlements, and his refusal to do so (Burge, 2002, August 7, August 6). The *Globe* impeached the statements that Law later gave at this hearing by asserting that his statements were inconsistent and contained misstatements or half-truths.

The investigative reporters tried to force Law to offer impeachable testimony. The more Law talked about how he handled priest sex abusers, the more he seemed to implicate himself through inconsistent and self-serving statements. For example, Law continued to say that "Never was there any effort on my part to shift a problem from one place to the next." This statement was inconsistent with the statements of his court depositions that said he knew about Geoghan's sexual abuse of children and reassigned him to work with children. Law made a feeble attempt to defend himself against the issues brought against him by the Spotlight Team. One of his attempts was to use the weak and inappropriate argument of blaming the victims. Law said that victims were "not in exercise of due care" and that their "negligence . . . contributed to cause the injury or damage" they suffered. He also blamed others for his mistakes, asserting that he did not have enough knowledge about sexual abuse and relied on doctors who did not understand the disorder (Paulson, 2002, July 27, p. A1). These attempts at self-defense, although typical for defendants involved in real civil cases, contradicted Law's earlier admission that he made grievous mistakes by assigning priests with records of sex abuse to other parishes. In the court of public opinion, Law's self-defense was unconvincing. The statements of self-defense implied that he was trying to cover up his mistakes by blaming others.

The climax constructed by the investigative reporters mimicked the adversarial drama created in real civil proceedings in which settlement negotiations take place at the same time trial attorneys try to prove divergent theories of the case, present compelling evidence, and impeach the witnesses of the opposition. This pseudo civil trial, however, differed from real cases because the investigative reporters created their own rules that differed significantly from rules in real court proceedings. The investigative reporters limited the testimony to church officials they considered relevant to their complaint and refused to undergo cross-examination from the attorneys representing the church. These differences allowed the investigative reporters to present prejudicial and one-sided evidence that would be excluded by the rules of a real civil court. Moreover, the Spotlight Team could present false testimony from publicity seekers who had not been sexually abused but who wanted to do harm to the church. As the coverage increased from weeks to months, the investigative reporters convinced their public audience that they had presented a stronger and more persuasive case than the church had done.

Resolution

The *Globe*'s case theory claimed the church and its leaders were negligent. To prove this theory, the reporters presented large amounts of evidence impeaching Law that signaled a major turning point in the new drama. The newspaper reporters wanted their serial news drama to produce a resolution in the form of a settlement, but this outcome did not come quickly. The resolution or denouement phase of a drama explains to audiences how the story turns out (Berger, 1997). The Spotlight Team took an active role in bringing this dispute to a conclusion. They made complaints, sought responses, outlined issues for a compromise, and demanded changes in personnel and church policy. The pseudotrial reached a resolution in part because the press set the conditions for a settlement, and the church reluctantly agreed to these conditions. Since public opinion and the pressures on the national leadership of the church favored the settlement described by the *Globe* reporters, the church had little choice but to comply with a number of the demands first issued by the Spotlight Team.

One reason that a settlement resolution in this pseudotrial did not come quickly was that the *Globe* kept adding new demands that had not been part of their original complaint. In real cases as in this pseudo case, settlements often stall because of demands not made in the original complaint. Through the negotiation process, about 90 percent of real civil cases settle without the parties going to trial. Parties to a civil dispute reach settlements through formal written agreements. Many settlements evolve out of pretrial negotiations, and others take place in a formal hearing or conferences in which a judge approves the terms of the settlement. A settlement typically means that the plaintiffs receive less than they demand. In some cases though, the settlement results in the defense fulfilling all of the plaintiffs' demands for monetary and other kinds of relief for victims. The end to the process depends on the willingness of plaintiffs to accept the offers of the defense. When one side provides a large quantity of compelling evidence that establishes negligence, then the pressure for the other side to settle increases.

Expanding the Complaint. In the resolution phase of the *Globe*'s pseudotrial, the settlement talks involved a number of parties that had not been part of the original complaint—attorneys for the abuse victims and the attorneys for the archdiocese, attorneys for the newspaper and attorneys for the diocese, the National Conference of Catholic Bishops, and even the pope. Victims' advocacy groups, priests, theologians, and members of churches exerted outside pressure on the negotiators to settle with victims and fix the problems in the church that had permitted the victimage to occur in the first place.

The investigative reporters portended to be participants in the negotiations although their main role was to report on what the attorneys for the victims in the real negotiations told them had occurred. The settlement with the victims involved monetary compensation and counseling provided at church expense, but the investigative reporters were not satisfied with these demands. They wanted Law to change institutional practices. The *Globe*'s role in the negotiations was to promote two issues that they thought should be addressed. First, the newspaper stressed the bad faith negotiations of the church, claiming Law reneged on a binding settlement and feigned his approval of the conditions of the settlement. Second, the *Globe* promoted a different settlement; they demanded Law's confession and resignation in addition to substantive changes in national church policies regarding sex offenders.

Forcing Compromise. Reporting on the settlements took place at several stages in the *Globe*'s coverage. The settlements, perhaps better named "forced compromise," evolved from the allegations of attorneys about the suffering of victims. The church was unable or perhaps unwilling to refute victims' allegations with evidence. In the pseudo case, the *Globe* identified the conditions for a settlement, such as the breach of trust created by the archdiocese with the people of Massachusetts. The *Globe* reporters appeared to make offers and accept counteroffers from the archdiocese even though no attorneys were present and no formal agreements resulted. The attorneys for the victims seemed to agree with the investigative reporters and made similar demands to the attorneys for the church.

In fact, real settlement negotiations lasted for months and the issues and demands changed. The *Globe* reporters detailed the adversarial and contentious nature of these negotiations. In March, Law's attorneys agreed to a multi-billion-dollar settlement with 86 victims that provided compensation according to the extent of the abuse suffered by the victims (Robinson, 2002, March 5). A few days later, Robinson (2002, March 12) projected the settlement would be $20 million. In another article, Robinson (2002, March 12, p. A1) reported that church attorneys had held up the settlement because they argued that the church was exempt from the civil liability that "applies to secular organizations because" they are protected "under the First Amendment and the Massachusetts Constitution." In April, Kurkjian and Robinson (2002) reported that if church defendants failed to pay victims as much as they deserved, a tremendous loss of public trust would ensue. In August, both sides participated in a court hearing to determine if the original settlement agreed to by Law in March was valid (Burge & Kurkjian, 2002). Shortly afterward, Rezendes and Carroll (2002, August 8) claimed the settlement talks were moving too slowly. But in mid-August, victims agreed to a settlement in which the archdiocese paid $10 million to 86 plaintiffs, a settlement significantly below the $20 million that reporters had predicted in March (Robinson & Rezendes, 2002).

Demanding Change. As part of its pseudo participation in the negotiations, the *Globe* kept insisting that Law make an honest, public confession to victims acknowledging that he was responsible for permitting sexually abusive priests to continue an active ministry. The newspaper also continued to demand Law's resignation (Spotlight Team, 2002, January 29). In December, Law resigned at the request of clergy and church members in the archdiocese rather than at the request of the Spotlight Team (Paulson, 2002, December 14). After the *Globe* had challenged and interrogated Law for 11 months, he confessed by admitting his personal responsibility for permitting priest sex abuse. In fact, Law seemed both defeated and contrite when he publicly acknowledged the extent and duration of the abuse, expressed personal sorrow, and asked forgiveness from congregations, priests, victims, and the public. Although Cardinal Law did not make his admissions to the public directly, a press release published in the *Globe* (Paulson, 2002, December 14) related Law's confession in the words that he used when he apologized to a church congregation:

> I did assign priests who had committed sexual abuse. . . . The forgiving love of God gives me the courage to beg forgiveness of those who suffered because of what I did. . . . Once again I want to acknowledge publicly my responsibility for decisions that I see were clearly wrong. . . . I acknowledge my own responsibility for actions which led to intense suffering. While that suffering was never intended it could have been avoided, had I acted differently. (p. A1)

Law chose a church rather than a public audience for the confession. This choice likely was intentional because he did not want to admit that the investigative reporters had the right to demand this kind of confession or that the *Globe* was the proper channel for the message, and he did not want to appear to cave into the demands made by the newspaper. The *Globe* asked for and indirectly received a confession from Law, even though negotiators made no such demand of him.

Even though one major settlement had been finalized by attorneys for the victims and the church, the investigative reporters wanted institutional change, and they believed that Cardinal Law's resignation would help make this change take place. They bolstered their demand by quoting church members and victims' rights advocates. Both groups agreed with the investigative reporters that Law lacked the moral character and leadership expertise to lead the church in new directions. In one article, reporters noted that 58 priests from the Boston archdiocese sent letters requesting Law to resign. One letter stated, "While this is obviously a difficult request, we believe in our hearts that this is a necessary step that must be taken if healing is to come to the archdiocese" (Paulson, 2002, December 10, p. A1). A Boston church group, Voice of the Faithful, petitioned the pope to seek and then approve the resignation of Law (Farragher, 2002, December 12). The *Globe* as well as its public allies called for a return to a virtuous leader and policy.

Nearly a year after the investigative reporters made their complaints against Law, the Vatican announced that the pope had accepted Law's resignation and that he had appointed a new interim archbishop to run the Boston archdiocese (Sennott, 2002). The *Globe*'s reporters achieved their goals—Law both confessed and resigned. During the dispute, the national church and the state adopted new policies for handling clergy sex abuse. After Law resigned, church members and the public at large rightly believed the press had coaxed Law's resignation. Paulson (2002, December 14) summarized the reasons for Law's resignation in this way:

> He tried to explain away his conduct as a result of insufficient understanding of the nature of sex crimes, as the result of bad advice from physicians, or as a result of bad record keeping. He apologized in a variety of ways . . . . But none of the changes were enough in the face of a year of astonishing revelations and disastrous public relations. There are now more than 500 people suing the Archdiocese of Boston, claiming to be victims of abuse by priests. (p. A1)

Law's resignation brought a "powerful leader to his knees" (Paulson, 2002, December 14, p. A1). The newspaper used its press power to reduce the power of the church, an outcome that reporters sought in the early months of 2002, but did not achieve until December of 2002.

In the pseudotrial, the process used to reach a settlement may appear especially contentious. But settlements in real cases also contain expanded complaints, stalled talks, forced compromise, and demands for institutional change. What made the resolution of this dispute seem so difficult was that the investigative reporters established some of the terms for the settlement and rallied public and church support and enforced those terms. In doing so, the *Globe* accomplished a feat seldom achieved by investigative reporters; they forced a powerful institution to change.

Epilogue

The last phase of a drama, the epilogue, consists of the commentary and explanation about what the drama means. In one sense, the epilogue to this long-running media drama initiated by the *Boston Globe* cannot be fully written. The effects on the clergy and parishioners of the Boston archdiocese as well as on the national church and the victims are yet to be assessed. Although the epilogue presented here is incomplete, it hints at several effects that the pseudo civil trial had on investigative reporters and church policy.

This chapter does not argue that the *Boston Globe*'s investigative reporters intentionally set out to create a year-long civil case in which it acted as pseudo plaintiff by filing complaints against Cardinal Law and the Boston archdiocese. The work of the Boston reporters was exceptional in its breadth and depth, unusual in the strength of the commitment to the issues, and remarkable in the outcome it created. Other press coverage has the potential to force public and private institutions to be accountable, but few newspapers have the resources or commitment to do what the *Globe* and its reporters did. The ability of investigative reporters to create a pseudo civil trial is unusual even in sophisticated and committed investigative reporting. The coverage of the priest sex abuse cases resembles the processes and procedures of a real civil case. The investigative reporters mimicked a civil case by filing complaints and responses, engaging in evidence discovery, and impeaching a key witness. The reporters made demands from the defense that exceeded what real attorneys for the victims sought in negotiating a settlement.

The *Globe* reporters helped forge a $100 million settlement between the Boston archdiocese and the victims (Burge, 2002, July, 27) and attracted the pope's attention to the problem (Spotlight Team, 2002, December 18). The coverage led to the appointment of a national commission to investigate church policy and uncovered sex abuse victims from as long as 50 years earlier. The commission eventually acknowledged 10,667 reported cases of sex abuse of minors by priests, and 6,700 of these accusations had corroborating evidence. The *Globe* set the agenda for both the secular and religious press to talk about the sex abuse scandal and the failure of church leaders and policies to deal with abusers and victims. The National Council of Catholic Bishops recognized that grave institutional problems existed and so they held an emergency meeting to discuss current and future church policies (Farragher, 2002, June 14; Paulson & Pfeiffer, 2002; Paulson & Farragher, 2002). Finally, the media's investigation promoted public discussions about church power, celibacy, lay activism, the academic preparation of priests, ordination of women, homosexuality in the priesthood, and the relationship of the church to the legal system.

LESSONS

The investigative reporters in this case acted as custodians of the moral conscience. The Spotlight Team called public attention to the breakdown and disorder in the Catholic Church and showed how this injustice created victims that needed compensation. The coverage revealed the vices of church leaders and eventually forced leaders to give up their power and accept change. The coverage created a sense of moral outrage that brought about significant change in the way the Catholic Church deals with priests and with victims. The pseudo civil case of the *Boston Globe* v. Archdiocese of Boston defined sex abuse among the Catholic clergy as an urgent moral issue that demanded resolution. One resolution was to compensate victims financially for their pain and suffering and to pay for counseling to help them recover. Another resolution was to force the church to change its leadership and its policies toward sex abusers. The investigative reporters sought and received the confession of Cardinal Law and secured his resignation. The coverage led to the National Council of Catholic Bishops' recommendations for a specific policy for dealing with sex abusers and a national council to address the problems of abuse.

This case study demonstrates that the press has the ability to uncover evidence of institutional malfeasance, force those with responsibility to answer to the public, provide a forum for the testimony of victims, and even change the policies of powerful institutions to make them accountable to the public. Some irony exists in the fact that the press took over some of the responsibilities that for decades had belonged to the church courts and civil courts. The *Globe*'s coverage got results. State legislators changed Massachusetts laws so that abusive clergy would be subject to the same legal actions as other abusers. Church groups met in an emergency session to develop a strong policy for handling abusers. The newspaper got the church to pay attention to the grievances of victims and of church members who demanded the resignation of Cardinal Law.

Although the public often blames the press for its failures, this analysis makes clear that investigative reporting has a central role in exposing the corruption of public and private institutions. Specifically, committed reporters can conduct a pseudo civil proceeding that creates real consequences for the parties in the dispute and the public as well. This case shows how investigative reporters exerted their press power as a watchdog to reduce the domination and control that church leaders had exerted over its members and how some church officials undermined the legal systems of the church and the state.

4

Moral Drama and Games in the Minnesota Tobacco Trial

For decades, civil attorneys tried to make tobacco companies compensate smokers for the illnesses they suffered from cigarette smoking, but they lost nearly all of their cases. Between 1992 and 1998, civil attorneys finally succeeded with the help of medical research documenting that 400,000 premature deaths occurred yearly as the result of smoking tobacco. John Grisham's fictional account of the tobacco litigation in his best-selling novel *The Runaway Jury* (1996), as well as Michael Mann's (1999) film, *The Insider,* captured some of the elements of the moral drama that ensued when the tobacco companies tried to defend themselves.

Tobacco litigation involved ambitious and crafty plaintiffs' lawyers fighting against wealthy and powerful tobacco defense attorneys. At the center of this drama were thousands of pages of evidence gathered from whistle-blowers and legislative hearings that exposed the greed and deceptive research of tobacco companies. The collection and use of the evidence were part of a strategic legal game that brought down Big Tobacco. After the tobacco companies realized the public no longer believed that cigarette smoking was safe, they settled a huge class action lawsuit with the attorney generals of 46 states, involving payments of $368 billion over a 25-year period. Before the settlement was complete, the State of Minnesota (joined by Blue Cross/Blue Shield) went forward with a civil trial in 1998. Just prior to summations and before the case went to the jury, the tobacco companies also settled with the Minnesota plaintiffs.

In ways similar to other civil actions, the tobacco cases evolved through time. No one person can take full credit for the plaintiffs' defeat of Big Tobacco. This chapter looks at the tobacco cases through the lenses of moral drama and games. Specifically, the analysis focuses on the Minnesota tobacco trial and explains (1) the pretrial morality play that instigated the trials, (2) the pretrial negotiation games, (3) the strategic and tactical maneuvers concerning the evidence, and (4) the lessons applicable to other civil actions.

THE PRETRIAL MORALITY PLAY

The tobacco cases replicated a morality play, a drama that enforces moral truths or lessons by means of the speech and actions of good characters who struggle against social vices and evil characters (Pollard, 1904). In the tobacco cases, the moral drama did not teach religious principles as medieval morality plays did, instead it promoted principles of social responsibility regarding safe products and honest marketing. The attorneys and witnesses from Big Tobacco represented evil forces in modern society, and the plaintiffs and whistle-blowers personified morally upright characters. The tobacco drama taught a dogma that businesses are obligated to tell the truth about their products. In ways that resemble a medieval morality play, the rising action of the tobacco drama presented the characters, setting, and disputed actions while the falling action provided reasons why the plaintiffs defeated the tobacco companies. In one sense, the pretrial morality play foreshadowed the issues and evidence resulting in the settlements. But in another sense, it concealed the extensive strategic and tactical gaming maneuvers that characterized the accumulation and presentation of evidence.

The first dramatic sequence centered on the suffering and death of smokers and the inability of seemingly good-intentioned attorneys to get a verdict against the tobacco companies. In the 1970s, attorneys sued tobacco companies on behalf of the families of clients who had died of lung cancer after smoking cigarettes. Derthick (2002) notes that out of 813 cases filed against tobacco, 23 went to trial, and no plaintiffs won. In these early cases, plaintiffs theorized that tobacco companies were responsible for the illness and death caused by tobacco and the chemically addictive additives (nicotine) in cigarettes. The plaintiffs' theory did not persuade jurors who decided that ill health and death were the smokers' fault, not the tobacco companies' (Zegart, 2000). For more than 25 years, plaintiffs continued to lose lawsuits against Big Tobacco because jurors were unwilling to make tobacco businesses liable for the suffering and premature deaths of smokers.

Even though plaintiffs lost cases, they amassed large amounts of evidence demonstrating that the tobacco industry knew its products were dangerous and engaged in fraudulent advertising to make them appear safe. For example, in the 1980s, New Jersey lawyer Marc Edell sued a tobacco company to recover damages for the estate of Rose Cipollone, a lifelong smoker who had died of lung cancer. Although the appellate court overturned the verdict in *Cipollone v. Liggett Group* (1986), attorneys had accumulated 1,500 internal documents that exposed Liggett's deception about cigarettes and health. This and other cases from the sixties, seventies, and eighties would play a significant role in the development of future cases.

In the 1990s the convergence of (1) evidence from whistle-blowers, (2) the congressional (Waxman) hearings on tobacco regulation, (3) class action lawsuits, and (4) negotiated settlements made it possible to force tobacco companies to accept responsibility for their products. The accumulation and use of evidence in the lawsuits and settlements involved carefully planned gaming strategies and tactics.

The Whistle-Blowers

Two whistle-blowers, Merrell Williams and Jeffrey Wigand, played virtuous heroic roles that vilified tobacco companies in a legal moral drama directed by Mississippi Attorney General Mike Moore. The whistle-blowers acted as morally good characters who exposed the wrongdoing, corruption, and deception of the tobacco organizations that had employed them and the evil actions of the tobacco industry. They claimed that Brown & Williamson knew, but publicly denied, that smoking caused cancer; deliberately increased the amount of nicotine and other chemical carcinogens in their products; and aggressively marketed cigarettes to youth. Moreover, the motives of Big Tobacco were to make profit at the expense of their customers' health. In the early 1990s, the evidence from Williams and Wigand revealed that tobacco manufacturers lied about their products and concealed the health dangers from smoking even though their in-house research had demonstrated the harmful effects resulting from chemically enhanced cigarettes.

The media and the public considered whistle-blowers as heroic figures promoting public accountability, but the tobacco organizations considered these same people as disloyal traitors who threatened the existence of the tobacco industry. Without "Merrell Williams and Jeffrey Wigand," Moore emphasized, "we wouldn't have been here today where we are with the $368 billion settlement without the courage of these two people" who stood "alone against one of the most powerful industries in the world" and [we] did "the right thing" (Bergman & Docherty, 1998).

The actions of whistle-blower Merrell Williams developed in an unusual way; he stole the evidence from Brown & Williamson while working as their employee. Williams was a heavy smoker and in poor health when he took a job as a paralegal for Brown & Williamson Tobacco Corporation in 1988. Although he had a Ph.D. in theater, he was unable to make a living for his family. A law firm in Louisville, Kentucky, hired him to file documents for their client Brown & Williamson Tobacco to ensure that the law firm would succeed in future litigation. While Williams worked at a warehouse sorting and filing documents, he observed that tobacco companies had concealed research and disseminated information contrary to their own research findings. He believed that the public needed to know about the malfeasance of the tobacco companies and the dangers their products caused. During lunch hours and breaks, Williams smuggled thousands of documents that showed the deceptive practices of Brown & Williamson. He copied a few documents at a time and mailed them to a friend in Florida for safekeeping. He later recalled that his copying of the documents seemed like a minor transgression of rules, rather than some major legal or moral evil. Shortly after Brown & Williamson discovered Williams had copied documents, they fired him. From the copies of the pirated documents, Williams produced elaborate manuscripts detailing the sins of Brown & Williamson Tobacco Corporation. One document, "Intent to Deceive" (a.k.a. "Affidavit in Expectations of Death"), gave elaborate details of the company's malfeasance (Zegart, 2000).

After Williams was fired, he continued to play a moral role even though his motives were not always clear. For example, he tried to sue Brown & Williamson by complaining that the company was legally responsible for the distress and health problems he suffered from working with the company's documents. In a predictable move, Brown & Williamson countersued and filed a court order forbidding Williams from talking about the company or his relationship to it (Zegart, 2000). Brown & Williamson, however, continued to play an evil role in the tobacco drama by covering up their transgressions and seeking revenge against Williams by following and threatening him. In what they conceived as a morally responsible reaction, Mississippi antitobacco lawyers, Don Barrett, Dick Scruggs, and Mike Moore, gave Williams refuge, agreeing to shelter and protect him from the surveillance of tobacco companies. In fact, Barrett found Williams's actions so helpful for their fight against Big Tobacco that he sent packages containing copies of the documents smuggled from Brown & Williamson to Professor Stanton A. Glantz at the University of California at San Francisco. The attorneys protected themselves from tobacco company retribution by using an ironic pseudonym, "Mr. Butts," as the return address on the packages of evidence. In turn, Glantz transmitted the evidence of the transgressions of the tobacco company by using a publicly accessible Internet archive, publishing a book that included some of the documents, called *The Cigarette Papers* (1996), and publishing several articles in the *Journal of the American Medical Association* implicating Big Tobacco in disseminating deceptive health information (Glantz et al., 1995; Hanauer et al., 1995; Slade et al., 1995).

Major newspapers, such as the *New York Times* and the *Wall Street Journal,* also diffused the evidence from Glantz to the public in an effort to demonize Big Tobacco. The evil actions of the tobacco companies revealed in the 4,000 documents circulated by Glantz became the centerpiece of congressional hearings led by California Congressman Henry Waxman (Regulation of Tobacco Products, 1994). The hearings presented the evidence pirated by Williams and disseminated by Glantz. Additionally, the hearing forced tobacco executives to testify about their beliefs and actions regarding the production of tobacco products. Later, the smuggled evidence and the testimony from tobacco executives at the Waxman hearings figured prominently in negotiated settlements and in the Minnesota trial.

Another whistle-blower, Jeffrey Wigand, took the role of a strong virtuous character in the tobacco litigation morality play. Unlike Williams who was a low-level employee for Brown & Williamson's law firm, Jeffrey Wigand worked in a high-paying position as vice president of tobacco research that allowed him to use his Ph.D. in biochemistry. After Brown & Williamson hired him in 1989 to help design a safe cigarette, Wigand and his

research team of 243 staff and researchers had a $40 million budget and con-
ducted research on the effects of cigarettes on health (Zegart, 2000).
Wigand discovered the deceptive actions of the company by accident. At first
he thought the company was morally responsible and really wanted to
develop a safe cigarette, but later he recognized that the company lacked
scruples. He learned the company wanted his researchers to produce a
potent cigarette that would increase smokers' addiction and, by implication,
ruin their health. After Wigand told Brown & Williamson's executives that
he knew about their immoral goals, they fired him. In order to have health
insurance for his family, Wigand reluctantly signed a confidentiality agreement with Brown & Williamson that prohibited him from talking about the
company's research. Then according to his attorneys, Wigand pursued a low-
paying and socially responsible job as a science teacher in the Louisville public schools.

Shortly afterward, Wigand accepted an undercover job of sorts; he
started working under a pseudonym as a consultant to the government about
the adverse effects of tobacco. One of his jobs was to provide information to
the Federal Drug Administration and to meet with Commissioner David
Kessler about the health effects of tobacco products. He conducted these
meetings under the code name of "Research" (Mollenkamp et al., 1998).
Eventually, Brown & Williamson suspected Wigand had consulted with the
enemy (government regulators). They decided this violated his confidentiality agreement with the company, so they "sued for millions of dollars of
fraud, theft, and breach of contract." When the company failed to silence
Wigand, they hired other people, company goons, to do this job. These company goons robbed Wigand's home, stalked him, and threatened to kill him.
The threats and intimidation were so extreme that Wigand hired personal
body guards to protect him from Brown & Williamson's hit men (Zegart,
2000). The public had more knowledge of Wigand's virtuous role in the dispute against tobacco companies than they did of Williams because of the
media attention Wigand later received.

Lowell Bergman, a producer of *60 Minutes*, elevated Wigand to a starring
role in the tobacco morality drama. Without revealing his identity, Bergman
paid $12,000 to Wigand for analyzing some documents regarding the devel-
opment of a fire-safe cigarette that his reporters had obtained from the Philip
Morris Tobacco Company. When his consulting came to the attention of lawyers at Brown & Williamson, the company filed another lawsuit against
Wigand for violating his confidentiality agreement, although the information
he gave to the producer was not directly related to that company. Philip Morris then secured a restraining order against Wigand and sued him for giving a
deposition in a case filed by the U.S. Justice Department accusing Philip
Morris of suppressing evidence. Bergman helped Wigand contact the Mississippi lawyers who had helped Williams. After legal threats from the tobacco
companies, CBS withdrew this negative portrayal of the Philip Morris
Tobacco Company. Wigand's analysis for that *60 Minutes* episode, however,

became part of a story in the *New York Daily News* (Mollenkamp, et al., 1998), and Wigand later gave a deposition for Dick Scruggs, a Mississippi lawyer, that aided the attorneys in bringing civil actions in Mississippi against tobacco companies. In this deposition, Wigand restated the conclusions he had made for *60 Minutes*. His continuing moral crusade against Big Tobacco intensified his feud with his former employer. The tobacco company hired investigators to gather "dirt" on Wigand in order to destroy his reputation. Brown & Williamson failed to accomplish their goal because the *Wall Street Journal* refused to publish these allegations (Orey, 1999).

Eventually, *The Insider* (Mann, 1999), a feature-length film, cast an actor (Russell Crowe) to play Wigand in a story about how the whistle-blower had sacrificed his job and family to expose the sins of Big Tobacco. For the most part, the movie accurately represented the heroic and morally upright role of Jeffrey Wigand and Big Tobacco's retribution against him. However, the film all but ignored Wigand's role in the tobacco litigation.

As part of the 1998 tobacco settlement negotiated in part by Dick Scruggs and other Mississippi lawyers, the tobacco companies dropped their lawsuit against Wigand in return for his promise to refrain from talking about tobacco during a cooling off period (Mollenkamp, 1998; Orey, 1999; Zegart, 2000). Wigand's biggest contribution to the tobacco drama was his willingness to testify against Big Tobacco and to serve as an informant to David Kessler and the Federal Trade Commission. Wigand's testimony was part of the Regulation of Tobacco Products (1994) and then became an important contribution to Glantz's evidence archive that implicated tobacco companies for engaging in deceptive practices and producing harmful products.

The Waxman Hearings

The Waxman hearings offered an important public forum for re-enactment of the moral drama that preceded it in the Mississippi litigation against tobacco companies. Clifford Douglas, an antitobacco activist, leaked documents from whistle-blowers to the media prior to the hearings, and he also encouraged the commissioner of the Food and Drug Administration, David A. Kessler, and Congressman Henry Waxman's Subcommittee on Health and the Environment to host hearings about the cigarette industry's manipulation of nicotine and their refusal to compensate sick smokers. The hearings took place from March 25 to April 14, 1994, and resumed again on April 28, May 17, and May 26, 1994 (Regulation of Tobacco Products, 1994; subsequent citations from the hearing cite the volume and page number of this document).

Under the auspices of the Subcommittee on the Health and the Environment, Waxman and 24 members of the House heard oral testimony from 28 people representing the government, the health care community, proto-bacco agencies, antitobacco activists, medical doctors, scientific researchers, and tobacco executives. The hearing received extensive TV and newspaper coverage. Congressional hearings are fact-finding forums that often precede legislation. This particular hearing produced a two-volume work with more than 1,400 pieces of testimony and documents relating to the product liability of cigarettes and the deception of tobacco company executives.

Congressman Henry Waxman's opening remarks gave credit to Commissioner Kessler for initiating the hearings and to previous U.S. surgeon generals for establishing the connections between nicotine intake by smokers and 430,000 deaths each year. The hearings implicated Big Tobacco as a morally irresponsible culprit. Waxman's argument foreshadowed the claims that plaintiffs would make in subsequent trials: "Nicotine is a powerfully addicting substance," "nicotine is the reason people smoke," and "tobacco companies have the capability of removing all nicotine from cigarettes." He emphasized that tobacco companies added chemically enhanced nicotine to make their products more addictive. Waxman supported the roles played by the whistle-blowers and plaintiffs at the same time he confronted the deceptive and demonic role of Big Tobacco. Waxman noted, "The tobacco industry denies the adverse health effects of smoking. They deny that advertising promotes smoking. They deny that nicotine is addictive . . . [and] that [they] enhance or fortify tobacco with nicotine" (Vol. 1, p. 2).

Commissioner Kessler also played a supporting role in the drama by presenting evidence that called attention to the deceptive practices of Big Tobacco. Furthermore, he promoted a legislative resolution to punish the cigarette companies, but this legislation never materialized. In his supporting role, Kessler delivered memorable lines that attorneys and witnesses opposing tobacco would frequently repeat. For example, Kessler noted that "430,000 Americans die" from smoking-related illnesses each year; "two-thirds of the adults who smoke say they wish to quit," fewer than "one out of ten succeed," and "as many as 74 to 90 percent [of all smokers] become addicted" (Vol. 1, p. 72). Kessler repeated one memorable line that "cigarettes are a nicotine delivery system," a statement that was originally made by a tobacco executive and discovered in the evidence leaked by the whistle-blowers (Vol. 1, p. 74).

The tobacco industry characters reinforced the moral deficiencies of their business when they asserted that nicotine was not addictive, while knowing full well that it was. When Congressman Ron Wyden posed the question: Is nicotine addictive? The executives repeated a familiar business line that they thought would save Big Tobacco (Vol. 1, p. 628):

> WILLIAM CAMPBELL (*Philip Morris*): I believe nicotine is not addictive.
>
> JAMES JOHNSTON (*R. J. Reynolds*): Cigarettes and nicotine clearly do not meet the classic definition of addiction.
>
> JOSEPH TADDEO (*U.S. Tobacco Company*): I do not believe that nicotine or our products are addictive.
>
> ANDREW TISCH (*Lorillard*): I believe that nicotine is not addictive.
>
> EDWARD HORRIGAN (*Liggett*): I believe that nicotine is not addictive.

THOMAS SANDEFER (*Brown & Williamson*): I believe that nicotine is not addictive.

DONALD JOHNSTON (*American Tobacco Company*): And I, too, believe that nicotine is not addictive.

In an effort to contrast the moral righteousness of health care providers with the moral weaknesses of Big Tobacco, Waxman asked the executives if smoking caused cancer (Vol. 1, pp. 620–627). Big Tobacco executives regurgitated lines that their attorneys had prompted them to use. James Johnson of R. J. Reynolds answered, "I don't know." Andrew Tisch of Lorillard answered, "I don't think so." William Campbell of Philip Morris responded, "We don't know what causes cancer." Their testimony contradicted the findings of health agencies, their own internal research, and some of their own written statements. The testimony showed that tobacco executives were willing to lie to government officials to protect company secrets. The pretrial drama scripted a plot in which the forces of good represented by whistleblowers, plaintiffs' attorneys, and government leaders struggled against the evil forces of Big Tobacco companies. This pretrial morality play foreshadowed the settlements that state attorney generals would make. This stage of the legal drama also generated new incriminating evidence that was used in subsequent legal actions against tobacco companies.

PRETRIAL GAMES

Legal coalitions eventually placed the morality play into the background and their bargaining and gaming strategies into the foreground. The prominent actions in the bargaining game were the strategical and tactical moves of the plaintiffs' attorneys and the countermoves of Big Tobacco. The strategic bargaining game resembled Schelling's (1960) idea of "variable sum games," in which the gains achieved for one side of a dispute forced losses on the opposing parties. In these types of games, Schelling explains, the actions of the players are interdependent because the choices of one party affect the choices others have to make. In variable sum games, however, the players may make moves that have various kinds of payoffs. Some moves benefit both sides, others help only one side, and still other moves result in unilateral or bilateral damages. In the bargaining games used to resolve the tobacco dispute, the plaintiffs were states who paid out large sums of money for the health care of smokers. The companies that made, marketed, and sold tobacco products were the defendants.

In the pretrial bargaining, the plaintiffs sought an out-of-court resolution by using gaming strategies, including: offensive empowerment, that is, building coalitions to enhance their bargaining position and to increase their resources of legal expertise and financial backing; refocusing their complaint; and divide-and-conquer, to weaken their opponents. Some of the tobacco defendants' moves presented weak responses to the plaintiffs' demands, because the defendants lacked a viable offensive strategy of their own.

Offensive Empowerment

The Castano coalition, a group of attorneys that started with lawsuits in the early 1990s in Louisiana, utilized the strategy of offensive empowerment, a plan they believed would deter the tobacco companies from winning future lawsuits. This alliance increased its power by consolidating many plaintiffs into one class action (a class action is a way of aggregating and consolidating several different cases together under one set of complaints [Rabin, 2001]), collecting legal expertise, and increasing the financial backing for antitobacco forces. Suits of this type attempt to "level the playing field" so that plaintiffs have enough financial resources to match those of the defendants. The Castano coalition first consisted of the alliance of two attorneys: Don Barrett circulated the smuggled documents of Merrell Williams to the public. With his associate, Wendell Gauthier, he initiated a class action lawsuit after his friend Peter Castano died of lung cancer at the age of 47. Gauthier added the names of other victims to the civil action. Although the plaintiffs in *Castano v. American Tobacco* (1996) lost their case, they built a coalition of 60 like-minded and reputable plaintiffs' attorneys from 25 firms who each gave $100,000, resulting in $6 million worth of financial backing to start the fight against the tobacco companies (Mollenkamp et al. 1998, p. 74). The Castano lawyers created one big lawsuit that sought $100 billion from Big Tobacco in compensatory and punitive damages for the reimbursement of state health providers for treating cigarette-smoking-related diseases.

The legal expertise and financial resources deterred tobacco attorneys from using the defense theory of blaming the smoking victim for getting sick. Deterrence means using power to persuade the opposition that it is in their own best interest to avoid a certain course of action (Schelling, 1960). The Castano coalition's offensive power moves helped convince tobacco attorneys that it was in their best interests to settle out of court. Subsequently, this coalition filed multiple class action suits against tobacco companies in several other states.

Refocusing the Complaint

In 1994, another coalition, an alliance of Mississippi attorneys, emerged with a focus similar to the Castano alliance. This Mississippi coalition sought to weaken the power position of the tobacco companies by switching the focus of their complaints. That is, instead of seeking damages for smokers, they sought compensation for states to pay for financial losses state health care providers suffered from treating smoking-related illnesses. Michael Moore and Dick Scruggs led the Mississippi coalition, and they eventually brought together attorney generals from several different states as a collective to sue the tobacco companies for the money that state-supported health systems had paid for treating smokers. Their idea was that the attorney generals would not try the cases but would hire private attorneys, such as those from the Mississippi and Castano coalitions. Rabin (2001, p. 183) explains that consolidating the tobacco litigants meant that attorney generals could sue on behalf of their various states "for the aggregate economic harm" that the states had "suffered as a consequence of the industry's wrongful conduct." Although this kind of massive lawsuit was unprecedented, the Mississippi lawyers believed this move would force the tobacco companies to be accountable to state taxpayers. The Mississippi alliance also demanded that tobacco companies change the way they advertised cigarettes: in particular, cease targeting children.

After the Mississippi alliance joined the Castano alliance, the new group refined the issues and changed the players. They wanted to force Big Tobacco to settle out of court rather than go to trial. This procedural maneuver refocused the complaint, strengthened the bargaining position of the plaintiffs, consolidated their evidence-gathering potential, and forced a response from Big Tobacco companies as a collective defendant. This move is similar to what Schelling (1960) calls "brinkmanship," that is, forcing the defendants into a downslope position, a vulnerable place where they could lose all of their grounding and eventually have no firm footing at all (p. 199) in a lawsuit. As a gaming strategy, the plaintiffs wanted to place the tobacco defendants in a vulnerable position that would keep them guessing about what the next move against them would be and whether their companies could survive the offensive moves directed at them by potent and united coalitions of plaintiffs. The plaintiffs believed their strategic moves would leave tobacco companies on the brink of financial disaster and force them to settle.

Divide-and-Conquer Tactics

In bargaining, one effective tactical maneuver is to divide the opposition in order to weaken its bargaining position. One significant achievement of the Castano-Mississippi-attorney general alliance was to broker a settlement with Liggett Tobacco Company, which separated from the other tobacco companies to avoid being sued by the attorney generals of various states. In 1997 Liggett agreed to label all cigarettes with a warning that smoking is addictive, admitted their executives lied in the Waxman hearings, and gave plaintiffs in-house evidence that showed Liggett concealed information about the health dangers of smoking. Attorney General Moore conducted the press conference that announced the Liggett settlement (Mollenkamp et al., 1998). After this victory, Castano and Mississippi attorneys met secretly with state attorney generals and tobacco executives from other companies. In June of 1997 Mississippi attorneys agreed to settle their tobacco lawsuit for $3 billion. Liggett's admissions had pushed the tobacco companies further down the slope of brinkmanship and forced them to pay for their irresponsible actions.

The plaintiffs' divide-and-conquer tactic had forced other tobacco companies to confess to similar malfeasant actions and brought a partial resolution to the morality play that preceded it by showing that the good characters (the plaintiffs) could force the bad characters (the defendants) to confess to their evil actions. This limited settlement gave plaintiffs hope that good would triumph over evil.

Minnesota Attorney General Hubert H. Humphrey III participated in the settlement talks, but he refused to join with the settlement because he wanted resolution to occur in a high-profile civil trial and had the intention of creating an even bigger financial liability for Big Tobacco. A trial of this type would be a zero-sum game with a definite winner and a loser. The trial, he thought, would show that good intentioned lawyers representing his state could force Big Tobacco to be accountable to Minnesota taxpayers.

THE MINNESOTA TOBACCO TRIAL

The attorneys in the Minnesota trial appropriated evidence, issues, and themes from the legal processes that preceded the trial. Minnesota Attorney General Humphrey had the opportunity to sue Big Tobacco in a public trial. The rules of a civil trial differ significantly from the norms for bargaining. The antitobacco plaintiffs and Big Tobacco defendants would have to conduct their morality drama and their strategic legal game according to the principles, procedures, and protocols of the civil legal system. The litigants had the burden of convincing a jury that their side had a preponderance of evidence. Unlike the secret negotiations that take place during settlement talks, a trial is a public and adversarial forum in which the judge has the power to rule what evidence is admissible and how attorneys can present and interpret the evidence. Additionally, the judge enforces the protocols of the court upon the participants, and jurors rather than attorneys decide if the complaints made by the plaintiffs have been proven. The plaintiffs in the Minnesota tobacco trial risked losing the whole case and foregoing a large monetary settlement. If they succeeded, however, they could gain more money from Big Tobacco than any of the states that previously had settled with tobacco companies.

State of Minnesota v. Philip Morris et al. (1998) was a civil action brought by the state of Minnesota, through Attorney General Humphrey and Blue Cross and Blue Shield of Minnesota, against the defendants of the tobacco industry, including Philip Morris Inc., R. J. Reynolds Company, Brown & Williamson Tobacco Corporation, B.A.T. Industries, P.L.C., Lorillard Tobacco Company, The American Tobacco Company, Liggett Group, Inc., The Council for Tobacco Research-USA, and The Tobacco Institute. The case took place in Ramsey County's Second Judicial District Court in St. Paul, Minnesota (filed as No. C1-94-8565), with Judge Kenneth J. Fitzpatrick presiding. Minnesota expanded upon the previous complaints to charge that tobacco companies also had engaged in antitrust conspiracy and consumer fraud. The plaintiffs first filed complaints in early 1994. The trial took place before 12 regular and 12 alternate jurors. The trial featured 40 witnesses testifying about 3,000 pieces of evidence, took 79 days, and produced nearly 16,000 pages of testimony (Rybak & Phelps, 1998).

Michael Ciresi, a prominent Minnesota lawyer, acted as the lead attorney for plaintiffs during both the pretrial and the trial, and he presented the opening statement and cross-examined most of the defense witnesses. Roberta B. Walburn, Thomas Hamlin, Susan Richard Nelson, Tara Sutton, Richard Gill, and Bruce Finzen from the law firm of Robins, Kaplan, Miller & Ciresi assisted Ciresi. Allan M. Katz conducted the pretrial discovery for the defense. Other attorneys conducted the trial, including Peter Bleakley representing Philip Morris, John Monica representing Lorillard Tobacco Company, David Bernick representing Brown & Williamson and B.A.T. Industries, and Robert Weber representing R. J. Reynolds. The tobacco companies also hired a few Minnesota defense attorneys to assist them. During most of the trial, 20 different attorneys were in attendance.

A typical civil complaint identifies problems with product liability, deception, and fraud. It constructs pertinent facts supporting those issues. The defendant's response, called an answer, either confirms or denies the complaint. When the trial began on January 26, 1998, Judge Kenneth J. Fitzpatrick summarized the complaints and responses in this way: Plaintiffs sought damages for (1) health care expenses from smoking illness brought about by defendants' misrepresentations and hiding of evidence related to the health hazards of smoking, (2) advertising that encouraged adolescent smoking, (3) deceptive advertising about addictive properties of nicotine, (4) failure to protect public health, and (5) violations of Minnesota's consumer protection and antitrust laws. Fitzpatrick constructed the defense case as a set of rebuttals to the plaintiffs' complaints; he noted the defense would claim the state (1) misrepresented evidence about the health hazards of smoking, (2) distorted the facts about nicotine content, (3) wrongly accused tobacco companies of violating Minnesota's consumer protection and antitrust laws, (4) misstated the advertising and marketing policy, and (5) falsely reported the financial damages to the state resulting from smoking-related illnesses (TR, 1998, January 26). (This chapter cites the trial record [TR] by date and from the transcripts downloaded from the Putnam Pit Web site.) In the middle of closing arguments, the tobacco companies agreed to a $6.1 billion settlement with the state of Minnesota and a $469 million settlement with Blue Cross and Blue Shield of Minnesota.

The Game Analogue

My analysis of evidence relies on an analogue of game theory (Davis, 1983; de Certeau, 1988; Duncan, 1968; Rapoport, 1970). Trials are decision-making processes in which the players (attorneys) try to meet their goals of winning or losing their cases through general plans of action called strategies and specific maneuvers called tactics. Attorneys employ calculated and reasoned moves to achieve their goals. A financial award or a financial punishment (called a payoff) results from the choices the attorneys make. The goals of the plaintiffs are intertwined with those of the defense. If the plaintiffs win, the defense loses; and if the defense wins, the plaintiffs lose. The judge and jurors can introduce elements of chance, factors unknown to the attorneys before the trial game begins. These chance factors can impede the attorneys' strategies and tactics to such a great extent that they have to change their goals and moves midway through the trial. Before attorneys make their opening moves in a trial game, they have utilities (human and financial resources) that influence the kind of moves they can make.

Attorneys make moves using strategies and tactics that they believe will persuade jurors. Strategies are general communication plans that attorneys use to navigate the legal rules and improve the probability that they will win the verdict. Tactics, specific communication and legal maneuvers, add to the persuasiveness of strategies. The moves in the Minnesota tobacco trial resembled a two-person non-zero-sum game (Rapoport, 1999) in which two legal teams, possessing substantial and somewhat comparable human and financial utilities, engaged in strategic interactions that resulted in payoffs. The subsequent analysis explains the chance factors, discovery strategies, case development moves, and evidence maneuvers that dominated the gaming strategies and tactics used in the Minnesota tobacco trial.

Chance Factors

From the beginning of the case, Judge Fitzpatrick restricted the strategies of the defense by inserting elements of chance that surprised tobacco attorneys. He made unusual moves in the trial that benefited plaintiffs and inhibited tobacco defendants. Fitzpatrick's moves created a home-field advantage for the Minnesota plaintiffs and forced the defense to change its strategy. First, the judge decided most of the 200 motions about evidence submitted prior to and during the trial in the plaintiffs' favor. Second, he permitted the seating of jurors who voiced their animosity toward the defense on juror questionnaires and during *voir dire*. Third, he provided extreme latitude to Ciresi, who repeatedly badgered the defense's witnesses and at times maligned the tobacco industry attorneys. He consistently sustained Ciresi's objections and overruled those of the defense attorneys.

The judge's pro-plaintiff actions created such a strong impediment that defense lawyers filed a motion to have Fitzpatrick removed from the case by the head judge of that jurisdiction, but their recusal motion was not granted. Defense attorneys strongly believed that Fitzpatrick's professional conduct was so aberrant that it would have provided grounds for an appeal had the case not settled. Defense Attorney Robert Weber told local reporters covering the trial that "I don't think there's any question that we're facing a hostile court. . . . The state basically has carte blanche for whatever it wants to do" (Rybak & Phelps, 1998, p. 303).

Fourth, Fitzpatrick paid out thousands of dollars for courtroom security and staff assistance that was unnecessary since defense attorneys posed no threat to the community. The fact that the security helped the plaintiffs, but not the defense, added additional controversy to proceedings. Finally, the judge videotaped the closing arguments of the defense without their permission, and after the trial was over, he invited jurors to his chambers to hear plaintiffs' summations (Rybak & Phelps, 1998). Fitzpatrick's pro-plaintiff actions were an aberration of legal rules that eventually led head trial judge Lawrence Cohen to reprimand him and force him to cease any action related to the case. Throughout the trial, the defense criticized Fitzpatrick for his partiality to the plaintiffs, but of course the plaintiffs' attorneys appreciated the advantage they gained from the judge's rulings.

Discovery Strategies

Since attorneys need to prove their case theories demonstrating a preponderance of evidence, it is not surprising that the evidence-gathering process, called discovery, is a key part of their overall strategy. Legal guidelines for discovery first surfaced in the Federal Rules of Civil Procedures in 1938 (Matlon, 1988). As a general rule, attorneys seek evidence that applies to the pleadings in a civil case or to the indictments in a criminal case. The rules of discovery permit access to all of the evidence that has been gathered by both sides of the case. The discovery process benefits both sides because it makes evidence available prior to trial. For example, the federal rules indicate that any information that is relevant to the subject matter and the pending case should be part of discovery. The rules for discovery promote a two-player non-zero-sum adversarial game. These rules give an advantage to the plaintiffs, but the defense can limit this advantage by manipulating the rules and supplying more or less evidence than the plaintiffs requested.

Consolidating Power. Processes of discovery produce evidence (also called documents) about facts related to the case through interrogatories, requests for documents, and requests for admissions. Interrogatories are written inquires from the attorneys from one side of the case about the testimony and evidence of the other side. During the discovery process, attorneys request documents that are relevant to the claims and responses of the lawsuit. The side that produces more and better evidence establishes a power position that can be used to outwit and deter its opponent. In a civil case, usually the side with the most and best evidence wins the verdict.

During the discovery process, plaintiffs also used military language to impugn the integrity of defense lawyers. Plaintiffs claimed that one of the tobacco companies engaged in "General Patton-style litigation" and used a "concerted national strategy of discovery abuse" when they delayed the delivery of requested documents, submitted masses of irrelevant and unusable information, used an excessive number of motions and protective orders, and filed false and misleading responses to the requests (Hatfield, 1996, p. 527).

After the plaintiffs requested all documents related to previous settlement agreements, the defense handed over some of the documents and withheld others. Plaintiffs claimed the tobacco companies utilized stalling tactics by saying that the documents were subject to attorney–client privilege, providing insufficient indices for the documents they submitted, and deliberately dumping documents in inaccessible, oversized repositories (Ciresi, Walburn, & Sutton, 1999). The defense made clear that their dominant strategy in discovery was resistance, and they planned to use all legal means available to them to make this strategy work for their advantage.

In this trial, plaintiffs' admission requests turned into demands that the defense admit or deny facts generated in previous trials, congressional hearings, and settlements. The defense's arguments showed that selling cigarettes to adults is legal, cigarette products are subject to regulations and taxes, and that Minnesota pays for public education programs to reduce youth smoking. The defendants admitted that tobacco causes health problems but qualified this admission by noting that the public has known about the health problems for decades, tobacco companies are in business to make profit, advertising is essential to profit, and tobacco attorneys have informed company executives about the health risks from cigarette smoking.

Plaintiffs manipulated discovery rules so they could obtain as much evidence as possible even though much of it was irrelevant to complaints. For example, in 1996 the plaintiffs requested pro-tobacco lobbying documents; the defense countered by requesting anti-tobacco lobbying documents. Even after the trial started, the plaintiffs demanded all internal documents from all of the tobacco companies involved in the lawsuit.

In addition to these aforementioned approaches for consolidating power, attorneys often use pretrial motions to prevent their adversaries from introducing evidence that may be especially prejudicial or damaging to a case. Motions are mini arguments, that is, requests supported with evidence and analysis, made by attorneys to the trial judge prior to the opening of the trial. In the Minnesota tobacco trial, for example, attorneys for both sides made pretrial motions to exclude or "quash" some evidence and prevent their adversaries from presenting it during the trial. In other words, pretrial motions follow the process of discovery and seek to limit the adverse effects of damaging evidence uncovered during the discovery process by attorneys that oppose them in the trial.

Late in the trial on April 7, the defense caved into plaintiffs' demands and Fitzpatrick's court orders seeking 39,000 additional pieces of evidence previously protected under defense's attorney–client privilege designations. The plaintiffs' requests affected the financial utilities of the defense by creating huge expenses. Rybak and Phelps (1998) reported that one of the tobacco companies, Philip Morris, had to hire "100 extra attorneys and paralegals to decide which company files they would turn over to the prosecution" (p. 29).

Reversing Roles.   Prior to the trial, attorneys for both sides took depositions. A deposition involves adversarial interrogation of potential witnesses for the purpose of gathering evidence and developing a case theory. A court reporter transcribes the deposition so that it can be used during settlement negotiations or in a trial. The videotaped depositions of some adversarial witnesses became important evidence in the trial. The plaintiffs' use of tobacco executives as adversarial witnesses proved to be an astute and clever move that forced defense attorneys to reverse their roles, harmed the adverse witnesses' credibility, and reduced the availability of defensive countermoves.

An example of reversing roles occurred when plaintiffs showed the videotaped deposition of adversarial witness Dr. Thomas Osdene, a former director of research at Philip Morris and vice president of the company. The video of Osdene showed that he was suffering health complications from years of smoking tobacco. Rybak and Phelps (1998) noted that Osdene suffered from many respiratory diseases and was "gray-faced, frail, and wheezing" during his testimony. He "had to pause frequently to catch his breath or to cough" (p. 180). Although the defense tried as best they could to have this deposition quashed because it was prejudicial, Fitzpatrick allowed the testimony. Osdene's deposition implicated rather than exonerated Philip Morris from charges of fraud and deception and reversed the roles of the attorneys in the questioning of the witness.

In his work for this tobacco company, Osdene had signed numerous documents that showed the company wanted to hide the addictive and carcinogenic ingredients of cigarettes from the public. When plaintiffs' attorneys tried to get Osdene to explain his previous statements, he took the Fifth Amendment 125 times. Taking the Fifth Amendment is not usually a privilege afforded a defendant in a civil case, but Fitzpatrick permitted the testimony anyway since Osdene appeared for the plaintiffs.

When plaintiffs' attorney Gordon asked if Osdene had served as research director for Philip Morris, he answered, "On the advice of counsel, I decline to answer based on my Fifth Amendment privilege against self-incrimination because there is an ongoing, parallel criminal investigation." Gordon asked if Osdene knew why people smoked, Osdene invoked the Fifth Amendment. Afterward, Gordon read documents that Osdene previously had written about the dangers of smoking. Gordon read one of these documents to Osdene in the deposition that said: "We're in the smoke business. It might be more pointed to observe that the cigarette is the vehicle of smoke, smoke is the vehicle of nicotine, and nicotine is the agent of a pleasurable body response" (TR, 1998, February 19). Although Osdene refused to answer the questions about this statement, jurors knew full well that this testimony hurt the defense's case. After the trial, Ciresi said that he called adversarial witnesses so that the jury could hear the statements of tobacco leaders "in the industry's words and documents" and so they (the jury) would recognize the contradictions and deceptions in those public statements (Rybak & Phelps, 1998, p. 444).

Case Development Moves

Case development processes lead to a case theory, and theories come from the facts based on evidence. Matlon (1988) explains that "events do not just happen as a matter of truth or fact. Events are subject to interpretation by the parties involved, and they all have different interpretations of what took place" (p. 86). Evidence is socially constructed; it is presented by attorneys who package and interpret what witnesses say so that it fits with facts that support a case theory. Attorneys can communicate their case theory through narratives, dramas, games, or other analogues, or they can just present themes. A case theory (1) encapsulates the facts, evidence, and stipulations uncovered in the discovery process and (2) abides by the procedural rules and protocols (Murray, 1995). The attorneys in the Minnesota trial built their case by borrowing theories and themes from previous cases.

Borrowing Case Theories.   The themes in the Minnesota trial resembled the themes of the moral dramas that preceded it. In *Ross v. Philip Morris* (1962), for example, plaintiffs argued that "the tobacco companies made people smoke" (Zegart, 2000, p. 45). Despite repeated losses to the tobacco defendants, plaintiffs continued to use this theory prior to the Minnesota trial. Since plaintiffs were unable to persuade jurors in the early trials that "tobacco companies made people smoke," plaintiffs in the Cipollone and Carter trials re-envisioned their theories about product liability and sought damages from fraudulent and deceptive advertising. For example, plaintiffs in *Cipollone v. Liggett Group* (1992) claimed the Liggett company was negligent for their false advertising of tobacco, and this negligence resulted in Rose Cipollone's death. The jurors faulted Rose Cipollone for causing her own death by smoking, but they awarded her husband damages based on deceptive tobacco marketing. In *Carter v. Brown & Williamson Tobacco Corp.* (1996), Norwood Wilner sued a tobacco company on behalf of smoker Grady Carter who had lost part of his lung to cancer. After the trial, jurors said the evidence showed fraud and deception by the tobacco companies, and they awarded Carter $750,000 in damages (Orey, 1999).

The Castano-Mississippi-attorney general group complained that Big Tobacco's violation of consumer protection laws made them liable for reimbursements to states for money spent on the care of ill smokers. These cases replaced the smoker-as-victim with the state-as-victim theory. These theories forced the defense to deny that states suffered financial losses from paying for smoking-related illnesses and to deny that their own marketing persuaded potential customers to smoke. In the Minnesota trial, plaintiffs used deception and fraud as the basis of their theory that Big Tobacco engaged in an antitrust conspiracy.

Appropriating Moral Themes.   Attorneys in civil cases often use moral themes to contrast the actions of victims with those of perpetrators. Ciresi's moral themes repeated what other plaintiffs had used in previous tobacco litigation. He said:

> Ladies and gentlemen, the evidence will show that this was an industry which conceived of a strategy of deceit and, through an arrogance of power, promoted and fortified that sanctuary of deceit for the sole pur-

pose of achieving their objective of the continuous recruitment of teen-
agers to a product which they knew was addictive and fatal. (TR, 1998,
January 26)

Ciresi emphasized the moral theme of ensnaring youth, and the defense was
unable to refute this theme.

Defense attorneys offered a four-pronged case theory using truncated
themes that concentrated on a denial strategy. Peter Bleakley denied the
plaintiffs' theory, saying they cannot prove that "health care costs of the
plaintiffs have been increased by smokers" (TR, 1998, January 26). John
Monica concluded that "cigarette advertising has its place, but advertising
cannot cause people to do something they don't want to do. . . . We advertised a legal product, we put the warnings on our brands . . . we complied
with the rules" (TR, 1998, January 26). David Bernick asserted that the
tobacco industry did not hide anything because it permitted its customers to
make "a choice based upon publicly available information" (TR, 1998, January 27). Robert Weber admitted the harms resulting from cigarette use and
noted that Liggett "acted appropriately" by selling cigarettes as a legal product. The defense attorneys countered the social and moral responsibility
theme of plaintiffs by introducing the ideas of personal responsibility,
emphasizing that "smokers choose to smoke" even when they know the
health risks. In this case, the attorneys appeared to use moral themes to conceal their gaming strategy. Although the personal responsibility theme had
worked well for defense attorneys in previous litigation, in this case the
theme was too narrow to address the breadth of the plaintiffs' complaints
and the defense lacked evidence about the personal behavior of smokers
whose health care bills had been paid by state taxes.

Evidence Maneuvers

Attorneys used tactical maneuvers for gathering and presenting evidence that could shift the balance of power, confuse the issues, and convey
the finesse and expertise of the attorneys. Both the plaintiffs and the defense
adapted to legal rules by piling up evidence, selecting dependable evidence,
amending court procedures, and following court protocols.

Piling up Evidence.   The amount of evidence accumulated for the Minnesota tobacco trial exceeded that of the other tobacco trials, resulting in a public
depository of 3.3 million separate pieces of evidence. Attorneys from both
sides had access to the evidence during the discovery process. In ways that differed from other civil trials in general and tobacco cases in particular, Judge
Fitzpatrick ordered in July of 1995 that parties in the trial create a "central
repository for discovery documents" in order to provide other plaintiffs suing
tobacco companies with access to the documents. Moreover, the order specified that the parties in the case would create the repository by systematically
organizing and identifying the documents and by sharing the cost of copying or
imaging the documents. Plaintiffs and defense attorneys added evidence to the

depository from its inception in 1995 until the last days of the trial in April 1998. The archive contained more than 20,000 numbered exhibits containing millions of pages of evidence (Tobacco Global Settlement Archives, 1999).

A common tactic for piling up evidence is to use many experts sequenced one after the other. This tactic gives jurors the impression that numerous experts will corroborate one another's testimony. Calling many experts also solidifies the attorneys' position of power by creating the impression that piles of evidence support their side in contrast to the paucity of evidence available to the opposition. The piling up of plaintiffs' health experts emphasized that they were people of good character who wanted to deter the evil actions of Big Tobacco. Among the 29 plaintiffs' witnesses were health experts Dr. Richard Hurt from Mayo Clinic in Minnesota, Dr. Channing Robertson from Stanford University, and Dr. Jonathan Samet from Johns Hopkins University. The quality and quantity of plaintiffs' experts outmatched that of the defense partly because Judge Fitzpatrick ruled that the defense could only call 11 witnesses, one witness for each of the tobacco defendants.

The defense could not provide a comparable number or quality of experts nor could they counter the evidence provided by plaintiffs; they called only two statistical experts, William Wecker of Stanford and Donald Rubin of Harvard. Nonetheless, the two experts served the defense well and perhaps their testimony helped to forge a settlement prior to the verdict. Both professors testified that plaintiffs' statistical models were flawed and the damages claimed by plaintiffs exceeded what the model projected. In general though, the plaintiffs piled up more evidence than the defense, and they also drew positive inferences about the moral character of witnesses and the relevance of their testimony. Jurors would likely have been convinced that the preponderance of evidence was on the side of the plaintiffs.

Selecting Dependable Evidence.   Evidence is dependable to the extent that it supports case theory, excludes vulnerable evidence, includes strong evidence, corroborates other evidence, and relates evidence to issues. Evidence that is redundant or extraneous prolongs the trial without adding relevant content. Selections of evidence depend on a variety of factors, such as what evidence can be introduced through available witnesses, what foundation can be established for the evidence, what communication purposes the evidence serves, and what probative value the evidence has (for example, does the evidence add substance to the case that outweighs the prejudicial value?). Although thousands of pieces of evidence were available, plaintiffs selected evidence that had proved successful in previous civil actions against Big Tobacco.

PLAINTIFFS' EVIDENCE

• *Statistics about cancer deaths.* In the Waxman hearings, Commissioner Kessler claimed that more than 400,000 Americans died of illnesses related to cigarette smoking. Ciresi repeatedly stated this figure through his health experts and pushed adversarial witnesses to admit that this statistic was a stipulated fact.

- *The Frank statement.* This statement consisted of a page-long advertisement that appeared in 448 newspapers in 258 cities throughout the United States in January of 1954. The ad, prepared by the Tobacco Industry Research Committee (a public relations firm hired by the tobacco companies), was a response to news reports that smoking causes cancer. The ad claimed tobacco companies had made a good faith effort to find the facts about smoking and health problems and employed scientists with "unimpeachable integrity and national repute" to conduct research (Glantz et al., 1995, pp. 34–35). Ciresi referred to the Frank statement with nearly every one of plaintiffs' witnesses to show that the tobacco companies never followed through with their promise and instead hid the findings of the research that implicated cigarettes as the cause of health problems.

- *The addictive features of nicotine.* The plaintiffs claimed that tobacco companies knew about addiction as early as the 1960s, failed to disclose the information to the public, and conducted research to increase rather than reduce nicotine effects. Plaintiffs also featured the evidence that Merrell Williams had stolen from Brown & Williamson as well as documents gathered from the Carter case against Brown & Williamson to show that the companies hid the evidence from the public. Plaintiffs introduced this evidence through contemporary health experts who commented on their own research about this subject.

- *The advertising of cigarettes to youth.* Plaintiffs stressed that cigarette companies targeted those less than 18 years of age to try to get them to start smoking. They based this claim on ads with cartoon figures, like Joe Camel, and the content of magazine ads and billboards. Plaintiffs introduced dozens of ads from the tobacco industry using adversarial witnesses to present this evidence.

- *The concealing of health facts by tobacco officials.* Plaintiffs' evidence presented hundreds of statements made by tobacco executives and researchers indicating that they knew about the harmful effects of smoking but did not inform the public. In fact, some tobacco companies dumped some of these documents in an overseas depository and marked other research "confidential" so that it would be protected by attorney–client privilege (Walburn, 1999).

The plaintiffs' selection of evidence forced the defense to admit that the companies they represented knew smoking was harmful and that they marketed addictive cigarettes. The defense selected some evidence that benefitted their case theory by emphasizing the legality of cigarette smoking, showing the existing regulations that restricted the sale and use of cigarettes, and pointing out the weaknesses of plaintiffs' statistical models about costs incurred by Minnesota taxpayers.

DEFENSE'S EVIDENCE

- *Public information about the risks of smoking.* Defense claimed that information about the health risks was publicly available through the surgeon general's warnings on tobacco packages, through popular magazines (*Readers' Digest*), through the National Cancer Institute and the American Medical Association, and through anti-smoking curricula in Minnesota public schools and in the communities of the state.

- *Alternative reasons for underage smoking.* Defense used the testimony of tobacco company advertising and marketing executives to show that advertising does not cause smoking. Instead underage smoking occurs because of rebellion, peer pressure, and the thrill of doing something forbidden by adults. Defense witnesses claimed that advertising affects brand preference, but it does not make people smoke.

- *Design of safer cigarettes.* Defense asserted that the tobacco companies continue to produce cigarettes that have a reduced tar and nicotine content, and they indicated that the surgeon generals' reports have acknowledged this fact. They argued that the companies continue to study nicotine and tar content and to use new technologies to reduce additives that harm the health of smokers. Defense witnesses gave evidence that tobacco companies have reduced the levels of bensopyren, phenol, tar, and nitrates in cigarettes and added filtrating systems based on recommendations of the health community.

- *Legitimacy and legality of cigarette advertising.* Defense witnesses cited evidence that the federal and state governments regulated the tobacco industry through various laws about the labeling, selling, taxing, and distributing of cigarettes. The federal government has banned the advertising of cigarettes on television for the past 25 years, and cigarette smoking is now legal and always had been legal. People choose to smoke despite their knowledge of health risks and despite the high taxes on tobacco products.

- *Problems with plaintiffs' economic analysis.* Experts testifying for the defense gave evidence that the statistical model presented by plaintiffs came from national statistics and did not apply to Minnesota. Their statistical experts noted that plaintiffs requested damages from hemorrhoids, schizophrenia, and broken bones rather than smoking-related illnesses.

Both sides effectively selected evidence that met their obligation to show a preponderance of evidence, supported their respective case theories, and related their evidence to the issues of the dispute. Given the extent of the complaints in the case, the defense had fewer options for selecting evidence than the plaintiffs did. They did the best they could under the factual and judge-created constraints of the legal situation. The accumulation of evidence from so many resources prior to the trial and Fitzpatrick's favorable rulings gave plaintiffs a distinct advantage that defense could not overcome. For this reason factors of both strategy and chance affected the outcome of the Minnesota trial.

Bending Court Rules.   Court rules require attorneys to introduce the evidence through their witnesses. In some cases, attorneys maneuver around the rules by using adversarial witnesses to present testimony that favors their side of the case, as plaintiffs did in this trial. This approach does not break procedural rules, but it involves what Posner (1990) calls, "navigating around the rules" (p. 60). Plaintiffs navigated the rules in this way: (1) They used their own witnesses to explain what the facts were about tobacco use and cancer; (2) they called adversarial witnesses to confirm the deceptive and fraudulent marketing practices, identify weaknesses in tobacco company research, admit that smoking does cause cancer, and acknowledge that tobacco companies added chemicals to increase the addictive capacity of cigarettes. This tactic allowed the plaintiffs to moralize about the evil actions of tobacco companies in contrast to the morally upright actions of their experts. The defense called no adversarial witnesses, relied on tobacco company employees to deny their employers had engaged in deceptive and fraudulent practices, and did not bend the rules of evidence. They provided evidence to defend the presumption that existing regulations and education about health risks are adequate means for warning people about smoking.

Another way that plaintiffs' attorneys successfully bent the rules was persuading Judge Fitzpatrick to allow jurors to examine evidence that was not presented through witnesses. In an unconventional move, Fitzpatrick allowed three different days for jurors to browse through documents not presented through trial witnesses. This tactic permitted jurors to look at evidence from previous civil actions and to decide which side had the preponderance of evidence. Fitzpatrick explained the process in this way:

> Members of the jury, . . . we're going to give you one more time and opportunity to review some of those exhibits. There will be three copies of each exhibit available to you for your review. . . . [You] will be asked to read those trial exhibits. There will be two counsel, one for plaintiffs and one for defendants, in the other courtroom during your review, along with a bailiff and security. . . . You can wander around the courtroom, review as you so choose. The purpose of the procedure is simply to allow you to review a large number of documents at one time. Some of the documents that you'll review are copies of newspaper articles, magazine articles, books and other materials on the topic of smoking and health that have been written by third parties. (TR, 1998, April 2).

One problem was that the judge's action favored the plaintiffs who submitted mounds of evidence, and some of it lacked a foundation and probative value. Moreover, the judge allowed jurors to decide what evidence they would examine and how much attention they would give to the evidence. This court bent the rules to favor the plaintiffs, and the defense also tried to the bend rules in their favor by offering evidence for their side under the same rules. For example, the defense asked the judge to add evidence that was extraneous to the issues and had little, if any, foundation. Defense attorneys justified the showing of this evidence by careless reasoning similar to that used by plaintiffs.

In what appeared to be a ploy to expose the self-serving and absurd nature of some of plaintiffs' evidence and reasoning, defense asserted without justifying their claims that some of their documents need not be introduced through a witness because they are "self-authenticating" and "probative." The documents should be included, defense attorneys said, because they show the state of mind of tobacco companies about additives and cigarette design. Plaintiffs expressed dismay that the defense had called their bluff and exposed the unfairness of Fitzpatrick's evidence browsing process. Since the trial never went to the jury, this browsing process had no explicit effect on the trial outcome.

Following Protocols. The courts have specific legal and communication protocols for introducing evidence. These protocols legitimize the evidence, show the attorneys' respect for the court and their witnesses, and allow attorneys to impress jurors that the evidence is authentic and relevant. The protocol follows explicit stages that recognize the sources and relevance of the evidence and enforce a particular way of communicating about the evidence.

PROTOCOLS FOR INTRODUCING EVIDENCE

- Qualify the witness by laying the foundation for the witness to identify the evidence.
- Request that the witness examine and recognize the exhibit.
- Offer the exhibit into evidence by referring to the exhibit number or letter.
- Respond to any objections made by opposing attorneys.
- Obtain the judge's ruling on the record.
- Show the exhibit to the jurors if admitted. (Fontham, 1995; Haydock & Sonsteng, 1994b)

An example of this protocol occurred with the plaintiffs' first expert witness, Dr. Richard D. Hurt (TR, 1998, January 28). Ciresi asked Hurt to identify evidence related to the history of tobacco use, the chemistry of cigarettes, and the reasons for addiction. First, Ciresi qualified Hurt as an expert.

C: Can you tell us what your present employment is?

H: I'm a consultant in internal medicine and director of the Nicotine Dependence Center at Mayo Clinic.

Ciresi asked Hurt more questions about his qualifications, and the information was more extensive than necessary since it covered more than 20 pages of the transcript and repeated information that was already in evidence. But the information about the witness's Minnesota connection (Mayo Clinic) probably impressed jurors and the judge. Ciresi inquired about his previous jobs, the results of each of his published studies, and his lectures to professional medical groups.

Next, Ciresi asked Hurt to examine an exhibit of evidence.

C: Now you've been asked to give your expert professional opinion on the following subject . . . whether nicotine is an addictive drug, correct?

H: That's correct. . . .

C: And do you at the clinic in the Nicotine Dependence Center utilize a historical perspective?

H: I have.

Ciresi showed the notebook that contained the evidence, identified it as Exhibit 300083, and then asked Hurt to describe the history of tobacco in this country, using the evidence in that exhibit. Before he could answer, defense attorney Bernick objected on the grounds that plaintiffs had failed to lay a foundation. Judge Fitzpatrick overruled the objection, and then Hurt continued giving lengthy testimony about the history of tobacco. Bernick objected again by claiming that the foundation for the exhibit had not been laid and that the historical content was not within the expertise of Hurt. Since Ciresi had not established Hurt's expertise in history or laid the foundation, Judge Fitzpatrick probably should have sustained defense's objections, but he allowed the plaintiffs to present the evidence they wanted. In any trial, the judge can tip the balance so that it favors one side. Judge Fitzpatrick favored the plaintiffs, and his rulings showed his biases. Even when attorneys play by the rules and follow protocols, judges can introduce an element of chance that impedes attorneys' strategical and tactical moves.

Judge Fitzpatrick allowed defense attorney Weber more latitude than other members of the defense team. Reporters covering the trial speculated that Fitzpatrick liked Weber more than he did other defense attorneys because Weber was not as critical as others were of the proceedings (Rybak & Phelps, 1998). The following example illustrates his practice of following protocols for presenting evidence. Weber, a capable and veteran defense attorney for R. J. Reynolds, questioned Lynn Beasley, the key person responsible for the tobacco company's marketing campaign and for its cartoon-like character, Joe Camel. Plaintiffs had argued that ads featuring Joe Camel encouraged underage youth to start smoking. Weber began by qualifying his witness (all of the following excerpts are from TR, 1998, April 20):

W: Mrs. Beasley, could you tell us by whom you're employed and where you work?

B: Yes. I'm employed by R. J. Reynolds Tobacco Company in Winston-Salem, North Carolina. . . . I'm executive vice-president of marketing for R. J. Reynolds. . . . I'm responsible for all of the marketing for all of R. J. Reynolds brands, all the advertising and promotion and packaging for all the brands.

Weber then introduced personal factors about Beasley that might be appealing to a Minnesota jury. He asked her about her family background. Beasley responded that she grew up on a dairy farm in Wisconsin, paid for her own college, and worked for the post office before she got her graduate degrees that enabled her to direct marketing at R. J. Reynolds.

After qualifying the witness, Weber laid a foundation by asking the marketing director to identify the ads and promotions.

> W: And what was your particular responsibility as assistant brand manager for Camel?
>
> B: When I was assistant brand manager on Camel, I was responsible for promotion development, things like sweepstakes where you can enter a sweepstakes and win something, and FSI promotions, which—you know when you get your Sunday newspaper and you open it up and a bunch of coupons fall out, that's an FSI promotion.
>
> W: Is there a difference between promotion and advertising?
>
> B: Well, yeah. The way we think about it is—advertising is like paid media that you place, so it would be magazines and newspapers and billboards, that's advertising, and then promotion is [one of the] things you do that provide an incentive for a competitive smoker to try the brand, so it might be a coupon, it might be a sweepstakes, it might be a buy-two-get-one-free in the store, but it's some more incentive rather than just an ad that has a message.
>
> W: Can you turn to tab one in your binder, which is Exhibit ASP000023? And let me ask you if you can identify that this is an ad from the Bob Beck campaign.
>
> B: Yes, it was.

Weber's tactic for admitting the evidence won a favorable ruling from Judge Fitzpatrick:

> W: Your Honor, I'd move the admission of ASP000023.
>
> F: The court will receive ASP000023.
>
> W: Now is that a representative example of that campaign's ads?
>
> B: Yes. Well this is actually a promotion ad.
>
> W: And how was this campaign perceived in the marketing department by the Reynolds's employees?

Ciresi objected to the way the witnesses reacted to the evidence by "saying this calls for hearsay." After Fitzpatrick overruled Ciresi, he permitted the witness to continue her testimony.

> B: Yes. When I was on the Camel brand then, the campaign was perceived as having problems because this guy in the ad, he was seen as kind of a loner, and smokers were seeing the campaign as kind of a—[I] hate to say it—bad imitation of Marlboro, that—you know, that it was—it just wasn't very compelling and motivating to particularly younger adult smokers.

W: That's a document already in evidence, Exhibit 12811. . . . And is this a marketing research report dated February 1, 1985, related to "CAMEL YOUNGER ADULT SMOKER FOCUS GROUPS"?

B: Yes, it is.

W: And does this memo report on focus group reaction to a variety of potential supplementary ad campaigns?

B: Yes, it does.

Both the plaintiffs and the defense had capable attorneys who implemented tactics that they thought would help them win the verdict. Weber demonstrated his finesse in following the protocols for presenting the evidence by focusing on the witness's Midwestern and working-class background, a way of enhancing her credibility with the jurors. He used Beasley's testimony to establish facts relevant to the defense's case by admitting that a marketing campaign existed, claiming that it was not directed to youth, and noting that focus groups of 18- to 24-year-old smokers indicated that this marketing strategy had failed to entice them to smoke the Camel brand.

Attorneys for both sides employed legitimate gaming strategies and tactics that navigated the rules about presenting evidence, and the judge used his discretionary powers to make new rules and enforce old ones. As is clear from the analysis of this trial, at times the trial outcome does not rely as much on existing procedures and protocols as it does on the judge's discretion for allowing attorneys to bend the rules.

In the final hours of the Minnesota trial in April of 1998, 39,000 confidential and incriminating tobacco company documents became public. These documents added intensity to other settlement talks. In May of 1998, after the summation of the defense and before the summation of plaintiffs, Minnesota settled with tobacco companies for a sum $6.1 billion over a 25-year period. The outcome reinforced the morality drama that had begun years before in out-of-court bargaining efforts that pitted the socially responsible actions of health care researchers and plaintiffs' attorneys against the evil actions of tobacco companies.

In November of 1998 the attorney generals of 46 states agreed to a "Master Settlement" of $206 billion to take place during a period of more than 25 years. The settlement restricted tobacco marketing and advertising, refused protection for Big Tobacco from liability in private or class action suits, and permitted no regulation of cigarettes by the Food and Drug Administration. The tobacco companies changed their marketing and doled out a few state financial settlements as early as September of 1998. This civil litigation game ended with a settlement, but legal moral dramas against Big Tobacco continue to be played out in other states nearly a decade after the initial settlements. Since the settlements, some states have turned into bad actors who have used money from tobacco settlements to build community centers or parks rather than to educate citizens on the harmful effects of tobacco as they had promised to do. The tobacco companies in a sense transformed their evil actions into socially responsible ones in which they restricted advertising, paid some penalties for their sins, and educated the public about the evils of tobacco. The success of the Minnesota plaintiffs made the theories and evidence of their trial available to subsequent plaintiffs. Settlements do not extinguish litigation, but often promulgate it.

Lessons

Readers can learn several lessons from this trial about communicating the law. First, attorneys often conduct civil actions in ways that resemble medieval morality plays. Instead of preaching about religious dogma, plaintiffs try to force defendants to engage in socially and morally responsible actions so their products and services benefit customers. Attorneys in civil actions often borrow the moral themes generated from media publicity and pretrial bargaining for their opening statements and for their summations. By the time attorneys face one another in settlement proceedings, the gaming strategies have already dominated the moral themes. The legal coalitions that engaged Big Tobacco in bargaining used power moves to deter opponents, procedural moves regarding issues to place opponents on the brink, and divide and conquer tactics that refocused the issues. Unlike a typical variable-sum bargaining game, the Minnesota trial resembled a two-person zero-sum game that favored the plaintiffs. The judge's actions created chance factors that enabled the plaintiffs to provide more and better evidence than the defense. The moves used in discovery allowed plaintiffs the opportunity to consolidate their power and force the defense to reverse their roles. These moves enhanced the quantity and quality of evidence that plaintiffs secured from witnesses. Since previous legal actions against Big Tobacco had tested case theories and themes with other jurors, plaintiffs selected a theory and appropriate themes that had succeeded in the past. Although attorneys for both sides adopted skillful tactical maneuvers to support their side of the case, the judge permitted more latitude to the plaintiffs to pile up evidence, a factor that helped them establish their burden to show a preponderance of evidence. Both the plaintiffs and defense selected dependable evidence and followed protocols in ways that showed their knowledge of the law and their skill in communication.

5

Narratives and Opening Statements in the McVeigh Trial

When the sun rose over Oklahoma City on April 19, 1995, none of the citizens who regularly worked, visited, or left their children at the Alfred P. Murrah Federal Building could have imagined the horror of the bomb blast that would kill 168 and injure 500 members of the community. The facts about how and why so many lives were ruined began to unfold just 75 minutes after the bomb blast when Timothy McVeigh was arrested north of Oklahoma City because his car had no license plate. In his car, police found guns and antigovernment literature. Residue from the bomb components was on McVeigh's clothes.

Several sources (Hoffman, 1998; Jones & Israel, 2001; Michel & Herbeck, 2001; Serrano, 1998; Stickney, 1996) explain the circumstances that led to the bombing. After a lengthy investigation into the life of this young veteran of the Gulf War, investigators discovered that McVeigh was deeply upset by the government's role in the deaths of the wife and son of white supremacist Randy Weaver at Ruby Ridge, Idaho, and in the deaths of 76 Branch Davidians in Waco, Texas, on April 19, 1993. Investigators also learned that McVeigh was obsessed with the plot of a novel, the *Turner Diaries,* and speculated that he may have modeled the bombing on its fictional plot. Prosecutors claimed that McVeigh, with the help of codefendant Terry Nichols, had purchased the components of the bomb—a ton of ammonium nitrate and explosive fuels. He placed the bomb ingredients in a Ryder truck that he had rented under a phony name in Junction City, Kansas, drove the bomb-laden truck to Oklahoma City, parked it at the entrance to the Murrah Federal Building, and ignited the bomb at 9:02 AM on April 19, the anniversary of the deaths of the Branch Davidians.

A grand jury indicted McVeigh and his friend Nichols for conspiring to use a weapon of mass destruction (the truck bomb) and for killing 168 people.

Specifically, the indictment contained 11 charges, including conspiracy to use a truck bomb to destroy the Alfred P. Murrah Federal Building and to kill and injure persons in that facility. Additionally, the government charged McVeigh with the first-degree murder of eight law enforcement agents, including four secret service agents, two customs agents, one drug enforcement agent, and one agent from housing and urban development. In response to pretrial motions, Judge Richard Matsch ruled that McVeigh and Nichols would be tried separately, the trial would be moved from Oklahoma City to Denver, and victims and their families could view the trial on closed-circuit television. Since eight of the victims were law enforcement agents killed while on duty, McVeigh was eligible under federal law for the death penalty. McVeigh lacked funds so the government appointed and paid for his defense. The defense bill was $13.5 million and the government paid more than $86 million for the prosecution attorneys, consultants, and federal investigators.

The trial took place in a federal court, a jurisdiction that had not permitted the death penalty since 1963. Federal investigators amassed huge amounts of information during discovery, including "30,000 government witness statements, 100,000 photographs, hundreds of video and audio tapes, 7,000 pounds of bomb debris, and 156 million telephone records" (Jones & Israel, 2001, pp. 152–153). Although 35 different attorneys and investigators worked for the defense, Stephen Jones served as McVeigh's lead trial attorney and presented the defense's opening statement and summation, and Robert Nigh Jr. helped prepare for the trial and for the posttrial appeal in case McVeigh received the death penalty. Joseph P. Hartzler led the 10-person team of prosecution lawyers and hundreds of federal investigators; he delivered the opening statement and summation on behalf of the U.S. government. Two years after the bombing, the trial of Timothy McVeigh commenced with opening statements on April 24, 1997. The trial lasted 36 days with the prosecution calling 151 witnesses and the defense calling less than a dozen. A formal sentencing hearing followed the guilty verdict; it featured the testimony of a few members of McVeigh's family and friends who argued that the court should spare McVeigh's life and 38 victims who urged the judge to give the defendant the death penalty. The jury sentenced McVeigh to death on June 13, 1997.

All citations from the trial transcript come from the trial record of the *United States v. Timothy McVeigh* (1997, April 24, the date when attorneys presented opening statements). Before the federal government executed McVeigh on June 11, 2001, he granted extensive interviews to reporters Lou Michel and Dan Herbeck from the *Buffalo News*. Michel and Herbeck (2001) published Timothy McVeigh's story under the title *American Terrorist*. Before this book was published, Stephen Jones and Peter Israel (2001) published their perspective of the trial to refute McVeigh's claims that Jones provided inadequate counsel.

This chapter (1) explains the case background and media coverage, (2) describes in general terms how legal rules and communication choices affect the narratives of opening statements, (3) analyzes the prosecutor's opening statement, (4) evaluates the defense's opening statement, and (5) identifies some of the lessons readers can learn from the trial's opening statements.

CASE BACKGROUND AND MEDIA COVERAGE

As the rescue efforts started, Timothy McVeigh drove away from the bomb scene and headed toward Kansas. Before he left Oklahoma and one and one-half hours after the bomb went off, an Oklahoma patrol officer stopped McVeigh for failing to display a license plate. When the officer searched him, he discovered that McVeigh was concealing a weapon, an action that violated Oklahoma law; had books chronicling the fictional bombing of a federal building; and possessed receipts from purchases of materials that could be used to make a fertilizer bomb. The officer took McVeigh into custody for failing to display a license plate and for carrying a weapon, but he had no idea that he had nabbed the bomber of the Murrah Federal Building. While McVeigh was in jail in Enid, Oklahoma, federal investigators accumulated evidence about who rented the truck containing the fertilizer bomb, phone records that linked McVeigh to purchases of ammonium nitrate and detonation devices, and testimony of Kansas business proprietors from whom the Ryder truck was rented and the getaway car was purchased. The discovery of this evidence became part of the media coverage prior to the trial and was central to the content of the opening statements during the trial.

The pretrial media coverage of the Oklahoma City bombing influenced the prosecution's opening statements in the McVeigh case by creating a public consciousness about the defendant's guilt and by presenting extensive evidence against him. For example, the coverage featured constant images of the destroyed face of the building, smoke-covered rescue workers holding injured and deceased babies, and crime scene investigators finding parts of bodies in the rubble of the federal building, evoking emotional outrage from the public. Defense attorneys also used the media to help them create public doubt about McVeigh's guilt. Jones recalled: "I called Peter Annin, the *Newsweek* reporter assigned to the Oklahoma City bombing. I told him my client wanted to do an interview. . . . I wanted Tim on the cover. I would be present during the interview and would record it" (Jones & Israel, 2001, pp. 84–85).

The media called attention to the reputations of the lead attorneys before the trial started. Prosecutor Joseph Hartzler was a federal prosecutor with a reputation as "a feisty tactician." The Illinois native volunteered to join the prosecution after hearing about the bombing. He had convicted members of terrorist groups who had blown up buildings in Chicago and was confident that he could convict McVeigh. The U.S. attorney general helped create the distinguished nine-member team of federal prosecutors that tried the case. Since Hartzler suffered from multiple sclerosis, he made his way around the courtroom in an electric scooter. This physical challenge, however, did not impede his rhetorical skill (Michel & Herbeck, 2001, p. 318). During his opening statement, Hartzler proved that he understood the jurors by the way he constructed his compelling story.

Stephen Jones accepted the role of the lead attorney for the defense after McVeigh's original court-appointed attorneys, Susan Otto and John Coyle, withdrew from the case. Jones was a country defense attorney with experience representing Vietnam protestors Abbie Hoffman and Keith Green in cases in Oklahoma, but he lacked experience on the national legal stage. Jones recognized how difficult it would be to defend a person who allegedly killed 168 of his fellow citizens. At the time he agreed to represent McVeigh, Jones had tried 15 death penalty cases in Oklahoma. Before the trial, he closed down his law firm in Enid, Oklahoma, and moved his office to Denver to work on the McVeigh case. By the time of the trial, Jones had recruited 34 attorneys and investigators to help him with the case.

Two years before attorneys presented their opening statements, the media constructed a strong case and presented mounds of evidence that implicated McVeigh and his coconspirator Terry Nichols. Using his rhetorical skill, prosecutor Hartzler's opening statements bolstered, named, framed, and elaborated the evidence that had been leaked to the media. The defense faced a major challenge because the media's evidence against McVeigh was so strong. In fact, prior to the trial in 1997, stories on the *Dallas Morning News* Internet site, in *Playboy* magazine, and on ABC television news reported that McVeigh had confessed to the bombing.

LEGAL RULES AND COMMUNICATION CHOICES IN OPENING STATEMENTS

Opening statements are speeches that preview the underlying story structure of the case and thereby establish a perceptual framework for jurors into which the rest of the trial fits. The U.S. Supreme Court has limited the scope of opening statements to informing "the jurors concerning the nature of the action and the issues involved" and noted that the purpose of the opening speech is to give jurors "an outline of the case" (Starr, 1983, p. 426) so that they can understand how the evidence they hear in the trial fits together (Fontham, 1995). Although attorneys cannot technically argue in opening statements, they can forecast and promise what is to come. In other words, opening statements are the quintessence of argument, for they persuade without appearing to.

Persuasive opening statements are not just descriptions, they are carefully organized, framed, and condensed stories that meet specific legal constraints. Describing the scene, characters/actors and their motives, disputed action, and outcomes of the action are not persuasive unless attorneys frame the descriptions as assertions that relate to themes, sequence the narrative into distinct story categories, draw causal connections between parts of the story, and establish direct connections between the elements of the story and the indictments or complaints. Prosecutors' narratives are designed to achieve their burden of proving guilt; plaintiffs' narratives address establishing a preponderance of evidence; and those of the defense seek to achieve their goal of creating doubt.

Prosecutors and plaintiffs usually create narratives that support a case theory, but defense attorneys need not offer an alternative theory because they can rely on refutation to deny the narratives presented by opposing attorneys. Attorneys for both sides need to interpret the evidence using some sort of narrative (Fontham, 1995; Haydock & Sonsteng, 1991; Jeans, 1993; Lubet, 1993; Mauet, 1992). Some research on juror decision making indicates that opening statements create such strong impressions that jurors often decide cases according to the initial impressions they formed from attorneys' opening statements (Haydock & Sonsteng, 1991; Schuetz & Lilley, 1999). Opening statements provide an opportunity for attorneys to teach jurors how to be fact finders and how to make sense of the evidence by envisioning the scene and the actions of the defendants in relation to the scene (Murray, 1995).

The procedural rules give more latitude to attorneys during opening statements than during other parts of the trial. However, the following rules of procedure still prohibit attorneys from referring to inadmissible evidence, overstating the evidence, talking about the facts their opponents will present, and providing extensive detail about the testimony of their own witnesses (Tanford, 1983). The opposing attorneys can object during opening statements if they believe their adversaries are violating these rules, and the trial judge then decides whether or not to enforce these rules. Some jurisdictions do not permit attorneys to talk directly about the law. The order of presentation is that the prosecution or plaintiff usually presents first and the defense follows. However, the defense can choose not to present an opening statement at all or decide to present it after the prosecutors or plaintiffs have presented their entire case. The length of the opening statement depends on the complexity of the case and the amount of evidence. Several procedural rules guide the construction and presentation of opening statements during a trial.

PROCEDURAL RULES FOR OPENING STATEMENTS

- Avoid partisan arguing, that is, asking jurors to resolve the issues or interpreting acts in ways that present two sides.
- Avoid discussing specific provisions of the law.
- Avoid referring to inadmissible evidence.
- Avoid overstatements of the evidence.
- Avoid talking about the opponents' evidence.
- Limit the details used to explain testimony of the witnesses for your side of the case.
- Avoid references to testimony that will not be presented at trial.

Even though opening statements are somewhat limited in content, carefully constructed narratives can overcome these limitations and produce persuasive outcomes with jurors (Haydock & Sonsteng, 1991; Iannuzzi, 1982, 1998; Murray 1995).

Attorneys expect their opening statements will communicate the facts and evidence that support their case theory and persuade jurors without overt argumentation (Schuetz & Snedaker, 1988). The following recommendations enunciate the important role of communication in opening statements.

COMMUNICATION IN OPENING STATEMENTS

- Tell an interesting story that engages jurors, using vivid language, including metaphors and imagery.
- Convert a case theory into an interesting narrative by depicting the crime scene, the characters, the nature of action, the plot, and a theme/point to the story.
- Connect the issues of the indictment or the complaints to the plot of the story.
- Humanize the victims when representing the prosecution; humanize the defendants when representing the defense.
- Link the narrative to the familiar values and experiences of jurors using familiar themes.
- Create persuasive narratives that conceal the argumentative substructure of the story.
- Frame, preview, and connect the parts of the story into a coherent narrative.

Attorneys present their opening statements before witnesses actually testify so attorneys have to project what they think the witnesses will say based on what they have said in depositions. As a result, attorneys try to interweave large amounts of complicated and disjunctive evidence and testimony using a thematic connective thread. Opening statements construct arguments under the guise of narratives, what Walter R. Fisher (1984, 1987, 1989) calls "narrative rationality." The narratives reconfigure the evidence so that it reconstructs crime scenes, characterizes perpetrators and victims, and construes criminal actions in relation to criminal statutes. Prosecuting attorneys draw inferences from the evidence to link defendants' motivations and planning to the indictments for the crime. Defense attorneys can create an alternative story or deny the prosecution's story. For both sides of a case, the narratives of opening statements contain arguments that do not appear in conventional inductive and deductive sequences. Nonetheless, the narrative of opening statements can provide a coherent and reasonable accounting of what happened, how it happened, how people acted, and what the context or scenes of the action was. In one way, the narratives of opening statements persuade jurors because they ring true with their experiences and values. In another way, narratives help jurors make sense of the evidence through recognizable themes, a coherent chronological structure, and a familiar story line. Attorneys' stories should transport jurors into the narrative worlds they have created in their opening statements.

In a sense, opening statements conceal the arguments under the veneer of the narrative that includes the story form and the language. Just as in any act of storytelling, the attorneys tell their story in opening statements through the use of powerful verbs, carefully chosen adjectives, and active voice. Additionally, though, the marks of an engaging story are its persuasive use of repetition, imagery, and metaphor (Schuetz & Snedaker, 1988). Repetition consists of repeating key phrases that reflect the point of the story—that is, reasons why, in a criminal case, the accused is legally either guilty or not guilty or why, in a civil case, a defendant is liable for damages. The narrative must also appeal to the attitudes and values of the jurors, and imagery and metaphors are vehicles that create and sustain jurors' attention and facilitate comprehension. Imagery consists of word pictures that call up a vivid mental representation about people, actions, and circumstances in the minds of the jurors. Whereas a prosecutor might describe the accused as a vicious animal that stalks victims in the night, the defense might paint a picture of that same person as a physically or mentally victimized person who lacks control over his or her actions. In ways similar to imagery, metaphors add vividness to the story, denoting one kind of idea or object in place of another and suggesting an analogy or likeness between them. Metaphors in criminal trials often compare the accused to demons and traitors and their acts to destructive accidents, storms, or devastation. In this way, language draws jurors into the reality of the stories told by attorneys during their opening statements.

ANALYSIS OF THE PROSECUTION'S OPENING STATEMENT

Since legal rules provide minimal restraints on the way attorneys present their opening statements, attorneys can use creative rhetorical approaches to these initial speeches of the trial. In criminal cases, the prosecution has a dual burden of proof, that is, the burden to prove guilt and the burden to prove the facticity and reliability of the government's evidence. Prosecutors have an opportunity to create a primacy effect, a first impression of the strength of the case that stays with jurors even after they have heard the opening statements from defense (Fontes & Bunden, 1980). Before the case ever begins, the prosecution has the advantage of using the resources of police and government investigators. Since the McVeigh trial was a federal crime, the entire Justice Department and the Federal Bureau of Investigation (FBI) gathered evidence, and federal crime laboratories linked the evidence to McVeigh. Additionally, the media had already presented evidence leaked from federal investigators that likely influenced jurors' expectations about how strong the evidence was and what the prosecutor would say in his opening statement.

Hartzler presented the one-sided argument of his case under the veneer of a compelling narrative. The prosecutor's story evolved in ways similar to chapters of a book. Each chapter served distinctive narrative functions and legal goals. In chapter one, Hartzler characterized the setting of the bombing in this way: "It was a beautiful day in Oklahoma City. . . . The sun was shining. Flowers were blooming. It was springtime." For him the story of the Garrett family tragedy served as a "representative anecdote," that is, "a representative incident that sums up a prototype of a situation." The anecdote implicitly contains the essential features of other similar stories (Burke, 1969a). The story of Helen Garrett and her son Tevin was a representative anecdote for the mothers and for all of the 19 children who died in the day care center in the Murrah Federal Building. Hartzler traced the movements of Helen Garrett and Tevin. She parked in the lot next to the building because she was running late. "When she went in, she saw that Chase and Colton Smith were already there . . . so was Zack Chavez. . . . When she turned to leave to go to her work, Tevin . . . cried and clung to her." She explained that when parents leave the day care center, they can look back and see their children through the plate glass windows. Hartzler concluded, "None of those parents ever touched those children again while they were still alive." He then linked this victim's story to the defendant by saying that at the same time as parents were leaving their children at the day care center, a legal process was taking place across the street when a Ryder truck bomb went off. He connected the bomb blast to a legal proceeding in that "both involved grievances." A legal proceeding resolves matters using "constitutional due process," Hartzler said, and the Ryder truck

> was there to impose the will of Timothy McVeigh on the rest of America and to do so by premeditated violence and terror, by murdering innocent men, women, and children, in hopes of seeing blood flow in the streets of America. . . . And the only reason they died, the only reason they are no longer with us, no longer with their loved ones, is that they were in a building owned by a government that Timothy McVeigh so hated that with premeditated intent and a well-designed plan . . . he chose to take their innocent lives to serve his twisted purpose. . . . In plain simple language, it was an act of terror and violence intended to serve [a] selfish political purpose.

In his first chapter, Hartzler's opening statement related a compelling narrative, a kind of flashback to the crime scene, that engaged the attention of jurors, outlined the theory of the case, linked his representative anecdote to the indictments, and humanized the victim and demonized the perpetrator. This chapter framed the case in terms of the experiences of victims at a horrific crime scene, a frame that would become the predominant cognitive category that jurors would use to interpret the subsequent evidence.

Hartzler's second chapter emphasized the motive and associated McVeigh's cowardly character with his ill-conceived and antigovernment beliefs. The prosecutor began this chapter by explaining the arrest of

McVeigh 75 minutes after the bombing and identifying the evidence that surfaced at the time of his arrest. McVeigh had earplugs in his pocket to "protect him from the loud noise of the bomb blast"; he had the "residue of undetonated explosives" on his clothing; he had a business card from a military supply company, a T-shirt advertising his hatred of the government, copies of book chapters, editorial commentaries on the *Turner Diaries,* and quotations from antigovernment literature. All of these material artifacts pointed to the character and motive of McVeigh.

Hartzler continued, saying the words on the T-shirt said, "The tree of liberty must be refreshed from time to time with the blood of patriots and tyrants"; the tree on the T-shirt showed "droplets of scarlet-red blood." The *Turner Diaries*, Hartzler emphasized, served as McVeigh's Bible. This was a fictional book that glorified an attack on the federal government using a truck bomb. McVeigh also possessed a handwritten quotation from American revolutionaries that said, "When the government fears the people, there is liberty." From these associations, Hartzler concluded, "We are not prosecuting McVeigh because we don't like his thoughts or his beliefs or even his speech; we're prosecuting him because his hatred boiled into violence, and his violence took the lives of innocent men, women, and children."

This chapter of Hartzler's opening statement emphasized that McVeigh used the plot from a novel as his manifesto for committing the crime, and this manifesto contained evidence that supported the indictment of conspiracy, weapons of mass destruction, premeditation, and murder. The prosecutor concluded this chapter by returning to the scene of the bombing. A maintenance man was walking toward his car to meet his wife when

> he heard a whirring sound, like the propeller of a helicopter, coming toward him. He pushed his wife quickly under the car to protect her as more than 250 pounds of twisted metal came crashing down on his car. . . . That piece of twisted metal was the rear axle of . . . a Ryder truck that Timothy McVeigh had rented two days before in Kansas.

In this part of his opening statement, Hartzler associated material evidence, especially the earplugs, with the defendant's cowardice. The earplugs showed that McVeigh wanted to kill hundreds of people with a massive bomb, but he carefully protected himself from the harm that could be caused by the sound of the bomb. The rules of the court permit attorneys in opening statements to reason by association, that is, linking together two different concepts with a common interpretation; the bomb blast and the earplugs signify cowardice. Hartzler used his chapter on motive to preview the evidence and introduce a narrative theme for his side of the case.

Hartzler's third chapter, premeditation, emphasized McVeigh's planning of the crime—"We will go back . . . from a certain stage in McVeigh's life and walk through the various details of what he was doing and how it all fit into his plan to kill people in the Murrah Building." This segment followed a detailed chronological order.

The Order of the Prosecution's Opening Statement

- McVeigh and Terry Nichols became friends when they served together in the army because both disliked the government.

- McVeigh's anger resulted from what he thought were misguided government interventions at Waco and Ruby Ridge and ill-conceived gun control laws.

- McVeigh became obsessed with the plot of the *Turner Diaries*, which served as a blueprint for the bombing of the Murrah Federal Building.

- McVeigh used the *Turner Diaries* for his "cookbook on how to make bombs." It served as "a step-by-step recipe about how to put together your fertilizer fuel-based bombs."

- McVeigh declared to friends and relatives in late 1994 that he was "finished distributing antigovernment propaganda" and "was ready for action" against the government so that "just like the main character in the book he would become the hero."

- Six months before the Oklahoma bombing, McVeigh built fertilizer bombs with his friend and coconspirator Terry Nichols.

- McVeigh's fingerprints were on the receipts for ingredients to make the bomb.

- McVeigh's phone credit card, under the name of Darrell Bridges, showed he purchased bomb ingredients.

- After purchasing the ingredients, Nichols and McVeigh stored the bomb chemicals in sheds in Kansas, and then they stole bomb detonators from a rock quarry close to Nichols's house.

- After securing and storing the bomb-making chemicals, McVeigh took up residence with his army buddy, Michael Fortier, and his wife Lori, in Arizona. Together they experimented with the bomb making.

- McVeigh left the Fortiers in early April and traveled to Junction City, Kansas, where he rented a Ryder truck and with the help of Nichols mixed up chemical ingredients into a bomb.

- McVeigh purchased a getaway car, drove to Oklahoma City, and left the car on a side street not far from the Murrah Federal Building.

- Days later, the defendant detonated the bomb at "one of the busiest times of the day while everyone was in their offices, business was being conducted, and the children were in the day care center."

My paraphrase of the narrative indicates that Hartzler related the stages of premeditation in a chronological order connected by a metaphor and potent imagery. According to the prosecutor, McVeigh's bomb building followed a recipe. He found the recipe in books he valued and then tried out the recipe at friends' houses by exploding bottle bombs. Eventually, the defendant secured the ingredients to multiply the basic recipe hundreds of times. When he finally gathered all of the ingredients, he called Nichols to help him mix the ingredients together in a fertilizer bomb. When the bomb concoction was ready, he detonated it so that it would kill the most people possible.

Hartzler carefully presented the evidence. In his presentation, he avoided using the repetitive phrase, "the evidence will show," a common and somewhat annoying refrain that attorneys sometimes overuse. Instead the prosecutor converted the evidence into an engaging narrative, used the recipe metaphor to connect the evidence to the indictments, and explained how McVeigh exerted effort and took time to premeditate the murder of people at the Murrah Federal Building. This commonly understood recipe metaphor condensed the evidence into a frame of reference that jurors could understand. Metaphors persuade without seeming to argue because they causally connect different actions into a unified process.

The fourth chapter centered on "a conspiracy" involving the complicity of Terry Nichols and Michael and Lori Fortier. The participants in the conspiracy were Nichols, a sidekick of McVeigh, who aided and abetted him but did not detonate the bomb, and the Fortiers, political pals of McVeigh, who underestimated the defendant's intentions and dismissed the seriousness of the defendant's threats to bomb the federal building. The government eventually tried Nichols in a separate trial, and he is now serving a life sentence. The Fortiers made a plea bargain that enabled them to give damning testimony against McVeigh in exchange for Michael's light sentence. Michael went to prison late in 1995 and was paroled in January of 2006; the government never charged his wife, Lori. The testimony of both of the Fortiers was crucial to McVeigh's conviction.

The prosecutor portrayed Nichols as a naive accomplice. He helped McVeigh rob a quarry to get bomb detonators, and then he stored the drill bits he used to break open the locks at the quarry in his basement. He stored the chemicals for the truck bomb in his own name in storage sheds close to his house. In Hartzler's narrative, McVeigh was the agent of the action, and Nichols naively followed McVeigh's requests. Since the Fortiers were Hartzler's key witnesses, he described the two as passive and friendly spectators who observed what McVeigh said and did so without understanding the consequences of the defendant's threats. Hartzler noted that in the fall of 1994, McVeigh sat in the Fortiers' living room and "drew a diagram of the bomb . . . outlined the box of the truck . . . drew circles for the barrels inside the truck" and showed them how "he would place [the barrels] strategically in the truck to cause the maximum damage." Later on, Hartzler explained that McVeigh demonstrated the design of the bomb by "placing soup cans on the floor." In order to safeguard some credibility for the Fortiers, the prosecutor ignored many of the details that implicated them in the bombing plot.

Hartzler added some evidence in his conspiracy chapter that did not fit, including the names of potential witnesses who rented McVeigh a motel room, who sold him a car, and who rented the Ryder truck to him just a few days before the bombing. He described McVeigh's movements but carefully avoided mentioning the names of witnesses who would testify about those movements. The prosecutor ended his conspiracy chapter by connecting it with the issue of premeditation and by repeating the recipe metaphor that he said McVeigh had followed from reading the *Turner Diaries*. Hartzler claimed:

> The *Turner Diaries* taught him how to mix the different ingredients, how to set up the bomb, right down to how to drill a hole between the cargo box and the cab of the truck, . . . so that the fuse could run into the cab of the truck, and he could fuse it from where he was sitting. . . . So he converted the Ryder truck from a cargo vehicle into a gigantic deadly bomb, and he drove it to Oklahoma City, and he detonated it on one of the . . . busiest times of the day. . . . The sound and the concussion of the blast rocked downtown Oklahoma City. . . . No one in downtown Oklahoma City could have missed the sound. It ripped the air, shattered windows. It was a terrifying explosion.

In the fifth chapter, Hartzler emphasized the explosion. At the beginning of his final chapter the prosecutor returned to the story of Helen Garrett and her son Tevin. Hartzler used additional "thick descriptions" to arouse jurors' feelings about the horror of the bombing and the deaths of innocent children. He said:

> When she heard the blast, she rushed outside and saw the entire face from the Murrah Building was missing. The plate glass window that the children pressed their hands and faces against was gone. . . . She ran to the scene and frantically searched for her son. . . . At one point, she climbed on a pile of debris in front of the building until the rescue workers begged her to leave. Then she went home and waited. . . . And when Tevin's body was found, it was taken to a funeral home and she never saw her son again.

This evocative description of the grieving mother and her dead baby concentrated jurors' attention on the effects of the bomb on victims' lives.

The rest of the chapter elaborated about the contents of the bomb components and the conditions under which the defendant purchased them. Hartzler concluded this segment by connecting the bomb blast to the recipe book found with McVeigh when he was arrested. In this chapter, Hartzler concentrated on Michael Fortier's crucial testimony by saying he traveled to Oklahoma City with McVeigh and "they drove around the Murrah Building. . . . McVeigh told Fortier that he wanted to bring the building down. And Fortier told him, 'Well, even if they as individuals are innocent, they work for an evil system and have to be killed.'" The prosecutor admitted that Michael and Lori Fortier could have contacted authorities and prevented the bombings. He also acknowledged that the Fortiers lied and used drugs for a time; however, they eventually told what they knew, an eventual moral action on their part. The conclusion to this chapter ridiculed McVeigh's conception of himself as a patriot and inferred that he was instead a coward: "Our forefathers didn't fight with women and children. They fought other soldiers. They fought them face to face, hand to hand. They didn't plant bombs and run away wearing earplugs."

The chapter on the explosion tied together the claims that Hartzler had presented earlier in the story about the scene, the weapon of mass destruction, the motive, premeditation, and conspiracy. The chapter was unconventional because it promoted a complex plot rather than a particular theme. Hartzler constructed a complicated action story in which a cowardly defendant engaged in premeditated and evil actions against innocent victims in order to resolve his anger against the government. By using the recipe metaphor, subtle associational arguments, a believable plot, and engaging imagery, Hartzler framed his narrative. The framing showed jurors that they could use their emotional reactions to the bombing to understand the legal indictments. From a legal perspective, the narrative framework forecast the evidence, interpreted what it meant, and avoided blatant argumentation.

As legal persuasion, Hartzler's first chapter also created a primacy effect and his last chapter created a recency effect. The primacy and recency effect mean jurors recall the first information and the last information they hear more than they do the information sandwiched in the middle of the attorneys' opening statements. The middle chapters packaged prosecutors' evidence using the recipe metaphor that brought together the causal sequences of a believable plot. In many ways, Hartzler's multichapter narrative is an exceptional example of the use of narrative in the opening statements of a criminal trial because his rhetorical skill brings together mounds of evidence in a believable plot.

ANALYSIS OF THE DEFENSE'S OPENING STATEMENT

McVeigh's trial attorneys faced more constraints than the prosecutors did, and these constraints forced the defense to tell a different kind of story than they wanted to tell. Moreover, the evidence gathered by the prosecution was not available to the defense to the extent it should have been, the defendant tried to control the content of the speech his attorney delivered, and the rhetorical skills of Hartzler exceeded those of Jones. Additionally, extensive media evidence created a public consciousness that McVeigh was guilty long before the trial started.

Defense Approaches

The defense has no burden to prove innocence, but it is often stuck with massive amounts of damning evidence from the prosecution. For this reason, the defense usually develops some kind of case theory. The principle guiding the defense is to create reasonable doubt, and this side of a case can choose from among several available approaches (Haydock & Sonsteng, 1991; Mauet, 1992; Schuetz & Lilley, 1999). One approach is to offer an alternative theory of the case and defend that alternative with a counternarrative based on new explanations of the scene, the characters, the action, the motive, and the outcome. During the two years preceding the trial, Jones pursued an alternative theory, claiming McVeigh was taking the rap for a radical Muslim-inspired conspiracy in which he was only a minor player.

Before the trial started, Judge Matsch ruled that Jones could not present this theory although he had spent months trying to gather evidence to support it. After he learned that he could not present this theory at trial, Jones wrote:

> The real story of the bombing, as the McVeigh defense pursued it, is complex, shadowy, and sinister. . . . It stretches, weblike, from America's heartland to the nation's capitol, the Far East, Europe, and the Middle East, and much of it remains a mystery. . . . The Oklahoma City bombing conspiracy may not merely be the crime itself but also the systematic, deliberate attempt of our federal government to prevent all of us from finding out what exactly happened on that terrible April morning. (Jones & Israel, 2001, p. xxii)

Whether or not Jones's conspiracy theory would have persuaded jurors is questionable since the prosecution's opening statement cleverly combined extensive circumstantial evidence with emotional testimony from victims. Presenting a narrative that blamed the government for covering up a large conspiracy likely would have incurred resistance from jurors because they saw the government as a victim of McVeigh.

Themetizing provides another approach for defense attorneys. The defense's opening statements can rely on one or more themes to refute the prosecution's story. A variety of trial advocacy literature recommends themes as the key to persuasive defense opening statements. For example, defense attorney Gerry Spence (1995) claims that defense attorneys should use a theme or a "slogan that represents the principal point of our argument." The theme should summarize a story or stand for the "ultimate point we want to make, a saying, as it were, that symbolizes the very heart of the issue" (p. 77). Trial consultant Ronald J. Matlon (1993) advises defense attorneys to embed the theme "in the minds of the judge and jury in the opening statement, emphasize it throughout the questioning of witnesses, and stress it once again in summation" (pp. 13–14).

In criminal trials, the defense can select from commonly used themes: the mental duress theme that concludes a defendant committed the crime because of physical or mental stress, the contrast theme that portrays the defense as limited by too few resources and too little time, the political theme that claims defendants are disadvantaged by the legal system when they espouse politically charged views that oppose the government, the mysterious stranger theme that concludes someone unknown is responsible for the crime, or a conspiracy theme that characterizes the defendant as a small player in a big conspiracy in which others are responsible for the crime. Prior to the trial, Jones tested many of these possibilities. He had the defendant take psychological tests to determine if he suffered from mental duress, but the tests gave no evidence of mental disability. To preclude charges that the defense lacked sufficient money and resources, the government paid for a huge defense team. Jones understated the political theme even though McVeigh pressured him to use it. He presented the mysterious stranger theme, but failed to connect the theme directly to the trial evidence.

Defense attorneys can combine several of the aforementioned themes rather than select one, but the problem is that too many different themes bog "a case down" and confuse "jurors" (Matlon, 1993, p. 11). The justification for using just one theme is that it condenses the story into repeatable phrases that jurors can easily understand. The goal of a defense attorney is to find a theme that raises so much doubt for jurors about the facticity and credibility of the evidence that they will acquit the defendant. The themetizing used by the defense in this case differed significantly from Hartzler's distinct chapter themes that converged in a plot sequence.

Denial provides a third viable approach for defense attorneys. Denial emphasizes direct refutation of the evidence outlined by the prosecution. This defense approach is not narrative in the formal sense of creating vivid depictions of the scene and victims, developing credible characters for witnesses, establishing the motive and premeditation of the action, constructing a persuasive plot, and explaining the defendant's role in a crime. The defense can choose from among several denial options to expose the flaws of prosecution's narrative by reinterpreting the scene while acknowledging the suffering of victims, redefining the motives of the defendant, denying the plot, diffusing the responsibility of the defendant, impeaching the character of opposing witnesses, disputing the details of action, reconfiguring the plot, and reordering the prosecution's narrative.

When defense attorneys adopt the denial approach, they should follow with their promised impeachment of the prosecutor's witnesses during cross-examination. Most courts allow defense attorneys to delay their opening statement until after the prosecution has presented its case. If the defense chooses this option after it has cross-examined the prosecution's witnesses, then the denial strategy evolves from actual testimony rather than speculation about what that testimony might be.

Jones opted for a denial approach without hearing the prosecution's evidence and without the benefit of having completed his cross-examination of the prosecution's witnesses. This choice forced him to speculate about whether witnesses would be called and what they would say when they testified. From a retrospective view, this approach weakened the content of Jones's opening statement. After the trial, Jones admitted that the prosecution never called the vulnerable witness he expected them to examine. Instead, they gathered testimony from only 151 witnesses on their list of 327, and they never called many of the witnesses in Kansas who claimed that two people—John Doe #1 and John Doe #2—rented the truck and stayed at the Dreamland Motel prior to the bombing. In fact, in his posttrial account (Jones & Israel, 2001), Jones listed 33 witnesses he had expected to cross-examine but could not because prosecutors never called them. Jones characterized the prosecution's approach as "daring" and "high-risk." He noted that he would never "have guessed that a case, already highly circumstantial . . . would leave the jury without a single witness to Tim McVeigh's whereabouts between Junction City, Kansas, on Monday, April 17, and Perry,

Oklahoma, at 10:30 AM on April 19" (pp. 316–317). Jones's opening statement referred to witnesses and evidence that never materialized; it was an
approach that disregarded the advice of most trial advocacy experts
(Fontham, 1995; Mauet, 1992; Tanford, 1983).

Constraints on the Defense

The preface to the trial story presented in opening statements enables
attorneys to repeat, extend, and defend their evidence during their summations. Attorneys rely on their knowledge of the evidence, their legal reputations, their experiences as trial lawyers, and their knowledge about jurors for
telling persuasive trial stories.

Storytelling Ability.   One constraint in this case was the difference in the
storytelling abilities of the attorneys. Attorneys for both sides of the
McVeigh case recognized the importance of telling stories, but Hartzler constructed a rhetorically compelling narrative in contrast to the disjunctive and
rambling narrative presented by Jones. The defense was unable to construct
a rhetorically persuasive narrative with an easy-to-follow form and persuasive content. I examine more closely Jones's storytelling ability in the section
"The Defense's Opening Statement."

Investigatory Resources and Discovery.   A second constraint came from
the disparate resources available to the prosecution and the defense. In this
case, as in many high-profile trials, the defense faced more impediments
than the prosecution did because federal and local law enforcement, including the Federal Bureau of Investigation (FBI), Alcohol, Tobacco, and Firearms (ATF), and Oklahoma and Kansas state and local police assisted the
prosecution. The defense expected that the prosecution would share all of
the evidence they had gathered under the rules of discovery and that the evidence would give direction to defense's own investigation. Jones lamented
the fact that he had to file dozens of motions to force the prosecution to turn
over evidence from their interviews with potential witnesses when this evidence should have been shared with the defense team under the federal
rules of discovery. More specifically, Jones claimed the government withheld
evidence that could have exonerated McVeigh (Jones & Israel, 2001).

Defendant's Involvement.   A third constraint for the defense was dealing with McVeigh on his terms. Prior to the trial in 1996, McVeigh wrote
what he called "a manifesto" to his defense attorneys.

> Let it be known that I do not approve of a trial strategy in which Terry
> Nichols is attacked, blamed, or otherwise implicated in any crimes. Fur-
> ther, I do not approve of pointing the finger of responsibility at anyone
> else who I know is not responsible or who is in no way deserving of such
> scrutiny. I have relayed this wish orally for 18 months—not only con-
> cerning Terry Nichols, but also addressing the foreign investigations and
> the "neo-Nazi" investigations. My oral requests have been basically

ignored for the past 18 months, and it is only recently that Judge Matsch
has forced the defense into a partial compliance with my wishes. (Jones
& Israel, 2001, p. 259)

Prior to and during the trial, McVeigh urged his attorneys to present
what he called "a necessity defense." This type of story, McVeigh believed,
would present legitimate and compelling political reasons why he committed
the crime to save himself and others from the unfair laws and zealous governmental actions that proscribed Second Amendment rights of gun owners,
resulted in the deaths of innocent Branch Davidians in Waco, and led to the
killing of Randy Weaver's family members in Idaho (Michel & Herbeck,
2001, p. 286). The defense attorneys recognized early on that this political
story would serve no legitimate legal or communication purpose, and in the
end they suspected such a defense would ensure that McVeigh would receive
the death penalty. As a result, Jones refused to present the necessity defense,
and after his conviction McVeigh used this fact to blame Jones for failing to
give him competent representation.

After the trial, McVeigh maligned Jones for his efforts to find a plausible story for the defense. Jones believed he had represented McVeigh the
best way he knew how given the circumstances that McVeigh had admitted
to his attorneys that he was guilty, but pled not guilty anyway (Jones &
Israel, 2001). McVeigh distrusted Jones because he kept creating alternative
theories, a process that in fact was a legitimate approach for Jones to take as
a defense attorney. While he was awaiting his execution, McVeigh referred
to his lead defense attorney as "Sherlock Jones" and said he tried to provide
a "Perry Mason defense" (Michel & Herbeck, 2001, pp. 295, 319). Dealing
with McVeigh's ongoing criticism before and during the trial placed Jones in
a double bind: if he provided an alternative story in opening statements, he
would offend the defendant, and if he did not provide an alternative story,
he had few options except for denial. From a retrospective viewpoint,
Jones's theory may have been stronger had he presented his denials after
rather than before the prosecution presented its case.

Defense's Evidence.   A fourth constraint existed in the evidence itself.
The bombing of the Murrah Federal Building was not an ordinary crime
with a recognizable plot; it was a horrendous act that defied any reasonable
explanation. The challenge for the defense was to present a story consistent
with its own investigations and at the same time create reasonable doubt
about the prosecutor's case. In the two years between the indictment and the
trial, the defense, assisted by the mass media, promoted a conspiracy theory
about McVeigh's involvement with foreign powers, probably Filipino Mus-
lim terrorists connected to Iraqis and white supremacists living in Oklahoma. Jones planned to argue that an unlikely group of conspirators
planned the attack on the federal building and used McVeigh to do their evil
deed. Jones speculated that Terry Nichols learned how to build bombs from
Filipino terrorists and that Nazis living at a compound in Elohim City, Okla-

homa, participated in the bombing. Although Jones spent time and money
and even leaked this theory to the national media, Judge Matsch would not
allow Jones to present this theory (Michel & Herbeck, 2001). As a result of
McVeigh's manifesto and Judge Matsch's ruling, the only narrative that
Jones had left for his opening statement was denial and a weakly supported
missing stranger theory.

Jones had a difficult task, and he deserves some praise for his effort in
trying to find a defense that would save his client from the death penalty.
Although Jones did not achieve this goal, he did work diligently to present a
defense that he believed would create reasonable doubt that McVeigh was
solely responsible for the bombing. His lack of rhetorical skill, however,
doomed his efforts. My subsequent analysis shows that Jones's opening
statement contained many of the same legal and rhetorical flaws that
plagued the remainder of the defense's case.

The Defense's Opening Statement

Jones's opening statement used a denial approach, but he also stated
that he planned to prove the defendant's innocence. He could have
sequenced the denial in chapters that reflected different problems with evidence, such as the inconsistencies of eyewitnesses, the altered stories of
Kansas witnesses, the contamination of the FBI labs, or the existence of
missing evidence. Jones, however, combined a denial approach with truncated and undeveloped themes.

Denial of Scene.   Jones's first sequence partially responded to the first
chapter of Hartzler's opening statement by addressing the setting of the
crime. Jones asserted that he would not "establish a reasonable doubt," but
would prove his client was innocent of the crime. This is a curiously worded
statement since the defense has no burden to prove anything and the
defense's broad approach was denial. This first defense claim committed the
legal faux pax of overpromising what the evidence would show. Jones said:

> It was a spring day in Oklahoma. Inside of her office in the Murrah
> Building, Dana Bradley was feeling the atmosphere a little stuffy and
> warm. . . . [As] she was looking out of the plate glass window, a Ryder
> truck slowly pulled into a parking place and stopped. . . . She saw a man
> get out. . . . Three weeks later she described the man . . . as short, stocky,
> olive-complected, wearing a puffy jacket, with black hair, a description
> that does not match my client. . . . And then in just a matter of moments,
> the explosion occurred. It took the life of her mother and her two chil-
> dren and horribly burned her sister. She is not a witness in this case.

Jones's description of what Dana Bradley saw has the potential to create
some doubt in the minds of the jurors about the prosecution's claim that
McVeigh parked the truck in front of the Murrah Federal Building. But
Jones's next statement about Bradley's loss was a first step toward validating
the prosecution's story.

Furthermore, Jones followed his alternative interpretation from Dana Bradley with a list of all of the names and, in some instances, the occupations of each of the 168 people who died from the bombing, thereby emphasizing the victims and the horror of the bombing. Then Jones compared the bombing to Pearl Harbor, saying, "For those of us from Oklahoma, the bombing of the Alfred P. Murrah Building is the event by which we measure time. It is to my generation in Oklahoma what Pearl Harbor was to my mother and father's generation." This kind of information seems inappropriate: why would the defense attorney emphasize the victims and stress that "this was the largest domestic terrorism act in the history of the country"? Focusing on the victims and the horrors of the bombing does not achieve a primacy effect for the defense. Instead, it reinforces the prosecution's primacy effect. From a retrospective viewpoint, the only justification for this kind of content would be that Jones was trying to bolster his credibility as a defense attorney by identifying with jurors and victims from his home state of Oklahoma. This approach seems ill conceived because it was inconsistent with the rest of his narrative, and it affirmed much of the content of Hartzler's opening statement.

Jones also suggested the metaphor of a puzzle, which could have been used to organize other content in his opening statement. He noted that both he and Hartzler were trying to "put together pieces of a puzzle so that you [jurors] may look at the puzzle and see whether, in fact, the pieces justify the way that we say they come together." A metaphor is often used to condense and explain the evidence presented in the opening statement, but unless the attorney develops the metaphor in detail, it cannot substitute for a clear thesis, for a preview of the organization of this opening speech, or for a unifying theme that gives coherence to the opening statement. Jones initiated the puzzle metaphor, but he did not elaborate it; he did not say what or how he was going to piece the puzzle together. At the very least, Jones should have enunciated what the parts of the puzzle were and how he planned to piece them together. Shortly after Jones floated the puzzle metaphor, he hinted at another metaphor, saying that the prosecution's puzzle was terribly wrong and that he would, like radio commentator Paul Harvey, tell the "rest of the story." In any trial narrative, a mixed metaphor diffuses rather than unifies the story the advocate is trying to present. After Jones tried these metaphors out, he never referred to either puzzles or the "rest of the story" during the remaining hours of his opening statement.

Defense attorneys, in ways similar to prosecutors, need to supply categories into which jurors can fit the evidence they will subsequently consider. Just as in any important courtroom speech, Jones needed a specific preview so that he could name, cluster, and repeat the categories to facilitate jurors' comprehension. Since Judge Matsch prohibited jurors from taking notes and Hartzler already had clearly mapped out his case, Jones needed to package the information contained in his opening statement with alternative and clear categories into which jurors could fit subsequent evidence.

Denial of Character.   In an attempt to humanize the defendant, Jones's second narrative sequence presented a short biography of Timothy McVeigh.

BIOGRAPHY OF THE DEFENDANT

- He was born April 23, 1968, in upstate New York.
- He has two sisters, and his parents worked in blue collar jobs.
- His parents were separated in June of 1984 when Tim was 16.
- He made good grades at Star Point High School "except for his senior year."
- He was awarded a college scholarship but didn't use it.
- He held several jobs, such as working at Burger King, an armored car company, a security service, and a hardware store.
- He entered the U.S. Army in 1991 and served in Operation Desert Shield in Iraq and received the Bronze Star and some other army medals.
- After returning from Iraq, he tried out for special forces in the army, but lacked the physical stamina to be admitted.
- After his army service was over, he roamed the country "buying, trading, and selling weapons in numerous gun shows."

Jones's biographical portrait of McVeigh described but did not interpret what this information meant or how it could cast doubt on the prosecution's case. Jones ended the biographical sequence with a mundane statement that this is "basically his background," a clue to jurors that Jones had presented a sterile story without persuasive impact for jurors. Jones's account could have humanized McVeigh by drawing inferences about his values, his relationships, or his intelligence. Jones did not embed the biological facts in a narrative that denied the prosecution's portrait of McVeigh as a self-absorbed coward who killed so many people in an effort to avenge government policies that he hated.

Jones inappropriately ended his short biography of the defendant by stating that "Hartzler said that he [McVeigh] has hatred for the United States and that he conspired with others to build a terrible explosive device which he ignited because he was angry at the government." Since Jones was obligated to defend his client, it seems odd that he would repeat the prosecution's demonizing language and assertions about McVeigh's motives just after he had provided biographical facts that could have been used to humanize the defendant.

Denial of Motives.   Another sequence of Jones's opening statement described McVeigh's antigovernment beliefs. Jones tried to reinterpret what the phrase on the T-shirt worn by McVeigh at the time of his arrest meant and connect it to ideological phrases associated with positive rebellious acts. Jones noted that revolutionary war patriots, like Robert Henry Lee and George Wyeth, had used the phrase, *sic semper tyrannis* (thus ever to tyrants, which happens to be the motto of the State of Virginia), to refer to independence from foreign powers. But then he dismissed the importance of the phrase, saying that "McVeigh was one of tens of thousands of people of his political persuasion who believed that something big was going to happen in April of 1995."

Jones then claimed that the defendant's extreme politics were the fault of the federal government because they had "executed 76 people at Waco" and McVeigh believed that the government "entrapped Randy Weaver into committing a crime in Idaho, in order to pressure him to be a government informant." When Weaver would not comply, ATF agents murdered Weaver's wife and child. Moreover, the defendant believed that the Brady Bill was a defective piece of legislation that repealed the Second Amendment rights of citizens to own guns.

Hartzler had claimed that McVeigh's political beliefs were his motive for blowing up the federal building, and so Jones needed to deny the connection between the defendant's beliefs and motives. However, instead of framing these beliefs to raise jurors' doubts about McVeigh's political motivations, Jones just concluded, "These were his beliefs." Jones described McVeigh's political views, but he never redefined or reinterpreted them with a denial that would lead jurors to doubt the prosecutor's characterization of the defendant's motives. One explanation for what seems to have been another defense error is that Jones was giving into McVeigh's demand that he present a "necessity defense." This interpretation seems more likely than a conclusion that Jones corroborated the prosecution's narrative about motive (the second chapter of the prosecutor's opening narrative) and deliberately failed to create doubt about the defendant's motives.

Denial of Evidence.   The last sequence of Jones's opening statement denied some of the prosecution's evidence—the role of the *Turner Diaries,* the components of the bomb, Michael and Lori Fortier's testimony, the prepaid telephone calls traced to McVeigh, and McVeigh's time in Kansas prior to the bombing. This denial consumed a great deal of time, and it seemed to be the centerpiece of Jones's narrative. In ways similar to the earlier part of his opening, Jones did not state a theme, explain how he had organized this denial sequence, or connect one set of denials with others. This lack of structure and connection likely gave the impression that Jones was wandering through the evidence rather than framing it so jurors could follow his narrative. Jones previewed his evidence in such excessive detail that it seemed to violate the brevity norm, but the prosecutors did not object since Jones's rhetorical oversights benefited their case. This sequence revealed Jones's lack of rhetorical skill; he talked too long, used unnecessary detail that did not fit with the defense's position, and failed to frame his story with categories or language that would help jurors understand the remainder of the defense's case.

The following analysis of Jones's refutation of the Fortiers' testimony illustrates some of the flaws in his denial approach. This sequence of testimony consumed seven singled-spaced pages of the transcript and nearly an hour of the opening statement. The explanation was needlessly long as well as overtly argumentative. Jones's refutation made several claims. (1) Michael Fortier entered into a plea bargain, and the defense had no say in that plea. (2) Fortier had met Nichols and McVeigh at the Ft. Riley army base in Kansas. (3) McVeigh lived with the Fortiers prior to the bombing. (4) "Michael and Lori Fortier's beliefs were very similar to Tim McVeigh's," especially those concerning the deaths of innocents at Waco and the abridgement of gun owners' rights in the Brady Bill. (5) From the date of the bombing until a month later, the Fortiers studied the media to discern what the prosecutors knew about them and their associations with McVeigh. During this time, however, the Fortiers publicly stated that McVeigh was innocent. (6) The Fortiers decided to cooperate with the government, supply state's evidence, because they feared they would be charged as coconspirators and receive the death penalty. (7) The Fortiers carefully gave statements that conformed with the evidence they had studied in the media. In fact, "Michael and Lori Fortier checked and double-checked to be sure that their statements were consistent" before they confessed to the FBI. (8) The Fortiers told the government what it wanted to hear in order "to save their own skins at the expense of truth."

In this sequence, the conniving Fortiers' segment, Jones listed the connections of Michael and Lori Fortier to McVeigh and noted their common interests in the bombing. Jones did not frame the inferences so that jurors knew where or how they fit with defense's case. By describing problems with the Fortiers' testimony, Jones implied that jurors should be cautious about believing what either of the Fortiers would say in their testimony. Jones could have chosen a theme for his denial, but did not do so. For example, he could have converted the puzzle metaphor into a theme claiming that McVeigh's Arizona friends were an important missing part of the conspiracy puzzle or that the Fortiers' involvement showed that many persons, other than McVeigh, had the motive and the capability of bombing the Murrah Federal Building. Jones also could have connected his denial of the Fortiers' testimony to a phrase that tied it together with other denials of evidence, such as "Not one single person ever saw McVeigh at the site of the bombing."

For the most part, this sequence seems to violate some of the norms for opening statements; Jones presented more detail than necessary about what the Fortiers would say at trial. Jones lacked the rhetorical skills to create a persuasive narrative; he used no themes, his speech lacked developed imagery or metaphors, and he failed to interpret the Fortiers' testimony using a subtle and suggestive argument based on inferences that connected their confession to the specific indictments of conspiracy, murder, and premeditation.

The final sequence of Jones's opening statement contained two mysterious stranger segments. Jones was using this approach to show gaps in the prosecution's evidence. This segment could have elaborated the puzzle metaphor by stating something to the effect that the prosecution's puzzle had so many missing parts it could never present a realistic picture of the crime. Or as an alternative, Jones could have named this sequence "the mysterious stranger explanation." Although Jones inferred that others were suspects for the bombing, he was unable to name, frame, and chronicle the mysterious stranger part of the story in a way that captured the attention of jurors. Rather, Jones rambled for too long about the prosecution's evidence regarding the phone calling cards. Hartzler had claimed that McVeigh and Nichols used a phone credit card to call vendors and to make purchases of bomb-making chemicals. Jones speculated that anyone (i.e., a mysterious stranger) could have made the calls and that it was impossible to trace the phone cards to McVeigh and Nichols as Hartzler had implied. Jones wandered through the maze of the phone card evidence, describing how people used phone credit cards, how credit cards differed from regular phone billing, and how it was impossible for McVeigh to have made the calls using the card. Jones quibbled about the time specific calls had been made. After this excessively long explanation, Jones never bothered to claim that a mystery person made the calls. Instead he said, "Our proof is that the Bridges's [McVeigh's] calling [card] summary is not what it purported to be and therefore should not be believed." Jones's mysterious stranger counternarrative never evolved because the defense attorney never: framed the evidence, used previews and transitions related to the theme, connected the counternarrative to indictments, or connected the narrative to a larger theme.

The second segment of the mysterious stranger sequence concerned the presence of others who were with McVeigh in Kansas prior to the bombing. Specifically, Jones claimed that several witnesses would corroborate the existence of John Doe #2, a figure whose face artists had portrayed for the media in the days following McVeigh's arrest. Jones speculated that John Doe #2 signed his name Robert Kling to the lease for the Ryder truck used in the bombing. For this reason, Jones implied, Kling was not an alias for McVeigh as Hartzler had claimed, but this was the alias for a mysterious stranger who actually rented the truck that contained the bomb. Unfortunately for the defense case, Jones promised that witnesses would verify the existence of John Doe #2, but these promised witnesses never appeared at the trial and therefore jurors never heard the evidence. Jones's promise of "fitting together the parts of a puzzle" and "telling the rest of the story" never materialized either in the opening statement or through the subsequent evidence presented by either side of the case.

After the trial and while McVeigh awaited his execution, he confessed to reporters that he committed the crime and that he had told his trial attorneys that he alone was responsible for the Oklahoma City bombing even though they did not believe him. The defendant said he pled "not guilty" because he wanted his attorneys to use the court as a forum for his antigovernment views and to expose the evil actions committed by federal law enforcement agencies against citizens. Before his execution, McVeigh acknowledged that he had planned the bombing for 9:00 AM to maximize the casualties because he believed large numbers of casualties would force the government to rethink policies about gun control and prevent them from violent actions against minority and antigovernment groups, such as the Branch Davidians and the family of Randy Weaver.

LESSONS

The speeches that attorneys present in opening statements are narratives that are subject to legal rules and dependent on the rhetorical skills of the attorneys. When attorneys fail to abide by the legal rules, opposing attorneys and the judge can redirect their narratives. When attorneys lack rhetorical skills for framing, connecting, and presenting the narratives, jurors lack understanding about what categories they are supposed to use to interpret the evidence. Narratives persuade to the extent that the stories connect the evidence and facts about the scene, the key characters, the plot, the action, and the point of the story to the indictments. Narratives provide a kind of persuasive veneer that conceals the underlying inferential argumentative structure of the opening statement.

Prosecutors use their narratives to demonstrate they have met their burden to prove guilt in a criminal case or to prove the preponderance of evidence in a civil case. Defense attorneys typically operate under a number of constraints that lead them to adopt one kind of refutational approach rather than another. Defense attorney Jones faced many constraints because McVeigh told the defense team prior to the trial that he was guilty but pled not guilty. Furthermore, the defendant wanted to control what his attorneys said, and Judge Matsch prohibited Jones from presenting a theory that the bombing was planned and carried out by an international conspiracy. Other factors may have influenced Jones's fragmented and disjointed defense narrative as well.

The end result showed that Hartzler presented a rhetorically complex and persuasive narrative, and Jones faltered when he presented his opening statement. The persuasiveness of Hartzler's opening statement told a believable story that created a primacy effect that continued when the prosecution presented the rest of its case. The unfocused and unpersuasive opening statement of Jones hampered the effectiveness of the remainder of the defense's case.

6

Narratives and Direct Examination in the Hauptmann Trial

Public spectators hoped that the execution of Bruno Richard Hauptmann would end the tragic story of the kidnapping of the child of Charles and Anne Morrow Lindbergh. The drama of the execution, according to George Waller (1961), matched that of the trial. Hauptmann walked from the death house to the execution chamber slowly. Two German-speaking clergy, reading aloud from the Bible, followed him. As he got closer to the electric chair, Hauptmann walked rapidly, sat down, and awaited the executioner.

> Robert Elliott came forward. He had been standing by with the leather cap and its electrode, already dipped in brine, and he fitted it neatly over the shaved head and fastened it under the chin. Then the executioner stooped down and clamped a second electrode to the leg through a trouser-slit. . . . Light bulbs blazed on the control panel and two thousand volts fled into Hauptmann's body and violently snapped it rigid. His compressed lips were jarred apart by the gigantic invisible fire and his clenched hands pulled and strained at the chair arms. (p. 591)

Within three minutes, Hauptmann was dead. Immediately afterward, one of his attorneys, Lloyd Fisher, told the press, "This is the greatest tragedy in the history of New Jersey. Time will never wash it out" (p. 592).

Before his execution, Hauptmann predicted the case would have a long legacy: "They think when I die, the case will die. They think it will be like a book I close. But the book it will never close" (Scaduto, 1976, p. 484). Decades after the execution, the debate surrounding the case had not yet ended. In 1982, public television produced a documentary entitled, *Who Killed the Lindbergh Baby?* In 1985, Ludovic Kennedy claimed that Hauptmann was framed by the zealous actions of Attorney General David T. Wilentz, who encouraged the police to withhold evidence from the defense. In 1986, Anna Hauptmann, the then 87-year-old widow of the defendant, urged authorities to reopen the

131

case and to exonerate her husband after previously concealed evidence
became public. Based on interviews he conducted decades after the trial, Noel
Behn (1994) speculated that the child was killed by someone in the inner circle of the Lindbergh family and that the family participated in the cover-up. In
the late 1990s, Court TV produced a documentary about the case that raised
questions regarding the fairness of the trial. The narratives about the kidnapping continue to unfold as Hauptmann prophesied. One of the reasons that
critics continue to float new theories about this kidnapping is that the trial created public doubt about Hauptmann's guilt. In particular, the unconventional
strategies used by defense attorneys during direct examination, the contamination of crime scene evidence, the questionable conduct of prosecutor
Wilentz, the showboating of Judge Trenchard, and the perjured testimony of
some witnesses caused critics to question the verdict.

Many of the early representational discourses about the trial expressed
certainty that Hauptmann was guilty (Condon, 1936; Haring, 1937; Whipple,
1937); subsequent sources argued that Hauptmann was framed by the police
(Kennedy, 1985; Scaduto, 1976). One of the least biased accounts of the trial
(Siedman, 1977) concluded that Hauptmann likely was guilty, but he did not
receive a fair trial because his lead attorney was often drunk and unprepared.

The investigation, arrest, and trial attracted public attention and
engaged media spectators because of the celebrity status of the Lindbergh
family, the negative public feelings about German immigrants, and the mysterious circumstances of the kidnapping and death of the child. In one sense
this case was extraordinary because of the involvement of the media and the
visibility of the family. In other ways, the direct examination and the legal
process were typical of trials of the 1930s in which the judge selected jurors
on the call man system, the media sometimes paid the fees of defense attorneys, the press had unlimited access to the courtroom, the judge and attorneys talked to the press during the trial, crime scene investigators lacked
sophisticated technology for solving crimes, and formal codes of professional
conduct did not exist. Both the extraordinary events surrounding the trial
and the flawed practices of the defense attorneys figure into my analysis.

The goal of this chapter is to explain the role of narrative communication
in the planning and conduct of direct examination and to understand the consequences of the strategies used by the attorneys. The chapter (1) describes
the circumstances of the crime and trial, (2) explains the role of narrative in
witness examination, (3) critiques the defense's planning of direct examination, (4) analyzes attorneys' strategies during witness examination, and (5)
notes lessons to be learned about narrative and direct examination.

CIRCUMSTANCES

In 1927, Colonel Charles A. Lindbergh was the first person ever to fly
from New York to Paris. This amazing feat put him in the public spotlight.

Five years after the flight, the spotlight once again was on Lindbergh because his 20-month-old son, Charles A. Lindbergh Jr., was kidnapped from the family home in Hopewell, New Jersey. The kidnapper left ransom notes demanding money for the return of the child. The American people empathized with the Lindbergh's tragedy and offered their support during the long investigation that preceded the arrest of Hauptmann. Some of this public support came from citizens who placed ads in the newspapers, supplied tips about potential suspects, and monitored the spending of marked ransom bills. For months the location and condition of the kidnapped child were unknown, and the police had no suspects. Crime scene investigators in the early 1930s lacked the technology and the savvy to conduct careful crime scene investigations of the caliber that many of us now watch on popular television programs such as *CSI*. At the time they investigated this kidnapping, police overlooked key evidence and examined only obvious features of the crime scene. This may explain why it took two years to arrest Bruno Richard Hauptmann for the crime.

The Lindbergh child disappeared from his crib in the nursery of his parents' New Jersey home on March 1, 1932. At that time, kidnapping was a relatively common type of crime; more than 200 instances occurred from 1922 to 1932 (Alix, 1978). However, the disappearance of the child of an American hero, the bizarre circumstances that resulted in the payment of ransom, a stranger's discovery of the child's body in a shallow grave, and the delayed investigation of the crime scene added mystery and intrigue to the case. For four years the public followed the mystery as it was unveiled in extensive newspaper and radio coverage. After the arrest of a German immigrant carpenter for the crime, the public's interest in the trial never wavered.

The case was a compelling true crime that outraged the community, shocked the country, and rallied the media. The celebrity status of the family contributed to the media attention because "Charles A. Lindbergh was one of the more adored, harried, photographed, and written about men in the world" (Ross, 1976, p. xi). He was a national hero who had gained fame for completing a transatlantic flight. Through her marriage to Lindbergh and her father's career as a United States senator and diplomat, the mother of the child, Anne Morrow Lindbergh, was a national celebrity in her own right. She had endeared herself to the American public by her quiet and demure manner and by her aeronautical assistance to her husband on his international flights.

The duration of and participants in the investigation of the case resembled a fictional crime story more than a true crime. During that time, Lindbergh, the police, mobsters, and public celebrities independently tried to solve the case. Most notably, an eccentric retired Bronx college professor, John F. Condon, decided he could nab the kidnapper through newspaper ads. Despite the fact that he lacked law enforcement training, Condon still took on the responsibility for locating and contacting the kidnapper. After someone (presumably the kidnapper) responded to Condon's advertisement with another ad, Condon personally contacted Colonel Lindbergh by letter and said he had arranged a time and date for paying the ransom to the kidnapper at a New York cemetery. Without the supervision or approval of law enforcement, Condon and Lindbergh delivered $50,000 in marked ransom bills, including $20,000 in gold notes, to a person (or persons) thought to be involved in the kidnapping. Shortly after Condon and Lindbergh delivered the ransom money, a truck driver discovered the decomposed body of the child in a shallow grave on the Lindbergh property.

During two years of investigation, the involvement of well-intentioned citizens frustrated law enforcement and compromised the official investigation. Nonetheless, it was an alert citizen, a gas station attendant, who recognized that the money he received in payment for gas was marked ransom money. He took down the license plate number of the purchaser's vehicle and immediately reported this information to law enforcement. The license plate number matched the registration number for Hauptmann's car and led police to his home where they discovered more than $14,000 in marked ransom money buried in his garage under the dirt floor.

The trial began on January 2, 1935, at the Herndon County Court in Flemington, New Jersey. Judge Thomas Whitaker Trenchard presided. The Hearst newspapers paid the fees of defense attorneys on the condition that Anna Hauptmann, the wife of the defendant, would grant exclusive interviews to them. Hearst's financial support permitted the defense to hire a Brooklyn attorney of some professional repute, Edward J. Reilly, and at the same time, it enabled the press to get inside stories from its newspaper chain. At the time, almost no legal restraints existed to protect the defendant from adverse media publicity. New Jersey attorneys C. Lloyd Fisher, Frederick Pope, and Robert Roscranz assisted Reilly. The state attorney general, David T. Wilentz, led the prosecution. Anthony J. Hauck, Joseph Lanigan, H. Dobson Peacock, and George Large assisted Wilentz. The trial lasted six weeks. The jury returned a verdict of "guilty" and recommended no clemency. After more than a year of appeals, the State of New Jersey executed Hauptmann on April 3, 1936.

NARRATIVES AND DIRECT EXAMINATION

The analysis of the opening statements of the McVeigh trial explained that narrative is the underlying form of persuasive legal discourse. The narrative of direct examination extends the story that attorneys preview in their opening statements. Specifically, the opening statement constructs a narrative preface to the entire trial, and the direct examination of each key witness bolsters the underlying reasoning of the narrative. The narratives of witnesses add details, a proof of sorts, about the setting, characters, and actions described in opening statements. Trial advocacy literature (Fontham, 1995; Jeans, 1993; Lubet, 1993; Mauet, 1992) recommends that direct examination should elicit testimony that sufficiently elaborates the facts so attorneys can persuade jurors that their story of the case is more probable than the narrative of the opposing attorneys.

Trial narratives do not depend entirely on legal principles, procedures, or protocols for their style and content, nor are narratives completely independent from these legal rules. Attorneys struggle to make sense of the fragments of witnesses' stories and to put these story parts together into a coherent case theory. In most segments of the legal process the discourse of the direct examination falls short of the ideals imposed by media representations. Conducting direct examination is difficult because attorneys are never sure about the stories they are constructing. A struggle, according to Paul Gewirtz (1996), is "played out in a narrative construction and reception—a struggle over what stories may be told at a trial, over the way the stories must be told and even listened to, over who should be the audience for the story" (p. 136).

Attorneys construct and frame narratives from the story fragments they gather from their witnesses' testimony and from opposing attorneys' cross-examination of those witnesses. The fragments of narratives and counternarratives that emerge during the process of witness examination challenge the sense-making abilities of attorneys and of jurors. Skillful attorneys shape and frame narrative fragments so that pieces of the testimony point to a story theme and fit with other fragments of testimony. Additionally, attorneys need to figure out how the counternarratives from opposing witnesses and attorneys will "disassemble" the stories they have created and how they can make sense of "multiple, conflicting, and partially overlapping versions" of their own stories (Gewirtz, 1996, p. 8). Opposing attorneys try to dislodge and distort the fragments of testimony gathered during direct examination, but procedural rules constrain this process.

In a broad sense the narrative fragments that evolve during direct examination resemble other stories because they include "the words and/or deeds—that have sequence and meaning for those who live, create, and interpret them" (Fisher, 1984, p. 2). In a trial situation, attorneys should connect the words and actions of the witnesses to the disputed issues of the case. Narrative requires "no more or no less than a teller and a tale," a storyteller and a story. In direct examination, each side of the case has a story to tell, and the attorneys and their witnesses jointly tell the story (Scholes & Kellogg, 1966).

Trial advocacy manuals (Brooks, 1996; Fontham, 1995; Haydock & Sonsteng, 1994a) indicate that the attitudes and images conveyed by the storyteller influence how jurors evaluate trial narratives. These sources give the following advice: storytellers (attorneys and their witnesses) should appear well prepared, convey a strong belief in the stories they tell, show a sincere attitude, and recount the story in an orderly and logical way. Although the transcript does not provide information about these performance factors in the Hauptmann trial, both film clips from the trial and interviews from those who observed the trial give some indications about how the trial storytellers performed. For example, Whipple (1937) reported that Reilly was a flashy dresser, had an aggressive manner, and expressed an arrogant attitude that alienated the rural New Jersey jurors. During an interview in 1982, juror Ethel Stockton recalled that most of the jury members disliked Reilly because he was aloof and boastful. She further recalled that he was unprepared and sometimes came to court drunk. In contrast, she remembered that Wilentz was articulate, well prepared, and convincing. Stockton also remarked that from the beginning of the trial jurors felt compassion for Lindbergh and disdain for Hauptmann. The content of the direct examination shows contrasts in the competence of the prosecution and the defense.

The effectiveness of direct examination depends on the attorney's planning skills in selecting witnesses whose stories relate to a case theory, ordering or sequencing the appearance of witnesses, and constructing a persuasive story for jurors.

PLANNING DIRECT EXAMINATION

One goal of direct examination is for attorneys to elicit stories from their witnesses. This part of the trial involves a creative process that permits attorneys to tell a story to a jury in a way that is most advantageous to their side of the case (Mauet, 1993). For some attorneys, direct examination is "the most important part of the trial" because it draws out the facts of the story. Because jurors draw conclusions from the narrated facts, it is essential that witnesses tell stories that are "clear, logical, and persuasive" (Tanford, 1983, p. 329). Attorneys should link the narrative fragments provided by witnesses to themes that they stress in their trial speeches. Although witnesses' narratives are selective interpretations, attorneys can piece different stories together using logical sequences that explain the disputed actions and focus jurors' attention on some characters and actions rather than on others. Additionally, attorneys can shape and frame their witnesses' stories by naming, clustering, and locating the facts and issues into a condensed narrative sequence. These condensed categories enable jurors to organize large amounts of information according to the exigencies of the scene, the motives and opportunities of characters, the disputed action, and clear themes.

The *Federal Rules of Evidence* (1991) provide broad judicial discretion for the oversight of direct examination. Rule 611, for example, identifies three general guidelines about how attorneys should conduct interrogation: direct examination should "ascertain truth," "avoid needless consumption of time," and "protect witnesses from harassment." Similar norms about telling the truth and protecting witnesses were in place at the time of the Hauptmann trial.

In a general sense, the attorneys for each side of the case tried to develop a believable theory of the case based on a compelling story. Because the state of New Jersey lacked a strong legal statute against kidnapping, the prosecution could not indict the defendant on that charge. Instead, the state charged Hauptmann for a first-degree murder committed in the process of burglary. The advantage to the state for filing a murder charge was that, if convicted of the crime, Hauptmann would get the death penalty. The disadvantage of the indictment was that the state had only circumstantial and hearsay evidence to link the accused with the murder of the child. To prove the indictment, the prosecutors needed to contrive a story that would show the defendant willfully killed the child while he was committing a burglary—stealing the child from the Lindbergh home. This indictment creatively supplemented the existing criminal statutes and reinforced the public view that Hauptmann should be executed for the death of the young child.

The defense's theory of the case was not always consistent; the theory repeated Hauptmann's claim that he had nothing to do with the crime and his explanation that he had received the ransom money through a strange set of circumstances. Although Hauptmann admitted possessing more than $14,000 of the marked ransom bills at the time of his arrest, he claimed he was taking care of the money for a former business partner, Isidor Fisch, who died during a visit he made to Germany shortly after the kidnapping had taken place. More specifically, the defense's story was that Hauptmann discovered the money in 1933 when he opened a box Fisch had left with him. After finding the money, Hauptmann decided to spend it because Fisch owed him thousands of dollars for business loans. The defense's direct examination of Hauptmann and other witnesses elaborated this version of events.

The story of the prosecution was that Hauptmann plotted the kidnapping of the child to secure ransom from the wealthy Lindbergh family. Because the poorly constructed ladder used by the defendant to take the baby from the upper level window collapsed, the baby died at the scene. According to prosecutors, this turn of events did not stop Hauptmann. He hid the baby in a shallow grave on the Lindbergh property and followed his plan to extort ransom money from the family even though he knew that the child was dead.

Witness Selection

In a typical trial, attorneys select from a wide variety of potential witnesses. The primary witnesses for the prosecution usually are the victim or the close associates of the victim, and the primary witnesses of the defense are sometimes the accused and/or those who can testify about an alternative perpetrator. The testimony of the primary witnesses is often the basis for the case theory, and attorneys expect these witnesses will present a thorough account of the actions, the scene, and characters. Expert, records, occurrence, and reputation witnesses add details to the testimony of primary witnesses. In the Hauptmann trial, the primary witnesses for the prosecution were Charles Lindbergh, the father of the dead child, and John F. Condon, the intermediary who talked to the kidnapper and helped to deliver the ransom money. The primary witnesses for the defense were Hauptmann and his wife Anna. Both sides introduced dozens of witnesses to corroborate what Lindbergh and Hauptmann said.

A second type of witness is the expert, someone with specialized knowledge of a scientific or technical nature, who can assist jurors in understanding the evidence or determining facts pertinent to the case (*Federal Rules of Evidence,* 1991, #707). Experts have "knowledge, skill, training, or education" that exceeds the credentials of other witnesses. Both the prosecution and defense relied on experts. Prosecution experts tried to link the defendant to the crime, and defense experts tried to implicate other people in the crime. The experts compared handwriting samples with the writing in the ransom notes and grains of wood from the ladder at the crime scene to wood purchased by the defendant and used in the construction of his home. Because expert witnesses often command high fees for their testimony, attorneys are limited in the number and quality of experts by what they can afford.

The Hauptmann defense did not select high-quality expert witnesses; they called handwriting and wood experts whose credentials were inferior to those of the prosecution's experts (Kennedy 1985; Scaduto, 1976). For example, John M. Trendley offered his testimony free of charge to the defense after seeing pictures of Hauptmann's handwriting samples in the newspaper. He examined 50 documents for two and one-half hours and then concluded the ransom notes were not written by Hauptmann. Additionally, the defense relied on testimony from Ewald Mielke, a mill worker who had worked with wood but had no technical training. The defense called fewer expert witnesses than the prosecution, and their witnesses had inferior credentials.

A third type of testimony comes from records witnesses who explain the contents of travel, work, bank, and/or investment records. The prosecutors called records witnesses to interpret complicated financial transactions concerning the defendant's payroll and bank records. After scanning the bank and stock market deposits and withdrawals over a five-year period, a bank auditor testified about the Hauptmanns' banking assets and liabilities. The defendant's employer explained how Hauptmann was paid, said that Hauptmann had not come to work on the day of the kidnapping, and stated that the defendant quit his job on the day after the crime. The defense did not present any records witnesses; rather, they relied on Hauptmann to explain his financial transactions. The defendant claimed that large sums of money, not accounted for by either his or his wife's salary, came from money given to him by Isidor Fisch. Throughout his three days of testimony about money transactions, Hauptmann tried to explain the irregularities in his finances that had been identified by the prosecution's records witnesses.

A fourth category, occurrence witnesses, testify about what they "saw, heard, or did" in relation to the crime (Mauet, 1992, p. 82). Occurrence witnesses support the story line of the primary witnesses by verifying the facts about the events others have reported and by heightening or sharpening certain aspects of the story for jurors. The persuasiveness of one occurrence witness differs from others depending on his or her confidence, ability to make precise statements, and trustworthiness. Most witnesses in criminal trials fit into this category.

The prosecution called several occurrence witnesses who offered key facts for constructing a narrative about Hauptmann's guilt. For example, John Wallace, a sergeant in the New Jersey State Police, arrested Hauptmann. Walter Lyle, a service station attendant, accepted a ransom bill from Hauptmann for five gallons of gas. William Mulligan, an employee from a stock investment company, regularly conducted business with the defendant. The defense introduced occurrence witnesses to prove that Hauptmann was at the bakery where his wife worked at the time of the kidnapping. For example, August Van Henke said he talked to Hauptmann about a dog that evening. Paul Vetterle recalled that he attended a birthday party with Hauptmann on the evening Condon delivered the ransom money. Louise Wollenburg claimed that she knew about Fisch and Hauptmann's business partnership.

Reputation witnesses testify about the truth and veracity of other trial participants' character. Both the prosecution and defense call witnesses of this type. Prosecutors ask reputation witnesses to comment on the credentials of other witnesses called by the state (Mauet, 1993). For example, Wilentz called a few reputation witnesses whose testimony referred to the positive reputations of Colonel Lindbergh, John Condon, and members of law enforcement. In these instances, Wilentz used the reputation witnesses to reduce the impact of the answers these witnesses had given during cross-examination that had questioned their motives and integrity. The defense typically uses reputation witnesses to bolster the credentials of the defendant as well as the defense's theory of the case. Reilly called Hans Kloeppenburg to testify that Hauptmann was honest, hard working, and a good family man. The defense also called several reputation witnesses, close friends and associates of Hauptmann and Fisch, to implicate Fisch as the perpetrator of the kidnapping and the person responsible for the death of the Lindbergh child.

Many of the defense's reputation witnesses testified about Fisch's financial dealings and his relationship to Hauptmann. The defense called several witnesses for this purpose, including Oscar John Bruchmann, Gustave Miller, Auguste Hile, and Gerta Henkel. All knew both Fisch and Hauptmann and corroborated the defendant's story that Fisch left a shoe box with him on the night before he left for Germany. However, Wilentz impeached all of these reputation witnesses, implying they lacked objectivity because they were German nationals and friends and associates of the Hauptmanns. The defense did not call independent character witnesses, such as Hauptmann's neighbors or work associates. As a result, evidence about the defendant's credibility came from the prosecution's witnesses as much as it did from those testifying for the defense.

Attorneys should choose a variety of different types of witnesses so they can develop the details of the narrative previewed in opening statements in a way that is persuasive to jurors. Since jurors often evaluate evidence based on the credibility of the witnesses (Kalven & Zeisel, 1971), attorneys should make sure that witnesses testifying for their side of the case are credible and that their testimony fits with the overall theme of the case theory. In this case, the prosecution called expert and records witnesses with strong credentials that made their testimony appear to be of superior quality to those presented by the defense. The defense witnesses provided less technical information, and the prosecutors successfully impeached their credibility during cross-examination. For example, Wilentz impeached several of the defense's occurrence witnesses by showing one was a former mental patient, a second was a former convict, a third was a professional witness, and a fourth was a bootlegger. The inferiority of the defense witnesses resulted from several factors: Reilly was not interested in the case and did not search for credible witnesses; the defense lacked the money needed to pay expert witnesses; and the prosecution intentionally withheld evidence from the defense attorneys, thus prohibiting them from calling some available witnesses (Kennedy, 1985; Scaduto, 1976).

Ordering of Testimony

Some persuasion research (O'Keefe, 2002) indicates that the sequencing of evidence affects how audiences interpret and value that evidence. Other research shows that jurors have a set of stock stories in mind, and they try to connect the testimony and trial evidence with familiar plots, characters, and themes of stories they already recognize and understand (Bennett & Feldman, 1981; Kalven & Zeisel, 1971; Weisburg, 1996). Trial narratives are not always relevant, nor are they consistent with other story fragments from other witnesses. For this reason, the formidable task for attorneys is to impose a theme, provide a chronology, and supply a framework to explain the disparate batch of narrative fragments gathered from their direct examination of witnesses. In ways similar to other coherent narratives, attorneys should call witnesses according to a chronological sequence that highlights the relevant evidence and validates the case theory. One strategy for accomplishing this goal is for attorneys to place in the foreground the testimony of primary witnesses that relates directly to the theories of the case and to place in the background the testimony that verifies and corroborates what primary witnesses have said.

Attorneys should structure their witnesses' testimony according to three principles (Sannito, 1981). The first is to arrange witnesses so that their testimony points to a common theme that creates a thread that binds together all of the testimony. The second principle is to order the most important witnesses first and last and place the less important testimony in between. This recommendation follows social science research that concludes that arguments in a controversy presented first and those presented last leave the strongest impression on audiences (Luchins, 1957; O'Keefe, 2002). Moreover, attorneys should exploit the emotional potency of different kinds of evidence: "Put emotional evidence first to get the primacy effect"; place "factual evidence last to gain the recency effect"; and insert the best evidence "first on each separate day of the trial." The final principle is the Von Restorff effect, a strategy for gaining and sustaining audience attention that interjects "unique or novel" ideas that "stand out and are virtually unforgettable" (Sannito, 1981, p. 32). Attorneys can achieve a novelty effect when the testimony of their witnesses confirms an unusual theme, presents striking evidence, or offers an unexpected twist to the stories presented by other witnesses. Although the prosecution did not construct a novel theme, they did allow Condon, an eccentric and colorful character, to rise from the witness chair, throw his arms in the air, and engage in hyperbole. Unless more than one witness can support the novel theme of the case, this tactic should not be used just to get jurors' attention.

In the Hauptmann trial, the prosecution developed their story by clustering the testimony of occurrence, expert, and records witnesses so that it confirmed the testimony of primary witnesses Lindbergh and Condon. After a very short appearance by his wife, Anne Morrow Lindbergh, Colonel Lindbergh testified about the circumstances in- and outside of the family home on the night of the kidnapping. He discussed the content and placement of the ransom note on the window and the broken ladder below the window of his child's bedroom. Condon verified the authenticity of the ransom notes and identified scenes where he made contact with the kidnapper and the kidnapper received the ransom money.

The argument was that Hauptmann committed the crime for money, extorted the ransom, and spent the money for his own pleasure. Charles Lindbergh's appearance at the beginning of the trial provided sufficient emotional evidence to gain the interest of the spectators and achieve the primacy effect. Arthur Koehler, the wood expert, created a recency effect when he appeared last. He traced the wood samples to a lumber yard where Hauptmann purchased wood and then to a missing link in the ladder brace found at the defendant's home. The prosecution presented their story in a chronological order that follows the advice of trial advocacy manuals and social science research.

The prosecution arranged witnesses in the sequence indicated below and then constructed questions that permitted each witness to give a coherent chronological accounting of their testimony and connect it with the theme of the case.

PROSECUTION WITNESSES

Lindbergh's Testimony:

- Described the activities inside of his house on the night of the crime (Later on in the trial, Betty Gow, his child's nurse; Anne Lindbergh, the mother of the baby; and Elsie Whately, the cook in the Lindbergh home, corroborated his testimony.)

- Depicted the scene outside of his home on the night of the crime (Later in the trial, state troopers, Frank Kelley and Nuncia De Gaetana; wood expert, Arthur Koehler; and Newark policeman, John Sweeney, corroborated this testimony.)

- Identified the ransom notes (Crime scene investigators, John Condon, and Lindbergh's friend Henry Breckenridge confirmed the colonel's testimony about the content and location of the ransom notes.)

Condon's Testimony:

- Identified the ransom notes at the crime scene and letters sent to him after the crime by the alleged kidnapper (The testimony of Condon's daughter, Myra Condon Hacker; police officers, Thomas Ritchie and James Finn; and handwriting experts, Thomas Sisk, Frank Wilson, Albert Osbourn Jr., Eldrige Stein, Herbert Walter, Harry Cassidy, William Souder, and Clark Sellers, validated the location and authenticity of this written evidence.)
- Described the events related to the transfer of ransom to the kidnapper (Taxi drivers, John Perrone and James O'Brian, and two friends, Milton Gaglio and Alfred Reich, who drove Condon to meet the kidnapper, confirmed Condon's story about the delivery of the ransom notes.)

The defense did not develop their story through a discernible pattern. Instead, Reilly's examination of 49 witnesses took place in a random sequence. Reilly called the defendant first, but the testimony of both Christian and Katie Fredricksen, owners of the bakery where Anna Hauptmann worked on the day of the crime, interrupted Hauptmann in the middle of his testimony. They testified that Mrs. Hauptmann came to work and was picked up by her husband the evening the child disappeared. After these two testified, Hauptmann returned as the primary witness, and his testimony continued for five additional days.

The chart below indicates the sequence in which defense witnesses appeared; Hauptmann testified first and other primary witnesses followed him.

DEFENSE WITNESSES

Hauptmann's Testimony:

- Related his personal background, including his criminal record in Germany (His wife Anna affirmed this testimony.)
- Claimed he had received the ransom money found in his garage from his former business partner, Isidor Fisch (Several friends of the defendant agreed that he received money from Fisch.)
- Interpreted his financial transactions by saying that Fisch gave him other money to put in his stock accounts, which amounted to more than what he and his wife made from their salaries (No witnesses corroborated this testimony.)

Order of Appearance of Other Defense Witnesses:

- Three witnesses saw Hauptmann on the day of the crime.
- Lou Harding saw a man with a ladder on the top of his car, but it was not Hauptmann.
- John Trendley, a handwriting analyst, said the ransom notes were not written by Hauptmann.

- Peter Sommer saw Fisch and a woman with a small child the night of the crime.
- Sabastian Lupica saw a car near Hopewell, but he said Hauptmann was not the driver.
- Hans Kloeppenburg remembered that Fisch brought a shoe box (later found to contain marked ransom bills) to Hauptmann's house in December of 1933.
- Anna Bonestell saw Violet Sharpe, a Lindbergh household maid who later committed suicide, at her restaurant the evening before the crime.
- James Dott and Carl Jeorg saw Fisch and a woman with a baby on the docks the evening after the crime.
- Paul Vetterle claimed Hauptmann could not have used the ransom money because he was not in New York when the bills were spent.
- Crime scene investigator Thomas Sisk, also called by the prosecution, said he measured the footprints of the kidnapper after the ransom money had been paid rather than the morning after the kidnapping.
- Police officer Schwarzkopf, previously called by the prosecution, explained that he did an experiment with a duplicate ladder to prove its instability.
- Philip Moses, the taxi driver who drove Lindbergh and Condon to the cemetery, saw three men, not one, the night the ransom was exchanged.
- Maria Mueller, niece of Hauptmann, claimed she saw the defendant at his home on one of the days when ransom money was spent.
- Ten witnesses testified about Fisch and his business relationship with Hauptmann.
- Three witnesses claimed that prosecution witness Whited had a reputation for lying.
- Four witnesses gave conflicting testimony about the wood patterns and the ladder used in the kidnapping.

This summary shows that the defense attorneys switched from one type of witness and one kind of evidence to another, mixed expert witnesses with reputation testimony, and failed to cluster witnesses so they corroborated the story of Hauptmann, the primary witness. Additionally, several defense witnesses, such as law enforcement officers, provided testimony that helped the prosecution more than it did the defense. This strategy created confusion rather than reasonable doubt.

Several factors explain the defense's failure to present witnesses in a coherent order. Quite clearly, Reilly did not schedule witnesses ahead of time because Judge Trenchard repeatedly warned the defense that their witnesses must be ready to testify at a particular time. Several times during the trial, defense witnesses unexpectedly appeared. When this happened, Reilly asked the person testifying to leave the witness stand and asked the unexpected witness to take the stand. In some cases, the defense recalled prosecution witnesses, apparently to fill time until one of their own witnesses showed up, even though the testimony did not relate to the defense's story of the case. Reilly showed his desperation about insufficient witnesses by soliciting testimony through the local newspapers prior to the trial. Five witnesses answered his ads and appeared at the trial. Wilentz severely impeached all of the newspaper-solicited witnesses partly because defense attorneys had not properly interviewed or prepared the witnesses prior to their appearance in the courtroom. If witnesses do not have something pertinent to say, they should not testify at all. The reason Reilly called these witnesses is unclear. One can speculate that Reilly wanted more witnesses in order to prolong the case and add to his paycheck.

To achieve the primacy effect among their witnesses, the defense placed Hauptmann, the most emotional witness, at the beginning of their case. Since Reilly called other witnesses in the middle of the defendant's testimony, this weakened the impact of the defendant's testimony, which in fact became the only consistent defense narrative in the trial. The final witness was a mill worker with weak technical credentials in wood analysis. He was unable to provide persuasive factual testimony needed for the recency effect.

Defense attorneys could have rearranged at least three clusters of testimony so that the witnesses' narratives would fit together in a coherent whole. A strategic arrangement of testimony could begin with Hauptmann; follow with testimony from witnesses corroborating Hauptmann's story about Fisch; continue with both occurrence and reputation witnesses placing Hauptmann at locations other than the crime scene; implicate Fisch as the likely kidnapper by testimony from expert, reputation, records, and occurrence witnesses; and deny prosecution's case by other occurrence and records witnesses. Reclustering and reordering these witnesses could produce a coherent arrangement that would make a persuasive defense narrative more likely.

Connections Between Stories

One way attorneys achieve coherence is by inferring that causal connections exist between the narratives of diverse witnesses. When attorneys arrange testimony according to similar facts, they can frame and shape the evidence into a persuasive story that can be used to refute the opposition during summations. Moreover, when attorneys embed sufficient proof in their stories, jurors can make sense of what evidence means in relation to the indictments and contrast and weigh this evidence during their deliberations. Attorneys add coherence to their case when they link witnesses together by exhibits, personal and professional relationships, shared contexts, similar values, and common experiences.

Real evidence refers to those kinds of proof that jurors can see or hear, including weapons, blood stains, photographs, diagrams, models, summary charts, recordings, and business records. Rules of procedure require attorneys to introduce an exhibit through the testimony of a witness who has knowledge about what the evidence is. After attorneys introduce exhibits, they can refer to the exhibit and later on ask other witnesses to explain how that evidence relates to their own testimony.

The prosecution supported its narrative that Hauptmann killed the baby, took the ransom, and used the money to live a good life by emphasizing the handwriting sample, the wood evidence, and the buried ransom money. The prosecution introduced more than 250 different pieces of evidence in its attempt to convict Hauptmann. Prosecutors featured the ransom notes and the wood samples as the most compelling evidence of Hauptmann's guilt. By referring to the ransom notes over and over again, Wilentz connected Lindbergh's testimony with that of Condon, police officers, and handwriting analysts.

The defense introduced less than 10 pieces of evidence and did not use the information to connect witnesses' stories, to support a theme, or to develop a coherent alternative case theory. Defense's obligation is to create doubt about the prosecution's evidence rather than present an alternative theory or to provide extensive evidence that exonerates the defendant. Nonetheless, a strong defense usually features the testimony of several witnesses that creates doubt about the prosecution's case. Many defense witnesses did not support Hauptmann's story, and other witnesses lacked sufficient credibility to create doubt about the testimony of the prosecution's witnesses. Reilly asked a few of his witnesses to testify about the prosecution's exhibits rather than to testify about evidence that would exonerate the defendant. Even if the defense uses a denial approach or presents an alternative theory, a coherent narrative will not develop unless the attorney's approach creates doubt about the prosecution's case.

A second strategy for linking the testimony of witnesses is through personal and professional relationships and associations. Attorneys can link witnesses by family ties, a common neighborhood locale, shared membership in social or cultural groups, or even as customers at the same business. Attorneys can also connect testimony through professional relationships, such as banker–customer, seller–buyer, doctor–patient, teacher–student, employer–employee, or counselor–client. Both the prosecution and the defense connected some of the 150 witnesses to other witnesses by the questions they asked during direct examination and later through their interpretations of testimony during summations. Establishing relationships between witnesses can corroborate, impeach, create credibility, establish causality, or refute causality. An astute attorney uses relationship connections to build the coherence of the story and show associations between the testimony. Attorneys can exclude references to relationships that show collusion between witnesses or suggest bias.

Certain relationship connections help tie testimony together. For example, Wilentz established the relationships between the Lindberghs, their servants, and the child. In contrast, the prosecutor omitted links between handwriting analysts to make their testimony appear independent and objective. For the defense, Reilly emphasized the friendship between

Hauptmann and his German associates, his relatives, and those acquainted with Fisch. However, Reilly ignored the relationships between the defendant and the records witnesses to preserve the appearance of the objectivity of that testimony.

A third link occurs when witnesses lack knowledge of each another, but they share knowledge about a time, setting, or action pertinent to the disputed issues of the case. Although many occurrence witnesses do not know each other, they often have separate information about the same context. An example in this trial was that several prosecution and defense witnesses had knowledge about the cemetery where Condon and Lindbergh delivered the ransom money to the kidnapper. Other witnesses reported knowledge about cars traveling on the road to the Hopewell residence on the night of the kidnapping. By placing the testimony of these witnesses next to one another in the direct examination and alluding to the corroborative testimony of witnesses from the other side of the case, attorneys can solidify facts about the context, characters, and actions.

Finally, attorneys fit the testimony of one witness with that of another through their personal, group, situational, and practical experiences. Although the persons testifying may not know one another or share information about the context, they still may share common experiences and perceptions that unify the narratives that attorneys are trying to construct. For example, several of the prosecution's police witnesses came from different law enforcement agencies, jurisdictions, and states, but they shared common duties and secured and interpreted similar evidence. Several witnesses for the defense related the same negative perceptions about one prosecution witness who claimed he saw Hauptmann in the vicinity of the crime on March 1, 1932. Making connections between witnesses adds cohesiveness to attorneys' case stories. These linkages can add a singular point of view to the narrative, verify the testimony of the primary witnesses, emphasize the evidence essential to conviction or acquittal, provide grounds for the refutation of the stories of opposing attorneys, and point to the motives for the disputed actions in the case.

To elaborate their story of the case, attorneys should select a variety of credible witnesses, order the witnesses in a logical way, and connect the testimony of the witnesses to others. Attorneys on both sides use direct examination to elicit evidence that elaborates the theme previewed in opening statements. Attorneys then frame and reshape these fragments of narrative gathered from witnesses into a story they can defend during their summations. No perfect fit exists among all of the evidence and the features of the story, but attorneys try to create inferences that connect the fragments elicited from testimony to the issues and indictments.

Reilly was unable to shape and frame a persuasive narrative or to even create a memorable theme, although Hauptmann emphatically asserted that Fisch committed the crime. Perhaps the defendant's persistent denial of guilt and emotional outbursts from his wife achieved some novelty, but generally the defense lacked a theme, made few connections between the testimony, failed to sustain the credibility of several defense witnesses, and produced no Von Restorff effect to engage the jurors and sustain their interest in defense witnesses' narratives.

Conducting Direct Examination

Conducting a strong direct examination is difficult because each witness knows only part of the whole story and the attorneys' questions can elicit a small segment of what the witness knows. Additionally, the rules of evidence at times defy common sense and permit contrived testimony that differs from everyday language and conversation (Conley & O'Barr, 1998). Objections from opposing attorneys disrupt the sequence and logic of the narrative and introduce irrelevant and inconsistent information that complicates or refutes the witnesses' direct examination.

Extracting a cohesive, relevant, and believable story from each witness requires skillful communication. The prosecution's direct examination usually relies on definitions, inferences, and validation, and the defense's strategy depends on appropriate redefinition and reconstruction. This section contrasts the prosecution's strategies for examining Lindbergh with the defense's approach for examining Hauptmann. (The quotations from the trial are from the Trial Record, Hauptmann, 1935.)

Prosecution Strategies

Definition.   Most prosecutors try to "elicit particular definitions of evidence from witnesses" (Bennett & Feldman, 1981, p. 118). To do this, they ask restrictive questions that require concise and particular responses. The goal of these definitions is to elicit narrow explanations of evidence that directly fit with the prosecution's story of the case, such as the kidnapper killed the child in the process of committing burglary. To prove this conclusion, Wilentz asked Lindbergh to define the circumstances at the time he heard the ladder break and the kidnapper supposedly drop the child. The questioning of Lindbergh proceeded in this way:

> W: Did you see any objects coming down past that window or in the vicinity of that window?
>
> L: I did not. . . .
>
> W: Well, sometime during that night did you hear some sort of noise or crash?
>
> L: Yes, I did.
>
> W: About what time was it and where were you?
>
> L: Sitting on the sofa in the living room during 10 or 15 minutes after we had come into the living room. At that time, I heard a sound . . .

like an orange box, the slats of an orange box falling off a chair, which I assumed would be in the kitchen.

W: That is sort of like the falling of a crate, a wooden crate?

L: The slats of a crate. . . .

W: Was it the sort of a noise that would come with the falling of a ladder?

L: Yes it was, if the ladder was outside. (TR, pp. 80–81)

Lindbergh's definition of the noise relied on the analogy of the breaking of an orange crate to identify the possible sources of that noise. The analogy implied the ladder was so poorly constructed that it was unable to hold the combined weight of the kidnapper and the child. The analogy associated the kidnapper both with the defective ladder and the death of the child, and Lindbergh was the only witness who associated the broken ladder directly with the noises he heard on the night of the kidnapping. In response to a leading question from Wilentz, Lindbergh defined the source of the noise. This excerpt shows how the prosecutor shaped and focused the content of the story with Lindbergh's cooperation. In this case, the attorney transformed "bits of evidence [the noise, the ladder, the time] into familiar language terms that fit" the theory and story of the prosecution (Bennett & Feldman, 1981, p. 125). Although the rules for direct examination prohibit witnesses from speculating about causes and effects, Reilly did not object to the line of questioning or to Lindbergh's response.

Inferences.   By itself, a clear definition does not produce sufficient or persuasive evidence to support the story of a case. Definition followed by inferences about the meaning, relation, and/or significance of the definition, however, can connect a fragment of testimony to the theme of the story. In most cases, the inferences from the definition require "blatant innuendos" (Bennett & Feldman, 1981, p. 126). In other words, the inferences, constructed jointly by questions of the attorney and the response of the witness, permit jurors to follow the reasoning and conclude that a single definitional fact holds together the whole story of the case.

Wilentz asked questions enabling Lindbergh to report hearing a sound resembling the cracking of wood and also to conclude that the cracking was the sound of the ladder breaking. Wilentz's phrasing of subsequent questions encouraged Lindbergh to assert that the broken ladder had been used by the kidnapper and the break was responsible for the fractured skull and the eventual death of his child. In the following excerpt, Wilentz used the definition about the noise as the basis of an inference that the kidnapper killed the child because the ladder broke, a fact the prosecution needed to establish to prove the indictments.

W: Colonel, you stated, too, that sometime during the evening through the flashlight of one of Hopewell's officers, you could see the ladder used in the distance?

L: Yes.

W: Eventually that ladder was brought into your home, was it not, that evening?

L: Yes it was. Whether it was before midnight on the evening or not, I am not sure, but during that night it was brought in. . . .

W: And will you tell us whether or not the ladder was strange to your premises?

L: It was a ladder I had never seen before. (TR, p. 98)

The identification of the ladder helped the prosecutor build a connection that had been made in his opening statement:

> He came there with the ladder, placed it against the house. He broke into and entered at night the Lindbergh home with the intent to commit battery on that child. . . . Then, as he went out that window and down that ladder of his, the ladder broke. He had more weight going down than he had going up. And down he went with the child. In the commission of that burglary that child was instantaneously killed. (TR, p. 9)

This preceding segment reveals how the prosecutor drew deliberate inferences that created a persuasive story about the defective ladder and the reckless actions of the defendant. The prosecutor confirmed the probability of the story using validation.

Validation.   Both definition and inference strategies establish the overall fit between the evidence in the case story. Validation adds to the persuasiveness of the story by emphasizing "the completeness, consistency, and plausibility" of witnesses' testimony in relationship to the story as a whole (Bennett & Feldman, 1981, p. 132). Completeness means that witnesses report all the information they know, consistency refers to the internal fit of the evidence, and plausibility means the information has logical and persuasive force. Attorneys can enhance the completeness of testimony by the strategic phrasing of the questions they ask, and they can add to the consistency and plausibility of responses by pretrial preparation and by use of exhibits that help witnesses recall what they said in their pretrial depositions.

Wilentz asked concise questions that promoted complete responses from Lindbergh. Lindbergh's testimony about the ladder was incomplete because he had not directly observed Hauptmann on the ladder. However, Wilentz filled in these gaps by calling police investigators who testified about the faulty construction and weaknesses of the steps on the ladder. He also called wood experts who confirmed that the collapsed ladder found at the crime scene was constructed from wood extracted from the attic of Hauptmann's home. The completeness of any one witness's testimony depends on available information, but other witnesses can validate information in ways that add plausibility to the story of another witness.

One reason Lindbergh's story seemed internally consistent was that he recounted his impressions in a clear chronological sequence marked by a precise time line. Lindbergh told the jurors he arrived home in the evening at 8:25, finished supper at 9:00, heard the wood-cracking noise at 9:15; and discovered the baby was missing at 10:00 (TR, pp. 79–85).

Lindbergh's reputation as a trustworthy person and heroic adventurer likely added plausibility to his part of the story. Some aspects of his testimony would not be credible if reported by an ordinary person, but because Lindbergh was the source, jurors likely believed him. From a retrospective reading of the direct examination transcript, Lindbergh's ability to positively identify Hauptmann from hearing two words, "Hey Doc," more than two years after he first heard those words from a distance of 60 feet is difficult to believe. Nonetheless, this quite remarkable recollection of the sound of words seemed reasonable to the jurors (Scaduto, 1976). At several points in his testimony, Lindbergh did not remember the chisel by the ladder, did not observe footprints in the mud below the child's window, and did not recall the people present in the home on the night of the crime. These omissions might have weakened most testimony, but jurors forgave these oversights because they recognized that Lindbergh was emotionally fragile after discovering that his child was missing (Kennedy, 1985).

Defense Strategies

The goal of the defense in direct examination is to develop a coherent story of their own and, at the same time, cast doubt on the stories told by the prosecution. The major risk of direct examination is for the defense to spend too much time refuting and too little effort on the development of a narrative alternative to the story of the prosecution. Some trial advocacy manuals (Fontham, 1995; Haydock & Sonsteng, 1994a; Jeans, 1993; Mauet, 1992) recommend that the defense frame their own distinct case story prior to direct examination, develop and support the story when they examine their own witnesses, and refute the story of the prosecution primarily during cross-examination and summation. The defense strategies in a civil case might be that the defendants acted in good faith based on what they knew at the time, a story used by the defense in the Minnesota tobacco trial and by Boston church officials.

In many criminal cases, defense attorneys do not have the evidence to present a persuasive alternative story. In the McVeigh case, for example, the defense resorted to refutation of prosecution's evidence without giving the jury a substantive alternative to the prosecution's story. Both in the presence and in the absence of a defendable alternative story, defense attorneys can redefine and reconstruct the testimony of prosecution witnesses.

Redefinition.   One way to create doubt about the stories of the prosecution's witnesses is to identify a story element that is ambiguous or missing and then to exploit the missing elements by showing they create such large gaps or holes in the prosecution's narrative that the case should not be believed (Bennett & Feldman, 1981). The success of defense's redefinition strategies depends on the prosecution's story. If few discernible ambiguities or gaps exist in the testimony of prosecution witnesses, if defense's redefinition does not pertain to the issues of the indictment, and if the redefinition does not contribute to an alternative story, the defense likely will be unable to create reasonable doubt in the prosecution's case.

Both the prosecution's story about the kidnapping and death of the Lindbergh child and Hauptmann's story about Fisch giving him the ransom money depended on circumstantial evidence. The prosecution made the most of the circumstantial evidence, but the defense mishandled some witnesses and failed to draw pertinent inferences from others. Specifically, defense attorneys were unable to construct persuasive definitions, make reasonable inferences, and supply sufficient credentials for witnesses, which could have contributed to a plausible and cohesive story. Clarence Darrow, one of the most famous defense lawyers of that time period, publicly commented that he believed Wilentz had insufficient evidence to prove a murder charge against Hauptmann, although he might have enough evidence to prove extortion (Kennedy, 1985; Scaduto, 1976).

Lead defense attorney Reilly, however, did not frequently emphasize the prosecution's lack of evidence for supporting a murder charge and the obvious inconsistencies between the testimony of witnesses, nor did he redefine the indictment into a lesser charge that could have prevented Hauptmann from receiving the death penalty. Reilly chose a different tack. In pretrial depositions, both prosecution and defense witnesses claimed that more than one person had been involved in the kidnapping. The prosecution intentionally ignored witnesses' references to other persons mentioned in the depositions of Condon and of two taxi drivers and in the statements of several occurrence witnesses. Condon and the taxi drivers indicated that they saw and/or heard more than one person when they turned over the ransom money to the purported kidnappers. Other witnesses stated they saw more than one person in the vicinity of the Lindbergh house on the evening of the crime. To his credit, Reilly occasionally noted these gaps and inconsistencies in the stories of prosecution witnesses and at other times he redefined the kidnapping as a conspiracy involving several persons.

Reilly appeared to be on the right track when he laid the foundation for a conspiracy story in his direct examination of Hauptmann. He also called on other witnesses to show that Hauptmann was not at the scene of the crime and inferred that the crime was likely committed by more than one person. Hauptmann had an alibi for the night of the crime, and Reilly asked him to explain this alibi during direct examination:

R: What time did you go back and call for Anna [Hauptmann's wife]?

H: I was there around seven o'clock.

R: Well, tell us what you did there that night.

H: When I came down, I usually got my supper first. I took the police dog [belonging to the owners of the bakery where his wife worked] out . . . on the street sometimes for half an hour. . . .

R: You remember meeting a man that talked to you about that dog?

H: I do.

R: On March first?

H: Yes.

R: At about what time of the night?

H: I would say it would be between eight and half past eight.

R: What did you do? Did you bring the dog back to the restaurant?

H: Oh yes.

R: What time did you and your wife leave there? . . .

H: It was after nine o'clock. I can't remember the exact time. (TR, pp. 2453)

Reilly presented four witnesses, immediately following the testimony of Hauptmann, who admitted the possibility of a conspiracy based on crime scene evidence and testimony. One witness claimed he saw a car traveling to Hopewell with a ladder attached to the top and two men inside. Another testified that he saw several sets of footprints beneath the window of the Lindbergh home where the ladder was found. Still another witness said that several sets of fingerprints were found on the ladder. Finally, on the night and at the location where Condon delivered the ransom bills and gold notes, one witness remembered seeing three different men. In this instance, the defense redefined the circumstances and suggested a conspiracy. However, the defense lacked sufficient evidence to make this alternative story credible because only four witnesses confirmed the story compared with dozens of prosecution witnesses who denied it.

Reilly's second strategy was to redefine the key evidence that implicated Hauptmann as the source of the ransom notes. More specifically, the defense tried to establish that the misspellings in samples of Hauptmann's writing were dictated by the police rather than spontaneous responses by the defendant.

R: Now, in the station what did they do to you if anything?

H: The first thing they required [was] the request writing.

R: Yes, now in writing did you spell the words of your own free will or did they tell you how to spell the words?

H: Some of them words they spell it to me.

R: How do you spell "not?"

H: N-o-t.

R: Did they ask you to spell n-o-t-e?

H: I remember very well they put an "e" on it.

R: How do you spell "signature?"

H: S-i-g-n-u-t-u-r-e.

R: Did they tell you to spell s-i-n-g?

H: They did.

R: N-a-t-u-r-e?

H: They did.

R: So when they were dictating the spelling, that was not your own free will in spelling, was it?

H: It was not. (TR, pp. 2526–2527)

Whether or not the defense's redefinition would persuade jurors depended on if they accepted Hauptmann's or the police's version of the interrogation. This part of the direct examination marked a small strategic victory for the defense. Their redefinition strategy responded to a gap in the prosecution's story, and it converted the gap into an alternative explanation of who wrote the ransom notes. This part of the defense case became an important issue for media commentators who later wrote books trying to exonerate Hauptmann. At the trial, however, Hauptmann's testimony lacked completeness and plausibility. No defense witnesses corroborated the claim that the police dictated the spelling to Hauptmann, and several officers denied they had told Hauptmann how to spell the words so they would correspond with the spelling in the ransom notes. For these reasons, the redefinition did not create the persuasive effect that it could have.

Reconstruction. The defense can reconstruct the stories of prosecution witnesses by repositioning "the central action in the context of an entirely new story to show that it merits a different interpretation" (Bennett & Feldman, 1981, p. 104). During the defendant's six days of testimony, the defense attempted to reconstruct the prosecution's story in three segments of approximately equal duration—Hauptmann's biography, Fisch's guilt, and Fisch and Hauptmann's financial transactions.

Reilly curiously began the reconstruction by focusing on the defendant's biography, a strategy that was unorthodox for several reasons. The biographical testimony emphasized the defendant's German background at a time when Hitler had risen to power in Germany and when Americans held strong anti-German feelings. The testimony also accentuated Hauptmann's criminal record, information that seemed to implicate rather than absolve him of involvement in the kidnapping. Finally, the testimony stressed the sporadic work history and the financial instability of the defendant. The excerpt below provides a sample of this segment of the defendant's testimony.

R: Now, during the period of reconstruction in Germany, about 1919 and 1929, you were convicted of some offense there, is that correct?

H: I was. . . .

R: And as a result of that, did you serve any sentence?

H: Yes.

R: Where?

H: Beuthen, Beutthen.

R: And afterward, you were paroled?

H: Yes. (TR, p. 2400)

The defense likely elaborated Hauptmann's biography to inoculate the jury about the existence of his criminal record, that is, to give jurors a weak dose of the arguments they had heard in the media and then explain away the importance of those charges (O'Keefe, 2002). However, by introducing these facts into direct examination, the defense enabled the subject matter to fall within the legitimate scope of Wilentz's cross-examination of the defendant.

Reilly's reconstruction strategy resulted in two disadvantages: First, it allowed the jury to hear negative information about his first and most important witness, Hauptmann. Second, the information likely created a primacy effect implicating the defendant, which jurors would remember. Hauptmann's testimony was the only available narrative alternative the defense had, but this information also may have hurt his credibility more than it helped build an alternative case theory. The negative biographical data tainted rather than enhanced the credibility of Hauptmann for the remaining five days of his testimony (Kennedy, 1985).

Reilly's reconstruction of the central action of the kidnapping and murder implicated Fisch. This defense approach was more persuasive than the biographical testimony was. By claiming Fisch committed the crime, the defense story could explain the unconventional spelling in the ransom notes since Fisch was a German national with a low level of competence in writing English. By placing Fisch in the role of kidnapper, the defense also could account for the German accent that Condon and Lindbergh heard when they paid the ransom. Establishing that Fisch had given Hauptmann a shoe box full of money helped explain why the police found ransom money, and why his stock transactions exceeded the amount of money he earned from his relatively low salary. However, the defense's reconstruction could not account for the wood from Hauptmann's attic that was used to construct the ladder at the crime scene, the crushed skull of the Lindbergh child, or Fisch's motive for committing such a horrible crime and framing Hauptmann. The defense evidence did not seem to add up to a narrative that would create reasonable doubt in the minds of jurors.

The defense's reconstruction began in this segment of the direct examination of Hauptmann:

R: Well, before he [Fisch] sailed did he leave anything with you to take care of while he was in Europe?

H: Well, he left two suit cases.

R: What else?

H: Four hundred skins, Hudson seals.

R: What else?

H: And a little box. . . .

R: Now this little box . . . what kind of box was it? . . . carton, cardboard?

H: Yes.

R: Now will you describe to the jury what circumstances it was [that] he left this shoe box with you? . . .

H: Well, of Mr. Fisch's request it was he was throwing a party when he left for Chermany [sic]. . . . We invited a couple of friends. . . . Fisch came out and got a little bundle under his arm. . . . He came out and we went in the kitchen and he said, "I leave it . . . if you don't mind, keep care of it and put it in a tight place."(TR, pp. 2447–2448)

In the testimony that followed, Hauptmann explained that after he took the money from Fisch, he placed it on the top shelf of his broom closet, and then he forgot about the box until after a rain storm produced a leak that damaged the box. When he discovered the rain-soaked box, the defendant said he opened it up and realized it contained $15,000 in gold notes. By the time he discovered the gold notes, he already had heard about Fisch's death in Germany. Because Fisch owed him several thousand dollars, Hauptmann decided to spend the money because he had no idea that it was ransom money. The defendant's connection with Fisch also provided an explanation for Hauptmann's large bank deposits and stock market transactions. But defense attorneys' attempts at reconstruction still could not explain where Hauptmann got the money to participate in large stock market investments at the time he was unemployed and prior to the time the ransom was paid.

In ways similar to the prosecution's narrative, the reconstructed defense story needed to define facts, connect the facts to legal issues by inferences, and present a credible story that was complete, internally consistent, and plausible. Although the defense reconstructed the story and put Fisch in the role of the perpetrator, the defense strategy fell short of creating a persuasive alternative narrative. Hauptmann defined his relationship with Fisch, and other witnesses corroborated that they had some kind of a relationship. No witnesses, however, could verify that the money really came from Fisch. The story required jurors to make some broad inferences from the fact that Fisch was a business partner to the conclusion that Fisch was the kidnapper who killed the Lindbergh child and took the ransom money. Because the story was incomplete, not corroborated by witnesses outside of the defendant's circle of German friends, and lacked internal consistency, the jury likely doubted the story. Wilentz showed the inconsistency of the story when, under cross-examination, Hauptmann admitted that he had told no one about the money, lied about having the money when he was arrested, and buried the bills in his garage to conceal them from police.

Jurors receive instructions from the judge that they should decide a verdict of guilty only when they are convinced "beyond a reasonable doubt." Therefore one inaccurate definition, ambiguous inference, or statement that leads jurors to believe the testimony is incomplete, inconsistent, or improbable has the potential to create reasonable doubt. If Hauptmann had innocently come by the money, Wilentz reasoned, why did he engage in such deliberate efforts to conceal it? In this way, Wilentz created reasonable doubt about the reconstructed narratives of the defense.

LESSONS

Considering that 1935 was the era of the Great Depression and of Hitler's rise to power, the prosecution's story about Hauptmann, a convicted burglar, a German immigrant, and an often unemployed carpenter, committing the crime made more sense than the competing story that Hauptmann came in possession of the marked ransom bills from a business partner who had since died. For jurors living during the depression, the story of someone discovering thousands of dollars in a shoe box, burying the money, and spending it without telling anyone the source of the bills, must have stretched their commonsense understandings of what was reasonable. The fact that the defendant had previously been convicted of burglary and that Lindbergh was a national hero likely enabled the prosecution to tell the story about Hauptmann's guilt in a way that had fidelity with the experiences of jurors.

This chapter describes how attorneys constructed and reconstructed their trial stories through the process of direct examination. Moreover this case study identifies the approaches used by the prosecution and the defense to shape and reconstruct their trial stories. In all cases, the social and legal situations enable and constrain what approaches the attorneys can use in constructing persuasive narratives. The conduct of direct examination should allow attorneys to develop the narratives prefaced in their opening statements. Attorneys can enhance the coherence, consistency, and plausibility of their stories by selecting a variety of competent witnesses, carefully sequencing witnesses' testimony, asking questions permitting witnesses to tell their stories in both a chronological and logical sequence, and linking the testimony of one witness to that of others. The analysis in this chapter illuminated some reasons why Wilentz's direct examination succeeded and Reilly's direct examination failed.

Prosecutors can approach direct examination by using definition, making causal inferences from those definitions, and validating the definitions and inferences with facts and evidence from other witnesses. The defense usually chooses to redefine the meaning of the evidence and reconstruct the scene and offer a plausible alternative narrative.

Finally, stories elicited during direct examination are persuasive to the extent that attorneys intentionally leave out testimony that they cannot substantiate with other evidence and include testimony that has fidelity with the values and experiences of jurors. The act of constructing and reshaping the fragments of the stories that witnesses tell is both an art and a skill. During direct examination, attorneys cannot tell persuasive stories unless witnesses cooperate, and witnesses are unable to tell the stories unless trial attorneys ask them the right questions.

7

Strategic Games and Cross-Examination in the Sacco-Vanzetti Trial

Police arrested Nicola Sacco and Bartolomeo Vanzetti on May 5, 1920, for the murders of Fredrick A. Parmenter and Alessandro Berardelli, the paymaster and security guard at the Slater-Morrill Shoe Factory in Braintree, Massachusetts. Assailants murdered and robbed the victims in the middle of the afternoon after they left building #2 carrying a payroll of $16,000. Three weeks later, police took Sacco and Vanzetti into custody at a garage where they had gone to pick up a vehicle that police had identified as the getaway car from the shoe factory crime scene. When they were arrested, the defendants carried guns and possessed papers identifying themselves as anarchists. In fact, Sacco's gun was of the same type as the weapon used in the murder of Berardelli. When police first interrogated the defendants, Sacco and Vanzetti lied about their actions and their whereabouts on the day of the crime.

The trial of Sacco and Vanzetti opened on May 31, 1921, in Dedham, Massachusetts. Frederick G. Katzmann, an ambitious advocate and a formidable adversary, led the prosecution team for the Commonwealth of Massachusetts. His assistants included Harold P. Williams, William F. Kane, and George E. Adams. Because of large financial contributions to the Sacco and Vanzetti Defense Fund, the defendants were able to hire experienced attorneys: Jeremiah J. McAnarney and Thomas F. McAnarney; a radical labor Chicago attorney, Fred H. Moore; and William J. Callahan represented the defense. William Thompson conducted most of the defense appeal. Judge Webster Thayer, a law and order judge with political ambition, presided at the trial.

After deliberating for only five hours on July 14, 1921, the jurors returned a verdict of "guilty of murder in the first degree" for both Sacco and Vanzetti. Even though the trial itself moved quickly to its completion in five weeks, the appeal process lasted six years and the state did not execute the defendants until August 22, 1927. The death of the defendants, however, did not close the debate surrounding the trial of Sacco and Vanzetti. Forty years after the execution, Justice William O. Douglas characterized the case in this way (all of the excerpts from and directly pertaining to the trial are from Trial Record, Sacco and Vanzetti, 1969):

> The Sacco-Vanzetti trial was a highly sophisticated affair. The judge, honest and dedicated, was fiercely partisan. The jury was picked as a "hanging jury." The community was saturated with fear of foreigners. . . . The trial itself was infected with extraneous, irrelevant, and highly prejudicial testimony. (TR, p. xv)

In fact, posttrial representations of historians and legal experts have continued to retry and reevaluate the case through a dozen books and scores of essays. These representations try to answer the question: Did Sacco and Vanzetti commit the crime? Some sources say "no" (Ehrmann, 1969; Feuerlicht, 1977; Fraenkel, 1931; Frankfurter, 1954; Joughin & Morgan, 1948; Musmanno, 1939; Young & Kaiser, 1985). Other sources acknowledge the guilt of Sacco, but they question the involvement of Vanzetti (Montgomery, 1960; Russell, 1971; Sinclair, 1928; Topp, 2005). Retrospective views agree that the trial featured unusual and questionable strategies, tactics, and practices that created uncertainty about whether the verdict and death sentences were just.

My goal is not to analyze the whole trial or to prove that the defendants were framed. Instead, the analysis focuses on how attorneys conducted cross-examination using gaming strategies and tactics. This perspective illuminates the intensity and complexity of the adversarial moves of the attorneys during cross-examination. Although some critics claim that the entire cross-examination process was poorly conducted (Topp, 2005), the trial record indicates this was not the case. Parts of the 1921 trial of Italian anarchists Nicola Sacco and Bartolomeo Vanzetti featured competent attorneys trying to outwit and outmaneuver each other in order to win a verdict. Some of the inconsistencies on the part of the attorneys may have resulted from the fact that evidence emerged and changed during the trial because discovery rules forcing attorneys to share evidence prior to the trial did not exist in Massachusetts at the time of the trial.

The chapter (1) explains the controversy about the trial, (2) locates the case in a politically charged setting, (3) uses the game analogue to explain the goals and refutation strategies of cross-examination, (4) analyzes the tactics of posturing, navigating rules, and maneuvering, (5) evaluates the unconventional strategies in prosecutions' cross-examination of Sacco, and (6) emphasizes lessons that can be learned about cross-examination from the Sacco-Vanzetti trial.

CONTROVERSY

Controversy marked the Sacco and Vanzetti case from the beginning. Judge Webster Thayer seemed to be on a mission to convict and execute

Italian anarchists. He first presided at a trial that convicted Vanzetti on robbery charges in 1920. Thayer insisted on presiding at the Sacco-Vanzetti trial even though he should have recused himself. Because of a Massachusetts law, Thayer also decided on posttrial motions after the verdict despite the fact that much of the evidence argued in the motions for a new trial involved the judge's own misconduct at the trial. Another aberration was that prosecutor Katzmann prosecuted Vanzetti in 1920 and then agreed to prosecute him again in 1921 when he was a codefendant with Sacco. Prior to the trial, Fred Moore encouraged the national and international labor movements to finance the trial, and he also sought additional political and financial support from the labor movement during the trial.

The conduct of the trial was inconsistent. The attorneys often engaged in contentious wrangling with the judge and at other times remained silent when they should have objected. In some segments of the trial, defense attorneys engaged in carefully maneuvered cross-examination, and in other parts of the trial their cross-examination seemed to lack a clear purpose. Prosecutors also compromised legal rules and communication norms. The zealous prosecutor changed the trial from an indictment of murder and robbery to a political charge of anarchy and hatred of the American government, coached witnesses to change their stories, and badgered defense witnesses (Feuerlicht, 1977; Frankfurter, 1954; Musmanno, 1939; Young & Kaiser, 1985). Justice Frankfurter (1954) even alleged that prosecutors bribed witnesses so they would change their testimony. The defense uncovered lies in the statements of prosecution witnesses, and prosecutors also discovered irregularities in the testimony of defense witnesses.

Prior to and during the trial Judge Thayer repeatedly made public comments that the two were guilty. During the trial Moore openly challenged several of Thayer's rulings as prejudicial, and the two engaged in numerous contentious verbal exchanges. Despite this fact, Sacco blamed Moore for the verdict and for spending too much money and fired him after the trial. Alibi and eye witnesses for both sides of the case significantly changed their statements at trial so that they were inconsistent with statements given to investigators and made in depositions prior to the trial. Wealthy Bostonians and prominent authors provided financial resources and offered opinions about the innocence of the defendants during the trial. After the verdict, other people confessed that they had committed the crime, but the execution of Sacco and Vanzetti still took place in 1927. Prejudices and feelings outside of the trial impacted the animosity and intensity of what occurred in the trial.

From a retrospective view, some features of the trial may appear highly prejudicial to the defendants. At the time of their arrest, police interrogated the defendants without an attorney present or without their rights being read to them, but Miranda rights did not become the law until 1966 (*Miranda v. Arizona,* 1966). During the trial, the defendants appeared at the trial in cages, a practice that has long since been abandoned by the courts, but one that was common for Massachusetts defendants in murder trials of the time. Comprehensive rules of evidence did exist at the time of the Sacco and Vanzetti trial, but codes of professional conduct did not (Cornelius, 1929; *Philadelphia & T.R. Co. v. Stimpson,* 1840). The lack of discovery rules at that time meant that neither side knew who was going to testify and what they would likely say. The law that allowed Judge Thayer to decide motions about his own misconduct was changed later, but the irregularity in the law clearly impeded defense's options to get a new trial based on the appeal. The subsequent analysis of the cross-examination identifies other courtroom practices of that time that may seem prejudicial and unethical to contemporary readers. Some of these practices, however, were aberrations of the legal rules that had been adopted to ensure convictions of anarchists and other immigrants; others were conventional practices that eventually changed.

SETTING

The social and historical setting helps to explain the controversy about the trial. The arrest and trial of Sacco and Vanzetti took place during the Palmer raids and the Red Scare at a time when the U.S. government deported hundreds of aliens under the sanctions of the Alien and Sedition Acts. Sacco worked as a shoemaker and Vanzetti as a fish peddler, and both men actively participated in anarchist groups. Prosecutors indicted Sacco and Vanzetti for the murder and robbery of a paymaster and guard at a shoe factory in Braintree, Massachusetts. After the verdict, the trial became a celebrated example of the martyrdom of innocent immigrant workers for the cause of the international labor movement. The case rallied the international and national labor groups in support of the Sacco-Vanzetti Defense Fund that in turn funded the trial and appellate defense attorneys. The guilty verdict in the trial encouraged thousands of laborers to protest against what they claimed was an unjust verdict based on circumstantial evidence and judicial and prosecutorial misconduct.

Six years after the trial and despite the vehement protests, the state of Massachusetts executed Sacco and Vanzetti in 1927. Most legal historians agree that the police arrested the defendants because they had profiled them as unpatriotic Italian anarchists. Some media reporters covered the trial as if it were a routine murder case until Katzmann's cross-examination of Sacco, at which point the press and the public recognized this was a political trial.

In the years that have elapsed since the execution of Sacco and Vanzetti, the case still demands attention because of the social and political features of the Red Scare, the Palmer raids, the labor unrest, and the Alien and Sedition Acts. In many ways the political climate of the 1920s resembles the climate in the United States since September 11, 2001. The fear of foreign nationals, the threats of violence and terrorism against Americans, and the creation of restrictive national laws (e.g., PATRIOT Act, 2001) characterize both eras as a time of "political hysteria."

Between 1919 and 1920, the American public became "completely pre-occupied with the Bolshevik menace" (Levin, 1971, p. 52). The signs of this menace took the form of 1,400 labor strikes occurring nationwide between March and August of 1919. This unrest became known as the Red Scare, the period of national hysteria resulting from public fear that communists, anarchists, and Bolsheviks threatened the American way of life. This labor unrest polarized the opinions and actions of strikers and nonstrikers, and immigrants and citizens (Murray, 1964). Moreover, the press contributed to this polarized atmosphere by fostering fears about foreign dissidents. The press maligned immigrant workers and tried to suppress the actions of the labor movement in the Boston area, close to the homes of Sacco and Vanzetti.

The Red Scare, according to Feuerlicht (1977), was part of a "national nervous breakdown" brought on by the increase of left-wing groups—communists, socialists, anarchists, and syndicalists; a flu epidemic that killed 500,000 Americans; frequent labor strikes; and the economic slowdown caused by reduced production after World War I. During this time, thousands of immigrants arrived in the United States from eastern and southern Europe; many, including Sacco and Vanzetti, came from Italy.

These demographic and political circumstances fueled labor activism and resulted in statutes that restricted the political activity of immigrants and aliens. In 1918, the Sedition Act made it illegal to "utter, print, write, or publish" any information using "disloyal, scurrilous or abusive language" about the United States government and to advocate "curtailment of . . . production or products necessary or essential to the prosecution of the war." The Deportation Act of 1918 legalized the expulsion of any aliens (noncitizens) who believed in anti-American ideas or belonged to anti-American groups. Federal law enforcement prosecuted and deported more than 2,000 persons under the provisions of these two acts (Chafee, 1969) and arrested hundreds of others on criminal charges resulting from their public expression of anti-American beliefs.

The Alien and Sedition and the Deportation Acts together became the legal basis for massive raids on the homes and workplaces of noncitizens. Under the leadership of United States Attorney General A. Mitchell Palmer, federal officers conducted raids, arrested immigrants without serving warrants, denied legal counsel to those arrested, and forced confessions from them (Feuerlicht, 1977). A few months prior to the jailing of the defendants, Palmer took credit for the arrest of 4,000 radicals, including some Italian anarchists who were close associates of Sacco and Vanzetti. Young and Kaiser (1985) conclude that the strong-arm tactics used by law enforcement officers during the Palmer raids also characterized the arrest and interrogation of Sacco and Vanzetti.

After World War I, the U.S. government developed repressive legal measures in response to an emotional political climate. For this reason, it is not surprising two Italian immigrants, active in anarchist causes, became suspects for an unsolved crime committed in the vicinity where the defendants lived. This political climate, according to Justice William O. Douglas

(TR, 1969), converted the Sacco-Vanzetti case into "an ideological trial that took place behind the facade of a legal trial" (p. xlvii). A close reading of the transcripts indicates, however, that much of the trial was not overtly ideological; the case became especially political after the defendants testified and even more so after the guilty verdict. Frankfurter and Jackson (1960) support this conclusion:

> Up to the time Sacco and Vanzetti testified to their radical activities, their pacifism, and their flight to Mexico to escape the draft, the trial was for murder and banditry; with the cross-examination of Sacco and Vanzetti, patriotism and radicalism became the dominant emotional issues. (p. 345)

GAMES AND CROSS-EXAMINATION

Although the testimony of the defendants during cross-examination was politically charged, most of the trial featured zealous attorneys engaged in a high stakes game of strategy and chance. The features of this kind of game were particularly evident during cross-examination when attorneys cooperated under the rules of the trial game and when evenly matched opponents pursued incompatible goals, made moves based on consequential reasoning, and engaged in calculated choices to produce desirable payoffs (Rapoport, 1970; Schelling, 1960). The goals and strategies of attorneys' cross-examination resembled the calculated choices described in game theory.

Trials involve a mixture of strategy and chance; the moves of attorneys for one side of the case depend on the moves of opposing attorneys, and uncertainty evolves from taking chances with witnesses. What appears to be the facts presented at a trial are only probabilities and attorneys' reasoned choices often create unpredictable payoffs and uncertain outcomes. Sometimes choices that seemed reasonable at the time in retrospect appear flawed and ill-conceived after they have been made (Rapoport, 1970). During this era, trials were games of chance with uncertain outcomes rather than games where the most reasonable strategies produced the most probable outcome.

In a trial, participants start with different utilities or resources, pursue incompatible goals, act within certain rules, calculate their choices, make moves based on consequential reasoning, and gain payoffs. During this process attorneys are expected to follow rules at the same time they make calculated choices resulting in creative strategic maneuvers that will help them win their case. When attorneys attempt to outwit each other and yet obey the rules, cross-examination becomes a carefully planned and executed refutation game in which they create clever maneuvers that they hope will result in their side gaining political, social, or financial payoffs, or an acquittal or conviction. At other times, violations of the rules turn reasonable moves into unethical tricks that subvert the purpose of the game.

Goals

Since cross-examination serves more than one goal, the payoffs from this process may be mixed. The process attempts to discredit the credibility of a witness, refute the facts resulting from the direct examination of a witness, and elicit responses favorable to the interrogators' case theory (Fontham, 1995; Haydock & Sonsteng, 1991, 1994a; Iannuzzi, 1982; Lubet, 1993). Instead of considering the process of adversarial interrogation using a war analogy in which opposing attorneys set out to destroy the witnesses of the opposition, the game analogy illuminates the strategic choices of attorneys that evolve from their careful analysis of the situations under procedural rules that limit their moves and those of the opposing attorneys in hopes of producing desirable payoffs.

During cross-examination, the attorneys' moves are intertwined with the outcomes. When attorneys for one side of the case choose a reasonable move based on available options during cross-examination, they receive some payoff (a desirable gain). The opposing attorneys make countermoves that attempt to reduce the effects or the type of payoff. In other words, if a prosecutor presents a credible eyewitness during direct examination who points to the defendant as the murderer, the defense can force that witness, through cross-examination, to retract statements and rethink his or her reasoning. In this way, the attorneys' moves during cross-examination can create reasonable doubt for jurors. The moves and countermoves that attorneys make during witness examination depend on the case theory they have presented during their respective opening statements and on the rules that govern the trial game.

Prosecutor Williams argued that the defendants committed murder in order to finish a burglary. He described how Parmenter and Berardelli received the payroll in the presence of two short, stocky Italian men who waited for them, then grabbed the cache of money, and before they escaped, shot the paymaster and guard in broad daylight in front of many witnesses. The defendants disappeared in a large, dark, getaway car. That alleged getaway car remained for 20 days in a private garage. The police staked out that garage and eventually arrested Sacco and Vanzetti when they came to get the car. Williams claimed that several witnesses identified the defendants as two of the men who had been at the scene of the crime at the shoe factory. He further asserted that the defendants lied at the time of their arrest to cover up their guilt (TR, pp. 2325–2334). Prosecutors pieced together the theory presented in opening statements using the testimony of 59 witnesses.

Defense attorney Callahan offered a competing theory during his opening statement. He began with brief descriptions of the defendants as hard workers and then he described what their activities were on the day of the crime. Callahan claimed that both men closely identified with their Italian heritage and they supported the political loyalties of their cultural community. On the day of the crime, Sacco traveled to Boston to get a passport to return to Italy to visit his sick mother, and Vanzetti sold fish in an area close to his home in Plymouth, Massachusetts. Callahan predicted that defense witnesses would testify that Sacco and Vanzetti did not commit the crime, and, in fact, the appearances of the criminals that were described by eyewitnesses differed from the defendants'. Furthermore, the prosecution witnesses lacked credibility because they had changed their stories several times prior to the trial. Defense attorneys admitted that the defendants lied at the time of their arrest but claimed they did so because they feared being deported for their radical beliefs (TR, pp. 2760–2765). The defense called 99 different witnesses to support their case theory.

Strategic Plan

A general plan for cross-examination is that attorneys identify which witnesses should be cross-examined, how they should be questioned, what vulnerabilities they have, and decide how opposing attorneys' countermoves can be restricted or impeded. Strategies are more than plans; they are also calculated uses of attorneys' power in response to the contingencies of a situation (de Certeau, 1988; Schelling, 1960). Attorneys show their hand during direct examination, and opposing attorneys use trump cards and make tricks to score points in the minds of jurors for their respective sides of the case. Michel de Certeau's (1988) concept of a trick is the ability of players in social games to take advantage of the opportunities afforded them by other players; some tricks are deceptions, and others are just clever maneuvers that allow one player to outwit others. During direct examination, the attorney deals the cards to the opponents by selecting witnesses, placing their testimony in a logical sequence, and limiting the scope of the examination. Cross-examiners have to play the hand they have been dealt during direct examination and make reasonable and deliberate choices that lead to savvy moves that produce desirable trial outcomes.

Attorneys make choices about whom they should cross-examine based on their assessment of several factors of the trial situation. First, they usually cross-examine only those witnesses who have done damage to their theory of the case. The only circumstance in which attorneys should cross-examine a witness who has not rebutted their case is if they suspect that witness knows additional facts not revealed during direct examination. Second, attorneys typically cross-examine witnesses who have a central role in the case because of their proximity to the crime, ability to give eyewitness accounts, experience as victims, inability to withstand accusations made against them by others, or other unique circumstances that pertain to a crime or complaint. Third, attorneys typically cross-examine witnesses whose testimony is incorrect, flawed, or incomplete. Specifically, attorneys can score points for their side when they cross-examine witnesses whose testimony is inconsistent with their depositions, uncorroborated by other witnesses, or refuted by other witnesses. Finally, attorneys discredit witnesses for testimony that is biased, inaccurate, only partially true, or contradictory to other trial evidence. This list indicates that attorneys should cross-examine most opposing witnesses, although the method and the focus of questioning change from witness to witness. Attorneys risk losing personal credibility when they cross-examine vulnerable witnesses who have suffered emotional trauma from the crime or who are psychologically fragile (Fontham, 1995; Haydock & Sonsteng, 1991, 1994a; Iannuzzi, 1982; Mauet, 1992).

Although the players in trial games are expected to play by the rules, they often circumvent the rules to gain advantage for their clients or themselves. The attorneys' definition of the legal situation often directs them to use one strategy rather than another. As the trial progressed, it seems that Sacco and Vanzetti's attorneys were convinced that they would not win the verdict on the factual issues so they tried to create a record for the appellate courts to show that the judge and prosecutors violated the defendants' rights.

Refutation Strategies

In ways similar to other games, the goals of cross-examiners are incompatible with those of direct examiners. Direct examiners elicit coherent, consistent, and probable statements from their witnesses, which support their theory of the case, but cross-examiners break up the statements of witnesses into separate parts, reveal inconsistencies, and show the errors of their reasoning. Bailey and Rothblatt (1971) claim "cross-examination is the most vital part of your case. In many cases, it is your only defense" (p. 17). Although historians have emphasized the unfairness of the interrogation of Sacco and Vanzetti, the trial transcript reveals that attorneys for both sides made moves and countermoves that produced different payoffs. Defense attorneys for Sacco and Vanzetti conducted a high stakes game that involved the life or death of their clients, the political goals of the labor movement, and the renunciation of flawed judicial practices.

The attorneys relied on two broad conventional strategies: (1) attacking the truth of witnesses' statements, and (2) attacking inconsistencies in the witnesses' reasoning (Schopenhauer, 1942). A cross-examiner can discredit a witness by showing that his or her statements are actually based on something other than the facts and evidence of the case as outlined in the opening statements and developed through the corroboration of other witnesses.

ATTACKING TRUTH

- Get witnesses to identify their own biases resulting from deep-seated cultural, political, and familial values.
- Uncover witnesses' motives and attitudes.
- Show that witnesses' testimony results from their self-interests, lack of common sense, and/or distortions of facts.

Attacking inconsistencies in witnesses' presentation of information, observations, or conclusions in the stories they relate during direct examination can involve several strategies. One of the strategies is to expose their flawed reasoning (Schuetz & Snedaker, 1988):

EXPOSING FLAWED REASONING

- Show that witnesses' conclusions are based on flawed premises and inferences.
- Show that witnesses' conclusions do not logically follow from the evidence.
- Show that witnesses' reasoning is circular—the evidence is true because the conclusion is true, or the conclusion is true because the evidence is true.
- Force witnesses to admit that they have drawn a hasty generalization from observations that are unrepresentative or ambiguous.

Other strategies in attacking inconsistencies involve showing that a prior statement made by a witness is inconsistent with his or her later testimony and forcing a witness to admit that his or her statements conflict directly with testimony of other witnesses.

Refutation permits attorneys to make strategic courtroom moves that achieve their goals. Strategies of refutation evolve from calculated choices of attorneys and open up options for other moves that will influence the trial outcome. Once they have attacked inconsistencies, cross-examiners can ask a witness to eliminate certain explanations for actions or events, thereby leaving room for the cross-examiner's alternative explanation; this strategy is called "method of residues" (Jensen, 1981).

The Sacco-Vanzetti defense's cross-examination of the prosecution's eyewitness, Louis Pelser, illuminates several different refutation strategies. The defense discredited both the logic and the character of Pelser, the prosecution's star witness, who claimed that he had seen Sacco commit the murder. One of Pelser's vulnerabilities was that he had presented a story to the prosecutors prior to the trial that differed from his testimony at trial. Nonetheless, prosecutors relied on Pelser's testimony to identify Sacco as the gunman who shot Berardelli. Defense attorneys Jeremiah McAnarney and Moore took nearly four hours to interrogate this witness. Moore's cross-examination began by questioning the witness on the grounds of self-interest:

> M: Mr. Pelser, you have no interest in the outcome about this case at all, have you?
>
> P: Any interest?
>
> M: Other than to see to it that due and proper justice is administered between the parties?
>
> P: I don't know what you mean.
>
> M: I say, you have no interest in this case other than to see to it that justice is administered in this court?
>
> P: Yes, sir.
>
> M: By this jury?
>
> P: Yes, sir. (TR, p. 297)

At the beginning of the interrogation, the witness claimed he had no self-interest in the trial, but eventually Pelser admitted self-interest, acknowledging that he felt he could become a celebrity of sorts by helping the government and by saying with certainty that Sacco was the gunman.

Next, Moore refuted Pelser on grounds that his story violated the principles of common sense because the opaque window from which he observed the crime blocked his view.

> M: Now, those windows in that building on that floor are opaque, are they not, that is, you can't see through the window?
>
> P: Yes, sir. You can't see through the windows.
>
> M: So that the windows have to be opened to see anything, is that correct?
>
> P: Yes, sir.
>
> M: At the time this affair started, what was the condition of that window or those windows where you were?
>
> P: Well, there was a little window open about that much.
>
> M: About three to four inches?
>
> P: Yes. . . .
>
> M: And the crack that you say was in the window—
>
> P: It was open.
>
> M: About that much?
>
> P: Yes, sir.
>
> M: And your statement to the jury is that you saw out through there and saw bodies lying in the street?
>
> P: Yes, sir.
>
> M: Inside of what would be the gutter line, or outside street line?
>
> P: Well, he was lying right in the middle of the sidewalk. . . .
>
> M: And that was the body of Mr. Berardelli?
>
> P: Yes, sir. (TR, pp. 297–298)

After pointing out Pelser's restricted view of the crime scene, Moore impeached Pelser by showing the inconsistency of his statements before and during the trial. Pelser originally stated that he did not see the shooting and that he only saw the body of Berardelli after the shooting. Moore read the witness's original statement and proceeded with this line of questioning:

> M: Was that a true statement of the fact?
>
> P: Well, yes, it was.

M: What?

P: It was.

M: It was? This is a correct statement of what you told Mr. Reid?

P: That I told Mr. Reid, yes, sir.

M: Now, is it a true statement of what you saw?

P: No, sir.

M: Why was it that you didn't tell Mr. Reid the facts?

P: Because I didn't want to tell my story.

M: Why?

P: Because I didn't like to go to court.

M: What has happened between now and then that you should tell to one side in this lawsuit one set of facts, and tell the other gentlemen in this lawsuit another set of facts? What has happened?

P: Well, I didn't know them well enough.

M: You knew them on March 26th just as well as you know them today, did you not?

P: Yes, sir.

M: Why then didn't you tell them what the facts were?

P: I didn't think I had to tell my story.

M: Did you tell Mr. Reid a falsehood in order to avoid being called a witness in this case?

P: Yes, sir.

M: In other words, you think so lightly of your word that, in order to avoid being called a witness, you deliberately told a falsehood, representing it to be the truth?

P: Yes, sir. (TR, p. 300)

This segment provides an example of how cross-examiners impeach witnesses by showing that they had lied because of self-interest.

Moore continued his relentless attack on Pelser's reasoning by claiming the witness made hasty generalizations based upon ambiguous and limited information.

M: Now you don't pretend or claim that you ever saw either of the men previous to this date, do you?

P: No, sir.

M: And you want the jury to believe that you stood in that window with the bullets flying in your direction—

P: I didn't say that.

M: And carefully inspected the man that was firing below to the point of being able to state that he had a pin in his necktie?

P: I didn't say he had a pin in his necktie.

M: Or pin in his collar. And the first time you ever told anybody these facts, or what you claim to be facts, is on this witness stand?

P: Yes, sir.

M: And you haven't any explanation to give to this jury for telling an entirely different story, without coercion, without any pressure or any force, in the sanctity of your own home, surrounded by your own family—you haven't any explanation to give for telling an entirely different story [when interviewed by defense attorneys], except that you didn't want to be a witness?

P: No, sir. (TR, p. 306)

By the time he finished with Pelser, Moore's refutation uncovered several flaws in Pelser's testimony based on self-interest, violations of common sense, inconsistencies, and hasty generalization. McAnarney provided reasons why jurors should doubt Pelser, such as it was humanly impossible for him to see the gunman and record the license plate number on the getaway car through a small crack in an opaque window during the course of a few seconds. In a typical trial, refutation strategies of this type create desirable payoffs by giving jurors a basis for reasonable doubt in the theories and facts presented by the opposing witnesses and by leaving open possibilities for defense's alternative explanations of the legal dispute.

TACTICAL MOVES IN CROSS-EXAMINATION

In addition to attorneys' calculated strategies of refutation, procedural maneuvers help attorneys gain desirable payoffs (Bailey & Rothblatt, 1971; Givens, 1980; Heglund, 1978; Mauet, 1992). A payoff may be refuting a fact, showing flaws in the reasoning of the witness, or damaging the credibility of a witness. Tactics help to bolster the impact of the refutation strategies. Some of the tactics are implicit in the procedural rules, but others evolve through the trial-and-error experiences of attorneys. The sources of attorneys' tactical savvy are less important than the payoffs they achieve by gaining a competitive advantage over opposing attorneys. Sometimes these tactics impeach the credibility of the witness, help bring about a desirable verdict, allow political views to seep into the record, and show off the skills of attorneys. In other cases, attorneys may lose the verdict but expose errors in the legal process, that is, create a record enabling the case to be appealed. Tactics include questioning postures, navigating procedural rules, and using maneuvers to outwit witnesses.

Questioning Postures

Postures are maneuvers that affect the attorneys' performances during cross-examination. Postures refer to professional manners and questioning techniques in relation to witnesses. Postures consist of showing an appropriate attitudinal orientation, properly sequencing and using questions, and using legitimate moves to impair witnesses' credibility (Schuetz & Snedaker, 1988). The standards for professional conduct were less defined in 1921 than they are today. However, conduct of attorneys that offended the public norms of that time would also offend present-day jurors. Several attorney postures likely influenced the Sacco-Vanzetti trial in ways similar to the kind of effect they would have on contemporary cases.

TYPES OF POSTURES

- Attorneys should be courteous and considerate to the witnesses they interrogate because jurors will sympathize with a witness they believe has been ridiculed or drilled too much by attorneys.

- Attorneys should maintain a calm and unemotional attitude and refrain from showing anger or disrespect to witnesses.

- Attorneys should create questions that will move the witnesses logically through cross-examination. This calls for establishing rapport with witnesses and reordering the sequence of testimony a witness has presented during direct examination.

- Attorneys should build rapport by asking innocent or neutral questions that will establish agreed-upon facts about a legal dispute.

- Attorneys should continue with leading questions that focus directly on testimony that has the potential to damage their side of the case.

- Attorneys should follow through with questions that connect witnesses' answers to their own theory of the case.

- Attorneys should object when their witnesses are being interrogated by opposing attorneys under the following circumstances (Ehrlich, 1970; Haydock & Sonsteng, 1991, 1994a; Iannuzzi, 1982):

  — The question is incompetent, because the witness lacks the knowledge or personal observation to answer the question.

  — The question is irrelevant; no relationship exists between an item of evidence and an attempt to prove a fact.

  — The question is immaterial; evidence does not relate to the issues of the indictment.

  — The question calls for a conclusion; the witness interprets rather than reports information.

  — The questioner argues with a witness by confronting or denying directly what the witness says.

— The question calls for hearsay evidence based on reports of others rather than the witness's own knowledge.

— The respondent provides information beyond what the questioner asks.

— The questioner asks the respondent to give self-incriminating testimony.

— The question lacks a foundation because the assumptions behind the question are not developed by the questioner.

— The question is unclear, complex, compound, or unintelligible.

The record of the Sacco-Vanzetti trial provides some clues about the use of these questioning postures, and other clues about the attitudinal postures and orientation of attorneys are found in posttrial commentaries. For example, one source notes that Moore "alienated and angered Judge Thayer from the moment he stepped into the courtroom." He violated the Bostonian's sense of propriety with his long hair and by removing his jacket and even his shoes in the courtroom. Moore came across as an outsider, but the reputable McAnarney brothers knew and respected the protocols of the court and the expectations of the community (Topp, 2005, p. 26). Another source noted that Katzmann conducted a ruthless cross-examination of Sacco, and Moore was harsh and threatening in his interrogation of Pelser, Goodridge, and Andrews (witnesses for the prosecution) (Joughin & Morgan, 1948). Others reported that Katzmann was an exceedingly skillful examiner who got by with mean-spirited questions because Judge Thayer favored the prosecution's side of the case (Ehrmann, 1969). Most sources agreed that Katzmann's cross-examination of Sacco and Vanzetti ensured the defendants would be convicted by the proprosecution jurors that Thayer had seated (Ehrmann, 1969; Feuerlicht, 1977; Joughin & Morgan, 1948).

A strong adversarial sentiment characterized the tactics of both sides. Katzmann's interrogation ridiculed defense witnesses and made them look stupid, and Moore's cross-examinations of Pelser, Goodridge, and Andrews was so harsh that the witnesses likely wished they had never testified at the trial. In a typical trial, the judge tries to enforce courtroom decorum, but Thayer did just the opposite. He fought with defense attorneys, interjected his opinions into the record, and allowed the prosecutors to do and say pretty much what they wanted.

The defense called their own expert on guns and bullets, James E. Burns, to refute the testimony of the prosecution's ballistics experts. Burns stressed that the bullets taken from the victim may have come from guns other than the one found in Sacco's possession. The following excerpt reveals how the questions used by Katzmann controlled one of the defense witness's answers:

K: Does the double marking at the upper end of those grooves on the bullet indicate anything to your mind?

B: Yes.

K: What?

B: A worn lead.

K: Anything else?

B: A neglected gun.

K: Anything else?

B: No, sir.

K: Does it indicate anything else as to the matter the bullet took the lead?

B: Not plumb. . . .

K: That is, it did not jump the rifling perfectly? That is what it means, doesn't it?

B: It did not go straight into the lead, perfect center. (TR, pp. 1433–1434)

Katzmann controlled Burns's responses so that the witness would not be able to exclude the possibility that the bullet came from Sacco's gun. Any question that solicited an answer indicating that it was possible Sacco's gun was used would significantly damage the defense's case theory. Therefore, Jeremiah McAnarney objected to Katzmann's leading question, which was: "You are talking and predicting your opinion, are you not, that this bullet . . . was not fired through the Sacco gun?" McAnarney objected on grounds that the question lacked a proper foundation, saying: "This witness has not said that bullet was not fired by the Sacco gun" (TR, p. 1439). Defense attorneys frequently objected during the cross-examination of Burns in order to create doubt that the bullet found at the crime scene was fired from Sacco's gun.

Navigating Procedural Rules

In addition to the postures of the interrogator, attorneys need to know the rules and also to understand what a particular judge will tolerate as legitimate communication in relation to the rules. Givens (1980) identified several of these rules.

PROCEDURAL RULES

• Cross-examiners should not ask for explanations, because these types of inquiry permit witnesses to justify responses.

• Cross-examiners should ask leading questions to keep control of the witness.

• Cross-examiners should include facts within their questions, including times, dates, names, and statements from depositions.

• Cross-examiners should select questions that expose the vulnerability of the witnesses, such as their contradictions, prejudices, or inaccuracies in their answers.

• Cross-examiners should not ask questions if they do not know what the answer will be ahead of time.

Moore asked leading questions, restricted the responses of the witness, and included facts within the questions. His questioning discredited the credibility of Lola R. Andrews, a prosecution witness, who claimed that she talked to Sacco while he laid beneath a car on the day of the crime. As she walked past the shoe factory on her way to an interview, Andrews claimed she observed a parked car with one man sitting inside and Sacco underneath the car. Moore's cross-examination of Andrews forced her to admit that she never saw the face of the person she had positively identified as Sacco.

> M: Why, Mrs. Andrews, did you speak to that man, directing your attention again to the man down underneath this car, rather than to the other man who was standing doing nothing at a point no farther removed from you than I am at this moment?
>
> A: You mean, why I spoke to him rather than the other man?
>
> M: Yes.
>
> A: Simply because I was standing there talking and I directed my conversation to him to ask him that question, instead of going back. . . .
>
> M: Yet, you couldn't see even the face of the man you were directing the questions to?
>
> A: Why sir, I saw his face when he got up.
>
> M: You had to call him up before you were able to see his face at all, didn't you?
>
> A: He was getting up when I spoke, getting up from the auto. . . .
>
> M: At the time you asked him the question, he was down on the ground under the car?
>
> A: His head and shoulder was under the car. . . .
>
> M: Mrs. Andrews, on the date that I talked with you [in the deposition prior to the trial], did you in any way, form, or manner identify Nicola Sacco as the man that you saw, or claim to have seen, on April 15, 1920?
>
> A: You mean, did I recognize him as the man? No, sir, I didn't tell you that way. (TR, pp. 2482–2487)

Moore included a fact favorable to his side of the case, that Andrews failed to identify Sacco in her deposition, as part of the leading question; this allowed him to control the witness so that she would answer the question in the way he wanted her to respond.

Maneuvering to Outwit Witnesses

In addition to postures and procedural rules, a third tactic commonly used in cross-examination consists of verbal maneuvers that raise doubts about the veracity of the testimony. These maneuvers consist of asserting uncertain or false premises, using tag questions, and eliciting "I don't know" responses. Each maneuver has the potential to confuse the witnesses and give jurors the impression that witnesses are hesitant and unsure about their testimony. These communication tactics permit attorneys to manipulate the witness in a way that does not directly violate procedural rules.

One maneuver occurs when attorneys phrase leading questions by asserting uncertain or a false premise and then asking a witness to agree with these assertions. For example, in Katzmann's cross-examination of defense witness Frank Burke, he included an uncertain statement within the question: "You got there about . . . twenty minutes past two, didn't you?" (TR, p. 2782). This was not the time stated by the witness during his direct examination, and the witness was unsure of the time, but he still agreed that the prosecutor's statement was probably true. Questions of this type work to the advantage of the questioner because witnesses, more often than not, believe that attorneys are stating facts rather than hypotheses in the leading questions they ask (Swann, Giuliano, & Wegner, 1982).

Tag questions are short, simple questions added onto an original question. In cross-examination, assertions of fact are followed by tag questions. Questions of this type appeared frequently in the cross-examinations of witnesses: "You didn't see them, did you?" "You don't remember, do you?" "You meant to earn money, didn't you?" In her research, Loftus (1980) found that witnesses answered tag questions in line with how attorneys wanted them to answer these inquiries.

"I don't know" answers help create doubt about the credibility of a witness's testimony. When interrogators try to discredit witnesses, they often are met with the responses "I don't know" or "I don't recall" (Dunston, 1980). When witnesses respond with "I don't recall," they usually continue to use this phrase several times because they believe it adds consistency to their testimony. During Moore's cross-examinations of Pelser, Goodridge, and Andrews, these witnesses answered many of the questions by saying "I don't know." The following sample of Moore's interrogation of Lola Andrews indicates how this maneuver helped cast doubt on her credibility as a witness.

M: What did you see about the car? . . .

A: It was a large car. . . .

M: Bright, clean, shiny?

A: I would not say.

M: Or dirty or grimy?

A: I could not answer that.

M: The make of the car. . . .

A: I do not know the names. (TR, p. 2452)

Beyond Tactical Moves

Cross-examiners achieve payoffs and add persuasiveness to their case by choosing postures, obeying procedural rules, and adopting verbal maneuvers that reinforce their theories of the case. These tactics enhance the refutational strategies and add potency to the moves attorneys make during cross-examination. In the Sacco-Vanzetti case, the defense and the prosecution attorneys frequently showed their competence and power to control the responses of unsophisticated and vulnerable witnesses. The adversarial duel in the trial featured impeachment of the testimony of three occurrence witnesses by Moore and two of Vanzetti's alibi witnesses by Katzmann. Prior to the cross-examination of the defendants, the weight of the testimony appeared to favor the defense because the eyewitnesses of the prosecution could not identify the defendants as the gunmen. Both sides called a total of 33 eyewitnesses. Only seven of those located the defendants in the vicinity of the crime before or after it occurred. Only Pelser identified Sacco as the gunman. The testimony of ballistics experts for both sides resulted in a draw.

Why then did the defense lose the verdict? Scholars (Ehrmann, 1969; Feuerlicht, 1977; Joughin & Morgan, 1948; Musmanno, 1939; Young & Kaiser, 1985) argue the reason for the verdict is that the defendants incriminated themselves during direct and cross-examination by recounting their political beliefs and activities. Whether the defense allowed Sacco and Vanzetti to testify in order for them to gain political payoffs from those who sympathized with the cause of labor, to give them voice as victims of an unfair legal system, or to create a record of legal violations for an appeal is not clear. The aftermath of the trial indicates that the defense achieved the political but not the legal payoffs they sought. Whatever the defense's goals were, the prosecution decided to exploit the defendants' testimony to persuade the jury that they should render a guilty verdict.

From the perspective of a game analogue, it is just as easy to conclude that the defense attorneys knew that the jurors would convict their clients early on in the trial so they chose to emphasize the politics of the defendants and the prejudices of the prosecutors. This move could have exposed the unfairness of the laws against immigrants, revealed the errors in the conduct of the trial, and allowed the victims to express their strong political views. This choice may have been the most viable strategy the defense had to save their clients from the death penalty.

Another perspective may be that the prosecution strongly believed that Italian immigrants were a threat to democracy, and they may have decided to emphasize the politics of Sacco and Vanzetti so they could ensure a verdict against the men. It is also plausible that the prosecution recognized that their witnesses were vulnerable and knew the defense attorneys were formidable opponents so they thought that the only way they could win was by exposing the anti-American and anarchists' beliefs of the defendants, beliefs they knew were contrary to those of the jurors and the community. Prosecutors may have perceived the trial more as a game of pure chance in which they had to take advantage of every opportunity they had to persuade the jurors that Sacco and Vanzetti were guilty. Katzmann also may have used the trial to promote himself as a deserving candidate for a more prominent role in the legal system. Whatever the justifications were, the trial remains noteworthy because of Katzmann's unconventional cross-examination of the defendants, particularly Sacco.

The Unconventional Cross-Examination of Sacco

The interrogation of Sacco was one of the "most extraordinary cross-examinations in a capital case that ever took place in a courtroom" (Ehrmann, 1969, p. 307). The prosecutor turned the trial from a criminal case of murder into a charge that Sacco and Vanzetti were traitors (Feuerlicht, 1977). Quite clearly, Katzmann's questioning of Sacco made the defendant appear to be both a liar and a threat to democracy. The prosecutor's unconventional refutation diverted the defendant's testimony and the entire court proceeding away from the issues of the indictment, altered the roles of the participants, and maneuvered the semantics. Although many of these diversions violated the procedural rules for cross-examination, the defense did not frequently object to these obvious violations. When the defense voiced objections, Judge Thayer overruled them. The record of the testimony of Sacco showed that he lacked English-speaking and comprehension skills, misunderstood what he had been asked, and yet conveyed his political views despite semantic and syntactic errors. His statements incriminated him as an Italian anarchist, disloyal to the United States. So many years after the trial, it is still not clear whether the defendant's incrimination of himself was part of the defense's strategy or whether it was an accidental move that Katzmann exploited for the advantage of the prosecution.

"Diversions" refer to strategies that draw the attention of the jurors, judge, and witnesses away from the normative goal of cross-examination, that is, to gather evidence that pertains to the indictments. In other words, cross-examiners alter the witnesses' course of testimony or insert information not previously presented in the trial. Since some attorneys' diversions seem legitimate and relevant to the facts, the issues of the indictment, and beliefs and values of the community in general and jurors in particular, the judge may fail to notice the deceptive quality of diversions or to ascertain their lack of relevance to the legal dispute. From a retrospective point of view, the diversions in the Sacco-Vanzetti trial appear to be overt violations of procedural rules for cross-examination. Nevertheless, these diversions helped convince jurors that the defendants were guilty. The appellate briefs filed after the trial argued that these diversions were so egregious that they violated the rights of Sacco and Vanzetti to a fair trial, and therefore the verdict should be overturned.

Issue Diversions

One of Katzmann's overt diversions was away from the charges of the indictment of murder and toward the charges that the defendants' beliefs endangered citizens and threatened the American way of life. Katzmann successfully sidestepped the murder indictment and reframed the charge so it was a violation of the Alien and Sedition Acts because the defendants were unpatriotic and subverted the goals of the federal government.

During the two days of his cross-examination of Sacco, Katzmann persistently and aggressively confronted the defendant about his radical beliefs and associations. Katzmann's diversion began by emphasizing Sacco's lack of patriotism.

K: Did you say yesterday you love a free country?

S: Yes, sir.

K: Did you love this country in the month of May 1917?

S: I did say, I don't want to say I did not love this country. . . . If you, Mr. Katzmann, if you give me that, I could explain—

K: Do you understand that question?

S: Yes.

K: Then will you please answer it?

S: I can't answer in one word. . . .

K: Did you love this country in the last week of May 1917?

S: That is pretty hard for me to say in one word, Mr. Katzmann.

K: There are two words you can use Mr. Sacco, yes or no. Which is it?

S: Yes.

K: And in order to show your love for this United States of America when she was about to call upon you to become a soldier, you ran away to Mexico? (TR, p. 1867)

The defense made no objections during this sequence of questions even though the questioning called for immaterial, argumentative, and self-incriminating responses. The explanation seems to be that the defense inquired about Sacco's trip to Mexico to avoid the draft during direct examination and this inquiry opened up a line of questioning for the prosecution. From the perspective of a naive reader of the trial record, this defense strategy seems to have been an extremely poor choice. However, defense attorneys may have calculated this move in order to entice Katzmann to change the direction of the trial. It is conceivable that the defense wanted Sacco to identify his political allegiances or that Sacco asked his attorneys to allow him to explain his beliefs. Interviews that Sacco gave and letters he wrote while awaiting execution affirm the authenticity of the views he expressed during cross-examination. From the point of view of gaming strategy, Sacco's intentional self-incrimination may well have been part of defense's strategic game plan to entice Katzmann to make legally risky moves that would overturn the verdict on appeal. Or the defense may have wanted Sacco to present the position so Moore could rally additional support from the labor movement.

Although the goals are not clear, one outcome is obvious. Katzmann stressed that Sacco was disloyal to the United States, evaded military service, and maligned American education. Early in the cross-examination, Sacco asserted that poor children could not receive the same educational advantages as children from wealthy families. The prosecutor emphasized this admission, although it had nothing to do with the criminal indictment.

K: Do you remember speaking of Harvard University?

S: Yes, sir.

K: Do you remember saying that you could not get an education there unless you had money? I do not mean you used those exact words. I do not contend you did, but, in substance, didn't you say that?

S: They have to use money in the rule of the Government.

K: No. You don't understand. . . . Did you say in substance you could not send your boy to Harvard?

S: Yes.

K: Unless you had money. Did you say that?

S: Of course.

K: Do you think that is true?

S: I think it is.

K: Don't you know Harvard University educates more boys of poor people [for] free than any other university in the United States of America? (TR, p. 1789)

The defense repeatedly objected to this line of questioning, but to no avail. Judge Thayer allowed the questions without explaining the reasons for doing so, saying "the question may stand and the answer as well." Even if the defense had managed to entice Katzmann to make this political move, Judge Thayer seemed to be unaware of the defense's strategy and supportive of Katzmann's moves.

Katzmann's diversions continued in questions about the type of literature the defendant read and possessed at the time of his arrest on May 5, 1920.

K: What papers did you read?

S: I read *Boston American* every night.

K: What other papers?

S: Some papers from Italy, too. Some other Socialist papers from Italy.

K: Some other Socialist papers from Italy?

S: Yes.

K: Were all those papers except the *Boston Globe* and the *Boston American*, copies of them, in your house?

S: No. . . . They all used to destroy when I finished reading. . . .

K: What papers did you have on May 5th in your house?

S: You mean books? . . . Just the papers?

K: I mean papers, newspapers, or periodicals?

S: I got some [of] every kind [of] literature.

K: All these kinds you have mentioned, *Le Mortello*?

S: Yes.

K: *Cronaco Soverseva*?

S: Yes.

K: The papers from Italy?

S: Yes.

K: Were they Socialist papers?

S: Yes, sir.

K: [Were] [t]hey Anarchistic papers? (TR, p. 1883)

The defense eventually objected to this line of questioning, but Judge Thayer permitted the questions and responses.

The prosecution's line of questioning continued, showing that Sacco associated with known anarchists and supported their views. Katzmann seemed eager to establish that Sacco was guilty of murder because he associated with political dissidents.

K: Did you know Fruzetti of Bridgewater, who was deported, you did?

S: Yes.

K: Did you know him personally?

S: Yes, sir.

K: Been to his house?

S: I met him lots of times.

K: In Boston?

S: In conferences.

K: Talked with him about anarchy, haven't you?

S: Certainly.

K: Did you know his views on anarchy? (TR, p. 1885)

Subsequent questions by Katzmann also connected Sacco with other known anarchists, such as Orcciani, Boda, Salsedo, and Elia. The prosecutor considered all of these men to be dangerous radicals, which proved Sacco was guilty of criticizing the U.S. government. Thayer allowed this line of questioning on the grounds that it pertained to the credibility of the witness.

The issue diversions altered the prosecution's story of the case by showing that one of the leading characters, Sacco, was unpatriotic and disloyal for having supported the doctrine of anarchy, which promoted the overthrow of the government of the United States. By diverting the issues from facts related to the charge of murder to the defendant's political beliefs and associations, Katzmann implied that Sacco was also a murderer. Under the rules for the game of cross-examination, attorneys' logical reasoning should be overruled by the judge when it is fallacious and irrelevant. But Judge Thayer signified through his failure to sustain defense objections that he approved Katzmann's flawed logic and supported his manipulation of rules.

Procedural Diversions

In addition to the shift from legal to ideological issues, Katzmann created procedural and logical diversions that shifted the burden of proof from the prosecution to the defense and asked the defendant to implicate himself in political guilt rather than permitting him to give reasons why he was innocent. Shifting the burden of proof means the defendants are expected to prove their innocence rather than the prosecution proving guilt. An example of shifting the burden of proof occurred when Katzmann asked Sacco about a cap found near the scene (Ehrmann, 1969). Prosecutors introduced a different cap into evidence, one that was found a couple of days after the crime a distance from the crime scene, and implied that the cap was the same as the one found near the crime scene. Hundreds of Boston laborers wore caps like the one found near the crime scene. Katzmann tried to deceive jurors by trying to get Sacco to say this was his cap.

> K: Mr. Sacco, do you know anything about that cap?
>
> S: That is my cap.
>
> K: When did you buy that?
>
> S: Last March?
>
> K: In 1920? (TR, pp. 1851–1852)

Afterward, Katzmann asked Sacco to model the cap for the jury and to state again that this was his cap. As the jury observed this activity, they assumed that he was modeling the cap found at the crime scene instead of one found at his home. In a gaming analogue, this diversion qualifies as a deceptive move, a trick used by the prosecutor to mislead jurors by making a cap seem like substantial evidence against the defendant when it didn't qualify as legitimate evidence at all. This logical trick shifts the burden of proof from the prosecution to the defense to prove this was not the cap found at the crime scene. The reader must wonder why an experienced prosecutor could get by with what seems to be blatant unethical conduct and clear violations of the rules of evidence. After the trial, various people stated that the cap presented at trial was not the one at the crime scene. The defense may have permitted this deceptive move so that it later could be used as one of the many examples of prosecutorial misconduct and legal violations that would be cited in the Sacco and Vanzetti appeal.

In addition to shifting the burden of proof, the prosecutor altered the normative roles of the trial participants. One shift of roles happened when Judge Thayer began interrogating defense attorney Jeremiah McAnarney after his objection to the ideological focus of the prosecutor's questions. Thayer interrogated McAnarney as if he were a trial witness.

> M: That claim is not presented in anything tantamount to the language just used by the Court, and in view of the record as it stands at this time I object to this line of inquiry.

> T: Is that not your claim, that the defendant, as a reason that he has given for going to the Johnson house, that they wanted the automobile to prevent people from being deported and to get this literature out of the way? Does he not claim that was done in the interest of the United States, to prevent violations of the law by the distribution of this literature? I understand that was the—

> M: Are you asking that as a question to me?

> T: Yes. . . .

> M: I am going to make whatever claim that is legitimate.

> T: I want to know what . . . you are going to claim in the argument—

> M: I am going to claim this man and Vanzetti were of that class called Socialists. I am going to claim that a riot was running a year ago last April that men were being deported, that twelve to fifteen hundred were seized in Massachusetts.

> T: Do you mean you are going to offer evidence of that?

> M: We have witnesses which we may introduce here. I do not know whether we will introduce them or not.

> T: Are you going to claim that what the defendant did was in the interest of the United States?

> M: Your Honor please, I now object to your Honor's statement as prejudicial to the rights of the defendants and ask that this statement be withdrawn from the jury.

> T: There is not a prejudicial remark made that I know of and none were intended. I simply asked you, sir, whether you propose to offer evidence as to what you said. (TR, 1873–1874)

From a gaming perspective, it appears that Thayer was trying to impeach McAnarney by claiming he supported activities of socialists. This was quite an extraordinary move on the part of Thayer, who inappropriately abridged his role as listener and courtroom umpire and adopted the role of prosecutor. McAnarney called his bluff and said in the presence of the jury that the judge's statements were prejudicial.

Another procedural shift occurred when Katzmann allowed the defendant Sacco to address the jury directly about his political views. The response by Sacco followed an open-ended question by Katzmann, an inquiry typically used during direct examination but not during cross-examination: "What did you mean yesterday when you said you loved a free country?" (TR, pp. 1875–1877). In his long narrative response, Sacco stated his political beliefs and simultaneously affirmed his immigrant status. He also showed jurors that he had a poor command of the English language.

> I was a Republican, so I always thinking [that a] Republican has more chance to manage education, develop, to build some day his family, to raise the child and education, if you could. But that was my opinion; so when I came to this country I saw there was not what I was thinking before, but there was all the difference, because I been working in Italy not so hard as I been work[ing] in this country. I could live free there just as well, work in the same condition, but not so hard, about seven or eight hours a day, better food. I mean genuine. Of course, over there is good food, because it a bigger country. When I been started work here very hard and been work thirteen years, hard worker, I could not been afford[ing] much a family the way [I] did have the idea before I could not put any money in the bank. I could no push my boy some to go to school and other things. I teach over here men who is with me. The free ideas gives any man a chance to profess his own idea, not the supreme idea, not give any person, not to be like Spain in position, yes, about twenty centuries ago, but to give a chance to print and education, literature, free speech, that I see it was all wrong. I could see the best men, intelligent, education, they been arrested and sent to prison and lied in prison for years and years without getting them out, and Debs, one of the great men in this country, he is in prison, still away in prison, because he is a Socialist. (TR, p. 1876)

This long response added a great deal of information about Sacco's attitudes toward immigrants and politics, but the information lacked relevance to the indictment of murder and burglary. None of the defense attorneys objected to the response. Instead, they allowed Sacco to express his political views and speak for many similarly situated immigrants. The defense's silence likely was intentional because Sacco's testimony would persuade other immigrants that the U.S. legal system did not treat people equally and that the government was making an example of Sacco in order to justify more arrests and deportations of immigrants.

Katzmann continued his unconventional approach to cross-examination. The prosecutor deviated from controlling the witness by allowing him to tell his own story in his own prosaic language in an uninterrupted manner. In his summation, Katzmann attacked Sacco vehemently for the statements the defendant had made under cross-examination.

These shifts of procedure changed the roles normally adopted by the trial judge, the cross-examiner, and the witness and resulted in Sacco incriminating himself. Katzmann did not seem to recognize that his moves—using open-ended questions and permitting Sacco to vent his beliefs—may have helped the defense achieve different payoffs than winning the verdict. The prosecutor's moves may have seemed to be a legitimate tactic to jurors who thought the defendants were guilty and agreed that the defendants' political orientation provided a motive for them to convict the men.

This trial was not a zero-sum game in which one side wins all, and the other side wins nothing (Rapoport, 1970). On the contrary, the cross-examination created a game of both strategy and chance in which opposing attorneys achieved some desirable payoffs and gave up others. One payoff for the defense was that Sacco's trial became a platform for expressing the grievances of many immigrant laborers against the United States. Another payoff was that the defendants became martyrs for the international labor movement. And still another payoff might have been that Sacco's testimony exposed the underlying motives of the government and the flaws of its legal system that permitted a biased judge and a zealous prosecutor to circumvent the rules of the legal system for political gain.

Outwitting the Opposition with Semantic Diversions

The trial also included semantic diversions; that is, cross-examiners calculated choices of language that construed the meaning of their questions. Katzmann's cross-examination, for example, diverted meaning through misleading analogies and strategic repetitions.

A misleading analogy occurs when the likenesses are inferred from a common word, rather than similar relationships (Jensen, 1981). In the following excerpt, Katzmann compared "love" of country with "love" of a spouse.

> K: What is your idea of showing your love for this country?
>
> S: (no response)
>
> K: Is that your idea of showing your love for America?
>
> S: Yes.
>
> K: And would it be your idea of showing love for your wife that when she needed you, you ran away from her?
>
> S: I did not run away from her. (TR, p. 1868)

This kind of semantic diversion is also a type of trick, a deceptive move intended to mislead the jurors about what the witness is saying.

Katzmann also used the semantic diversion of repeating emotional words. Given the context in which the crime appeared, words such as "radical," "draft evader," "socialist," and "anarchist" had strong negative connotations for the public at large and presumably for the jurors. In Burke's (1970) theory, all of these terms qualify as "devil terms," that is, terms of repulsion that designate enemies and evils in a culture. The procedural diversions led others to charge that Katzmann was vicious in his cross-examination. By allowing such diversions, Thayer permitted the prosecutor to use prejudicial language to present the evidence. Additionally, defense attorneys showed negligence in failing to object to these prejudicial questions and responses.

The prosecutor's unconventional gaming moves emphasized Sacco's ideology, impeached his credibility, and changed the issues on which the jurors were expected to decide the verdict. Thayer enabled Katzmann to carry through with these procedural diversions. The judge's sympathy with the prosecution's approach seemed to be fed by his hostility toward the immigrant anarchists. This ideological standpoint caused him to disregard the procedural rules and fail to carry out his assigned role as an unbiased courtroom umpire. Most likely, Thayer was so committed to the government's mission of ridding the country of radicals who threatened the American political system that he justified his own behavior during the trial. He viewed Sacco as a threat to the community and wanted to put him out of circulation and knew he had the power to do so. It is conceivable that Thayer was naive about the strategic and tactical moves the attorneys made at trial and unaware of the political payoffs that the defense sought and received.

Lessons

An analysis of the cross-examination conducted by the prosecution and defense in the Sacco-Vanzetti trial explains how the attorneys' interdependent strategic and tactical moves created different payoffs from the trial. Some of the attorneys' moves fell well within the range of procedural rules and codes of conduct of the era. Other moves resembled tricks that attempted to deceive witnesses and mislead jurors. Still others showed reasoned choices that counteracted the opposition's moves and achieved desirable outcomes for themselves and their clients.

This chapter argues that cross-examination resembles games. It suggests that the defense (especially Sacco's attorneys) recognized that the political climate and the prejudices of the citizen jurors would make a conviction probable even before the case went to trial. After conducting a rigorous cross-examination of many of the prosecution's witnesses, the defense allowed Katzmann to conduct an unconventional cross-examination of Sacco in which the defendant incriminated himself as a disloyal American and an avowed anarchist. Several features of the gaming analogue—reasoned choices, strategic and tactical moves, payoffs, outcomes—make sense of the cross-examination practices in the Sacco-Vanzetti trial and explain the moves and countermoves that took place in this part of the trial.

The climate of opinion in which the case was tried, the values of the jurors, the skill of the attorneys, and testimony presented during direct examination influenced the direction and content of the cross-examination. These conditions contributed to the verdict against Sacco and Vanzetti. Considering the trial as a whole, the transcript offers numerous examples of skillful interrogation from attorneys on both sides of the case. This skillful cross-examination contained moves similar to those used in complicated games of strategy and chance. Attorneys made reasonable moves that adapted to the constraints of the legal and political situation. Sometimes the outcomes the defense seeks in a trial come long after the verdict.

In 1977, 50 years after the execution of the defendants, the then Massachusetts governor issued a proclamation declaring the defendants had not received a fair trial and that the prosecutors and Judge Thayer abused their power during the trial. In 1997, Boston Mayor Thomas Menino dedicated a memorial featuring the faces of Sacco and Vanzetti facing a tilted depiction of the scales of justice, a public acknowledgment that Sacco and Vanzetti did not receive a fair trial (Topp, 2005).

8

Media Stories, Trial Narratives, and Summations in the Simpson Trial

The crime resembled a number of others just like it: a woman is murdered at her home and police arrest the ex-husband for the crime. The fact that a celebrity was arrested for the murder made this crime extraordinary. At approximately 10:15 PM on June 12, 1994, a vicious killer slashed the throat of Nicole Brown Simpson and stabbed Ronald Goldman. In the early hours of the next morning police found the victims. Two days after the bodies were found, and after televised, live coverage of the high-speed chase of Brown Simpson's former husband, sports celebrity O. J. Simpson, on a California freeway, he was arrested for both murders.

The O. J. Simpson trial provides a compelling example of the impact of media narratives on the trial. The crime itself, the pretrial coverage, the televised trial, and the posttrial events, including a civil trial, produced extensive media narratives about the case. The prominence and excess of the media stories often relegated the trial itself to the background. During summations, the media narratives and the trial narratives converged.

The trial cost Los Angeles County an estimated $9 million and Simpson $10 million. The judge sequestered the jury of 12 regulars and 12 alternates for 266 days. The prosecution examined their witnesses for 99 days and the defense for 34 days (Schuetz & Lilley, 1999). It is not a surprise that the Simpson trial surpassed the Hauptmann trial in the amount and excess of coverage. A reported 150 million viewers tuned in to see the Simpson verdict on television. What the viewers did not see during the trial was the contentious wrangling between the attorneys, the charges and countercharges of unethical conduct, and the conversations during jury deliberation that led to a quick verdict.

My analysis takes seriously what distinguished French philosopher Jean Paul Sartre said about understanding stories: "Narrative, as opposed to living, really starts with the end of the story. The narrative," he said, "is there from the beginning, but we can only make sense of what the story means from its outcome" (cited in Brooks, 1996, p. 19). This chapter tries to make sense of the attorneys' summation narratives in relation to the media stories and the trial outcome. This analysis (1) begins with a scenario of the case, (2) describes the media narratives related to the trial, (3) explains general features of trial narratives, (4) identifies the rules of summations, (4) presents a summary of the summations, (5) analyzes how these summations affected jurors and trial spectators, and (6) notes lessons to be learned from the study of this trial.

CASE SCENARIO

Two days after police found the bodies, they took into custody Brown Simpson's former husband, sports celebrity O. J. Simpson. The trial started on January 28, 1995, and the jurors gave their verdict on October 2, 1995. The summations began on September 22 and ended with rebuttal arguments on September 29. The jury deliberated less than four hours before they announced the verdict of "not guilty." African American women and men screamed for joy, while white Americans called the verdict "an outrage" ("The Simpson Legacy," 1995).

In the Simpson trial, the prosecution had the burden to prove that a murder occurred, the killing was unlawful, and the killing was done in a "will-ful, deliberate, and premeditated" manner (*California Penal Code*, 1994). Because of the extensive pretrial publicity and the television coverage inside the courtroom, Judge Lance Ito sequestered the jurors during the entire trial. Prior to deliberation, the stress of sequestration and the opportunity to leak information to the press resulted in the judge replacing some of the original jurors with alternates. The chief prosecutors for the state were Marcia Clark, Christopher Darden, William Hodgman, Cheri A. Lewis, Hank M. Goldberg, and Brian R. Kelberg. Clark and Darden presented the summations for the prosecution. The chief attorneys for the defense were Johnnie Cochran, Robert Shapiro, F. Lee Bailey, Gerald Uelman, Alan Dershowitz, Peter Neufeld, Barry Scheck, Carl Douglas, Robert Blaiser, and Sara Caplan. Cochran and Scheck presented defense's summation. The prosecution called 72 witnesses, and the defense called 54.

The ethnic background of jurors in the criminal case included nine African Americans, two Anglos, and one Hispanic. Even prior to the start of the trial, the large number of African American jurors, according to media accounts, was an advantage for the defense. In their summations, African Americans Darden and Cochran directly addressed the jurors by quoting African American leaders, such as Frederick Douglas and Martin Luther King Jr., and by recognizing the problems of racism in the Los Angeles police department. Not long after the jury decided the defendant was not guilty, Simpson held a party at his home for the jurors.

MEDIA NARRATIVES

Media coverage was extensive before, during, and after the trial because the audience showed an insatiable appetite for information about the case. The media allotted major resources to cover the trial, including 120 video feeds, eight miles of cable, 19 television stations, eight radio stations, 23 newspapers and magazines, 850 telephones, and 2,000 reporters (Darden, 1996). Millions of viewers watched CNN's and Court TV's year-long live coverage. After the trial, Simpson defense attorney and law professor Gerald Uelman (1996) said that adding television cameras in the Simpson murder trial was "like throwing gasoline on a fire." It transformed the proceedings "into a sort of hype heaven" (p. 94). Media narratives dominated television news and also infiltrated public conversation. These stories hyped the trial drama by portraying the characters as either especially good or evil, speculated about motives and the plot of the crime, and created personal and social themes in order to attract the interest and sustain the attention of media spectators. Media narratives of popular trials have common traits with the Simpson case (Surrette, 1992), but no trial has matched the media coverage and public attention given to the Simpson murder trial. The traits of media narratives differ from those of trial narratives.

MEDIA NARRATIVES

- Take the form of info-tainment
- Stereotype trial participants into good and bad characters
- Emphasize sex, drugs, love, lust, lies, fame, wealth, beauty, and obsession
- Stress conflict and personalities
- Tell one-sided stories
- Use unnamed sources as evidence
- Produce profit from their coverage of crime
- Conceal trial rules and procedures
- Ignore the central role of reasoning and evidence in the trial

Much of the media coverage of the Simpson trial fit with the traits described here. Because the coverage dragged on for months on end, journalists faced the formidable task of attracting and sustaining the attention of public audiences using hundreds of metanarratives—stories that interpret, challenge, and elaborate the meaning of the dominant media narrative. Entertainment and informational narratives deserve further explanation.

The most prominent media narrative was the entertainment story. Entertainment themes, according to Surrette (1992), concentrate on (1) abuses of power by the defendant, attorneys, and judge; (2) exposure of the foibles of the sinful rich; and the (3) presence of evil strangers. The trial spectators seeking entertainment want information about the rich and famous and enjoy hearing about what they believe was their immoral or unethical behavior. Spectators gain satisfaction from learning about the foibles of the rich, such as their infidelity, drug use, social conflicts, bad relationships, greed, and deception. These audiences also enjoy stories about the flawed conduct of public officials, attorneys, judges, and police. Through the early months of the Simpson case, the media stressed these entertainment themes: Simpson's money, lifestyle, and celebrity status; Simpson and Brown Simpson's kinky sex life, their drug use, and their extramarital sexual relationships; and the possibility that an evil stranger or a drug cartel member committed the murders. In an article for *Vanity Fair*, author Dominick Dunne (1995) characterized the trial as being

> like a great trash novel come to life, mammoth fireworks displays of interracial marriage, love, lust, lies, hate, fame, wealth, beauty, obsession, spousal abuse, stalking, brokenhearted children, the bloody knife slashing homicides, and all the money that justice can buy. It had the ingredients of a real live cross channel soap opera.

Two network news anchors at the time, Dan Rather and Peter Jennings, expressed dismay about the entertainment themes, claiming they showed the media had engaged in "wretched access" (Dunne, 1995, p. 48).

Not all of the stories were about Simpson. Some talked about prosecutor Marcia Clark's neglect of her children and the recent problems in her marriage. Some blamed Nicole Brown Simpson for her own death, saying she used drugs and had sexual relationships with dangerous men. These entertainment themes appealed to a voyeuristic audience who thought they were getting a rare glimpse into the backstage world of people with money, fame, and power. Voyeuristic audiences thrive on tabloid journalism and seldom question the claims or the evidence of the entertainment themes (Furno-Lamude, 1999).

Televising trials heightens other dramatic elements by attributing heroic or demonic qualities to the trial participants. This dramatic veneer stresses personal conflicts and hides the legal procedures and trial arguments, emphasizes dramatic actions and emotions, concentrates on contentious interactions among trial participants, and portrays people and events in exaggerated ways. As the media coverage developed, the trial began to resemble a made-for-television movie more than it did a typical state murder trial. Defendant O. J. Simpson was a legendary football player and a popular spokesperson for Hertz Rent A Car. Cochran noted in his summation that Simpson "was the best"; he won the Heismann trophy which is "emblematic of the best football player in America" (TR, 1995). The media made clear from the beginning that the defendant was an African American millionaire sports celebrity living in an affluent white neighborhood, married to a white woman, and associating with the rich and famous.

Media narratives measure trial success according to the eccentricities of trial performers. Some of the attorneys' and witnesses' performances resembled celebrity appearances on television talk shows because the attorneys talked about their other starring roles in other prominent trials. Nine active defense lawyers who had achieved their reputations by representing celebrities constituted the defense "dream team." In media stories, the prosecutors were hardworking, but were neither as famous nor as competent as the "dream team." Although prosecutors tried their best to win a guilty verdict, they suffered from personal conflicts and witnesses' actions that were out of their control. In fact, prosecutor Marcia Clark had a major personal distraction because she was fighting her ex-husband for custody of their children and he claimed that the trial had prohibited her from spending enough time with them. Judge Ito, the spectacle ringmaster in the trial, was satirized on weekly broadcasts of NBC television's *Saturday Night Live* and in newspaper comic strips for failing to keep the media circus under control.

The performances of trial participants became so important that some jurors became offended. For example, juror Willie Cravin recalled:

> They were playing to the media. They were playing to the public, and caused a lot of delays as far as the trial was concerned. I can recall beepers, cellular phones going off in the audience. People were laughing. It was like a show for a while there. The judge would make comments, and the audience would laugh. Some of the attorneys would make comments, and the audience would laugh. (Cooley, Bess, & Rubin-Jackson, 1995, p. 205)

The incessant objections of opposing attorneys made during their adversaries' summations added to the media conflict and distracted attention from legal issues and evidence. After the trial, attorneys discussed their performances in extensive detail (Clark 1997; Cochran, 1996; Darden, 1996; Dershowitz, 1996; Goldberg, 1996; Shapiro, 1996; Uelman, 1996).

Some trial participants gave especially flawed legal and media performances. For example, Detective Mark Fuhrman was a cheat and a liar, a despicable racist cop, who found and, according to the defense, planted a bloody glove at the murder scene. The bumbling criminalists, Dennis Fung and Andrea Mazzola, tainted the crime scene and ruined the opportunity for prosecutors to adequately perform their legal roles. The flawed performances of the prosecution's witnesses loomed large in the defense's summation narratives and created reasonable doubt for jurors. The focus often deviated from the facts, such as when, in his summation, Cochran compared Fuhrman to Adolph Hitler. This comparison stirred intense feelings and ignited a firestorm of complaints from the Jewish family members of Ron Goldman and from some of the other defense attorneys.

At times the media coverage featured information rather than entertainment themes. According to some producers, televising the Simpson trial live for months helped inform the public. First, the coverage affirmed the "public's right to know" about celebrities and crime, allowed citizens to monitor the criminal justice process, and permitted the public to vicariously participate in the trial and talk about the social issues it raised. Steve Brill, a pioneer in Court TV, explained that cameras in the courtroom educate the public about the justice system and increase public support for the courts. A position paper from Court TV emphasized:

> Television coverage of trials tells the whole, real, true story about a complicated, often misunderstood and underreported subject. It allows the participants in a democracy to judge for themselves how well the government institution that makes the most fundamental decision that any government makes—liberty or prison—is working. (quoted in Caplan, 1996, p. 203)

Court TV broadcast the trial proceedings live every day for eight months, and cable channels CNBC and CNN, as well as the major networks, devoted hundreds of hours of coverage to the trial. The result was that almost no person who watched television during 1995 could ignore the trial.

Legal themes nearly always took a secondary role in the media narratives, but the legal content had the potential to improve audiences' understanding of legal practices and processes. The media inserted legal content into the coverage during the down time created when attorneys engaged in endless conversations, unheard by the jury, about motions to quash evidence and to reprimand opposing attorneys for their unprofessional conduct. Media discussions of the law functioned like metanarratives, footnotes of sorts that interpreted and elaborated some aspect of the trial story. Various media outlets invited members of the legal profession to explain why the trial had deteriorated into an entertainment forum, with potential witnesses appearing on tabloid talk shows and forfeiting their opportunity to testify at trial; why attorneys and the judge gave news conferences; and why the victims' family members consented to media interviews.

The stories from legal professionals often acted as a corrective to the dramatic excesses of entertainment narratives. Some legal commentators stressed the professional code of conduct for attorneys, explained what the objections made during the trial had to do with the rules of evidence, and explored conventional argumentation strategies used in the trial discourse, such as what an attorney should and should not say about the evidence in opening statements or what impeaching a witness means. The media attempted to dignify this kind of coverage by certifying the credentials of legal commentators as reputable law professors or experienced attorneys with professional expertise about legal principles, procedures, and protocols. The interviews with legal authorities had the potential to improve the legal understanding of trial spectators interested in legal practices. For example, they could learn about why jurors were sequestered in hotels for months, find out why some jurors had been dismissed, figure out why certain kinds of evidence presented in the media were not admissible in the proceedings, ascertain the purpose of motions, evaluate the strengths and limitations of technical evidence, and decipher the norms for crime scene investigations.

As the trial continued, the metanarratives from legal commentators became redundant. In order to avoid losing viewers, producers decided to spice up these commentaries by featuring fights among legal experts over trial issues. Legal analysts Greta Van Susteren and Roger Cossack started an evening program on CNN called *Burden of Proof,* and other cable networks created similar programs that featured attorneys and law professors haggling over the legal and communication issues that were surfacing in the murder trial. Long after the trial ended, this kind of programming remained as a familiar television news genre. CNN, MSNBC, and Fox offer specific programs on legal topics and events, anchored by individuals who all got their start as television personalities when they reported on the O. J. Simpson trial.

During the trial, legal narrators risked harming the credibility of their profession by ranting and raving about the missteps and bad moves of the prosecutors, Simpson's attorneys, and Judge Ito. Some spectators faulted the legal professionals for appearing on television at all, and others blamed them for expressing subjective viewpoints. Nonetheless, legal narrators carved out a specialized and information-oriented niche that appealed to an audience interested in legal content and that enabled trial spectators to learn something about the intricacies of the California criminal courts, the complexity of trial practices and procedures, and the importance of the communication that occurs inside and outside of the courtroom.

TRIAL NARRATIVES

Trial narratives lack the evocative power of the media stories. Anyone who has attended a real trial recognizes that the proceedings frequently are tedious, redundant, and difficult to follow, and the documents and transcripts of the proceeding are just as difficult to read and understand. The thousands of state criminal trials that take place every year have some similarity to the trial narratives from the O. J. Simpson case because attorneys are often inarticulate and ill prepared, judges tune out, and motions and objections interrupt the trial so frequently that audiences forget the importance of witnesses' testimony. The following are elements common to all trial narratives:

TRAITS OF TRIAL NARRATIVES

- Argument resides within trial narratives.
- Jurors are supposed to base their deliberations on trial narratives.
- Theories of the case are transmitted in the trial narratives.
- Trial stories evolve and change as the trial unfolds.
- Trial narratives are questioned by counternarratives and refutations from opposing attorneys.
- Trial narratives are subject to the constraints of legal principles, procedures, and protocols.
- Trial narratives are constructed from fragments of witnesses' testimony.

- Trial stories help to establish the prosecution's burden of proof and defense's reasonable doubt.
- Trial stories connect the facts and evidence with the indictments.

The actual Simpson trial proceedings generated far less interest for trial spectators than media stories did. Public spectators gave most of their attention to commentaries on the Internet, television highlights on the nightly news, the tabloid newspapers' emphasis on personalities, and the symbolic implications of visual depictions on the front pages of newspapers and magazines (Furno-Lamude, 1999). Although court reporters made it possible for Internet users to read the transcripts as the trial developed, the public paid more attention to what the media said about the transcripts rather than to the trial record itself. The public showed interest in the media highlights of the trial that emphasized interpersonal and adversarial conflicts and the opening statements and summations. They also focused their attention on the testimony of weak prosecution witnesses, including detective Fuhrman and criminalists Fung and Mazzola, because these parts of the trial fit with their voyeuristic interests of seeing and hearing about the flawed conduct of public officials.

Both jurors and public audiences pay attention to the narratives in trial speeches with a set "stock of stories in their minds," and then they decide whether the trial narratives ring true with the stock stories they know and understand (Gewirtz, 1996, p. 8). These stock stories contain the social knowledge of the audiences and serve as their interpretive frame of reference. Attorneys recognized that they could use racial issues to identify with the experiences and beliefs of the predominantly African American jury and to identify with spectators who had experienced racial profiling and police malfeasance. According to the accounts of trial jurors, the issue of racial injustice was the main reason for their doubt in the prosecution's case (Cooley, Bess, & Rubin-Jackson, 1995). During summations, African American attorneys Darden and Cochran enunciated racial themes, explained how these themes entered into their stories of the case, and repudiated the testimony of Mark Fuhrman.

Trial narratives differ from media narratives in several ways. In contrast to trial narratives, media stories are not constrained or limited by legal principles, procedures, or protocols. Audience interests and television ratings and newspaper sales influence the content of media narratives, whereas legal goals, rules, and evidence determine the content of trial narratives. The majority of media narratives are one-sided dramatic portrayals that include extensive character evidence and little technical evidence. In the trial speeches in the Simpson murder case, the prosecutors concentrated their narratives on real and technical evidence from the crime scene, but they said very little about the character of the victims. The defense narratives emphasized the good character of the defendant and the bad character of the crime scene investigators in their attempt to refute the prosecution's evidence.

During opening statements the prosecution told a quite common crime story by claiming that Simpson's murder of his wife was predictable given the long history of domestic abuse she had suffered at his hands. Prosecutor Clark's opening statement concentrated on the time line of the crime, pointed to the opportunity that Simpson had to commit the murder, and foreshadowed the testimony of witnesses with information about the crime scene and the stormy relationship between Simpson and his ex-wife. Prosecutor Darden claimed that the murder was the culmination of a long history of abuse between the defendant and his ex-wife, and he tried to deconstruct O. J. Simpson's celebrity status by claiming that his public persona differed from his private behavior. He noted the defendant "controlled, was controlling, wanted to be in control," and he had such a strong need for control that he abused his wife and eventually killed her. Goldman died because he happened onto the scene while Simpson was killing his ex-wife. The prosecutors' opening statements included a large number of facts and evidence embedded in their story of domestic abuse (TR, 1995, January 24). Although the opening statements paid little attention to the victims, this initial trial speech constructed a theme, provided a motive for the crime, and established a time line showing the defendant had the opportunity to murder his ex-wife (Lilley, 1999).

Cochran's opening statement emphasized that the prosecution had rushed to judgment by stating that Simpson was guilty and had also contrived evidence to prove this claim. He noted further that the prosecution's evidence was contaminated, compromised, and corrupted. Cochran characterized the prosecution's case in this way: "You put in garbage and you get garbage out." Besides condemning the crime scene investigators, Cochran described Simpson in glowing terms: he acted "within a circle of benevolence, he shared his wealth, he loved his family, and he was a great athlete" (TR, 1995, January 30). Cochran's style was compelling, but he presented a familiar defense story by claiming that the prosecution's evidence was mishandled and that the defendant was a person of character who would not commit this kind of crime.

The seemingly endless and detailed technical testimony of the prosecution's DNA evidence gave the defense an evidential basis for reasonable doubt and challenged the media to create a useful informational metanarrative. Several criminalists and DNA experts testified that Simpson's blood and hair were found at the crime scene, in his white Bronco, on his clothing, and at his home. Although this evidence bolstered the prosecutors' case, the media interest waned during this time. The DNA evidence provided a scientific resolution to the murder story, but this kind of technical evidence appealed to a narrow, scientifically informed audience rather than to voyeuristic audiences interested in entertainment themes. The technical evidence helped prosecutors establish their burden of proving Simpson's guilt, but most jurors failed to acknowledge the importance of the trial evidence. Some television spectators, however, learned a great deal about DNA and the imprint this type of evidence leaves at the crime scene, because legal commentators explained in media narratives how the technical evidence was gathered and why DNA was compelling evidence of guilt.

In the trial, the prosecution depended too much on the technical evidence; they implied that science does not lie and therefore Simpson must be guilty. A communication problem that any public speaking teacher would recognize plagued prosecutors. The problem was that presenting hours and hours of tedious numerical graphs and complicated DNA models indicating statistical probability likely put the jurors and public audiences to sleep rather than sustained their interest. Media storytellers did a better job than the attorneys and witnesses did in explaining the DNA testimony. In fact, many media narratives resembled a documentary for the Discovery Channel that translated and visualized technical evidence and interpreted the DNA models in ways that informed public spectators about the features and importance of DNA evidence. Unfortunately prosecutors did not interpret DNA in ways that appealed either to jurors or to television viewers. Ironically, the prosecution's communication mistakes and the informative media stories regarding DNA taught prosecutors in subsequent criminal cases how to present this evidence so that it persuaded jurors of the guilt of other defendants.

Another legacy of the DNA evidence was that the defense exposed flaws in gathering evidence that should be avoided by students and teachers conducting scientific research. Audiences who paid attention to Scheck's cross-examination of technical experts and his summation learned that the results of data analysis produce probabilities, not truths, and that the validity of the evidence depends on the way it is collected and processed. The defense's cross-examination of crime scene investigators emphasized their sloppy evidence gathering processes and inferred that these flawed methods created cross-contamination. The murder scene investigators in this case lacked the sophistication of those we now see on television programs, but resembled many other real crime scene investigators whose practices and procedures are often botched or flawed. From the defense's refutation of technical evidence, media audiences learned about the value of DNA evidence as well as the strategies that should be used in the cross-examination of technical experts. The prosecutors' inability to communicate the importance of the DNA evidence limited how Clark could use this evidence in summations, and Scheck's poignant cross-examinations of technical experts aided the persuasiveness of his summation.

Darden and Cochran used testimony about Fuhrman and his racism as the basis for racial themes in their summations. After the trial, defense attorney Gerald Uelman wrote, "The lesson of the Fuhrman tapes will resound in American courtrooms, perhaps even longer than the Rodney King tapes. The lesson is that racism is alive and well, and it affects the way citizens are treated by police officers" (Uelman, 1996, p. 154).

The following excerpt from defense attorney Bailey's cross-examination of Mark Fuhrman shows how the issue of racism emerged during Fuhrman's testimony:

B: Do you use the word "n. . . . ." in describing people?

F: No, sir.

B: Have you ever used that word in the past ten years?

F: Not that I recall, no.

B: You mean if you called someone a "n. . . . ." you have forgotten it?

F: I'm not sure I can answer the question the way you phrased it? . . .

B: I will rephrase it. I want you to assume that perhaps at some time since 1985 or 1986, you addressed a member of the African-American race as a "n . . . . ."

F: No, it is not possible. . . .

B: And you say under oath that you have not addressed any black person as a "n . . . . ." or spoken about black people as "n. . . . ." in the past ten years, Detective Fuhrman?

F: That's what I am saying, sir. (TR, 1995, March 15)

Although Bailey did not succeed in forcing Fuhrman to admit his racism during this initial cross-examination, he emphasized the racial theme and case theory that police prejudices influence how they perceive suspects and investigate crimes. It was not until September that several defense witnesses testified Fuhrman had lied in March about his use of racial epithets. In fact, when Cochran asked one defense witness if she had ever heard Fuhrman use the n-word, Laura McKinny replied that she recorded conversations in which Fuhrman used the n-word 42 times (TR, 1995, September 5). On that same day, Bailey examined defense witness Valerie Singer; she recalled that Fuhrman had once said to her that "the only good nigger is a dead nigger" (TR, 1995, September 5). Judge Ito permitted the court to hear some of the taped conversations between McKinny and Fuhrman in which he used the n-word.

This testimony electrified the racial theme in the trial proceedings and generated numerous media stories about police racism in particular and social racism in general (e.g., Race in America, 1995). The defense narrative about police racism dominated the next three weeks of the trial. For black audiences, race had existed all along as a kind of hypertext (a link for making cross-references that connect the unseen subtexts of the crime story to the media entertainment stories). In retrospect, the racial injustice theme was present even in the initial crime story about an affluent African American man and his white ex-wife and in footnotes about the fact that nine of twelve jurors were African American. Some of the trial attorneys, witnesses, and jurors had experienced firsthand racial profiling, and others knew from hearing secondhand that L.A. police often profiled and sometimes abused minority suspects. Defense attorney Cochran had represented a number of African American defendants by claiming they had been framed by L.A. police. For some trial spectators, *Time* magazine's provocative picture of O. J. Simpson with darkened skin and a sinister facial expression also exposed the racial subtext of the trial story. During the summation phase of the trial, the race theme dominated so much that it overshadowed the domestic abuse theme. After the trial, the metanarrative about race in media narratives was no longer a footnote but the dominant media and trial story. African Americans around the country generally believed all minorities needed to fight against police racism. White Americans did not grasp the theme until after the trial, when they decried the verdict and African Americans celebrated it as a victory for them (Dyson, 1996).

Understanding the narratives presented in summations depends more on the trial stories than those presented in the media. Final summations take on added dramatic importance in trial and media narratives because the public anticipates that these trial speeches will offer conclusive proof about what the verdict should be. Media commentators promote summations as essential to the determination of the verdict. Media hype about the importance of summations elevates public expectations about the potential persuasive impact of the arguments, the likelihood of intense adversarial refutation, and the necessity for attorneys to give dramatic performances. In the Simpson trial, the summations held even more significance than is usual for a routine trial because the trial had lasted for eight months, used so many attorneys and witnesses, produced a great deal of DNA evidence, and featured Fuhrman's racism. These factors elevated the importance of the final arguments and pressured the attorneys to present stunning speeches that would capture the attention of jurors as well as media spectators.

RULES OF SUMMATIONS

Effective summations condense, cluster, and draw persuasive inferences from the evidence and testimony. The goal of summations is to emphasize favorable evidence, present the position the jury is to adopt, rebut the allegation of the opposition, suggest ways the jury should resolve conflicting testimony, explain the law, and demonstrate how the evidence mandates a favorable verdict (Haydock & Sonsteng, 1994b; Lubet, 1993; Mauet, 1992; Schuetz & Snedaker, 1988; Tanford, 1983). Specifically, rules of criminal procedure direct attorneys to argue the applicable rules of law that control the case (as long as fairly presented), the testimonial evidence adduced from the witnesses, the exhibits admitted into evidence, and the inferences that may be deduced from the testimony and exhibits (Fontham, 1995; Haydock & Sonsteng, 1994a, 1994b; Jeans, 1993; Mauet, 1992; Stein, 1985). Attorneys can state stipulations of fact or matters of common knowledge, even though they may not have developed this content during the trial. Attorneys can use visual aids to enhance the clarity of the evidence and arguments. It is improper for attorneys to ask jurors to put themselves in the positions of victims, ask them to base their decision on broad social issues, or refer to jurors by name. The judge decides the order of presentation for summations, but typically, the prosecution presents theirs first, then the defense presents theirs, and the prosecution presents a rebuttal, if they deem it appropriate.

Judges usually do not give instructions about the rules for summations because they expect attorneys to know the rules and abide by them. When rules are not followed, the opposing counsel objects, and the judge decides if a particular rule or procedure is being followed. During summations, more so than at any other time of the trial, an attorney acts as an advocate. In the interest of promoting this advocacy function, judges often give attorneys some latitude in the way they present closing arguments, but they restrict the rebuttal part of summations to the content and issues presented in their closing and to lines of reasoning that pertain to issues and exhibits already in the court record. In the Simpson trial, the controversy and wrangling that occurred between the prosecution and the defense during the trial continued throughout the summations, disrupting the continuity of the arguments, interrupting jurors' concentration, and lengthening the trial. Since the summations at times rambled, interruptions from opposing attorneys probably contributed to the lack of cohesiveness of the final arguments.

The summation is the last opportunity for advocates to address the jury. Moreover, it is the psychological culmination of the trial. Summations present an excellent opportunity for attorneys to explore the full realm of logic, eloquence, and persuasion. Effective summations condense, cluster, and draw persuasive inferences from the evidence and testimony. These final speeches can affirm the beliefs of jurors who have already made up their minds, persuade undecided jurors, or change the minds of those who, up until that point, had made a different decision. Understanding the argumentative content and persuasive style of summations leads to knowing why some summations succeed and others fail. In a sense, the Simpson trial was an anomaly because attorneys appealed to the emotions and prejudices of jurors, asked jurors to make decisions based on social issues, and maligned opponents in the summation arguments.

SUMMARY OF THE SUMMATIONS

Both sides divided their closing arguments between two attorneys. For the prosecution, Clark presented first and Darden followed. For the defense, Cochran presented first and Scheck followed. The following summary gives a glimpse of the content, the organizational pattern, and the issues presented in the summations. The prosecution's summation consisted of two parts: closing argument and rebuttal.

Clark's Closing Argument

Clark stressed the scene of the crime and the circumstances in which the murders occurred. She clustered her arguments into the categories of a time line and evidence.

TIME LINE

- Neighbors heard screams at about 10:20 in the evening on June 12, 1994, the day of the murder.
- At that same time, neighbors heard Brown Simpson's dog barking and later on saw the dog covered with blood.
- Friends of the defendant and Brown Simpson saw and heard them fighting with one another.
- At the time of the murder, the defendant was not at his home.
- Shortly after the time of the murder, Simpson's houseguest, Kato Kaelin, heard thumping sounds on the wall near Simpson's guesthouse.
- Kaelin later saw cuts on Simpson's hands.
- Simpson was late for a 10:45 PM call to limousine driver Allan Park to pick him up to take him to the airport.
- When Simpson was told about Nicole's death in a telephone call to his hotel in Chicago on June 13 at 6:00 AM, Simpson never inquired about how she died or expressed grief about her death.

EVIDENCE

- Investigators found Simpson's blood at the crime scene, on the bodies of the victims, in the defendant's bedroom, on the door to his home, and in his Ford Bronco.
- Investigators found Nicole Brown Simpson's blood on the socks O. J. left in his room the night of the crime.
- Investigators discovered O. J.'s hair on a cap left at the scene of the murder.
- Investigators found Nicole's blood and hair and Goldman's hair on a leather glove found behind Simpson's house.
- Investigators found blue cotton fibers from Simpson's sweat clothes on Ron Goldman's shirt, on the bloody glove at Simpson's home, and on some of Simpson's socks found in his home.
- Bloody footprints at the scene of the crime and in Simpson's Ford Bronco matched Simpson's Bruno Magli size-12 shoes.
- The size of the bloody glove matched what Simpson wore, and a receipt from Bloomingdale's showed that Simpson purchased the gloves. Pictures of Simpson at a football game showed that he had worn the gloves.
- Simpson killed Brown Simpson and Goldman by stabbing them multiple times and by slitting Brown Simpson's throat.

Clark concluded her long closing argument by claiming

> these murders did not occur in a vacuum, they occurred in the context of a stormy relationship, a relationship that was scarred by violence and abuse. And this important evidence completes the picture of the defendant's guilt as it explains the motive for these murders. (TR, September 26, 1995).

Darden's Closing Argument

Darden emphasized Simpson's motive as jealousy and rage resulting from his divorce from one of the victims, and he stressed the defendant had no explanation for his whereabouts at the time of the crime. He clustered his arguments according to credibility and motive.

CREDIBILITY

• Justice demands that celebrities be treated just like other criminals.

• Fuhrman's racism was not the only issue.

• Simpson's celebrity status hid his history of domestic violence and the bad side of his character.

• Simpson lied about past abuse, showing him to be untrustworthy and dangerous.

MOTIVE

• Simpson's violence against his former wife Nicole was extensive.

• The murders were personal; Simpson had a score to settle with Nicole.

• Police recorded eight different domestic abuse charges by Nicole against Simpson in 1985, 1989, 1992, 1993, and then he murdered her in June of 1994.

• Simpson stalked, bruised, beat, and ridiculed Nicole before murdering her.

• At the time of the murder, Simpson was consumed with anger, jealousy, and rage.

• When Nicole told Simpson to get out of her life for good, he became so enraged that he slashed her throat and killed Goldman, who accidently witnessed the murder.

• The defense promised they would establish Simpson's alibi, but this never occurred.

• The defense's evidence was "a bunch of smoke and mirrors" distracting from the real evidence.

Cochran's Summation

Cochran's summation concentrated on police malfeasance and Fuhrman's racism. He refuted the time line presented by Clark. He offered reasons for jurors to doubt the prosecution's evidence because Simpson had an alibi, investigators had contaminated some evidence, and L.A. police had planted other evidence.

TIME LINE

• The prosecution's time line was based on circumstantial evidence.

• The prosecution's witnesses cannot be trusted about the time they heard the dog or heard voices.

- Simpson could not have committed the crime because he was having a hamburger with witness Kato Kaelin at the time prosecution says the crime was committed.
- When jurors use common sense, they will realize that Simpson did not have the time to commit the crime in the way alleged by the prosecution.
- Simpson did not have time to commit the crime, dress, and show up for his limousine ride to the airport between the time of the crime at 10:20 and the time he got into the limousine at 10:50.

EVIDENCE

- Simpson could not have dropped the bloody glove so the glove must have been planted.
- The glove does not belong to Simpson because it did not fit when he tried it on, and "if it doesn't fit, you must acquit."
- The receipt of his purchase of the gloves at Bloomingdale's cannot be trusted because many people bought gloves of this type.
- Simpson would not have bumped into the air conditioner or entered a side entry way behind his guesthouse as prosecution witnesses have alleged.
- The knit cap at the crime scene was not his. (Cochran put the cap on his own head in an attempt to show that the cap could not have been a disguise for the defendant.)
- Simpson's bags were outside of the house prior to the arrival of the limousine so he could not have hidden the clothes worn by the perpetrator of the murders.

EVIDENCE PLANTING

- Detectives Vannatter and Fuhrman planted the glove and blood to frame Simpson.
- L.A. detectives, especially Fuhrman, are prejudiced liars who tried to make Simpson look guilty because he is an African American celebrity.
- Since the detectives are corrupt, the case of the prosecution should be doubted.

Scheck's Summation

Scheck's closing argument claimed "the prosecution's case is built on perjurous [sic] testimony of police officers, unreliable forensic evidence, and manufactured evidence" (TR, 1995, September 28), and his summation emphasized the unreliable and circumstantial evidence.

UNRELIABLE AND CIRCUMSTANTIAL EVIDENCE

- Criminalists failed to document how they collected evidence.
- The blood evidence was improperly retrieved and documented.

- Fuhrman is a "liar and genocidal racist," and his testimony cannot be believed.
- Criminalist Mazzola testified that a large amount of blood was drawn from the defendant but admitted that she lost track of where all that blood went.
- There is a "cesspool of contamination" of all of the blood evidence.
- Prosecution's DNA evidence was contaminated.
- Simpson had no bruises at the time of his arrest that indicated he had been involved in a fight.
- Simpson did not cut his hand and bleed at the crime scene, but he cut his hand when he was at his Chicago hotel the day after the crime when he smashed a glass.
- The glove found at Simpson's house was covered with Goldman's blood because Fuhrman planted the blood there.

Prosecution's Rebuttal

Prior to the prosecution's rebuttal argument, the defense and prosecution clashed with the judge about how to proceed during the summation. The attorneys contested what the trial evidence actually said and whether the opposing attorneys had drawn reasonable inferences from this evidence. Judge Ito allowed prosecutors to proceed as they had planned. Darden began his rebuttal arguments by repeating his domestic abuse theme. He told jurors they would see this evidence for its value if they moved through the "smoke screens" presented by the defense. He claimed that neighbors residing close to the crime scene, the limousine driver, the crime scene investigators, the testimony of old friends of the defendant, as well as the DNA from the victims' blood and clothing in and outside of Simpson's home demonstrated that only the defendant could have committed the murders. Clark's rebuttal condensed and focused issues more clearly than she had done in her closing argument. She stressed that the DNA evidence—the hair evidence on the cap, the fibers from Goldman's shirt in the Bronco and on Simpson's socks and gloves, and Simpson's blood at the crime scene—proved beyond a reasonable doubt that Simpson was guilty. She noted that the lies of Simpson and the misrepresentations of defense expert Dr. Michael Baden, about wounds on Simpson's body at the time of his arrest, further implicated the defendant. Clark ended by urging jurors to think logically about the evidence. What Clark did not do was reestablish the evidence that Cochran and Scheck refuted during their closing, nor did she directly refute the racism charges.

Contrasts in the Summations

Since prosecutors have the burden to prove guilt, they want their approach to evidence and witnesses to be clearly organized and presented in an easy-to-follow sequence so jurors have no problem seeing how this burden is met. In order to create reasonable doubt, the defense may intentionally shuffle the prosecutors' order of evidence and restructure their arguments to get jurors to focus on a different approach to evidence and to be aware of different inferences.

Clark did not cluster her arguments around the specific elements of the indictment, and she did not provide explicit previews or summaries of her arguments. Her organization was unclear. Since Clark said that she was going to establish a time line for the murders, the jurors and spectators likely expected her to develop her interpretation of the evidence chronologically. Some of her segments were chronological, but she jammed other parts together in ways that lacked connection to issues, the time line, or the testimony of the prosecution's witnesses. She stated that the evidence "explains the motive," but the elements surrounding the motive had not yet been presented by Darden. (See the section "Analysis of the Summations" for a more detailed interpretation of Clark's summation.)

Darden did a better job than Clark. He followed a chronology and summarized evidence pointing to the defendant's motive and premeditation. However, his summation lacked information about the victims, their lives, their families, or their fight with the perpetrator at the crime scene.

Cochran's legal goal was to establish reasonable doubt; he did not have to prove Simpson's innocence. Although Cochran rambled, he did establish a theme that associated evidence with his line of reasoning and he had a clever rhetorical style that covered up some of his disorganization. His narrative of police malfeasance persuaded jurors because it confirmed their experiences and beliefs about police racism.

Although Scheck did not discuss the perjury committed by police officers introduced in his summation's claim that "the prosecution's case is built on perjurous [sic] testimony of police officers, unreliable forensic evidence, and manufactured evidence," he did elaborate on the evidence, and at the end of his closing argument he appropriately listed 16 questions about disputed evidence. This list summarized the sources of reasonable doubt he had raised, shifted the burden of proof back to the prosecution, and challenged his adversaries to use their rebuttals to answer the questions.

The condensed summaries of the closing arguments above may indicate that Clark and Cochran followed a clear organizational pattern—but this was not the case. Both of them moved from one idea to another in no particular order. Both attorneys would introduce a particular piece of evidence, get sidetracked by something else, and then go back to explain an issue they had forgotten to address when they initially brought up the evidence. At inappropriate times during their summations they would tell jurors how much their service was appreciated and how much knowledge and common sense they had. Although attorneys typically compliment the jury and interject legal instructions, Clark and Cochran did so in ways that intruded on the development of their arguments.

It is easy to attribute the muddled organizational patterns of Clark and Cochran to the length of the trial, the length of the speeches, the amount of evidence, the mid-trial revelations about Fuhrman's racism, the interruptions from opposing counsel, and the propensity of both attorneys to perform for the courtroom cameras.

Although Clark's effusive style and Cochran's clever rhetorical performances got the attention of media commentators at the time of the trial, Darden's and Scheck's arguments offer better examples of clear organization, cogent reasoning, and careful use of evidence than do Clark's and Cochran's. Darden and Scheck organized their closing arguments in line with established norms. Both gave a preview and a summary of their arguments and related their narrative in a chronological sequence. Darden and Scheck focused the content of their arguments using evocative language and repetitive themes. Darden stressed the domestic abuse motive as it was documented prior to and after the murder. Scheck reiterated the theme of the botched investigation using a chronological arrangement that showed how the theme proved to be true at all stages in the investigation.

ANALYSIS OF THE SUMMATIONS

Attorneys use narratives during summations to explicate and defend their theories of a case. In any trial, but especially in televised trials, the summations stress the character and personality of defendants, victims, and witnesses and emphasize the disputed action by using believable themes and memorable language. Even if summations lack a clear organizational pattern, they can still persuade jurors with narratives that are easy to recall (Brooks & Gewirtz, 1996). The summation narratives in the Simpson murder trial resembled media stories in that they established settings, developed characterizations of people, identified sequence and motives for action, reported characters' dialogue, presented themes, and constructed a recognizable plot in which characters' actions had a clear purpose. These narratives lacked the blatant entertainment themes that appeal to voyeuristic audiences but included the informational themes that appealed to audiences interested in the law.

Usually summation narratives rely on arguments and evidence rather than on conflict and emotion. Narratives enable jurors to keep track of the testimony because they merge together different stories using one theme and connect that theme to the crime scene, the perpetrators and victims, and the criminal act. Attorneys have a difficult task bringing together large amounts of evidence into a coherent story because they have to present their narratives in installments over a long period of time, the stories come from many witnesses and are reconstituted by more than one storyteller, and procedural rules restrict the emotional content. In this case, the attorneys had to adapt their stories for television audiences and jurors simultaneously. A particular challenge for attorneys in the Simpson case was to present their summations in segments over a four-day period that was disrupted by lengthy objections, television time-outs, and court recesses.

Narrative Cohesiveness

The plot of the prosecution's story was that O. J. Simpson committed the first-degree murder of his ex-wife Nicole Brown Simpson by slashing her throat because he was jealous of her. Prior to the murder he had stalked her, verbally maligned her, and beat her. Simpson murdered Goldman when he unexpectedly arrived on the scene to return the glasses that Brown Simpson's mother had left at a restaurant where he worked.

Clark's summation described more than argued. Her narrative emphasized the setting and the relationship of evidence to the place and time of the crime. The prosecutor used the testimony of crime scene investigators to establish the place as an alleyway leading to Brown Simpson's front door. Relying on the testimony of neighborhood witnesses who heard voices, heard the victim's dog barking, and saw blood on the dog, Clark asserted the crime occurred at 10:20 PM. During her summation, Clark repeatedly referred to a visual model that associated different events at the scene with particular times, but she inadequately explained what the time line meant in terms of criminal charges. Instead, Clark described the times out of the order in which they appeared on the visual. Furthermore, she did not point to the times on the visual when she talked about the evidence related to that time frame but instead moved to the next important time sequence and explained it with other evidence. She should have emphasized that the time line proved that O. J. Simpson had the time and the opportunity to murder both Brown Simpson and Goldman, but she did not do so.

Clark's narrative lacked cohesiveness, as exemplified by the following segment from the trial record:

> Let us begin with a very brief review of the movements of Ron and Nicole, and we are going to start with the recital in the later afternoon. Let's begin with the recital in the late afternoon. I am sure that you recall the recital for Sydney at Paul Revere High School. Nicole left the recital and went to the Mezzaluna [a restaurant where Ronald Goldman worked] near her home, along with her parents and friends and her children, Sydney and Justin, and she arrived . . . at approximately 6:30 PM. . . . Now you recall at the end of the People's case there was a stipulation that we entered into and you recall that the Judge had told you that a stipulation is to be accepted by you as an undisputed fact. (TR, 1995, September 26)

Clark harped on the fact that Nicole's mother left her glasses at the restaurant and that she had called the restaurant at 9:30 and alerted the bartender about her lost glasses. The bartender searched for and found the glasses, and then put them in an envelope that Ronald Goldman delivered to Nicole Brown Simpson. Clark assured jurors that "those phone calls are a matter of stipulation," and an "undisputed fact." She reported that Ron Goldman took the glasses, went to his house to change clothes, and then attempted to deliver the glasses to Nicole about 10 PM. Clark's explanation of the return of the glasses was needlessly long and detailed.

Clark followed this part of the story with a lengthy digression in which she told the jury why she was telling them about the dinner and lost glasses. Clark then qualified her earlier explanation even though it was not important to the chronology of the crime itself.

> But what we don't know is exactly what time he left his house. We know he left his house in time to be murdered, and we will talk about that shortly and in time for him to be there with the dogs barking. We have to make inferences, okay? We have to make an inference from the evidence that we know about as to when he got to Bundy [Brown Simpson's home]. Now, you can draw an inference that is reasonable or you can draw an inference that is unreasonable. (TR, 1995, September 26)

The excerpt represents only a short part of Clark's narrative, but this kind of communication is typical of how she told the story of the crime. Clark added much more detail than was necessary for jurors to understand the setting or the time line. She disrupted the flow of her story by including irrelevant details that had nothing to do with Simpson's guilt by repeating words and adding phrases, and by referring to people and things that did not pertain to the criminal charges. Instead of constructing a compelling story about the guilt of Simpson, she presented a redundant and disjunctive narrative.

Clark could have created a more persuasive narrative had she presented the facts through the words of witnesses and repeated the themes that emphasized premeditation and the brutal and senseless killing. A retrospective viewing of the video and reading of the transcript of the summations revealed that Clark's rapid delivery, use of mixed metaphors, and digressions and clarifications impeded a coherent narrative and likely caused jurors to tune out. Juror Cooley reacted to Marcia Clark's closing argument in this way: "Jesus Christ. Please. Somebody help me. Get these people to understand that I am not totally illiterate here. That we don't need this" (Cooley, Bess, & Rubin-Jackson, 1995, p. 137).

Narrative Fidelity

Trial narratives that ring true with the stories courtroom audiences know and understand, that have recognizable characters and familiar plots, have the most significant persuasive effect (Gewirtz, 1996). In the Simpson trial, the majority of the jurors had social knowledge that consisted of stories resembling the defense's narrative, not the story of the prosecution. Darden constructed a summation narrative about domestic abuse from story fragments found in police records and from the testimony of Brown Simpson's family and friends. Cochran contrasted the defendant's heroic actions and personal affability with the demonic and despicable character of the police. Simpson was a famous football player and loving family man; the L.A. police were deceptive and they hated African Americans so they lied about the crime scene and planted evidence to frame Simpson. The defense's police malfeasance story fit the stock stories of jurors more than the prosecution's domestic abuse narrative did. After the trial, one juror remarked that she didn't understand why the prosecution was harping on domestic abuse because this was a case about murder. She could not follow the causal inferences Darden had made that domestic abuse frequently leads to the murder of one spouse by the other. On the other hand, the defense's story about white men framing black men was what the trial was all about in the mind of several jurors (Cooley, Bess, & Rubin-Jackson, 1995; "O. J. Verdict," 2005).

One feature that adds emotion to the prosecutors' summations is to contrast the character of the victims with that of the defendant. Prosecutors at times demonized Simpson and faulted their own witnesses, but they said very little about Brown Simpson and Goldman. Darden told jurors Brown Simpson had two children, was divorced from O. J. Simpson, and had suffered domestic abuse from the defendant. But the prosecutors included few details about the victims that would evoke positive emotional reactions about their character, their relationships, and their values. Cochran said that both Brown Simpson and her husband "loved their children," but for Cochran, Brown Simpson was not an individual with emotions and rights, she was only the mother of Simpson's children. She got tickets and held a seat for him so he could attend their daughter's recital, and in Cochran's narrative, Simpson's life and values were more important than hers. Clark and Scheck claimed that Goldman put up a struggle with the perpetrator, but prosecutors did not emphasize Goldman's virtues and character, they just stressed that his blood had a distinctive DNA pattern. For the defense and the prosecution, he was a body at a crime scene who suffered from 30 stab wounds after fighting with the perpetrator.

After some witnesses testified about the dissected bodies and the autopsies that had been performed on Brown Simpson and Goldman, the prosecutors chose not to revive memories about the victims, envision the lives they could have led, or address the loss suffered by their families. Instead, prosecutors concentrated on the victims as dead bodies that supplied blood and fiber evidence. Neither the prosecutors' narratives during their opening statements nor their summation narratives put a human face on the victims.

Why the prosecutors said so little about the victims is unclear, especially because testimony from friends and family members permitted this kind of information to be used in the summations. It is possible, but unlikely, that the prosecutors eliminated references to the victims to avoid playing on the sympathies and prejudices of jurors, a legal recommendation for summations. Since Ito allowed so much leeway in summations, it is unlikely he would have prevented prosecutors from talking about the victims if they had chosen to do so. The prosecutors' failure to create visceral themes, use powerful language, and establish empathy with victims in ways that would affect "jurors at the gut level," a factor that Ball (1997) emphasizes as essential for persuasive summations, was a rhetorical mistake.

While both sides avoided either positive or negative characterizations of the victims, both the prosecution and the defense emphasized the characters of Simpson and Fuhrman. The prosecution acknowledged Simpson's celebrity status. Darden noted:

> All along I have asked you to be open-minded, to be open-minded about this man and who he is, and . . . I think we have proven to you that he is not the person that you see on those TV commercials and at half-time in those football games. . . . We have a very, very important example of who this man is, of who he is at home, of who he is in his private life. (TR, 1995, September 27).

On the day of the crime, Darden said, Simpson had been rejected by his girlfriend Paula Barbieri, and he was "simmering with anger"; he had lost his control, his fuse was short, he blamed Nicole for his problems. He was "brooding." Darden asserted that "he [Simpson] is a murderer" but at the same time he once was "one hell of a great football player," but "he is still a murderer." Darden enunciated, "This relationship between this man and Nicole, you know, it is like the bomb ticking away. Just a matter of time, just a matter of time before something really bad happened" (TR, 1995, September 26). According to one of the jurors, many of the other African American jurors had trouble believing this theme because of the celebrity status of the defendant. They could not conceive of Simpson being a murderer and a sports hero at the same time (Knox, 1995).

Cochran characterized Simpson in glowing personal terms as a hero and a happy family man. His rhetorical flair drew inferences about the defendant's character that went well beyond what the evidence established. Much of the characterization exaggerated the testimony from Simpson's daughter from his first marriage, his mother, and his sister. Cochran told the jury that "you have heard evidence about O. J. Simpson's great life." Later he asserted Simpson was attached to his dog, gracious to his tenants, a good father, and a good son. He tried to get back together with Brown Simpson. On the day of the crime, he "isn't brooding. He is not angry. He kisses these family members. He is laughing and joking. He is playing with his son Justin." He suffers from arthritis. He is always traveling for the Hertz rental car agency and giving his ex-wife money to help her out with the children. He sits on the couch and holds his mother's hand.

At other times it seemed that Cochran himself was giving testimony when he said that it was his honor to defend Simpson. "He's Orenthal James Simpson. He's not just the defendant, and we on the defense are proud, consider it a privilege to have been part of representing him in this exercise and this journey toward justice, make no mistake about it." Simpson has "conducted himself with dignity throughout this trial" (TR, 1995, September 26). Although Cochran's narrative was both biased and brimming with self-interest, Judge Ito permitted Cochran to personalize and glorify the defendant in this way.

Both prosecutors admitted that Fuhrman was a bad character because he made racist remarks about African Americans. Clark inquired, "Is he the worst LAPD has to offer?" And then she answered, "Yes." She continued, "Do we wish that this person was never hired by LAPD?" And again she answered, "Yes." "Should such a person be a police officer? No. In fact, do we wish there were no such person on the planet? Yes." Darden also acknowledged his embarrassment about Fuhrman, claiming, "We're not hiding Fuhrman. He's too big, especially now, to hide. So hey, Fuhrman testified" (TR, 1995, September 26). Prosecutors clearly faced a dilemma. They were damned if they used Fuhrman's testimony, and they were damned if they didn't. His testimony about the bloody glove, the path of blood in front of Simpson's house, and the blood in the defendant's SUV was the core of their case. Early on in the trial, prosecutors placed great faith in Fuhrman. After his testimony was impugned by writer Laura Hart McKinny and others, the prosecution's story started to dissolve. It is not an overstatement to say that Fuhrman's racist remarks turned the case inside out. Both the media stories and the trial narratives were no longer about the murder or the perpetrator, they were about the evil character of Mark Fuhrman and, by association, other detectives from the L.A. police department who investigated the crime.

One-third of Cochran's summation concentrated on demonizing Fuhrman by calling him the "personification of evil," "America's worst nightmare," "a liar," "a racist," and "one of the worst people in . . . history like Adolph Hitler." Cochran also implicated Philip Vannatter as being a partner with Fuhrman in the framing of Simpson, although the trial evidence did not support this type of conclusion. Cochran asserted:

> That is Mark Fuhrman. And he is paired in this case with Phil Vannatter. They are both beacons that you look . . . to as the messengers that you must look through and past. They are both people who have shown that they lie, will lie, and did lie on the stand under oath. . . . This is really a case about a rush to judgment, an obsession to win, at all costs, a willingness to distort, twist, theorize in any fashion to try to get you to vote guilty. (TR, 1995, September 28)

Cochran later asserted that other detectives had conspired with Fuhrman to frame Simpson:

> Why did they then all try to cover for this man, Fuhrman? Why would this man, who is not only Los Angeles' worst nightmare, but America's worst nightmare, why would they all turn their heads and try to cover for him? . . . There is something about corruption. There is something about a rotten apple that will ultimately infect the entire barrel. (TR, 1995, September 29)

This segment of Cochran's summation certainly played on the emotions and appealed to the prejudices of jurors, a strategy that judges usually prohibit in summations. Judge Ito gave no response to these violations of the rules of summation. The prejudicial content of Cochran's narrative also fit with jurors' social knowledge about the L.A. police. For example, trial juror Carrie Bess recalled her reaction to Fuhrman in this way:

> When I heard those things about the n-word, it was like a hot flash hit me. It just made me realize how badly I hate that word. For him to sit up here and pretend that he never used it, it made me feel like just jumping up and slapping him down right then and there. (Cooley, Bess, & Rubin-Jackson, 1995, p. 105)

The attorneys' characterizations of Simpson and Fuhrman in their summations paralleled the media portrayals of these two characters. This similarity shows a convergence between media and trial narratives.

Narrative Style

Trial attorneys, in ways similar to other speakers, present their messages using a particular style. Style consists of the way speakers express the trial story through a compelling theme, evocative language that depicts action, memorable words and phrases, and rhetorical devices. In many trials, little difference exists between the styles of the attorneys, but this was not the case during the Simpson trial. During his summation, Cochran's eloquence outshined that of the other attorneys. His fluent and forceful style captivated television audiences just as it did jurors. He presented the defense case using evocative language and memorable phrases. Cochran maligned and trivialized the prosecution's case by claiming it was "speculative and cynical," "contemptuously distrustful," "gloomy," "a contorted version" of reality because they "had an obsession to win," engaged "in a rush to judgment," and had a desire to "to win at any cost." He concluded the case was "totally ridiculous" and "completely preposterous," inferring that the prosecutors kept changing the case to "make it fit, but it doesn't fit, so you must acquit" (TR, 1995, September 28).

Prosecutors could not match Cochran's style and rhetorical flair, but they did attempt to use analogies. For example, Clark told jurors that they had to act like a sculptor—to take the evidence as if it were a whole piece of marble, and then like the sculptor, weed out what was not relevant, so they could get an accurate portrait of the crime. This analogy failed to identify substantive parallels between the sculptor and the process of jury decision making or to embellish the prosecution's narrative. Clark also faulted the defense by using the analogy that the defense was headed up false roads: "There were false roads. They are false roads because they lead to a dead-end. The false roads were paved with inflammatory distractions" (TR, 1995, September 26). But this analogy also lacked sufficient details and evocative images to sustain attention or add passion to the prosecutor's story.

The summation narrative of Darden featured the analogy and imagery about a fuse burning through a long history of domestic violence, the same rhetorical device he had presented in his opening statement. This imagery stressed Simpson's motive of domestic abuse and also maligned Simpson's character. This excerpt illustrates how he reiterated the analogy and imagery in his closing argument:

> This relationship between this man and Nicole . . . it is like the time bomb. . . . You see that the fuse is lit in 1989. . . . It is burning October 25 of 1993, and Nicole doesn't know it at the time, [but] she knows [later] he is going kill her. . . . There are certain things that can set him off, that can set that fuse to burning. . . . The fuse is becoming shorter. . . . It is the day of the recital . . . and the fuse got shorter. . . . After the recital, the fuse is getting shorter, and there is going to be an explosion. (TR, 1995, September 26–27)

Darden's style was more poignant than Clark's but not as compelling as Cochran's was.

Cochran's rhetorical savvy produced persuasive effects. For example, he repeated the defense theme of a "journey toward justice," an analogy that he presented in opening statements. He also refuted the prosecutors' imagery and analogies by adding cleverly worded contrasts. For example, he referred to the prosecutors' statement, "a fuse was burning," and then he said, "the fuse kept going out" because there was "no triggering mechanism." He noted that the prosecutors said they have given you "oceans of evidence," and then he said they really have offered only "little streams" (TR, 1995, September 27).

An appealing style aids memory and assists recall. The style of summation narratives should help jurors "imagine an event in a particular way" and lead them "to think that event is more likely" than the ones portrayed in the competing narratives (Rieke & Stutman, 1990, p. 209). One strength of Cochran's style was the evocative and memorable language that focused on the flaws of the prosecution and the lies of the police rather than on the defendant's weaknesses of character. What the jury remembered were Cochran's assertions about the racist police and the evocative language in which he expressed his narrative themes. What they did not remember was Darden's conclusion that domestic abuse leads to murder or Clark's imagery about false roads and sculptors. Repeating and restating themes does not result in persuasion.

In a trial, jurors decide whether or not themes, analogies, and images are persuasive. If the content of the story does not fit with the jurors' experiences and social knowledge, then the rhetorical embellishments will not change their minds. If the content of the story fits with their social knowledge, rhetorical embellishments can reinforce what jurors already believe to be true.

Judge Ito seemed to believe that media narratives could have no effect on the sequestered jurors in the Simpson murder case. But in an underlying way they did: the media narratives helped the defense attorneys figure out what themes and issues would make their summations persuasive.

LESSONS

Several lessons can be learned from Simpson's murder trial. Media narratives differ in substance and style from trial narratives. In this case, however, the summations of Cochran resembled media narratives more than trial narratives. Cochran portrayed the defendant as a benevolent hero and the police as prejudiced liars who framed Simpson because they hated successful African Americans. Cochran's summation story did not prove that other people committed the murder as he promised to do in his opening statement. Instead he described how police conspired and plotted to frame Simpson. He contrasted the personality of the defendant with the personalities of the police. He exaggerated the testimony and the meaning of the evidence using theatrics and overstatement. Cochran performed the narrative to enhance the dramatic effect for both jurors and media spectators. He ignored some of the procedural rules that usually constrain the content of summation when he overtly appealed to the feelings and prejudices of jurors, addressed public spectators in the television audience, and ridiculed the prosecutors and their case. The eloquent defense attorney presented a one-sided story with strong contrasts between good and bad personalities involved in a race-based plot. The type of story he told was common in media entertainment stories, but uncommon for murder trial summation narratives.

Prosecutors attempted to follow the norms of trial narratives, but they had to deviate from this plan because they failed to cast the celebrity Simpson in a believable role of a vicious murderer. Several reasons affected the effectiveness of their narrative. First, jurors doubted the police evidence implicating the defendant because of the actions of inept criminalists and racist police. Second, jurors doubted the prosecutors' stories of abuse because they did not understand why domestic abuse was a motive for murder. However, they did understand the defense story that police often profile and frame African American men. Third, jurors paid more attention to the dynamic communication of the defense attorneys than to the facts and evidence presented by the prosecutors. Although the prosecutors presented huge amounts of evidence to the jurors, the two attorneys did not relate the evidence clearly to the indictments so they could construct a coherent and probable story.

The end of Cochran's summation surprised the prosecutors. They had no response to what Cochran asked jurors to do. At the end of his summation, Cochran departed from the goal that he seemed to pursue at the beginning of the summation of creating reasonable doubt. He changed the purpose of the narrative so that he was not persuading jurors to acquit Simpson of murder charges, but he was asking them to convict the police of misconduct. At this late point in the trial, Cochran became the lead character in his narrative when he told jurors they had the right and the responsibility to "police the police." Their acquittal of Simpson was not so much about setting him free as it was about forcing the L.A. police to suffer the consequences of their racist policies.

I cannot say for sure that the prosecutors would have met their burden to prove Simpson's guilt if they had communicated more effectively by organizing and emphasizing evidence favorable to their case, refuting allegations of the opposition, suggesting ways the jury should resolve conflicting testimony, explaining how the evidence applied to the law, characterizing the victims, and demonstrating that they had met their burden of proof. But if they had communicated more effectively, I believe jurors would have paid more attention to the evidence pointing to guilt. Prosecutors never recovered from the evidence about Fuhrman's racism, evidence that affirmed the pre-existing beliefs of jurors. From the start of this murder trial, it is possible that prosecutors recognized that the defense's dream team had more legal and rhetorical skill than they did. But their posttrial stories do not support this viewpoint (Clark, 1997; Darden, 1996). To the contrary, prosecutors believed that they had met their burden and obeyed all legal requirements ("O. J. Verdict," 2005). The prosecutors for the most part seemed to follow the trial rules and created many strong arguments justified by relevant evidence, but their communication of the evidence and arguments was inferior to that of the defense. Perhaps the circumstances of the courtroom situation were such that the prosecutors' narratives never would seem reasonable to jurors. The defense constructed and performed their unconventional narratives so well that they seemed reasonable to jurors even though many trial spectators did not agree with the verdict.

9

Courtroom Drama and Judicial Conduct in the Chicago Eight Trial

In 1969, eight defendants gathered in a Chicago federal court to be tried for conspiring to riot during the 1968 Democratic National Convention. The Chicago Eight trial originated with politically motivated indictments that resulted from questionable laws that attempted to restrict dissent. The unusual legal proceeding that followed became a burlesque drama that subverted the conventional legal rules and practices. Specifically, the attorneys and witnesses for both the prosecution and the defense mocked the cherished ideals of the court by using vulgar speech, satirical actions, and disrespectful behavior. Furthermore, by not exerting appropriate control over the legal participants, Judge Julius Hoffman contributed to the disorder of the court and the distortion of the legal process. This chapter explains how the legal participants mocked the codes of conduct and violated the rules. In doing so, the trial participants transformed what should have been a dignified court proceeding into a mockery of the legal system.

This deviation from the traditional norms of courtroom practices occurred as the result of exceptional legal and political factors that forced a test of the existing legal rules and codes of conduct. Trial participants constructed the eccentric dramatic form of burlesque to thwart the legal proceedings, and the trial judge stepped out of the traditional judicial role and became part of the burlesque drama. The deliberateness of the performers and the effects of the hypertheatrical drama are not unique to the Chicago Eight trial. For example, the legal actions against Zacharias Moussaoui for his involvement in the terrorist bombings on 9/11 showed some similar features to the Chicago Eight trial, but the judge in that trial kept the courtroom in better control than Judge Hoffman did in the Chicago Eight trial.

This chapter (1) describes the political situation that led to the trial; (2) explains standards for judicial and attorney conduct; (3) shows how the dramatic analogue applies to the trial; (4) describes the burlesque dramatic form that emerged from trial participants' definitions of the situation, creation of scripts, enactment of roles, attention to performances, and staging of the trial; and (5) identifies lessons learned about professional conduct and subversive dramatic legal actions.

THE POLITICAL SITUATION

In the late 1960s and early 1970s, protests were part of a general social and political upheaval in the country. In 1968, assassins killed black civil rights leader Martin Luther King Jr. and Democratic senator and candidate for president Robert Kennedy. The American casualties from the Vietnam War rose to 40,000 dead and 250,000 wounded. President Lyndon Johnson's action to increase troop strength in Vietnam from 20,000 to 500,000 provoked antiwar sentiment among many activist groups. Young men decided to resist the draft, and college campuses became hotbeds of dissent where antiwar protestors organized sit-ins, strikes, and demonstrations, and they burned buildings and the American flag. Many protestors—Yippies, Students for a Democratic Society (SDS), the Black Panthers, other New Left antiwar activists—believed that they were part of a revolution that would bring down the government. Prior to the National Democratic Convention in Chicago, more than 100,000 activists had staged protests at the United Nations in New York and 50,000 demonstrated at the Pentagon near Washington, D.C. The problems with these previous demonstrations served as a warning to officials that they should beef up security at the National Democratic Convention, while the Chicago Eight defendants worked with leaders of antiwar groups to organize more than 10,000 demonstrators that would eventually gather at the site of that convention.

Prior to the convention, organizers of the antiwar demonstration sought permits from the city of Chicago to assemble, march, and camp near the site of the political convention. After the city refused to issue permits for the protest groups to demonstrate, city officials anticipated confrontations from the protestors and proceeded to mobilize hundreds of city policemen and members of the Illinois National Guard to keep the peace. When the convention commenced, an estimated 10,000 people camped, marched, demonstrated, presented antiwar speeches, and defied law enforcement. Most encounters between law enforcement personnel and protestors were contentious. Eventually, law enforcement retaliated against the protestors by using tear gas and billy clubs and by making mass arrests. Day after day the television media broadcast live video of the demonstrations and reported on police–protestor hostilities. Many citizens who watched the convention paid more attention to the conflicts outside of the convention hall than to the political events that occurred inside.

Ramsey Clark, the U.S. attorney general at the time, considered prosecuting the leaders of the demonstrations, but he changed his mind after his legal advisers told him that the recent legislation, called the antiriot law, might be unconstitutional. This law, called the Rap Brown Statute, was added to the 1968 Civil Rights Act to give the government power to restrain the "rebellion of black residents" who had protested against government policies (Kunstler, 1994, p. 4). This law made it a federal offense to cross state lines with the intention of inciting, promoting, or participating in a riot. If convicted, the penalty for this offense was a $500 fine and five years in prison.

After Richard Nixon won the presidential election in the fall of 1968, he and his newly named attorney general, John Mitchell, decided to bring charges against eight leaders of the August demonstrations outside the Democratic Convention. The justice department indicted Abbie Hoffman, Bobby Seale, Rennie Davis, Tom Hayden, Lee Weiner, John Froines, Dave Dellinger, and Jerry Rubin on charges that they conspired to riot. Midway through the trial, the judge severed Bobby Seale from the proceedings, and for the rest of the trial only seven defendants appeared in court. The trial, however, retained its name of the Chicago Eight.

The real reason for the arrest of the defendants, according to one of the defense attorneys (Kunstler, 1994), was that the defendants were symbolic representatives of

> all aspects of the counterculture of the sixties: irreverent rejection of the establishment, pacifism, strident militancy, opposition to the war in Vietnam, and rejection of racism. The government's strategy in joining the leaders of the nonviolent antiwar and civil rights movements with militant blacks was to create in the public mind the idea that the burgeoning antiwar movement was an integral part of the Black power movement. (p. 4)

Others agree with Kunstler; they claim that the government's motive for trying the defendants was to show the nation that it would no longer tolerate radicals seeking social change or movements that questioned the power of the establishment (Bowers, Ochs, & Jensen, 1993).

Thomas A. Foran and Richard G. Schultz served as the United States attorneys prosecuting the case. William Kunstler and Leonard Weinglass led the defense. Judge Julius J. Hoffman presided. After the trial concluded, Kunstler (1970) used hyperbole to describe the high level of tension and conflict in the trial. He noted that Judge Hoffman could not understand the defendants or their motivations. And as a result, the judge "used the judicial process against them exactly as Don Quixote had flailed his spear against a windmill's rotating vanes, destroying, along the way, his own credibility and undermining the very system he thought he was saving" (p. xvi). The case took place in a federal court because the indictment stated that defendants crossed state lines with intent to riot.

The trial commenced on September 26, 1969, and lasted nearly five months. The trial record consumed 22,000 pages of testimony. Attorneys called more than 100 witnesses. The jurors acquitted all of the defendants on charges of conspiring to incite a riot. The jury convicted Hoffman, Rubin, Davis, Dellinger, and Hayden on lesser charges of organizing and promoting a riot, and they acquitted Weiner and Froines on all charges. In a contempt hearing that followed the trial, Judge Hoffman sentenced Kunstler to four years and thirteen days in jail, Weinglass to nearly two years, and the five convicted defendants to the maximum five years and fined them more that $58,000. In 1972, the U.S. Court of Appeals reversed all of the contempt citations, and a federal court retried and convicted Kunstler on lesser contempt charges.

STANDARDS OF PROFESSIONAL CONDUCT

Judge Hoffman violated the norms of judicial conduct, and the defendants as well as many of the witnesses, spectators, and attorneys acted in a contemptuous manner opposing the traditions and decorum of the court. The combination of all these unorthodox behaviors produced mayhem in the courtroom. When viewed through the lens of standard trial procedures, the actions and behaviors of the Chicago Eight trial participants are incomprehensible. If we use the perspective of burlesque drama to view the trial participants' behavior, their characters and actions appear in a different light; the defendants, in cooperation with their attorneys, engaged in performances that followed the scripts used by popular guerilla theater groups of the era.

The American Bar Association adopted a formal code of conduct for judges in 1972 that was based on federal legal statues (28 U.S.C.A. 144), a 1943 professional code, and Supreme Court decisions from the nineteenth century. Some of the following canons of judicial conduct would have applied to Judge Hoffman in 1969.

> *Canon 1:* A judge should participate in establishing, maintaining, and enforcing, and should himself observe high standards of conduct so that the integrity and independence of the judiciary may be preserved.
>
> *Canon 2a:* A judge should respect and comply with [professional] conduct . . . at all times in a manner that promotes public confidence in the integrity of the judiciary.
>
> *Canon 3:* A judge should be faithful to the law and maintain professional competence in it [and] . . . should be unswayed by partisan interests, public clamor, or fear of criticism. A judge should maintain order and decorum in proceedings before him [her].
>
> (1) A judge should be faithful to the law and maintain professional competence in it. He [she] should be unswayed by partisan interests, public clamor, or fear of criticism.
>
> (2) A judge should maintain order and decorum in proceedings.

(3) A judge should be patient, dignified, and courteous to litigants, jurors, witnesses, lawyers, and others with whom he [she] deals . . . and should require similar conduct of lawyers . . . staff, court officials, and others subject to his [her] discretion. (Model Code of Judicial Conduct, 1972)

The legal system holds federal judges to a high standard of ethical conduct that enforces legal procedures and courtroom protocols. Judge Hoffman did not behave according to these standards, but neither did the prosecution and defense attorneys.

The preliminary statement in the Model Code of Professional Responsibility (1980) establishes principles that underlie what they say is "an inspirational guide to the members of the profession" and "a basis for disciplinary action when the conduct of a lawyer falls below the required minimum standards stated in the Disciplinary Rules." The code considers a number of responsibilities regarding qualification to practice law, including service to clients, advertising, and confidentiality. Some provisions deal specifically with attorney conduct applicable to the attorneys in the Chicago Eight trial in 1969.

Canon 1.5: A lawyer should maintain high standards of professional conduct and should encourage fellow lawyers to do likewise. He [she] should be temperate and dignified . . . and refrain from illegal and morally reprehensible conduct. Because of his [her] position in society, even minor violations of law by a lawyer may tend to lessen public confidence in the legal profession. Obedience to law requires respect for law.

Canon 7.1: The duty of a lawyer, both to his [her] client and to the legal system, is to represent . . . zealously within the bounds of the law the Disciplinary Rules and enforceable professional regulations.

Canon 7.24: The expression by a lawyer of . . . personal opinion as to the justness of a cause, the credibility of a civil litigant, or as to the guilt or innocence of an accused is not a proper subject for arguments.

Canon 9.24: Every lawyer owes a solemn duty to uphold the integrity and honor of his [her] profession; to encourage respect for the law and for the courts and the judges thereof; to observe the *Code of Professional Responsibility*; . . . to reflect credit on the legal profession and to inspire the confidence, respect and trust of his [her] clients and of the public. (Model Code of Professional Responsibility, 1980)

Subsequent analysis shows that although the attorneys in the case met some of these responsibilities, they violated others by disguising their performances as politically legitimate and engaging in burlesque drama to mock the court.

DRAMA AS ANALOGUE

Many sociologists and rhetorical theorists use drama as an analogue for understanding social interaction. This body of theory is known as "dramatism." Simmel (1968) notes that dramatic art forms resemble the structure and function of actual social interaction, and Burke (1968) says that the "difference between staged drama and the drama of real life is the difference between obstacles imagined by the artist and those actually experienced" by persons in their daily lives (pp. 444–450). In dramatic social interactions, persons enact their roles in order to change, modify, or sustain the social order (Combs & Mansfield, 1968; Duncan, 1968).

In a trial drama, attorneys reconstruct the real crime, portray the conflicts of lived experience, and use witnesses to re-create the reality of their lived experiences for the courtroom audience. Much of this dramatic action of the trial evolves according to the principles, procedures, and protocols of the legal profession. When trial participants seek to advance personal and social goals without considering the legal rules, distortions of normative legal processes and communication practices result. Drama can be a lens for looking at both conventional and unconventional legal proceedings.

Criminal trials often epitomize social dramas because the trial becomes "a dramatic thing put to legal use" (Harbinger, 1971, p. 122). Acting as directors, skillful attorneys dramatize the setting, characters, themes, and actions of a trial to capture the attention and involve the emotions of jurors and public spectators. (The courtroom drama can be a relatively simple explanation of each stage in the evolution of a conventional trial, or it can reveal the intricacies and outcomes of complex theatrical performances.) In a sense, the trial is one play within another play, and each play persuades audiences in a unique way. The most obvious play is the external drama—media articles and reports generated from the internal drama: from observing or speaking with courtroom participants, from assessing trial transcripts, and through sketches produced by courtroom artists (Okpaku & Sadock, 1970).

In the Chicago Eight trial both the defendants and the trial attorneys engaged in frequent communication with the media about what was going on in the internal trial drama. Their goal was to persuade trial spectators about what the trial means in social and political terms and to influence public opinion about what is going on inside of the trial. When the attorneys trying cases communicate with the media during the trial, they usually are trying to influence public opinion, bolster their own credibility, and promote their version of the case.

The trial was not televised, but the defense attorneys, the judge, and the antiwar demonstrators inserted their interpretations of the internal trial drama by talking with media reporters. Additionally, television audiences saw demonstrators and antiwar posters near reporters who presented daily reports about the trial. During the trial, the defense attorneys and the defendants conducted mini news conferences on the steps of the courthouse, attended fund-raising parties, and presented speeches about their radical political beliefs on college campuses throughout the country. On one occasion, defendant Jerry Rubin left the proceeding on the ruse that he was going to the bathroom when in fact he left so that he could make a flight to California and present a speech that night.

Defense attorney Kunstler (1994) was an especially popular speaker who told his audiences that the judicial system was "repressing and stifling people's rights" rather than "protecting people's rights." Kunstler relished the opportunity to speak to public audiences about what was going on inside of the trial. He said, "These speeches were so exhilarating that I was never tired. After I walked on the stage, the audience would stand up and cheer as if I were a superstar" (p. 35). This may have been Kunstler's concept of one part of the Model Code of Professional Responsibility that encourages attorneys to zealously defend their clients, but this behavior seemed manipulative and unprofessional to other attorneys. This media-savvy defense attorney's speeches also ridiculed and showed disrespect for the federal legal system.

It is curious that the defendants and their attorneys had unlimited access to the press and the public during the trial, especially since the trial occurred after the Supreme Court decision about media publicity in *Sheppard v. Maxwell* (1966). Did Judge Hoffman fail to issue silence orders on trial participants because the jurors were sequestered? Did he think that imposing these restrictions would fuel more controversy about free speech rights of the protestor-defendants? The answer is not clear. What is clear is that the external play that took place outside of the courtroom promoted the political issues that the defendants desired to convey in the internal play occurring in the trial.

The internal play centers on the communication and legal actions that take place inside the courtroom. The purpose of this internal play is to persuade jurors through the accounts of witnesses and through the evidence and argumentation that attorneys piece together from testimony and present in their opening statements and summations. In the internal play, attorneys present the trial story artistically by trying to appeal to the imagination, experiences, and understanding of jurors. In a typical trial, attorneys imbue their communication with a dramatic veneer that they hope will sustain the attention and interest of jurors and persuade them to decide the verdict in line with the facts and evidence that presumably supports their case theory. The internal drama differs from the external drama in several respects. The internal drama deals with what is happening live and in real time in the courtroom and creates an immediate persuasive effect on jurors. In the internal trial drama, the witnesses typically play supporting roles to attorneys and create the impression that "dramaturgical loyalty" exists among members of the prosecution, plaintiff, or defense team. The public learns about the internal play through the trial transcripts or through the reports of courtroom spectators.

The internal drama of this case evolved from several sources, including the actions and reactions of attorneys, the judge, and defense witnesses. Clues about the direction and purpose of the internal drama surfaced on the first day of the trial. On this day, Hoffman ordered the arrest of four pretrial defense lawyers after the attorneys telegraphed the judge, saying that they were resigning from the case. The actions of the pretrial attorneys angered

Hoffman because he viewed them as a sign of personal disrespect to him. That same day, Hoffman refused to delay the trial even though Charles R. Garry, attorney for defendant Bobby Seale, had entered the hospital for surgery and therefore could not appear at the trial. He appointed Kunstler to be Seale's attorney rather than postponing the trial or allowing Seale to represent himself. Prosecutors and defense attorneys presented their opening statements on this day as well. The defense introduced a strong political agenda for the trial when Kunstler noted:

> The real conspiracy in this case is . . . the conspiracy to curtail and prevent the demonstrations against the war in Vietnam and the related issues that these defendants and other people, thousands, who came here were determined to present to the delegates of a political party and the party in power meeting in Chicago; that real conspiracy was against these defendants. (TR, p. 16)

In his opening statement, Weinglass blamed city officials for refusing to meet the "reasonable demands of young persons who wanted to exercise their rights to free expression and assembly" (TR, p. 19; all TR citations refer to Trial Record [Chicago Eight], 1969). Hoffman engaged in a long conversation admonishing Weinglass for arguing rather than previewing the evidence. This beginning to the trial foreshadowed the contentious internal drama that would evolve during the next five months.

In the Chicago Eight trial, the attorneys and defendants had major roles in both the performances of the internal and external dramas. In the internal drama, the burlesque content introduced and sustained by the defense buried the plot of the prosecution's crime story about conspiracy to riot. The defense also directed the external drama by placing their own political spin on the processes and practices of the internal trial drama. Instead of refereeing the internal trial drama and restraining the external drama as judges usually do, Hoffman became a star performer in both dramas. As the two dramas evolved, the trial participants paid more attention to their own satirical performances than to the facts and to the interests of the jurors. The eccentric performances of many trial participants diminished the importance of the trial drama and magnified the importance of the political drama.

BURLESQUE DRAMA

Courtroom interaction can be classified according to a variety of dramatic modes, ranging from morality plays, tragedy, melodrama, and realism to burlesque. The Boston sex abuse lawsuits and the tobacco litigation resembled morality plays. The trials of McVeigh, Hauptmann, and Sacco and Vanzetti qualified as tragedies. The Simpson trial turned into a drama of racial realism. The Chicago Eight trial resembled burlesque, a type of satirical drama in which the conventional form of an activity or forum is subverted by unconventional subject matter. Burlesque takes two forms: a travesty, which subverts accepted or standard procedures by representing a lofty or serious subject with vulgarity (Burke, 1964; Holman, 1972; Styan, 1973); and a parody, which satirizes established practices by treating inconsequential subject matter with dignity. A trial is a travesty when the attorneys repeatedly mock the cherished ideals of the court by using vulgar speech and inappropriate manners and by displaying an unprofessional appearance. A trial is a parody when the attorneys raise inconsequential matters that make the trial itself seem irrelevant. In the Chicago Eight trial, the defense demanded that many inconsequential matters be treated as if they were important.

Burlesque drama can challenge or subvert legal principles, procedures, and protocols. The burlesque mode: (1) features language (slang, informal address, vulgar words, and words with private meanings) that mocks the formality and clarity of professional discourse; (2) subverts traditional procedures, as when participants adopt a demeanor that is sarcastic, disrespectful, and offensive; and (3) undermines legal protocols, exemplified by participants' unorthodox dress, posture, and gestures. When a combination of these factors becomes so pervasive and disruptive that the traditional legal process disappears from the view of audiences and the real goal is eclipsed, the trial turns into a burlesque drama.

The work of Goffman (1959) identifies several factors that help explain courtroom interaction as burlesque drama. He notes that persons plan their communication so that it fits with the norms and expectations of a context. Trial participants define the legal situation, develop their characters to fit with the definitions, select staging using appropriate verbal and nonverbal communication, and adopt the roles that allow them to manage impressions through performances.

Definitions of a Situation

When participants define a situation in a certain way, that definition predicts the behaviors that are to follow (Goffman, 1959). Usually trial participants consciously respond to the legal situation by following the established norms and rules associated with that context. The examination of witnesses relies on two definitions of the courtroom situation. The first is the implicit and mutually agreed definitions whereby the judge, attorneys, jurors, witnesses, and defendants agree to abide by the rules of the jurisdiction where the case is being decided. The second definition is that attorneys present a theory of the case that serves the interests of the clients they represent.

Most trial participants agree to follow the legal standards for "reason, objectivity, fairness of purpose, diligent preparation and presentation of evidence, clear, just rules, an orderly proceeding, and, at least, modest efficiency" (Clark, 1970, p. vi) so that the trial can be a formal and dignified fact-finding process. However, if participants define the situation as a political event or an opportunity for dissent, they can transform the formal judicial proceeding into a dramatic spectacle that ridicules the legal system.

The participants converted the Chicago Eight trial from a case involving charges of conspiracy to cross state lines to riot, into a political forum featuring confrontation between the "legal order" and the "new radicalism" (Kalven, 1970, p. xi). Instead of the state assuming its burden to prove the defendants' guilt, they ended up defending the legal process and the tactics that police had used to suppress the demonstrators. Rather than the defense upholding the presumption of innocence for the accused, they advocated an end to the war, acceptance of unorthodox lifestyles, and the rejection of authority.

These unusual definitions of the situation were one factor that contributed to the unreasonableness, subjectivity, and disorderliness of the trial. Although it was unreasonable to refuse to delay the trial when Seale's attorney could not participate, Judge Hoffman did so. Moreover, the defense attorneys and witnesses introduced matters for discussion in the court that were inconsequential and irrelevant to the trial, such as having a birthday party for defendant Seale, gaining bathroom privileges for the defendants, and making motions to delay the trial to attend a peace rally in Washington, D.C.

A second factor contributing to the burlesque function of the trial appeared in the case theories advocated by both the prosecution and defense. Procedural rules ask attorneys to present their theory of the case using a theme or detailed explanation to "create a cohesive and logical position" (Mauet, 1992, p. 9). Attorneys usually preview their theory in a narrative form during opening statements, develop this theory with the testimony of witnesses, and reiterate the theory in summations.

At the beginning of the Chicago Eight trial, the prosecution presented a defendable case in their opening statements. Richard G. Schultz, for example, argued that "The Government will prove that each of these eight men . . . united and conspired together to encourage people to riot during the convention." He explained the defendants did so in three stages: using the antiwar issue to get people to Chicago, inflaming the people against the police, and encouraging resistance to police action (TR, p. 11). Prosecutors adopted a plausible position, but the testimony, evidence, and argumentation that followed failed to prove these allegations. Instead, they used their theory to explain how the aggressive actions of Chicago officials and law enforcement personnel against demonstrators were justified.

The first part of the defense's theory emphasized a reasonable legal approach to the case. Kunstler outlined the theory in his opening statement:

> But we are going to show the real conspiracy is not against these defendants as individuals; the real attack was on the rights of everybody . . . to protest under the First Amendment to the Constitution; to protest against a war that was brutalizing all of us. (TR, p. 16)

The defense's testimony, evidence, and argumentation, however, did not develop the legal theory; instead the trial content explained the ideology of the various protest groups. Moreover, the defense never created reasonable doubt about the guilt of the defendants, but assumed a burden to prove the government engaged in malicious and violent acts against the demonstrators.

After opening statements, various anomalies in the trial evolved and neither side presented facts related to the indictments. Instead, attorneys dealt with issues external to the case, such as the rights of African Americans, the justifications for pacifism, and the subservient role of women in society, and both sides distorted the principle of the burden of proof. As a result, the case turned into a debate about the legitimacy of police action versus the rights and ideology of the New Left. The debate concentrated on the moral issues of the war from the point of view of the defendants and ignored the legal issues that the court was supposed to decide.

Since trial participants adopted unconventional definitions of the courtroom situation, the norm to "avoid conflict and to develop a working consensus" among interactants (Goffman, 1959) never occurred. The participants adhered to a dramatic standard, and the trial became a satire about the criminal justice system. The judge allowed the defense's definitions to legitimize changes in courtroom rules. Judge Hoffman did not exert authority over the attorneys and witnesses or maintain order. He did nothing to stop the defense from forcing himself, the prosecution, and spectators of the internal dramas to follow their burlesque form.

Scripts

The satirical drama affected the practices and processes that the attorneys used to elicit the testimony from their witnesses, develop evidence, and construct arguments. Traditionally, attorneys help construct the scripts of witnesses by the way they phrase questions during direct and cross-examination. In the Chicago Eight trial, however, the witnesses often directed the attorneys. This type of script altered the content and style of attorneys' trial speeches; their questioning of witnesses; their interactions with each other and the judge; and their approach to protocols, including their appearance, gestures, and manner.

The prosecution and defense attorneys followed a few of the procedural rules but violated others. The government called 70 witnesses; many were policemen, FBI undercover agents, and city officials from Chicago. The direct examination followed a routine of asking witnesses their name and occupation, what they were doing during the time of the demonstrations, and what observations they made of the speech and actions of the defendants during the convention demonstrations. In the beginning, prosecutor Schultz tried to conduct routine direct examinations, but his questioning was frequently interrupted by the defendants. As the trial developed, the prosecutors' involvement in unorthodox scripts evolved from the circumstances surrounding witnesses' testimony and the actions of the defense and the judge.

The scene contained an odd mixture of reports about the defendants' use of obscene and violent language, rude interruptions and emotional outbursts from the defendants when they commented on the testimony of others, and ridiculous motions initiated by the attorneys. When they reported about the behavior of demonstrators, both the defense's and some of the prosecution's witnesses used obscene and politically offensive language. For example, policeman Robert Murray recounted his recollections of Jerry Rubin's words at the demonstration: "'He says the pigs are in our park. They're—the same word I used before—motherfuckers, they're shitheads'" (TR, p. 57).

Interruptions and emotional outbursts frequently erupted in the court-room. Seale, Dellinger, A. Hoffman, and Rubin ridiculed Judge Hoffman. For example, after the judge addressed the jury with the greeting, "Good morning," the defendants mocked his tone and demeanor and repeated the greeting back to him. The defendants refused to rise when the judge entered, made satirical comments, calling the trial "ridiculous" and "unfair," and inserted sounds, such as "oink, oink," which reinforced that character-ization of law enforcement officers as pigs (Clark, 1970). Defense attorneys' lengthy motions protesting the trial proceedings further trivialized the legal process. For example, defense attorneys sought the removal of one court-room marshal because he barred Seale's wife and child from being specta-tors in the court. The defense's actions distorted the reasonableness of the prosecution witnesses' stories and ruined the continuity and believability of their scripts, characteristics fitting with burlesque drama. Schultz could not conduct direct examination according to legal procedures because the defense attorneys, their witnesses, and the judge devalued the content of their testimony and ridiculed their character.

When the defense questioned witnesses, they emphatically and deliber-ately violated the rules of direct examination. The defense called 113 wit-nesses in a random order so that the responses of one witness had little, if any, connection to the testimony of the persons who preceded and followed. The content of the testimony bore only faint resemblance to the defense's case theory. Furthermore, the defense laid no foundation for the evidence they introduced. As a result, the prosecution made hundreds of objections, and although the judge sustained most of them, the lack of continuity and con-stant interruptions made the proceedings farcical. The presentation of testi-mony highlighted the ideology of the antiwar dissidents, clearly differentiating the character and beliefs of the defense's from the prosecution's witnesses.

Whereas the defense forcibly altered the scripts of the prosecution and their witnesses, they molded unconventional scripts for their own witnesses so that the resulting style and content mocked the orthodox law-and-order stories of prosecution witnesses. The defense repeatedly ridiculed the proce-dures for introducing logical evidence relevant to the indictments by intro-ducing philosophical and artistic evidence pertaining to the defense's political ideologies. Defense witnesses included folk singer David Ochs, who testified by singing a song; Allen Ginsberg, who talked about Yoga and East-ern religion and chanted mantras; Abbie Hoffman, who read the demands of the Yippie demonstrators to have access to illegal drugs and free love; Cora

Weiss, who lamented the evils committed by U.S. soldiers in the My Lai massacre; and Judy Collins, who recited words to her popular war protest song, "Where Have All the Young Men Gone?"

The defense introduced a parade of New Left leaders and activists as their witnesses. As the trial progressed into the fourth and fifth months, the scripts of the defense witnesses became increasingly confrontational and mean spirited, and Kunstler encouraged this type of contentious testimony. For example, he asked witness Paul Krassner to identify spectators, mocking the fact the prosecution's witnesses identified the defendants. This witness interrupted Kunstler to mock the way the judge had previously complained that Kunstler had interrupted him (TR, pp. 448–450).

In a conventional trial, direct examiners create the script for their side of the case, and cross-examiners alter the script. Script altering tactics used by cross-examiners force "yes" and "no" answers, preview questions with contradictory testimony, point out omissions and oversights in the testimony, and use questions that elicit "I don't know" responses (Haydock & Sonsteng, 1994a; Heglund, 1978; Iannuzzi, 1982; Kuvin, 1965; Mauet, 1992). The defense did not follow legal procedures when they challenged the scripts of the prosecution's witnesses during cross-examination. Two maneuvers of Kunstler and Weinglass promoted the burlesque trial drama. First, the attorneys tried to force every prosecution witness to say that the police harassed and beat up demonstrators. Kunstler's interrogation of Chicago policeman Kenneth Carcerano illustrates this strategy:

K: Did you see the police use night sticks on demonstrators?

C: Yes, I did. . . .

K: Did you see any other type of wound on the demonstrators outside of the head injuries?

C: I saw demonstrators limping, holding parts of their bodies. (TR, p. 117)

Although court rules forbid trial participants from showing disrespect to the judge, the defendants made off-color verbal comments and obscene nonverbal gestures during the cross-examination of the prosecution's witnesses. For example, they raised their middle finger, pointed to the judge and witnesses; jeered witnesses, saying "that's a lie"; held up radical newspapers; and called the rulings of the judge "pathetic" (TR, pp. 125–133). These maneuvers emphasized the defense's disdain for the police and judicial system, distracted the jury and judge from understanding the content of the testimony, and reinforced the ideology of the political left.

The prosecution's cross-examination was particularly difficult because the scripts constructed by defense witnesses were not relevant to the indictment. Both Schultz and Foran tried to address omissions and oversights and to preview their questions with contradictory testimony. Since defense witnesses gave irrelevant answers and belittled the questioner, the cross-examiners could not get the trial back on a legal track. The following excerpt from

Schultz's interrogation of Abbie Hoffman illustrates how this witness's satirical responses frustrated the prosecution.

> S: Did you see some people urinate on the Pentagon? . . .
>
> H: I didn't get that close. Pee on the walls of the Pentagon? You are getting to be out of sight, actually. You think there is a law against it? (TR, p. 368)

Later in the examination, Schultz tried to establish Hoffman's whereabouts on August 22, 1968:

> S: Do you recall having coffee with some police officers?
>
> H: With the policemen that were tailing me from the Chicago Red Squad? Yes. They bought me breakfast every morning and drove me around.
>
> S: Do you recall while having coffee with—
>
> H: I don't drink coffee. . . . It is one of the drugs I refrain from using. (TR, p. 370)

In ways similar to A. Hoffman, other defense witnesses refused to act as if the questioning process was a serious way of gathering facts pertaining to the indictments. One of Schultz's obligations was to impeach the credibility of defense's witnesses, and this task was easy because most of the witnesses volunteered information that damaged their own credibility. The cross-examination of witnesses produced little evidence pertinent to the indictments, but it added scripts filled with irrelevant and irreverent subject matter that affirmed the trial drama was partly a travesty. In this case, the prosecution's interrogation of defense witnesses created a satirical reversal of legal processes and procedures that concentrated on irrelevant, ill-conceived, and trivial subject matter.

Roles

Roles constitute a third element of this trial drama. Whereas the definition of the situation predicts the content and issues, and scripts create the discourse, roles are the way that various individuals participate in the courtroom action. More simply, roles are the positions people occupy in a social drama. The testimony of witnesses usually begins with questions that reveal to the jury the witnesses' roles. In a conventional trial, each participant performs his or her role so the trial can accomplish its legal goals: judges decide legal issues, attorneys advocate the best possible case for their clients, witnesses tell the truth as they see it, and jurors decide the outcome of the case. The roles of all courtroom participants affect all others (Haydock & Sonsteng, 1994a; Heglund, 1978; Jeans, 1993; Mauet, 1992). In a typical case, legal principles, procedural rules, and protocols constrain the roles that trial participants can play, but these constraints had little effect on the Chicago Eight trial.

The rules of the court accord a high degree of respect to the judge. The architecture of the courtroom centers on the judge who sits on a pedestal above other participants, and the court operates under the power of the judge. The judge's black robe accentuates the authoritativeness of his or her role, and courtroom protocols dictate that trial participants rise when the judge enters or leaves the courtroom and that all trial participants address the judge as "Your Honor" (Jeans, 1993). Additionally, the Model Code of Judicial Conduct (1972) specifies that a judge should be "courteous" to counsel, "studious to avoid controversies" that are apt to obscure "the merits of the case," and "avoid interruptions of counsel" in arguments.

In this trial, the judge incurred the wrath of trial participants rather than their respect because his behavior was "arrogant without dignity, wisecracking without wit, a combination of Torquemada [an enforcer of the Spanish Inquisition] and Borscht-circuit tummler [a comic entertainer]" (Macdonald, 1970, p. xi). After the trial, Kunstler (1970) reflected on Hoffman's behavior in this way, "One of his favorite techniques in seeking to attain this goal was that of discreditation [sic]. . . . No insult was too gross, no humiliation too excessive, no degradation too cruel" (p. xiii). Judges should facilitate reasoned legal decisions and respectful behavior. As a referee in the court, the judge should moderate disputes rather than create conflict and controversy (Model Code of Judicial Conduct, 1972). Because Judge Hoffman violated the rules of legal fairness and interjected his personal values and feelings, he contributed to the burlesque mode of the trial.

A number of Judge Hoffman's decisions called into question his competency. For example, the judge failed to grant a change of venue despite massive trial publicity in Chicago, refused a motion to delay the trial so that Seale's attorney could be present, conducted a cursory *voir dire* that failed to eliminate prejudiced jurors, did not sequester jurors until four days after the start of the trial, arrested pretrial lawyers, removed African American spectators from the courtroom, sustained more than 90 percent of the objections of the prosecution and only about 2 percent of the defense's, and gave unreasonable sentences for contempt to defense attorneys and defendants. Prior to and during the trial, these actions impaired his ability to "uphold the integrity and independence of the judiciary," avoid the "appearance of impropriety," and perform his duties "diligently and with impartiality" (Model Code of Judicial Conduct, 1972).

Another role violation occurred when Judge Hoffman engaged in petty and unnecessary conversations with defense attorneys and defendants by quibbling with them and using linguistic ploys to annoy them. Throughout the trial, Hoffman quibbled with defense attorneys by insisting that they make irrelevant and unnecessary distinctions about some of the testimony and evidence. For example, Kunstler reminded Hoffman that it was 12:30, the time for a noon recess. Instead of finishing up and recessing the trial, the judge quibbled, "I know. I am watching the clock. You leave the time-watching to me, Mr. Kunstler. I will watch the clock for you . . . I will determine the time we recess. I don't need your help" (TR, p. 42).

Many times during the trial, Judge Hoffman used linguistic ploys, such as intentionally mispronouncing defense attorney Weinglass's name, calling defendant Dellinger "Derringer," and inserting puns into his responses to defense objections. An example of Hoffman's puns occurred after Weinglass had objected to a tape-recorded speech of one of the defendants on the grounds that it produced "a chilling effect" on free speech. Hoffman retorted, "Through this trial you have almost frozen the Court up here by repeating the word 'chilling' so often" (TR, p. 233). These linguistic ploys elevated petty matters to a level of importance they should not have had. The content of Hoffman's satirical responses was suitable for a burlesque drama, but not for dignified legal proceedings.

The attorneys also trivialized their roles. In the legal tradition, courtroom attorneys should advance "a legal cause in a legal setting, restrained by rules of procedure, confined to theories of discovery and defense, and gentled by the awareness of conscience" (Jeans, 1993, p. 3). The version of the Model Code of Professional Responsibility (1980) existing at the time stressed that attorneys "should represent their clients zealously, preserve the secrets of their client . . . prevent interference with the administration of justice," refrain from engaging in "undignified or discourteous conduct," refuse to use perjured testimony knowingly and refuse to assist clients in giving fraudulent testimony. Moreover, attorneys should adopt "an attitude of professional respect toward the judge, opposing counsel, witnesses, defendants, jurors, and others in the courtroom" (Karlen, 1971, p. 1024).

In the Chicago Eight trial, both the prosecutors and the defense attorneys undermined their roles as advocates by engaging in disputes and interjecting extraneous issues that lacked legal relevance. Extraneous disputations refer to verbal controversies or quarrels about nonlegal matters. For example, Kunstler made a motion indicating he believed the government was involved in sending threatening letters to the jury. Prosecutor Foran responded, "The Government objects to the totally frivolous, idiotic proposal that you have hearings to determine inferences of possibilities of circumstantial evidence . . . of a totally ridiculous charge. . . . I wish the showboat tactics would stop" (TR, p. 38).

Additionally, the attorneys engaged in other disputations with Judge Hoffman. This example took place after Kunstler made a motion to suspend the court session to observe "Vietnam Moratorium Day," a motion irrelevant to the case indictments but pertinent to the defendants' political agenda. Foran responded, saying the motion was cynical and that the defendants were trying to gain publicity. Kunstler then accused Foran of giving a political speech. Hoffman countered saying Kunstler's speech was also political. Kunstler attacked Foran, saying that his comments were abrasive to all American citizens. Judge Hoffman responded, "You just include yourself [rather than including everyone in the category of American citizens]. Don't join me with you. Goodness!" (TR, p. 88).

Finally, the prosecutors engaged in quarrels with the defendants. Schultz's examination of Chicago Deputy Police Chief Riordan tried to get this witness to talk about defendant Dellinger.

S: Did Dellinger say anything when this announcement was made?

R: I did not hear him say anything.

S: Did you see where he went?

R: He left with the head of the group that was carrying the flags.

D: Oh bullshit. That is an absolute lie. . . .

At this point, Kunstler inserted the comment that "sometimes the human spirit can stand only so much. I think Mr. Dellinger reached the end of his . . . ."

S: No further questions.

D: You're a snake. We have to try to put you in jail for ten years for telling lies about us. (TR, pp. 529–530)

These quarrels occurred in the presence of the jury and compromised the attorneys' legitimate legal roles because they engaged in undignified and discourteous conduct and ridiculed the seriousness and respectful decorum of the court.

Witnesses enact other roles. Jeans (1993) notes that in a conventional trial most witnesses consider themselves to be unbiased reporters of the truth. Even if they are partial to either the prosecution or the defense, they want to tell the truth as they know it. Jurors expect witnesses to be informed and accurate reporters of the truth, and most witnesses report the facts to the best of their ability. For this reason, attorneys usually select, coach, and arrange their witnesses so that their testimony offers evidence essential to case theories and helps prove or disprove the indictments.

In this case, the aberrant behavior of defense witnesses contributed significantly to the burlesque drama of the trial. At first glance, the roles of most of the prosecution witnesses seemed conventional. These witnesses reported incidents as they remembered them, but their roles were altered by the defendants and courtroom spectators who responded during the prosecution witnesses' testimony, saying "right on," "liar," and "shut up."

Much of the testimony did not relate the legal issues of the case, but it did enhance the burlesque courtroom drama in several ways. First, a number of radical witnesses testified about their ideology and beliefs, a satirical reaction to government witnesses who testified about their values of law and order. Second, Judge Hoffman's refusal to allow several defense witnesses to explain their testimony encouraged the defense to call other witnesses who presented irrelevant remarks and satirized the evidence-gathering process. Finally, the wide spectrum of witnesses, ranging from the Reverend Jesse Jackson to singer Judy Collins, supported defense's antiwar political agenda. In this way, the defense justified their claim that the antiwar demonstrations did not involve a conspiracy to riot on the part of the defendants but resulted from protestors' moral commitment to change government policies. Thus, the defense succeeded in making issues external to the legal process central to the internal trial drama. The unorthodox roles played by witnesses enabled the defense team to turn the standard legal procedure upside down so that the defense charged the state with a crime rather than the state charging the defendants.

Performance

The situational definitions, scripts, and roles contribute to the content of the drama, and the quality of the performance enhances the persuasive effect. The performance is the means social actors use to foster favorable or unfavorable impressions (Goffman, 1959). Sincere trial performances should incorporate the accredited values of the American court system by conveying respect, tactfulness, and decorum. Cynical performances show impropriety and disrespect, indicate a lack of concern for other participants, and discredit the norms of the court.

Courtroom performance consists of manner and appearance. A person's manner conveys the attitude and tone of interaction, such as acting apologetic, anxious, or haughty. In addition to manner, appearance—dress, posture, eye contact, gestures—has a significant effect on audience impressions. A person's manner works interdependently with appearance to create favorable or unfavorable impressions. In a courtroom, these impressions often have a greater impact on jurors than what was actually said. Although jurors might forget much of the content of the trial discourse, they can usually recall general impressions and attitudes that then enter into their decisions (Colley, 1981). This may be the reason attorneys pay attention to their own appearance and manner as well as that of their witnesses (Fontham, 1995; Jeans, 1993; Kuvin, 1965).

Performance teams are "any sort of individuals who cooperate in staging an event" (Goffman, 1959, p. 79). The attorneys and witnesses appearing on behalf of the prosecution act as one team, and the attorneys and witnesses of the defense act as another team. In the courtroom, the teams take turns being the protagonists and the antagonists. Courtroom performance teams work together to foster a common impression. In a conventional legal proceeding the teams of attorneys try to impress jurors about their belief in and commitment to their case theories. To do this, the teammates define the legal situation similarly, use compatible scripts, and adopt appearances and manners that are consistent with those of other team members.

Audience teams differ from performance teams since they react to rather than create the drama (Goffman, 1959). Courtroom audience teams consist of the judge, jurors, spectators, and usually members of the press. Courtroom audiences judge the facticity, credibility, and relevance of scripts, roles, and impressions of team performances. The judge sets standards for the behavior of the other members of the audience team and reprimands them when they violate the standards.

In the Chicago Eight trial, prosecutors wore their hair short and dressed in formal attire, and some of their witnesses dressed in their law enforcement uniforms. For the most part, the prosecution's witnesses acted in a respectful manner and tried to observe the rules of the court. Although the prosecutors acted with civility and respect during much of the questioning of their own witnesses, they often got out of team character by failing to sustain a positive impression; at times they showed arrogance and vilified the defendants, defense attorneys, and defense witnesses. An example of this kind of vilification surfaced when the defendants continued laughing during Schultz's examination of a witness. Schultz made this request, "I would ask the Court again if he would direct the marshal to direct the defendants and their lawyers to stop laughing out loud as they just did. Mr. Kunstler was probably more guilty of it than any of the defendants." Judge Hoffman responded by ordering a marshal to quiet the defense team and stated emphatically: "This is a trial in the United States District Court. It is not vaudeville theater." Kunstler defended what he had done by saying, "Your honor, we are human beings too. You can't make automatons out of us, or robots; we are human beings and we laugh. . . . I don't really see how that really becomes a court matter." Schultz's recognition of the purpose of Kunstler's remarks is evident from his response, "Mr. Kunstler is laughing so he can influence the jury with the impression that this is absurd" (TR, pp. 208–209).

The defense team intentionally ridiculed and satirized the trial and succeeded in conveying a unified, negative impression of the judge and other trial participants. The defense successfully converted the respectful setting into a disrespectful forum, elevated inconsequential matters and vulgar actions to places of importance, and adapted an irreverent and discourteous manner and appearance.

In various ways the defense expressed contempt for the decorum usually shown to the court. They used diminutive first names rather than formal titles and last names, slang and poor grammar, obscenities, name calling, irreverent puns, and vulgar words. Moreover, their manner showed contempt through interruptions of the court's procedures, insertions of malicious and derogatory comments, disregard for sustained objections, and failure to answer questions in a serious way.

Kunstler and Weinglass contributed to the performance by making silly motions and suggesting they were completely serious, such as requesting that the judge allow them to place a Viet Cong flag beside the American flag in the courtroom. Defense attorneys skillfully directed the burlesque performances of other members of their team, producing a consistent and thorough impression of their political beliefs by consistently adopting the speech, appearance, and manner of disruptive and out-of-control antiwar demonstrators.

The trial was not televised, but appearance still was important to the defense team's performances. They accentuated the trappings associated with radicals and dissenters, such as bringing marijuana into the court, displaying peace symbols, wearing beads and black arm bands, and having long uncombed hair and beards. Additionally, they brought a guitar and displayed poems and pacifist literature as evidence of their connection to antiwar activists and counterculture. Body postures also contributed to the mockery of the court. The defendants sat on the floor, some defense witnesses slouched in their chair, others sauntered to the witness stand, and still others faced the defense table rather than the judge. Members of the defense team made exaggerated and sometimes obscene gestures to indicate their disgust with the prosecution team. The gestures of pointing the middle finger, plugging their ears with their fingers, picking their noses, and brushing one finger across another to indicate shame disparaged the prosecution team and ridiculed the judge. These gestures, however, bolstered the defense's performances in this burlesque drama.

When trying to respond to the defense's burlesque drama, prosecutors faced a double bind. If they ignored the behavior of the defense team, they might give the impression of not caring or not respecting courtroom norms. On the other hand, by challenging the defense team's behavior, they exhibited a disparaging and belittling attitude that spoiled the impression of respect and formality toward the court, thereby giving the impression that they had joined in the burlesque performance. When the behaviors of one part of the performance team lack consistency with other members of the team, the entire group risks having their performance misinterpreted (Goffman, 1959).

The defense's appearance and manner promoted the burlesque drama and also justified some kind of contempt of court charges after the trial. In the contempt proceedings, Judge Hoffman emphasized defense's ridicule of the court. He said,

> No record can adequately portray the venom, the sarcasm and tone of voice by a speaker. No record . . . can adequately reflect the applause, the guffaws, and other subtle tactics employed by these contemptors in an attempt to break up the trial. (Clark, 1970, p. 43)

The following excerpts from Weinglass's direct examination of Abbie Hoffman demonstrate how one defendant performed his burlesque and deserved contempt charges.

> H:　My name is Abbie. I am an orphan of America. . . .
>
> W:　Abbie, what is your last name? . . .
>
> H:　My slave name is Hoffman. My real name is Shaboysnakoff. . . .
>
> W:　Where do you reside?
>
> H:　I live in Woodstock nation. . . .
>
> W:　Between the date of your birth November 30, 1936, and May 1, 1960, what if anything occurred in your life?
>
> H:　Nothing. I believe it is called American education. (TR, p. 344)

Adopting an appearance and manner befitting a burlesque performer, Abbie Hoffman's three days of testimony created one of the best-executed burlesque performances for the defense team. He dressed in the hippie garb of purple pants and an Indian head band, flashed the peace symbol, and sat either on the courtroom floor or on top of the table in front of his attorneys. A few times, he wore a judicial robe for the proceedings (Macdonald, 1970). Whether he was on the witness stand or at some other location in the court, A. Hoffman satirized the legal process and his role in it.

The audience team also contributed to this burlesque drama. Judge Hoffman, relegated by rules of procedure to membership on the audience team, frequently acted as though he was a member of the performance team by trying to upstage the attorneys and their witnesses, rather than performing his designated role as stage manager or referee. He constantly reprimanded the members of the defense team, and then they poked fun at his reprimands. To integrate himself into a performer-team role, Judge Hoffman at times portrayed himself as an omniscient and omnipotent director of the court. He played this role by presenting authoritative responses to attorneys' objections and motions.

Many of Judge Hoffman's remarks fostered the impression that he was a powerful, experienced, efficient, and fair judge. Hoffman emphasized the omnipotent nature of his judicial role in the following response to a defense motion requesting that the pretrial lawyers for the defendants be removed from the case. He asserted, "I will determine the disposition of this case. . . . They are now held in contempt. . . . I will impose a sentence. I am not going to let these men play horse with the court as some of these men have done with me" (TR, p. 25). At another time, Hoffman informed the court about his superlative record "with Negroes," a record resulting in a "discrimination free" court. Using the trappings of his judicial office—garb, gavel, and seat of importance in the court—he moved from a stage manager role to the performance team. In his performances, the judge mimicked the insults, name calling, and emotional outbursts of the defense team performers. Inserting this kind of undignified judicial performance into what should have been a respectful legal forum contributed further to the burlesque features of this trial drama.

Courtroom spectators played performer roles, although court rules forbade the participation of any members of the audience team. The spectators who were packed into the large federal courtroom included sympathetic antiwar dissenters, law enforcement officers, city officials, and members of the defendants' families. Despite the legal restrictions, these spectators clapped, laughed, commented on testimony, and jeered law enforcement officers and Chicago city officials. The 14 court marshals attempted to control the crowd and maintain the decorum of the proceeding, but their presence encouraged rather than discouraged the spectators from joining in the performance. These unorthodox spectators challenged the legal rules, applauded and cheered defense witnesses, and pointed their thumbs down and booed prosecution witnesses.

The only members who acted in accordance with their prescribed roles as one of the audience teams were the jurors. Despite the courtroom confusion, the length of the trial, and the unconventional scripts, the jurors managed to uphold their audience roles as respectful adjudicators abiding by the rules of the court.

Although excluded from the courtroom, members of the press made their reactions known through their reports to the media and their use of sketches drawn by courtroom artists that showed the participants' actions inside the courtroom. The transcript of the trial was not available to the public until a year after the trial ended. Given the polarized political climate in 1969 and 1970, it is not surprising that the conservative press lauded the performance of the prosecution and Judge Hoffman, and the liberal press applauded the satirical performances of the defendants and condemned the actions of Judge Hoffman (Dee, 1985).

One way to assess the courtroom performances is by interpreting them according to the context and audience. The trial context centered on political rather than legal issues. The performers created both a parody and a travesty that satirized the ideals of the litigation process. According to political standards of the antiwar and New Left movements, the trial demonstrated to the public and the judge the truth of defendant Dellinger's words, "Justice is more important than decorum" (Kalven, 1970, p. xiii). For the most part, left-wing and liberal audiences of the time enjoyed the burlesque drama because it furthered their political cause, but the government and conservatives abhorred the satirical content, conceiving it as an attack on America and its system of justice.

Staging

A final element of this dramatic analogue is the staging of the trial performances. Front stages are regions where the performances intended for audience teams are staged (Goffman, 1959). Participants in the court can perform front stage behavior in- and outside of the courtroom through their statements in the official trial record and their public responses to the media. Backstages are regions where trial participants can be themselves, where the impression designed for the consumption of audience teams is "knowingly contradicted" (p. 112). Participants may spoil the favorable impressions they have earned if they present backstage behavior in the front region. In a typical trial, audience teams glimpse backstage behavior when they see participants say and do things outside of the courtroom that are contrary to the scripts, roles, and performances they follow inside of the courtroom.

In this case, the trial performers repeatedly and willfully transposed backstage behavior onto the front region in order to subvert the principles, procedures, and protocols expected in federal courts. The defense's satirical responses so degraded and belittled other participants that they were unable to perform according to the norms of the appropriate courtroom region. This burlesque drama turned expectations upside down, converting one set of norms into another by ridiculing conventions associated with courtroom manners and overtly violating the rules of procedure. Adopting this dramatic mode encouraged performers to present what would normally be backstage behavior in the front region, where it was observed by courtroom and public audiences.

Many of the staged behaviors of the defense were so egregious they became grounds for the contempt charges after the trial. For example, Dellinger called the judge a "fascist"; Davis accused the court marshals of "torturing" him; Hayden refused to sit at the defendants' table; Rubin charged the judge with interrupting a defense attorney; Weiner referred to the judge as an "executioner"; and Froines said prosecutor Schultz was a "tattletale" (Clark, 1970). The 175 contempt citations identify some of these backstage behaviors (Levine, McNamee, & Greenberg, 1970, pp. 287–289).

A second instance of transposing backstage behavior onto the front stage occurred at the out-of-court appearances during the trial of Kunstler, Weinglass, and the defendants. The defense team's commentaries outside of the courtroom about their inside performance functioned as a theatrical interlude, that is, as intervening episodes performed between the acts of the main drama for the benefit of public spectators. This interlude permitted the media to report what they learned about the trial from inside sources, and this reporting gave the defense an alternate venue to re-present their burlesque drama. Judge Hoffman joined in the interlude by giving interviews to newspapers and magazines. In all of these instances, trial participants intentionally transferred backstage behavior, which should have been outside the hearing of jurors and hidden from spectators, to the front region for everyone to see and hear.

A striking example of this type of staging of behavior occurred during the trial when Jerry Rubin interrupted the examination of a witness to protest that a marshal was removing Rubin's wife from the courtroom.

R: Bill [Kunstler], they are taking out my wife . . .

K: Your Honor, must we always have this force and power of government? . . .

R: They are dragging my wife out—will you please—

K: They like to strike women, your Honor, we've seen that constantly here. (Clark, 1970, p. 191)

When heard and seen by the jury, staged performances of this kind conveyed the impression that conduct in the courtroom was out of the control of the judge and in the control of the defense who promoted the pandemonium as a way of showing that the legal system had no authority over their behavior. Judge Hoffman was aware of the prejudicial effect of this kind of behavior and at times tried to remove jurors from the courtroom so they would not have to observe the continual wrangling that was happening on the front stage of the trial. The repeated action of removing jurors, however, left a negative impression, similar to what Kalven (1970) calls "a sense of crisis after crisis" (p. xxiii).

In a third instance when backstage behavior entered onto the front region, performers served as a "studio audience" for the defense team. A number of instances exemplified the intrusion of performers in their own trial drama. For example, defendant Dellinger interrupted the testimony of defense witness Riordan and called Judge Hoffman "a liar" for revoking the defendant's bail. Dellinger then presented a short speech asserting that the defendants were fighting for "all the rest of the people in this country who are oppressed." Spectators also took their performances to the center stage of the trial by adding their appraisals of the testimony, saying, "Damn right, assert yourselves," "Right on," and "I agree" (Clark, 1970, p. 66).

Judge Hoffman's remarks offer a fourth example of how his own back-stage behaviors entered into the burlesque staging of the drama. On the way to the courtroom, media reporters overheard the judge saying, "Now we are going to hear this wild man Weinglass." After Judge Hoffman directed his remarks to the defense, they asked him to enter his remark into the official trial record so they could use it later as evidence of judicial misconduct, a justification for a mistrial. Another time, Judge Hoffman confronted Kunstler about the frequent laughter from the defendants, defiantly asserting, "I will not sit here and you must know it by now, certainly—and have defendants laugh at my rulings, sir. And I will not hear you on that" (Clark, 1970, p. 184). Hoffman frequently directed some of the marshals to remove courtroom spectators, to quiet and restrain witnesses, and to seize objects from the defendants and spectators. These punitive measures intruded so strongly into the legal proceeding that at times the legal features of the trial disappeared from the view of the courtroom and public spectators.

One of the most extreme measures that the judge took was to bind defendant Bobby Seale's hands and feet, gag him, and tie him to a chair in the courtroom. Since Hoffman could not silence the defendant by ordering him to be quiet, he decided he would have the court marshals silence him by these ridiculous methods. These kinds of outrageous punitive actions showed that Judge Hoffman was staging actions on the front region of the courtroom that had no legitimate place in any dignified legal proceeding. The judicial code of conduct does not permit prejudicing jurors by these kinds of actions, and the common sense of most judges dictates that such staging is inappropriate and damaging to the court.

On many occasions, the advocates showed out-of-character behavior not meant to be seen by the audience team. Jeans (1993) recommends that trial lawyers should be combative about legal issues while they maintain a genuine commitment to the welfare of their clients. In this trial, the confrontations between the attorneys and the judge transformed what should have been fact-finding and adversarial argument leading to a verdict into ridiculous bickering about issues of no consequence that had no place in a trial. For example, in several instances, Kunstler rose while Weinglass was examining witnesses, and Judge Hoffman demanded that Kunstler remain seated; Kunstler refused:

    H: Sit down.

    K: I am not going to sit down unless I am directed.

H: I direct you to sit down.

K: Am I to be thrown in the chair by the marshal if I don't sit down?
(Clark, 1970, p. 187)

Other more serious ethical disputes took place as well. Instead of making dignified and serious attempts to resolve these disputes, the attorneys
changed the focus to trivial matters that should never have been presented
in a court. At one point, Kunstler asserted that Schultz and Foran were making derogatory personal references when they said the defense resembled
television actors who engaged in theatrics (TR, p. 54). The defense attorneys
tried to magnify the importance of these trivial disputes by claiming that they
were justifications for motions for a mistrial. Regardless of who initiated
these silly actions, jurors should not have had to tolerate this kind of behavior. But the defendants chose to behave in this way in front of jurors because
they wanted to perform a burlesque drama in which they could demean the
government by ridiculing legal practices and protocols.

Drama, Communication, and the Courts

After five months of name calling, personal insults, and legal challenges,
the Chicago Eight trial came to an end on February 12, 1970. When the trial
ended, reporters characterized the case as "horrendous provocation" and
"guerilla theater" ("Chicago Trial," 1970, p. 38); *Newsweek* called the case a
"wild eccentricity" filled with "pyrotechnics" ("Judgment in Chicago," 1970,
p. 27); and *Nation* concluded that the proceeding attempted "to suppress
dissent" and "intimidate" protest (1970, p. 5). The theatrical form of the trial
detracted from the fact that the case was one of "the most important political trials of the century" (Arbetman & Roe, 1985, p. 151). However, *Newsweek* offered this generous evaluation of the trial, saying it was a case that
tested the judicial process and proved the value of the American jury system.
The magazine claimed that the trial went astray because the "American judicial process is a form of unscripted drama that works on the tacit agreement
of everyone concerned to play by the rules and trust the outcome to be just"
("Judgment in Chicago," 1970, p. 25). Reporters did not recognize that the
trial was indeed a carefully scripted burlesque drama. Clearly though, the
external and internal burlesque drama was so dominant that it concealed the
legitimacy of the trial proceeding.

This case illustrates two types of burlesque drama—parody and travesty.
Parody surfaced only a few times in the trial. For example, the preoccupation
of Judge Hoffman with the defense's use of diminutive names, such as Billy,
Abbie, and Rennie, raised that trivial issue to a level of extreme importance.
Kunstler also used parody when he made several motions about the trivial
nonissue of securing bathroom privileges for the defendants. But the predominant type of burlesque was travesty. This mode of drama was pervasive,
repetitive, and directed to the singular purpose of subverting the traditional
goals, roles, and protocols of decorum and respect. Travesty was part of the

defense's definition of the trial situation, the development of the scripts, the enactment of roles, the impression the performers tried to make, and the staging of the trial.

The analogue of this trial as burlesque drama gives a more complete evaluation of what occurred in the case than the verdict does. Through the defense's definition of the situation, use of scripts, and enacting backstage performances on the front stage of the courtroom and in view of the public audience, they satirized the government's charges against them so much that the conspiracy charge seemed ridiculous. The drama also showed that defendants can use a trial as a platform for presenting the ideological beliefs of the political left, criticizing the judge, government attorneys, and witnesses, and ignoring legal principles, procedures, protocols, and codes of conduct.

LESSONS

Trial performers in this case seemed to recognize that the external and internal trial drama can be directed in ways that achieve their goals. They understood that good performances persuade audiences in- and outside of the courtroom. At one point during the trial, defendant Jerry Rubin quipped: "I like being here. It is interesting. . . . It is good theater, your honor" (Macdonald, 1970, p. xxiii). At another point, prosecutor Foran lamented:

> I feel like one of the characters in Alice and [sic] Wonderland that just went through the looking glass. I have never, your honor, in twenty years of practice, heard attorneys like Mr. Kunstler and Mr. Weinglass refuse to direct their clients with decency and courtesy in the courtroom. (TR, p. 161)

At still another point, Judge Hoffman warned the defendants: "This is not a guerrilla theater" (TR, p. 207), but clearly that is what the trial turned out to be. Additionally, many of the witnesses presented mini performances by establishing their credentials, elaborating their roles, and promoting their political points of view. Clearly, the trial participants knew that the trial could be turned into a theater to promote their political views, and they performed the roles and delivered lines from scripts that would achieve this purpose.

Analyzing trials as drama has several advantages for persons interested in how the law is communicated. First, this perspective accounts for what seem to be unethical interactions and distorted relationships among attorneys, the judge, jurors, spectators, and witnesses; it demonstrates that the verbal and nonverbal action of each trial performer affects and is affected by other performers and by the goal of the drama. Second, this perspective identifies the patterns of verbal communication created by the scripts of witnesses, showing that jointly constituted messages require the cooperation of attorneys, their witnesses, the judge, and courtroom spectators. Third, investigating trials as a satirical dramatic genre provides an alternative explanation for why participants enjoy engaging in what at first seem to be blatant unethical practices. Fourth, the analysis raises questions about whether zealous attorneys can follow professional codes of legal conduct if judges themselves are unable to abide by the judicial codes. Fifth, a retrospective analysis of the trial shows that zealous conduct on the behalf of clients can compromise attorneys' responsibilities to the legal system. Finally, using an analogue based on an unconventional dramatic genre is a lens for viewing the mistakes, bad performances, errors in staging, inappropriate roles, and negative impressions that surface in many different legal proceedings. This exposé of the distorted practices of the Chicago Eight trial illuminates the kind of disarray that results when judges fail to monitor and enforce procedural rules, codes of conduct, and protocols.

Even though the burlesque drama achieved some of the political goals of the defendants, it left only a temporary scar on the legal system. The defendant's success was fleeting because the public viewed the performances as too bizarre and offensive to be legitimate for the legal setting. By failing to play their designated roles, produce legitimate legal scripts, give believable performances, and stage their behavior in an appropriate region, the judge, attorneys, defendants, and some witnesses hurt their credibility as legitimate political activists and legal participants (Karlen, 1971). In a strictly artistic sense, the defense achieved its dramatic purpose by satirizing the legal proceeding. The defense demonstrated to their followers that political ideology was more important than decorum, and to some extent the appellate court accepted this idea when it overturned Hoffman's contempt sentences for the defense attorneys. This satirical theatrical genre achieves a dramatic reversal when it changes the traditional way of thinking. The defense probably did not change the traditional way of thinking about the law, but they did seem to change some of the political thinking about the rights of demonstrators and antiwar activists.

10

The NAACP's Legal Campaign in *Brown v. Board of Education*

More than 50 years after the U.S. Supreme Court decided *Brown v. Board of Education of Topeka* (1954, 1955), the decision and its impact on race relations in the United States remain difficult to assess. *Brown* began with graduate school test cases, continued in five trials related to segregation in public elementary and secondary schools, and progressed to the five school desegregation cases being consolidated and heard by the Supreme Court. The National Association for the Advancement of Colored People (NAACP) and its Legal Defense Fund (LDF) first constructed test cases to challenge segregation laws in higher education in Texas and Oklahoma. After the Supreme Court struck down segregation in graduate schools, the LDF attorneys conducted civil lawsuits to challenge public school segregation in South Carolina, Kansas, Virginia, Delaware, and the District of Columbia. The judges in some of the five trials ordered school officials to upgrade black school facilities, but other judges allowed segregation to continue. The NAACP lawyers appealed the decisions of the public school cases, and the U.S. Supreme Court consolidated the appeals from five trials under the generic title of *Brown v. Board of Education*.

The Supreme Court agreed to hear the cases because they recognized that elementary and secondary school segregation created a divisive social issue, and they also questioned the legality of some previous court decisions that allowed segregation. The appeals to the Supreme Court evolved from a systematic campaign conducted by LDF attorneys to eliminate school segregation laws. After the Court first heard oral arguments from attorneys opposing and supporting school segregation in 1952, the justices withheld a decision and asked both sides to reargue their cases in 1953 with an emphasis on how the equal protection clause of the Fourteenth Amendment applied to school segregation. After deciding that segregation violated the

245

Fourteenth Amendment rights of African American public school children in 1954, the Court requested another round of arguments to help them establish guidelines for desegregating the public schools. The texts of lower court decisions, the attorneys' briefs, and the oral arguments are published in Friedman (1969) and Kurland and Casper (1970). In ways similar to other decisions that seek legal and social change, the *Brown* decision ignited major conflicts. Many school districts refused to integrate, others forced the bussing of children from one school to another, and still others dismantled the black schools and fired black teachers (Cashin, 2004).

Numerous scholars have examined the legacy of the *Brown* decision in terms of the racial strife that followed the decision. For example, some historians (e.g., Martin, 1998) noted that the decision reinforced attitudes of black inferiority by implying that blacks could learn best under the direction of white teachers in predominantly white classrooms. They claimed the decision insulted some black teachers and administrators, devalued black culture, and reduced the self-esteem of black students. Others emphasized that the decision was a strong and positive step toward a more egalitarian society. The decision did not produce an immediate change in educational spaces or an alteration of the place of blacks in society, but it influenced the "rights consciousness" of the public and inspired "judicial activism on the part of oppressed minorities" (Tushnet & Lezin, 1991, p. 1187). Most critics agree that the outcome of the case changed "America profoundly" (Kluger, 1977, p. 26). Jack M. Balkin (2002) emphasized the importance of the *Brown* decision when he noted that it is the

> single most honored opinion in the Supreme Court's corpus. The civil rights policy of the United States in the last half century has been premised on the correctness of *Brown*, even if people often disagree . . . about what the opinion stands for. No federal judicial nominee and no mainstream national politician today would dare suggest that *Brown* was wrongly decided. (p. 4)

My purpose is not to assess the legacy of the decision, since others ably have done so, but to explain how a well-planned and well-orchestrated legal campaign using conventional legal reasoning and following established appellate procedures can develop U.S. law. Specifically, the chapter explains how NAACP attorneys created test cases and utilized the narratives presented in federal civil trials to construct persuasive appellate arguments showing that segregated schools violated the constitutional rights of black students. This case study emphasizes the development and content of the oral arguments rather than the decision itself by (1) describing the processes NAACP attorneys used to mount a legal campaign against segregated schools, (2) explicating the role that plaintiffs' narratives had in establishing facts in the five trials that preceded the *Brown* decision, (3) summarizing the arguments in the attorneys' appellate briefs, (4) explaining the legal principles and communication procedures and protocols followed in the attorneys' oral arguments, and (5) noting lessons to be learned about conventional appellate argumentation from this study.

THE LEGAL CAMPAIGN OF THE LDF ATTORNEYS

In ways similar to other campaigns, attorneys organized their legal effort to desegregate public schools "from the top down" (Stewart, Smith, & Denton, 2001). The leadership created a goal for their campaign, planned the type of legal methods they would use to achieve their goals, raised money to support the attorneys participating in the campaign, and designated the roles attorneys would play in the campaign. The legal campaign proceeded by establishing goals, following processes of appellate review, overturning precedents that impeded their goals, and creating test cases in which the Supreme Court overturned some of the precedents that permitted segregation.

Establishing Goals

The decision in *Brown* was the culmination of a deliberate effort on the part of the LDF attorneys of the NAACP. The goal of the LDF attorneys was to mount "a legal assault" on segregated schools. Jack Greenberg, an LDF attorney, explained that the goal for the campaign originated in 1939 as part of an organizational charter written by Thurgood Marshall:

> (a) To render legal aid gratuitously to such Negroes as may appear to be worthy thereof, who are suffering legal injustices by reason of race or color . . . and (b) To seek and promote the educational facilities for Negroes who are denied the same by reason of race or color. (Greenberg, 1994, p. xvii)

According to Paul E. Wilson, an attorney representing the Kansas defendants and appellees, the states knew full well that the case against them was being led by Marshall and supported financially by the LDF (Wilson, 1995).

In this campaign, attorneys planned how they would use legal processes to bring about changes in the segregated education. They developed a specific legal plan with the following objectives: (1) overturn precedents that impeded school integration, (2) create new precedents that forbid separate but equal schools, (3) sue states that prohibit black children from attending white schools, and (4) persuade the Supreme Court to overturn segregation laws. This campaign showed that the LDF attorneys understood the appellate process and knew how to make it work to achieve their goals. They understood that in order to make new laws, they had to overturn precedents.

Following the Appellate Review Process

The basic justification for the Supreme Court review process is the need to create uniformity of decisions among the various jurisdictions. Three prominent functions of the judicial process are error correction, law development, and doing justice. Error correction protects a person or group from arbitrariness in the administration of justice. In some of the trials that preceded the *Brown* decision, judges ruled that state laws needed to be changed to make black schools equal to those attended by white students. In doing so, they corrected errors in the way states implemented the laws.

Law development has several features: it allows the law to change to meet social and cultural needs, permits the appellate courts to change unjust laws, protects the previous legal interpretations of judicial and legislative bodies, and sometimes attempts to change social or institutional practices. The law development function usually results from appeals about constitutional or statutory provisions that are in need of interpretation or from case precedents that are in need of revision (Carrington, Meador, & Rosenberg, 1976; Martineau, 1985; Parker, 1950). LDF attorneys wanted to develop the law by overturning precedents that permitted segregation and by creating new precedents that would result in integration of public schools.

Doing justice means that judges make decisions that remedy injustices suffered by particular people in specific situations and apply them to all similarly situated citizens. The LDF attorneys emphasized the harm caused to black plaintiffs in five states, but they expected that the Court would apply the law to all black children in all of the 17 states in which segregation was legal. In order for their campaign to succeed, LDF attorneys first had to find a legal means to overturn the precedent of separate but equal facilities (*Plessy v. Ferguson,* 1896), the primary justification that states used for segregating schools.

Three Precedents to Overturn

The doctrine of precedents, called *star decisis,* means that courts are bound to follow the decisions that courts of appeals have made in prior cases. When attorneys rely on precedents, they use analogical reasoning to persuade appellate judges that the precedents they are using show sufficient similarities to a new case so that the old precedent should be applied to that new case (Savellos & Galvin, 2001).

The Precedent Set in Plessy.   During the first half of the twentieth century, states justified school segregation using the precedent of *Plessy v. Ferguson* (1896). The ruling in *Plessy* did not deal with schools at all, but it addressed the legality of segregated public accommodations, specifically the legality of Louisiana officials ordering blacks to ride in separate rail cars from those occupied by white passengers. In New Orleans, the Citizens' Committee to Test the Constitutionality of the Separate Car initiated a lawsuit against the state of Louisiana. Before the case could go forward, Albion Tourgee and James C. Walker initiated a complaint on behalf of Homer Adolph Plessy, a 78-year-old man who was one-half white and one-half black. Tourgee and Walker asked Plessy to board a train and sit in the white coach in order to be arrested. After his arrest, his attorneys sued, claiming that Louisiana segregation laws violated Homer Plessy's rights. After a New Orleans criminal court upheld the legality of the segregation laws, Tourgee and Walker appealed their case to the Supreme

Court, but the justices ruled that Plessy's rights had not been violated because the rail cars provided separate accommodations for blacks that were equal to those available to white citizens.

In this case, the Court affirmed that separate accommodations for blacks and whites in railroad cars were legal if they were equal. The decision was called a "Jim Crow" law because it sanctioned segregation. Two senses of the word "segregation" appear in legal discourses. *De facto* segregation means separation of races in social settings, and *de jur* refers to legally sanctioned segregation achieved through a variety of legal restrictions, such as zoning laws, school bus routes, location of new schools, and drawing of school district lines (Patterson, 2001, p. xx). *Plessy* upheld the right of school districts for *de jur* segregation. When applied to schools, "to segregate means to apportion school children differentially according to discriminatory criteria. . . . The apportionment is either to a specific building, away from a specific building, or a combination of both" (Weinberg, 1967, p. 3).

The Supreme Court ruling in the *Plessy* precedent created a formidable obstacle that the LDF attorneys had to overcome in order for their legal campaign to succeed. If this separate but equal doctrine remained settled law, then the attorneys would be unable to develop new law to achieve their goal of desegregating the public schools. However, the dissenting opinion in the *Plessy* case offered a glimmer of hope that the *Plessy* decision might someday be overturned. Justice John Marshall Harlan's dissent opined:

> In view of the Constitution, in the eye of the law, there is in this country no superior, dominant, ruling class of citizens. There is no caste here. Our Constitution is color-blind, and neither knows nor tolerates classes among citizens. In respect of civil rights, all citizens are equal before the law. (*Plessy v. Ferguson,* 1896, p. 537)

The metaphor of a color-blind Constitution raised the hope of LDF attorneys that they could eventually overturn school segregation laws on constitutional grounds.

The Roberts Precedent.   LDF attorneys feared that states would justify their retention of segregated schools by using a decision that predated *Plessy* named *Roberts v. City of Boston* (1850). This decision concluded that separate schools did not deny black children their legal rights or expose them to undue "logistical difficulties and degradation." The justices ruled that racially segregated schools were legal if they served the "reasonable racial and social interests" of a community. Attorneys representing segregated schools in South Carolina and Virginia used this as a precedent in their 1952 arguments before the Supreme Court in the *Brown* appeal.

The Gong Lum Precedent.   Another decision, *Gong Lum v. Rice* (1927), applied the separate but equal doctrine to schools. After the state of Mississippi forced a nine-year-old Chinese girl to attend a black school because she was not white, her father, Gong Lum, sued, claiming that his daughter had a constitutional right to be assigned to a white school because she was not a member of the black race. The Supreme Court, however, decided that the practice of classifying all school children as either white or black was legal. The justices affirmed *Plessy* and noted that Lum's child should attend a segregated black school because this facility was equal to the white school. LDF attorneys were not involved in this case, but they saw it as an unfortunate decision that misapplied *Plessy* to children in public schools. The opposition would also use this decision to support their appeal arguments.

The Graduate School Test Cases

In order for their appellate campaign to succeed, LDF attorneys decided to initiate test cases based on some plaintiffs' compelling stories about segregation in state-supported graduate schools. A test case is a legitimate legal means that attorneys can use to find out whether or not the appeal courts will decide that a particular case violates or upholds the law and if old precedents should be applied to the new fact situation established in the test case. Test cases do not start with the plaintiffs filing complaints against the government as most constitutional cases do. Rather, attorneys instigate test cases to force judges to make a decision about whether or not existing laws violate plaintiffs' constitutional rights.

The success of this part of the LDF's legal campaign, their test cases, depended on whether LDF attorneys could persuade the Supreme Court to overrule the separate but equal doctrine of the *Plessy* decision and rule against state-supported segregation in the graduate school cases. If LDF attorneys succeeded, the decisions in these test cases could be used as a new precedent that would support their legal campaign to desegregate elementary and secondary schools. When the LDF attorneys set out to overturn *Plessy,* they stressed the issue of "inequality rather than attacking segregation itself." They concentrated their lawsuits on graduate education because blacks at that time had extremely limited opportunities to attend graduate schools (Greenberg, 1994, p. 63).

LDF attorneys initiated their test cases by soliciting qualified black students to apply for admission to segregated graduate schools. In order for the test cases to be legitimate, the attorneys needed to document legally and socially appropriate narratives that proved violations of black students' rights. First, they had to locate persons with educational aspirations for attending graduate school and with good moral character. A black person with poor educational credentials or a flawed character would only limit the success of their campaign. In order for the case to go forward, the black student had to fill out the appropriate application for admission to a graduate program, the state-supported institution then had to admit the black applicant, and deny the admitted student access to the all white graduate program. After the institution denied the black student the right to attend one of the white graduate school programs, then LDF attorneys could create a narrative scenario using facts that served their legal goals. Although the narrative scenarios for the different graduate cases had some unique features, the characters, actions, institutional responses, and settings were similar.

The narratives centered on the strong moral character and educational motivation of graduate school applicants. In these test cases, LDF attorneys contrasted the positive character of the plaintiffs with the defective character of white state education officials who used their position of white privilege to conceal their race-based motivation. In addition to character, the LDF attorneys established narrative details about the unequal features of the physical setting created by state officials for black students to meet the provisions of *Plessy.* The trial narratives presented in these test cases included facts that served several of the legal purposes of LDF attorneys. For example, the narratives demonstrated that plaintiffs did not get an equal education, the facilities were neither adequate nor comparable, and state education officials supported segregation for race-based reasons. The purpose of these contrived legal cases was to assemble and present facts that would prove black students lacked access to graduate schools, black schools were not equal to those attended by white students, black students suffered personal harm from segregation, and this harm proved that they did not get constitutional protections equal to white graduate students. Three of the test cases reached the Supreme Court.

Sipuel v. Oklahoma State Board of Regents (1948).   Ada Lois Sipuel was an educationally motivated and morally upright black woman who wanted to attend law school. Sipuel had graduated at the top of her class from the State College for Negroes in Langston, Oklahoma, but the segregated University of Oklahoma refused to let her attend their law school. The lower court ruled that the state had to set up a separate school, and the state complied by roping off an area in the state capitol and designating the space as a law school for blacks. This response provided an even more absurd resolution than the LDF lawyers could have imagined. As a result, LDF attorney Thurgood Marshall appealed the case to the Supreme Court, arguing that segregation was unconstitutional because it failed to provide black graduate students equal legal protection. The Court returned the case to the civil court and asked it to make another ruling about whether or not the makeshift law school was equal. The Court also ruled that Oklahoma must provide Sipuel with a legal education that conformed with her Fourteenth Amendment right for equal protection. Because the institution got tired of the legal and political hassles, Oklahoma lawmakers gave up their fight to keep Sipuel out of the University of Oklahoma and finally admitted her.

The Court never ruled that segregation was illegal, but the decision provided a victory of sorts for the NAACP campaign because LDF attorneys convinced the Supreme Court that separate facilities did not add up to equal educational opportunities for black graduate students nor did it afford black students the same equal protections that white students received.

Sweatt v. Painter (1950).   The trial narrative of this test case centered on Herman Marian Sweatt, a committed and capable black student who sought admission to the University of Texas Law School in Austin. The school rejected his admission because of his race. After LDF attorneys Thurgood Marshall, W. J. Durham, and James M. Nabrit filed a complaint with the Travis County Court alleging that Sweatt's rights had been violated, this court ordered the University of Texas to create a separate law school for black students within six months. In their feeble effort to comply with the court, the university created a makeshift law school for blacks in the basement of a petroleum building in Austin. The space consisted of a few small rooms and a toilet; it lacked a library, study materials, or other amenities for learning.

After the University of Texas created its so-called separate but equal law school, LDF attorneys immediately filed a complaint claiming the rooms did not constitute a law school by any stretch of legal educators' imagination. In this case, the NAACP attorneys expanded the arguments they had used in *Sipuel* by emphasizing that unsuitable facilities impeded black students' rights. To prove this point, LDF attorneys called numerous experts from the disciplines of education, sociology, psychology, anthropology, and law to support their arguments. The trial court predictably ignored the plaintiffs' evidence and ruled that makeshift basement rooms were equal to the white University of Texas law school.

This court's ruling, however, offended the white students at the university. After Herman Sweatt refused to attend the makeshift law school, more than 2,000 students, educators, and community members rallied to support him and demanded that the University of Texas integrate their graduate programs. As a result of the unpopular and ill-constructed decision, the Supreme Court agreed to hear the case. In their appeal, LDF attorneys argued that segregation violated Sweatt's constitutional rights.

The Court ruled in 1950 that under the equal protection provision of the Fourteenth Amendment, Sweatt must be admitted to the white University of Texas Law School and receive instruction in the same classes with white students because "no makeshift law school would in any way be equal to any long-standing law school" (*Sweatt v. Painter*, 1950; Williams, 1998, p. 185).

McLaurin v. Oklahoma State Regents for Higher Education (1950). In ways similar to the cases of *Sipuel* and *Sweatt*, the story of George McLaurin centered on the lack of legal justification for a university to refuse admission of a capable black student to a graduate program. After Professor McLaurin was denied entrance into a doctoral program at the University of Oklahoma in 1948, LDF lawyers filed a complaint with the federal district court, which ruled that the state must provide McLaurin with a graduate education. The Oklahoma governor recommended that state universities admit black students to white graduate programs only if the degrees they sought were unavailable at the black colleges. After the University of Oklahoma admitted McLaurin, professors forced him to sit in a back area of the classroom, segregated from white graduate students. LDF attorneys appealed the case to the Supreme Court, arguing that Oklahoma had denied McLaurin equal protection by singling him out because of his race and creating a "badge of inferiority" for this student.

The Court ruled that the placement of McLaurin in the back of the classroom inhibited his ability to learn, created a stigma, and denied his rights. The Court ordered the university to treat McLaurin the same way the institution treated white graduate students.

Each of the aforementioned test cases and the appeals resulting from them relied on fact-disseminating narratives that revealed how short-sighted state and school officials violated the constitutional rights of capable and motivated black graduate school applicants and students. The decisions overturned the separate but equal doctrine established in *Plessy:* the Supreme Court eventually agreed that separate but equal graduate educational facilities violated the first provision of the Fourteenth Amendment of the Constitution. This constitutional provision states:

> All persons born or naturalized in the United States, and subject to the jurisdiction thereof, are citizens of the United States and of the States in which they reside. No State shall make or enforce any law which shall abridge the privileges or immunities of citizens of the United States; nor shall any State deprive any person of life, liberty, or property, without due process of law; nor deny to any person within its jurisdiction the equal protection of the law.

After LDF attorneys persuaded the Supreme Court that the actions of state school officials did not provide equal educational facilities or equal protection to black graduate students, the first stage of LDF's campaign was complete. The attorneys expected that the precedents decided on behalf of Ada Sipuel, Herman Marion Sweatt, and George McLaurin would help them achieve the goal of desegregating elementary and secondary schools, and this expectation later proved to be correct.

TRIAL NARRATIVES IN THE CONSOLIDATED CASES

In 1950, 17 states and the District of Columbia enforced school segregation, and at that time, the segregation of hotels, restaurants, and public transportation was the norm in most of these states. Black parents complained on behalf of their children that government and educational agencies violated the rights of black children by forcing them to attend segregated schools. The legal campaign to overturn *Plessy* and school segregation intensified at the beginning of 1951. LDF attorneys continued to pursue their campaign goals by agreeing to help plaintiffs win lawsuits in five different jurisdictions. The facts presented in the narratives of these cases resemble those in the graduate school cases because they centered on violations of the rights of black public school students, their lack of opportunity to get a quality education, and the failure of the states to protect their constitutional rights. This next crucial phase of the campaign relied on the narratives from plaintiffs that related how they had been adversely affected by segregated black elementary and secondary schools. In these new cases, LDF attorneys assisted parents and students who already had decided on their own to challenge segregation. The trials featured testimony from children, parents, and expert witnesses about the harm they had suffered from school segregation.

In ways similar to the graduate cases, these trials juxtaposed the good character and positive educational aspirations of black parents and their children with the racist motivations and discriminatory policies of public education officials. The setting—the black school facilities—was central to the witnesses' narratives, which conveyed that black schools were unequal to white facilities. The lack of resources and the inadequate facilities in black schools contrasted with the abundance of resources and quality of learning environments in white schools. In addition to the contrasts of character and settings, the trial narratives emphasized a racial theme. For example, some defense witnesses admitted that the reason they did not want integration of schools was because they feared the social consequences of mixing the races, such as interracial dating and marriage. The explicit and common theme corroborated by the narratives of LDF's witnesses was that institutional racism promoted segregation that in turn stigmatized black children and stifled their education.

SUMMARY OF THE FIVE SEPARATE COMPLAINTS

1. Plaintiffs in Bolling petitioned Congress to terminate segregation in the District of Columbia based on due process provisions of the Fifth Amendment.
2. Plaintiffs in Briggs complained that the unequal and segregated practices of schools in Clarendon County, South Carolina, impeded black children's educational opportunities.
3. Plaintiffs in Brown contested state-supported segregation in Topeka, Kansas, claiming their children were burdened by travel to black schools outside of their neighborhoods.
4. Plaintiffs in Belton and Bulah sought legal entry into the white secondary schools in Delaware, claiming that black schools were inferior and segregation violated black children's rights to equal protection.
5. Plaintiffs in Davis challenged the systemic practices of segregation and unequal facilities and inferior instruction in black schools in Prince Edward County, Virginia.

LDF attorneys played a central role in all of these cases by using the graduate school precedents to overturn the separate but equal doctrine of *Plessy* and to declare segregation illegal. The cases featured testimony of black parents and children about the struggles they experienced with segregation as well as the testimony of experts about the psychological and sociological harms to black students.

The Bolling Trial

The legal campaign started in the nation's capital when LDF attorneys used unique legal arguments supported by a narrative about the features of post–Civil War history. The legal complaint first evolved from a demonstration by black students and teachers who protested the fact that they could not pursue their education at a new school in Washington, D.C., because they were black.

In 1951, LDF attorneys Spottswood Robinson and James Nabrit demanded the federal court abolish the school segregation policy in Washington, D.C., and admit their client Spottswood T. Bolling to the new white Sousa Junior High. They argued that segregation was illegal, but they did not address the inequality of facilities. Specifically, Robinson argued that the U.S. Congress should never have condoned segregation in the District of Columbia in the nineteenth century, and his colleague Nabrit asserted the District's segregated schools violated the due process clause of the Fifth Amendment, and this clause implicitly contained an "equal protection component." Milton Korman defended the segregation policy by saying that the intention of Congress in the nineteenth century had been to create public rather than segregated schools. He quoted from *Dred Scott v. Sandford* (1857) to support his position. Judge Walter M. Bastion dismissed Robinson and Nabrit's complaint on the grounds that LDF attorneys had failed to provide evidence that black and white schools were unequal. The judge never ruled about whether or not segregation was unconstitutional.

Shortly after Nabrit filed his case with the U.S. Court of Appeals, the Supreme Court granted *certiorari*, agreed to hear the case, and added the Bolling appeal to the other four appeals related to segregation. This complaint touched the nerves of some Supreme Court justices, likely because they worked in Washington, D.C. During a Court conference, for example, Justice Felix Frankfurter noted that "The District of Columbia is the nation's capital. I am prepared to vote today that segregation in the District of Columbia violates the due process clause" (Dickson, 2001, p. 650). The legal proceeding on behalf of Bolling was unique because it relied exclusively on historical narrative rather than on testimonials from black children or expert witnesses about the harm brought about by segregation.

The Briggs Trial

The concerted legal campaign intensified with cases in the deep South, a region where education for black children was not a social priority, but keeping the races separate was. The Briggs trial took place in May of 1951 in the United States District Court for Eastern District of South Carolina in Charleston. Harry Briggs and other parents of black children served as plaintiffs in the case, and the trial narrative emphasized that black children suffered adverse consequences from segregation. A three-judge panel of John J. Parker, Waties Waring, and George Bell Timmerman heard the case. The plaintiffs sought an injunction banning segregation in Clarendon County. LDF attorneys Thurgood Marshall, Robert L. Carter, and Spottswood Robinson represented the plaintiffs, and Robert Figg represented the schools of Clarendon County, South Carolina. Before the trial commenced, Figg conceded that inequalities existed in facilities, curricula, and opportunities in Clarendon County's black schools.

Some of the plaintiffs' evidence came from adversarial witnesses, L. B. McCord and Roderick W. Elliott, who were county school officials. Both witnesses admitted deficiencies in black education. Plaintiffs' expert witnesses related persuasive narratives that showed black schools were unequal and that segregation harmed black children. For example, LDF attorney Carter examined Matthew Whitehead, a Harvard professor of education, about the conditions in black schools in Clarendon County. Under direct examination, Whitehead noted conditions that were unfit for inhabiting, let alone for learning:

> There is no running water at all, nor any urinals in any of these places for boys. At Scott's Ranch School, the same situation prevailed, only to a greater degree of disgust on the part of the one who made such a survey, to see 694 students serviced by two toilets for boys and two toilet seats for girls, of the same out-of-door type of construction, no running water, no urinals.
>
> In a kitchen, there were cracks. They [the kitchen tables] were supposed to be used for instructional purposes for students to write on and read on, and there were actually holes in the tables. . . . The chairs were dilapidated, and the children could not sit in them. (Kluger, 1977, pp. 350–351).

This testimony clearly showed that black schools were unequal. Other testimony noted that these poor facilities impeded children's ability to learn. For example, David Krech, a psychologist from the University of California, affirmed that unequal segregated schools harmed children psychologically. Krech concluded that "legal segregation of education is probably the single, most important factor to wreak harmful effects on the emotional, physical, and financial status of the Negro child" (Whitman, 2004, p. 62).

Later in the trial, Kenneth Clark testified about his doll experiments. When he showed black and white dolls to children, he said, the black children expressed positive attitudes toward white dolls and negative ones toward black dolls. From these experiments, Clark concluded: "My opinion is that a fundamental effect of segregation is basic confusion in the individuals and their concepts about themselves conflicting in their self images" (Whitman, 2004, p. 50).

Despite what seemed to be compelling testimony about the impact of poor facilities on children, Judge Parker denied the requested injunction to ban segregation, but he asked the school district to take immediate steps to equalize facilities. The dissenting opinion by Judge Waring, however, encouraged LDF attorneys in their campaign against segregation. The judge emphasized that "segregation can never produce equality" and that it is "an evil that must be eradicated" (*Briggs et al. v. Elliott et al.,* 1951, p. 548). The two other judges emphasized *Plessy*'s separate but equal doctrine and ignored the narrative testimony of expert witnesses about the barriers that black children faced in segregated schools. Although the federal court decision favored South Carolina defendants, the fact-based narratives of plaintiffs' witnesses established grounds for an appeal to the Supreme Court.

The Brown Trial

The legal campaign to overturn *Plessy* continued in Kansas, an unlikely location because this state had welcomed runaway slaves and prohibited slavery during and after the Civil War (Wilson, 1995). The plaintiffs consisted of 12 parents and their children. They protested that the children could not attend schools close to their homes because blacks were not permitted to attend white neighborhood schools. The case took the title of Brown because it was the last name of parent Oliver Brown and appeared first on the complaint. The trial commenced in 1951, one month after the Briggs trial. LDF attorneys Robert L. Carter and Jack Greenberg and Topeka attorneys Sam and John Scott represented the plaintiffs. Lester Goodwill led the defense for the Topeka school board. A three-judge panel consisting of Walter A. Huxman, Arthur J. Mellott, and Delmas Carl Hill presided at the U.S. Court of Appeals for the Tenth Circuit in Topeka, Kansas. More than 100 witnesses testified in the case, including a few black children—Katherine Carper, Linda Brown, Lucinda Todd, and Silas Hardrick Fleming. Even though the judges did not find that the schools were unequal, the expert testimony from educational and social science experts convinced them that children suffered psychological harm from segregation.

The trial featured narratives from some of the children adversely affected by segregation. For example, 10-year-old Katherine Carper testified that she had to walk a dangerous path to catch a bus that took her to a black school 24 blocks from her home. She said that the bus was overcrowded and that she lived in an integrated neighborhood and played with white children but could not go to a nearby school with them (Irons, 2004).

The testimony of the experts apparently was more important to the Kansas judges than the children's testimony was. The testimony of Luisa Holt, a sociology professor from the University of Kansas whose children attended Topeka schools, impressed the judges. Carter asked her during direct examination, "Does enforced legal separation have any adverse effect upon the personality development of the Negro child?' Holt responded:

> The fact that it is enforced, that it is legal, I think, has more importance than the mere fact that segregation by itself does because this gives legal and official sanction to a policy which is inevitably interpreted both by white people and by Negroes as denoting the inferiority of the Negro group. Were it not for the sense that one group is inferior to the others, there would be no basis . . . for such segregation. . . . A sense of inferiority must always affect one's motivation for learning since it affects the

feeling one has of one's self as a person. That sense of ego-identity is built upon the basis of attitudes that are expressed toward a person by others who are important. (Kluger, 1977, p. 421)

Holt's narrative about why segregation harmed black children was a determining factor in the judges' decision. Five weeks later, Judge Huxman said that Topeka schools were equal, but he also ruled that segregation was harmful to black children:

Segregation of white and colored children in public schools has a detrimental effect upon the colored children. The impact is greater when it has the sanction of the law; for the policy separating the races is usually interpreted as denoting the inferiority of the Negro group. A sense of inferiority affects the motivation of a child to learn. Segregation with the sanction of law, therefore, has a tendency to restrain the educational and mental development of Negro children and to deprive them of some of the benefits they would receive in a racially integrated school system. (*Brown. v. Board of Education*, 1951, p. 797)

Huxman's conclusion gave support to the goals of the LDF's campaign, and it provided key evidence for their appeal to the Supreme Court.

The Belton and Bulah Trials

LDF's legal campaign continued its attempt to overturn segregation by conducting trials in the East Coast region of the U.S. Their most successful trial evolved from the cases filed by the parents of Ethel Louise Belton and Shirley Barbara Bulah against Gebhart, a Delaware state official. The lawsuit originated after Sarah Bulah wrote a letter to the Delaware Department of Instruction complaining that she had to drive her daughter Shirley two miles to a black school when a bus passed in front of her house taking white children to a neighborhood school a few blocks from the family home. Delaware school officials eventually told Bulah that they had no remedy for her because the state required separate schools for white and black children and that law also prohibited black children from riding on school busses reserved for white children.

At about the same time that Bulah complained to school officials, Ethel Belton's mother complained to state officials that her teenage daughter should be attending a nearby high school, but because of the segregation laws, she had to be bussed for two hours to a remote and rundown black high school. Ethel Belton, Shirley Bulah, and other black students applied to their white neighborhood high schools, but the schools refused to admit them. Parents of Bulah and Belton asked Louis Redding, the only black attorney in the state, to help them. Shortly afterward, Jack Greenberg answered Redding's request to the NAACP for help in trying the Delaware cases. The attorneys sued the state of Delaware for violating the equal protection rights of black secondary students by forcing them to attend distant and inferior black schools.

The trial took place in the Delaware State Chancery Courts in Wilmington in the fall of 1951 with one judge, Chancellor Collins Seitz, presiding over the court. Greenberg and Redding attempted to prove that segregated schools and bussing black students violated their constitutional rights, and Attorney General Hyman Albert Young defended the Delaware schools. At the trial, the plaintiffs called an academically distinguished group of expert witnesses to testify that segregation harmed black children. Frederic Wertham from New York University, Jerome Bruner from Harvard University, and Kenneth Clark led the list of plaintiffs' experts.

Wertham testified about the interviews he had conducted with black students in Delaware. He said one student complained about long hours on a crowded bus, another said that white children make fun of blacks, and another child remarked that white Protestant children exhibited more prejudice that Jewish, Catholic, German, and Italian children did. Wertham also noted that a few of the white children in his study sympathized with black students and reported that other white students repeatedly bullied and belittled the black students. After reporting his data from the interviews, Wertham blamed segregation for these attitudes:

> It is the fact of segregation in general and the problems that come out of it that to my mind are anti-educational, by which I mean that education in the larger sense is interfered with. . . . Most of the children we have examined interpret segregation in one way and only one way—and that is they interpret it as punishment. There is no doubt about that. Now, whether that is true, whether the state of Delaware wants to punish these children, has nothing to do with it. I am only testifying about what is in the minds of the children. (Kluger, 1977, p. 444)

Just as he had done in previous trials, Clark appeared as one of the plaintiffs' experts and testified about additional doll experiments that he had done with 41 black children from Delaware. By a large majority, Clark testified, black children said black dolls were bad and white dolls were "nice" and "good." He concluded that black schools promoted stereotypes that led black students to believe they were inferior because of their race (Kluger, 1977, p. 46). In general, the narratives of plaintiffs' witnesses contrasted with defense witnesses who insisted that black schools were equal to white schools.

This trial was unique in several respects. After hearing testimony, Judge Seitz and plaintiffs' attorneys traveled to see some of Delaware's segregated schools. Five months after the trial, Seitz issued a complex opinion that faulted the state for segregating schools, acknowledged the psychological hardships experienced by black children, concluded that segregation created inequality, and ordered white high schools to admit blacks. His opinion showed that the facts asserted in the narratives of LDF's experts had influenced his decision. He claimed that Negro children had been denied equal protection of the law because of inferior school facilities and declared that Ethel Belton and Shirley Bulah and other similarly situated students must be admitted immediately to white public schools. Seitz concluded:

The evidence demonstrates that the refusal to permit plaintiffs and members of their class to attend schools for white children similarly situated, results in their receiving educational opportunities markedly inferior to those offered white children. This consequence flows . . . solely from the fact that they are Negroes. . . . Legally enforced segregation in education, in and of itself, prevents the Negro from receiving educational opportunities which are "equal" to those offered whites. (*Belton v. Gebhart* and *Bulah v. Gebhart,* 1952; Friedman, 1969, p. 589)

The defense appealed the decision to the Supreme Court on the grounds that Seitz had wrongly decided the case. This chancery trial court decision gave the plaintiffs even more reason than the Kansas court decision did to believe that the Supreme Court would declare elementary and secondary school segregation unconstitutional.

The Davis Trial

By the time the LDF attorneys tried the Davis case, they had learned from their failures in Bolling and Briggs trials and from their successes in Brown, Belton, and Bulah. LDF's legal campaign had to overcome a significant challenge from the defense. The trial resulted from student-created protests and strikes over the deplorable conditions at Moton High School in Virginia. When the students met with a local Baptist pastor to try to get something done about their school, he told them to contact Spottswood Robinson from the NAACP and its LDF legal team. Robinson and Oliver Hill met with the students, asked them to return to school, and agreed to sue Prince Edward County on their behalf. The first name on the list of plaintiffs was Dorothy E. Davis, a 14-year-old attending Moton High School in Prince Edward County (*Davis v. County School Board of Prince Edward County*, 1952).

This trial started at the end of February in the U.S. District Court in Richmond, Virginia. Plaintiffs wanted the panel of judges to declare the schools in Prince Edward County unequal and to overturn the Virginia state statute mandating segregation. The defense attorneys relied on a historical narrative and concluded that segregation was a central feature of the history of the state and assured the judges that this practice met the needs of both black and white citizens. Robert L. Carter, Spottsman Robinson, and Oliver Hill, LDF attorneys, represented the plaintiffs. Archibald G. Robinson, J. Lindsay Almond, and T. Justin Moore represented the Prince Edward Schools. The panel of three federal judges hearing the case consisted of Armistead Dobie, Sterling Hutcheson, and Albert Vickers Brian. Just as in previous proceedings, most plaintiffs' witnesses were experts on education and social science (Irons, 2004; Kluger, 1977).

On behalf of the plaintiffs, S. Robinson submitted hundreds of documents showing that the black Moton High School was inferior to the white Farmville High. Based on the success of previous trials, Carter called expert witnesses to testify about the adverse effects of segregation on students. The testimony of M. Brewster Smith, a psychologist from Vassar College, provided an especially potent argument about how segregation harmed black students. When Carter asked him about the effects of segregation, the witness responded:

> [T]he effects of segregation . . . make the Negro, on the average, more like the common, prejudiced conception of a Negro, as a stupid, illiterate, apathetic but happy-go-lucky person. . . . Children, whether they be white, Negro, or any background, who grow up knowing that they are despised by the people around them, . . . [think that they are] not as good as the people around them. [They] are growing up with conceptions of themselves as being, in some way, not worthy. . . . [S]egregation is, in itself, under the social circumstances . . . a social and official insult and . . . has widely ramifying consequences on the individual's motivation to learn. (Kluger, 1977, p. 491)

When Carter asked another expert whether segregation had an adverse effect, Isidor Chein answered: "I would say yes, definitely, yes." Chein also noted that school segregation produced worse effects than other kinds of segregation because it stamped prejudice and other racial stigmas on the minds of children (Kluger, 1977, p. 494). Kenneth Clark reported the results of his experiments conducted in Prince Edward County schools with black and white dolls. The results he reported replicated those given by children in South Carolina and Delaware.

What was new in the Davis trial was that the defense recruited expert witnesses of their own to rebut the testimony of the plaintiffs' experts. Defense's witnesses consisted of the school superintendent, a representative of the Virginia Department of Education, Colgate Darden, a former governor of Virginia, and psychologists John Nelson Buck and Henry Garrett. The defense contested the narratives of plaintiffs' witnesses and adopted a bold theme, asserting that segregation benefitted both black and white children (Irons, 2004; Kluger, 1977).

Even the Southern segregationist justices agreed with plaintiffs that the black schools did not have equal buildings, curriculum, and transportation. They maintained, however, that the long history of racial segregation in Virginia was part of the state's tradition and culture and for this reason should be maintained. The judges concluded, "We have found no harm to racial segregation" and asked local authorities to upgrade black schools to satisfy the provisions of *Plessy.* The judges agreed with the defense's historical justification that segregated schools should continue because for "generations this has been the mores of the state" (*Davis v. County School Board of Prince Edward County*, 1952; Friedman, 1969, p. 552).

The testimony of plaintiffs' witnesses did not always produce the kind of decisions that LDF lawyers wanted. However, these witnesses contributed fact-based narratives that were essential to the Supreme Court appeal because they provided evidence about violations of the rights of black students, inequities in black school facilities, harm to black students' motivation, institutional racism, and the psychological stigmatizing of black students. The record from the trials demonstrated inequality of facilities in some cases and violation of students' constitutional rights in others.

THE APPELLATE PROCESS

By the time the trials had ended, the LDF attorneys believed they had made significant progress in their legal campaign to overturn *Plessy* and to show that segregation violated the constitutional rights of black parents and their children. This section describes the appellate process by outlining the order of action for a Supreme Court appeal and discussing the steps attorneys took in the first stages of the appeal, by highlighting the participants in the consolidated appeal, later decided as *Brown v. Board of Education*, and by looking at the argumentation the attorneys used in their briefs.

Attorneys first presented oral arguments before the Court in 1952, reargued the cases in 1953 on Fourteenth Amendment constitutional questions, and argued issues of implementation in 1955. My analysis emphasizes the 1952 appellate arguments because the reasoning and evidence presented at that time reappeared in the rearguments that took place in 1953 and 1954.

Steps and Participants in the Appeal

Arguments before the Supreme Court typically take place in six procedural actions:

THE ORDER OF ACTION FOR A SUPREME COURT APPEAL

1. The Court grants the petition to hear the case.
2. The parties to the case prepare elaborate briefs that give the factual background of the case, cite the major legal or constitutional issues in a point-by-point analysis, and provide justifications for violations of appellants' constitutional rights.
3. Petitioners file their briefs with the Court at least three weeks prior to the time the case is heard, and respondents must file at least one week before the case is heard. In contemporary appeals, attorneys file their briefs several months before they are heard.
4. The Court requests that appellate attorneys provide "learning aids," such as a "three or four page" summary of the issues of the appeal, the arguments set aside by numbers and titles, and a readable script, with an intricate and thorough citation of applicable precedents (Stern, Gressman, & Shapiro, 1986, pp. 556–557; Weiner, 1967).
5. An individual or an organization, not directly involved in the case but interested in the outcome, can file an *amicus curia* brief supporting either side of the case. (Seven groups filed briefs in support of overturning *Plessy* and making segregation illegal.)

6. Attorneys present their cases in oral arguments before the Supreme Court justices during either the spring or fall term designated for hearing oral arguments.

The typical appellate process starts when attorneys file briefs to persuade the Court to grant a *writ of certiorari,* permission to hear arguments. However, for *Brown,* four of the five cases—Brown, Briggs, Davis, and Gebhart (Belton and Bulah)—took a direct route to the Court, based on a procedure allowed by the Judges' Bill of 1925. This legislation permitted a small group of cases to be given automatic review by the Supreme Court when issues and evidence from the lower courts jointly produced compelling reasons for hearing the case. To prevent too many cases from coming by this route, the Court required the parties to file petitions explaining the jurisdiction, issues, and the importance of the case just as they would have done in appealing a single case. After filing the petitions, at least four justices needed to agree that the cases were sufficiently important and involved substantial constitutional matters that should be heard (Weiner, 1967; Whitman, 2004). After the Supreme Court justices agreed to hear Briggs, Brown, Gebhart, and Davis, they added Bolling because this appeal also involved constitutional rights and public school segregation.

Participants in the Appeal

In legal jargon, attorneys appealing the case are called petitioners, and they represent appellants; attorneys resisting the appeal are called respondents, and they represent appellees.

Petitioners and Respondents

- Petitioner Robert Carter represented the children and parents in Brown et al., and Paul Wilson responded for the State of Kansas.
- Petitioner Thurgood Marshall represented Briggs et al., and John W. Davis responded for the Clarendon County School District.
- Petitioner Spottswood Robinson argued the case for Davis et al., and Justin Moore and J. Lindsay Almond responded for the State of Virginia.
- Petitioners George Hayes and James Nabrit represented Bolling et al., and Milton Korman responded for the Washington, D.C., school district.
- Petitioner Albert Young represented the Delaware schools (Gebhart) and Louis Redding and Jack Greenberg responded on behalf of Belton and Bulah.

Appellate Briefs

All of the briefs filed by LDF attorneys argued that segregated schools violated the rights of black children under the Fourteenth Amendment and that the separate but equal doctrine in the *Plessy* precedent should not be applied to schools. The respondents to these briefs claimed that segregation should be retained, states and localities should maintain control of schools, and school districts should continue to upgrade black schools to make them equal with white institutions. The appeals emphasized the adverse effects of segregation in elementary, junior high, and high schools.

Vision. According to Delaney (1998), appellate briefs map the legal landscape and present a vision about what rights citizens should have. Petitioners and respondents in these cases promoted different visions about what public education should be. This appeal was about the quality of educational facilities and the availability of educational opportunities in segregated elementary and secondary schools.

LDF attorneys presented a progressive vision in the sense that they wanted black children to attend schools that would meet their psychological and social needs and motivate them to learn. The visions of attorneys upholding school segregation were conservative; they favored the status quo and the continuation of *Plessy* as the standard for legal segregation. In appellate argumentation, attorneys often create "two divergent construals of the meaning . . . two incompatible renderings of the legal landscape. When read side by side, it can be seen how each takes account of the other." One attorney "foregrounds what the other might ignore," and the opposing attorney "puts at the center of the argument what the opposing side" places at the margins (Delaney, 1998, p. 26). The petitioners took account of the visions of the respondents, and the respondents understood petitioners' visions.

Arguments. Appellate arguers sequence their reasoning and evidence in a deliberate order. The following summaries contrast the arguments in the briefs of the LDF attorneys with those of the attorneys supporting school segregation. These summaries appear in the order the appeals were argued in the Supreme Court.

SUMMARY OF ARGUMENTS IN BRIEFS

The Brown Case
Petitioner Carter:
1. Segregation denies educational opportunity under the Fourteenth Amendment.
2. State statutes permitting segregation violate the constitutional provision of equal protection.
3. Federal courts should have applied precedents from *Sweatt* and *McLaurin.*
4. Segregation harms black children psychologically and socially.

Respondent Wilson:
1. The Kansas statute permitting segregation is legal.
2. No substantial inequality exists between black and white schools in Kansas.
3. The Kansas statute does not violate the Fourteenth Amendment.

The Briggs Case
Petitioner Marshall:
1. Segregated schools violate the Fourteenth Amendment rights of black children.
2. Unequal schools deny the equal protection of black children.
3. Segregation deters the development of children's personalities.
4. The lower court decisions should have applied the precedents of *Sweatt* and *McLaurin.*
5. The South Carolina statute mandating segregation is unreasonable.

Respondent Davis:
1. The lower court rightly held that South Carolina school districts should upgrade black schools.
2. The school districts have spent money to upgrade some black schools.
3. The lower court opinion is cogent and complete.
4. The framers of the Constitution did not intend for the Fourteenth Amendment to apply to schools.
5. The trial testimony of social scientists that segregation harms black children is flawed.
6. South Carolina knows best what to do with its public schools.

The Davis Case
Petitioner Robinson:
1. Virginia segregation laws violate the due process rights of children.
2. Virginia segregation laws violate the equal protection provisions of the Fourteenth Amendment.
3. Black schools in Virginia are not equal to white schools.
4. Race-based laws are unconstitutional and unreasonable.
5. The reasonableness or unreasonableness of segregation has not yet been tested.
6. The equalization decree ordered by the lower court erred because it sanctions segregation.

Respondents Moore & Almond:
1. Virginia is spending money to make black schools equal to white schools as required by the lower court's equalization order.
2. Black children have not suffered social and psychological harm from segregation.
3. *Sweatt* and *McLaurin* do not apply to elementary and secondary schools.
4. The history of Virginia provides a rational basis for segregation.
5. Negro teachers would not be employed in desegregated schools.
6. Desegregation would hurt white and colored students in Virginia.

The Bolling Case

Petitioners Hayes & Nabrit:

1. Congress mandated segregation in Washington, D.C., public schools.

2. Segregation violates the due process provisions of the Fifth Amendment, the equal protection provision of the Fourteenth Amendment, and the Charter of the United Nations.

3. Segregation denies children admission to quality white schools.

4. Congress created segregated schools solely based on race, and these statutes forbid this kind of discrimination.

Respondent Korman:

1. Congress provided black public schools in the District because the District previously supported only private schools for white children.

2. Congress rightly provided the District with school boards, taxation, and teachers for public schools.

3. Congress can pass discriminatory laws because there is no equal protection clause in the Fifth Amendment.

4. The equal protection clause does not limit congressional jurisdiction over the schools in the District.

5. Separation by sexes is legal in many jurisdictions so separation of races should also be permitted in Washington, D.C.

The Gebhart (Belton & Bulah) Cases

Petitioner Young:

1. Segregation in Delaware should continue.

2. The Delaware Supreme Court erred in issuing an injunction forcing white schools to admit black children.

3. The Delaware Supreme Court misapplied the equal protection provisions of the Fourteenth Amendment to justify the injunction.

4. The Delaware appellate judges wrongly relied on *Sweatt, Sipuel,* and *Gaines.*

5. Delaware has pursued a plan to correct inequalities in the black schools.

Respondents Redding & Greenberg:

1. Race-based classifications for educational facilities are arbitrary and unreasonable.

2. Delaware has never ratified the Fourteenth Amendment.

3. The Delaware statute providing for separate but equal schools should be overturned.

4. The Delaware Supreme Court rightly decided Bulah and Belton.

5. Inequalities in education in the black schools are severe, and the state attorney general's plan for fixing them will not work.

6. Affirming the lower court decisions will prevent further denial of black children's right to an equal education.

The petitioners' brief for Brown, Briggs, Davis, and Bolling and the respondents' brief for Gebhart summarized the reasons behind LDF's campaign to overturn *Plessy* and end segregation. LDF's appeals relied on the precedents from the graduate school cases, emphasized the social stigmas and psychological impediments to learning suffered by black students, stressed that *Plessy* does not apply to school segregation, and praised the parts of some lower court decisions that supported their goal. The briefs supporting segregation asserted the relevance of the *Plessy* doctrine of separate but equal for schools, emphasized the applicability of precedents upholding segregation from state and federal appeals' courts, utilized the precedents from *Roberts* and *Gong Lum,* stressed historical reasons for segregation, and ignored the precedents in the graduate school cases. Some of the claims and evidence presented in the written briefs were emphasized in the oral arguments in the consolidated cases under the name of Brown.

ORAL ARGUMENTS

The oral arguments in a Supreme Court case are a high point in the legal drama because attorneys present their evidence and reasoning to the most distinguished judges in America. Moreover, the decision that the judges make can change the course of history. Few attorneys have the opportunity to argue cases before the Supreme Court.

Attorneys' oral arguments should (1) establish a legal standpoint, (2) provide the evidence for the assertions that are made, (3) construct clear and cogent sequences of reasoning, and (4) present a persuasive performance. Legal arguments provide plausible explanations about what the constitutional law means based on evidence from the record of the case as constructed by witnesses and from judicial rulings (Clary, Paulsen, & Vanselow, 2004). Unlike the prevalence of narrative in the trial argumentation, oral arguments place reasoning and evidence about constitutional issues in the foreground and relegate narrative testimony to the background where the arguer notes the adverse effects suffered from violations of individuals' constitutional rights. The legal procedures and communication practices provide standards for evaluating the oral arguments in this appeal.

Procedures for Oral Arguments

Appellate advocacy manuals give different opinions about the nature of oral arguments. For example, Cooley (1989) emphasizes that oral argument requires both artfulness and fine-tuned critical thinking skills. Delaney (1998) concludes that oral argument is a strategy in which "all participants seek to simplify the complex and to clarify the ambiguous" points of their briefed arguments. This process may involve "distorting" some aspects of the facts and the legal precedents addressed by compressing them into a narrow set of legal and social categories. Conversely, arguments may draw conclusions that expand the facts and precedents far beyond the territory they should consider (Delaney, 1998). Making too broad or too narrow interpretations of the law can distort appellate reasoning. Specifically, appellate attorneys can simplify the argument so much that they leave out what should be included, expand the argument beyond what the evidence warrants, or show a disregard for the lower court record by arguing only legal issues. The oral performance of attorneys can reduce or enhance the persuasiveness of oral arguments.

Communication of Oral Arguments

The oral arguments seek to persuade appellate judges about constitutional issues. In an appellate situation in which multiple attorneys argue a single case in separate segments, as was the case in *Brown*, attorneys should emphasize the unique issues of their particular segment, making sure their arguments and evidence are consistent with that of the other appellate attorneys pursuing the same legal goal. Subsequent analysis shows the LDF attorneys adopted a focused legal standpoint, consolidated and streamlined their arguments, made use of trial narratives, and concentrated on a narrow range of constitutional issues. Attorneys arguing for upholding segregation stressed their efforts to uphold the doctrine of *Plessy*, expanded their arguments to focus on culture and history, emphasized their willingness to equalize black schools, and showed commitment to the position of the appellees/appellants they represented. Appellate arguers always deviate from the detailed reasoning and evidence presented in their written briefs because the judges interrupt them and ask them to focus on issues or explanations not addressed in the briefs.

Appellate attorneys should "find a persuasive theme, articulate it up front, and refer to it throughout the argument" (Clary, Paulsen, & Vanselow, 2004, p. 99). In their entire legal campaign, the LDF attorneys repeatedly emphasized the theme that segregation harmed students by stigmatizing them and violating their rights to equal protection. The attorneys upholding segregation presented several themes, but they did not present their themes in a unified way.

Oral arguments are subject to time restrictions; each attorney is usually allotted one hour. In all of the arguments except for Brown, both petitioners and respondents took their full time. Stern, Gressman, and Shapiro (1986) give the following advice about how the oral argument should be delivered: rather than reading their briefs, attorneys should extemporize the main ideas that they believe will be controversial for the justices and engage in a responsive dialogue based on the questions directed to them by the justices.

It is not surprising that in 1952 the Court directed more questions to petitioners than to respondents. In a sense, petitioners have a burden to prove that issues of law have been wrongly decided by most of the lower court judges and that (in the cases where the LDF attorneys were the petitioners) they had inappropriately relied on *Plessy*. The justices asked Paul Wilson, respondent for the Topeka board of education and the most inexperienced attorney, very few questions. They grilled Carter, Marshall, Robinson, Moore, and Almond, attorneys with experience before the Court. Prior to this appeal, John W. Davis, who represented South Carolina in this case, offered advice concerning the performance for attorneys arguing before the Supreme Court. He recommended that the attorneys adopt the mind-set of the Court; emphasize only a few points that the justices will remember; read only pithy and pertinent phrases, but otherwise extemporize; show confidence by knowing the complete record of the case; and avoid any negative remarks about people involved in the cases (Kluger, 1977). Subsequent analysis shows that Davis did not follow his own advice.

A positive performance helps attorneys to achieve their legal goals, show their knowledge and preparation, exhibit their reasoning ability, and adapt their arguments to the questions asked by the justices. A strong performance by inexperienced attorneys can enhance their credibility and reduce the power disparity they might have in relation to an experienced and well-known attorney. The subsequent discussion of the oral arguments concentrates on the legal and communication processes and refers to performances when information is available.

Evaluation of the Oral Arguments

Reasoning and evidence dominate the content of oral arguments, but trial narratives also offer key facts that verify violations of appellants' legal rights. Attorneys and judges dialectically construct the argumentation through a combination of reporting on the content of the brief and responding to questions asked by the justices. The attorneys in 1952 presented several hours of oral arguments on consecutive days—beginning on December 9 and ending on December 11. The oral arguments from attorneys opposing segregation frequently referred to the narratives of their witnesses, but the attorneys supporting segregated schools made few references to facts from the testimony because they had called few witnesses to establish a trial record favorable to their side of the cases. The arguments on behalf of Davis were the exception. Appeal arguments are grounded in the evidence supplied from the trial record (Stern, Gressman, & Shapiro, 1986; Weiner, 1967). Attorneys argued the cases in this order: Brown, Briggs, Davis, Bolling, and Gebhart. The transcripts of the oral arguments show some disparities in both the content of the arguments and the performance of attorneys. (Unless otherwise noted, all of the citations for the *Brown* arguments are from Friedman [1969].)

Oral Arguments from the Brown Trial.   In the Brown appeal, attorneys for both sides presented condensed and focused arguments, shorter than the oral arguments for the other cases. Carter cited witnesses' narratives from the trial record and emphasized Judge Huxman's ruling about harms from segregation. The trial record supported Carter's theme that Kansas laws should be overturned because segregation caused psychological harm to black children. Carter skillfully enforced his legal standpoint during his oral argument. Carter emphasized:

> [R]acial segregation, as practiced in the city of Topeka, tended to rele-gate appellants and their group to an inferior caste . . . lowered their level of aspiration . . . instilled feelings of insecurity and inferiority . . . retarded their mental and education development. . . . It was impossible for the Negro children who were set off in these four schools to secure, in fact or in law, an education which was equal to that available to white children. . . . The sole basis for our appeal here on the constitutionality of the statute of Kansas is that it empowers the maintenance and opera-tion of racially segregated schools . . . [in which] Negro children are denied equal protection of the law and . . . they cannot secure equality in educational opportunity. (Friedman, 1969, p. 17)

Justice Burton then asked Carter about the adverse impact of segregated schools on children.

> B: Is it your position that there is a great deal more to the education process even in the elementary schools than what you read in the books? . . . .

> C: Yes, sir. We say that the question of your physical facilities is not enough. The Constitution does not . . . give equal protection of the laws with regard to equal educational opportunities, does not stop with the fact that you have equal physical facilities, but it covers the whole of the education process. . . . (p. 17)

Justice Vinson continued the questioning by asking Carter about whether Kansas provided transportation to the black students.

> V: And the only item of discrimination . . . [was] transportation by bus for the colored students without that facility for the white students. . . .

> C: These are the physical factors the court found, and then the court went on to show how segregation made the educational opportuni-ties inferior, and this, we think, is the heart of the case. (p. 18)

Carter referred to his legal standpoint when he answered the questions from the justices. He repeatedly emphasized that the lower court record supported his legal standpoint that segregation was harmful. He appropriately empha-sized the parts of the Huxman decision that faulted segregation and claimed black schools created psychological harms to black children, and he astutely downplayed the judicial findings about equal schools and transportation.

Oral Arguments from the Briggs Trial.   The Court may well have expected that the oral arguments on behalf of Briggs would dominate the entire appeal because both Marshall and Davis had a strong record of success arguing before the Supreme Court. Marshall had recently succeeded with his arguments in the graduate school cases, and he also had established credibility because he was the founder and principal attorney for the LDF legal effort. Davis had been a member of Congress and a U.S. solicitor general and had argued dozens of cases before the Court. Some historians (e.g., Irons, 2004) claim the eloquence of Marshall and Davis was superior to the other oral arguers.

It is difficult to assess their performance since oral recordings were not available at the time and the written transcripts contain only a few clues about the quality of their performances. Jack Greenberg (1994), who responded for Gebhart and was in the Court for the oral arguments, recalled:

> Thurgood . . . hovered imposingly over the lectern as he addressed the justices familiarly, but respectfully. He had been before the Court many times and the justices knew him well and trusted him. . . . Thurgood spoke slowly, for him, on this occasion, making sure to articulate his words in an educated Southern way, rather than in the country style he often used. (p. 169)

Greenberg (1994) also recalled that Davis was a "legendary" legal figure of "medium height, with white hair, thoroughly at home in the Court having argued there more than any other living lawyer" (p. 170). He came dressed in formal attire, a club coat and striped trousers. Since the Briggs trial did not feature much defense testimony, Davis relied on arguments that had worked for him in the past. He claimed that the original intent of the equal protection provisions of the Fourteenth Amendment had nothing to do with segregation and that South Carolina was doing the best it could to equalize segregated schools. To show that segregation did not harm black children, he quoted literary sources.

The transcript indicates strong contrasts in the content of Davis's and Marshall's oral arguments. Just as other LDF attorneys, Marshall's argumentation stressed constitutional principles, the graduate school precedents, and the harms suffered by children in black schools. He cited evidence from plaintiffs' experts in the Briggs trial, saying that their testimony proved that segregation deprives children of "equal status in the school and the community," "destroys their self-respect," "denies them full opportunity for democratic social development," and shows that "they were injured as a result of segregation" (p. 28). Most of Marshall's argument centered on the common theme and legal standpoint of the LDF campaign—that segregation violates the constitutional provisions of equal protection in the Fourteenth Amendment and *Plessy* should be overturned.

A direct clash between issues did not exist between the oral arguments of Marshall and Davis as much as it did in the oral arguments of the other appellate attorneys. Some of the justices engaged in systematic interrogation of Marshall, but asked Davis very few questions. Davis argued in broad generalizations without applying what he said to the decisions in the lower court cases or to trial testimony. When he did speak about South Carolina schools, he chronicled their history and achievements. Davis's conclusion illustrated the indirectness of his legal approach:

> What is the great national and federal policy on this matter? Is it not a fact that the very strength and fiber of our federal system is local self-gov-

ernment, in those matters for which local action is competent? Is it not of all the activities of government the one which most nearly approaches the hearts and minds of people, the question of the education for the young? Is it not the height of wisdom that the manner in which that shall be conducted should be left to those immediately affected by it? (p. 61)

Davis posed questions in his conclusions rather than asserted answers. He inferred the centrality of his states' rights argument rather than stating it directly. He emphasized broad rather than narrow constitutional issues.

Justice Frankfurter directed a large number of questions to Marshall after the justice asserted that the traditions of segregation "are part of the historical conflict of the South." To this Marshall responded: "I do not think that segregation in public schools is any more ingrained in the South than segregation in transportation is." Frankfurter agreed that the problems of segregated schools were more complicated than issues about segregated transportation were. Marshall emphasized, "I agree that it [segregation] is not only complicated. I agree that it is a tough problem. But I think that it is a problem that has to be faced" (p. 46). Other justices asked Marshall why the graduate school precedents applied, but the precedent in *Roberts* (see p. 249) did not. He responded that public schools must abide by the law. Historians characterized the oral arguments for Briggs as the most compelling of the whole case, but the transcript lacks evidence for this conclusion. Perhaps those who attended the oral arguments concentrated more on the character and delivery of the attorneys than on the content of their arguments.

Oral Arguments from the Davis Trial.   In the appeal from the Davis trial, Spottswood Robinson made a clear and cogent legal argument based on facts of the trial and the legal problems with the decision. He succinctly stated his legal standpoint—the "segregation laws of Virginia are invalid" because these laws violate the rights of "the due process and equal protection clauses of the Fourteenth Amendment" for black citizens (p. 71). He made effective use of trial narratives from the lower court record, saying that the trial witnesses had demonstrated that segregation produced inequalities, these inequalities "handicap Negro students in their educational endeavors," and make it "impossible for Negro students to obtain educational opportunities and advantages equal to those afforded white students" (p. 71).

Respondent Moore was a formidable opponent for Robinson because he directly refuted Robinson's arguments. Because defense witnesses had confronted the plaintiffs' witnesses head-on in the trial, Moore cited defense testimony from the trial as evidence that Virginia's segregated schools would soon meet the separate but equal dictate of *Plessy*. He bragged that Virginia was following the injunction of the lower court to equalize black schools, saying "[t]here is no doubt about it, no question from this record, that the funds are in hand, the buildings are going up, and the facilities will be equal by next September." Later, Moore explained that Virginia had been a victim of sorts because they had to cope with such large increases in enrollment in the black schools. But he assured the justices again and again that segregation was not based on discrimination, but on tradition. Moore addressed directly the conservative Southern justices on the Court, saying that Virginia was doing its best to meet the provisions of *Plessy*, but the state just needed more time to upgrade its schools.

Respondent Almond's argument lacked relevance to the reasoning of either Robinson or Moore. He pleaded with the justices to recognize the state's long history of segregated schools and to sympathize with state taxpayers who had spent so much money on black schools. He warned the justices that if Virginia had to desegregate its schools, this process would "destroy the public school system in Virginia" (p. 99). From a retrospective analysis, Almond's oral argument was the weakest of all the appellate arguments because he did not adopt a clear legal standpoint, his reasoning was not relevant to the disputed constitutional issues, he ignored trial testimony and the record of the lower court decision, and he built the argument on a curious theme based on circular reasoning—segregation should be preserved because public funds are being spent to save segregated schools.

Justices Vinson and Reed challenged Robinson's claim that race-based legislation violated the Constitution, and Justice Jackson rebutted Moore's and Almond's conservative states' rights position. Reed asked Robinson to explain the "purpose of the enactment of the [Virginia] statutes." Robinson responded: "I think from the historical viewpoint . . . the original notion behind the school segregation laws was to impose upon Negroes disabilities," and they could do this prior to the ratification of the Thirteenth, Fourteenth, and Fifteenth Amendments. Justice Reed then asked what "disabilities" meant. Robinson stressed that disabilities for blacks still exist in Virginia because of "inequalities" that "handicap Negro students' experience when they are stifled in their educational pursuits." Vinson continued by asking Robinson what he thought the lower court should have done. Robinson responded, "The Court should have immediately entered an injunction which would have prevented the school authorities from assigning school space in the county on the basis of race" (pp. 76–78).

Vinson also questioned Almond about the content of the Virginia segregation statutes. Almond admitted the statutes provided for equal facilities, but, he said, this provision has not been met in the past, and "it is our determination" to support equal facilities. "That is our program today, and that is the program that we want to go forward with" (p. 97). Vinson asked Almond why he opposed desegregation, and Almond answered that desegregation would hurt Negro teachers "who would not be employed to teach white children," undo all of the progress being made in equalizing schools, and "would stop the march of progress" (p. 99). Even though Almond's original oral argument was weak in content, his responses to the questions from some of the justices permitted him to assert his strong commitment to the segregated schools in his state, a theme that probably resonated with the school officials he represented and the southern justices.

Oral Arguments from the Bolling Trial.   The arguments in the Bolling case contained only a few references to the harm done to plaintiffs. Instead petitioners Hayes and Nabrit concentrated on the meaning of the language and the applicability of legal principles to Washington, D.C., public schools. They argued that Congress lacked the power to segregate schools in the District. Korman responded, saying that history and tradition gave Congress the power to decide how public schools served the District. Korman defended the segregation policy because, he said, the District was a federal territory and not subject to the Fourteenth Amendment. But Hayes and Nabrit noted that the due process clause of the Fifth Amendment did apply to the District and the Fourteenth Amendment guaranteed equal protection to all U.S. citizens regardless of where they lived. The weakness of arguments for both sides was twofold. First, the arguments were so narrow in scope that neither side really dealt directly with school officials prohibiting the admission of black students to white schools or with the inequality of the black schools that black students had been forced to attend. Second, the arguments got bogged down in explaining the history of the jurisdiction of Congress over the District of Columbia.

Oral Arguments from the Gebhart Case.   By the time the attorneys argued the Gebhart (Belton and Bulah) case, the LDF attorneys had developed a strong coordinated assault on segregation. As a result, the NAACP attorneys had a relatively easy task of defending the favorable opinion that Chancellor Seitz had rendered in Delaware because it validated their legal standpoints. Redding asserted that race-based educational facilities are "arbitrary, unreasonable, and unconstitutional" (p. 161). He featured the testimony of expert witness Frederic Wertham, emphasizing that "segregation, state-imposed segregation, created an important inequality in educational opportunity" (p. 164). Greenberg enumerated the many types of inequality in Delaware schools. He noted that traveling long distances is especially harmful because it "induces fatigue and irritability" and takes portions of the students' time that should be used for learning. Other inequalities existed in the buildings, teachers' preparation, curricula, extra curricular activities, and teacher-to-student ratios (p. 166). When questioned by Justice Jackson about whether Delaware should be given more time to obey Chancellor Seitz's injunction, Greenberg replied that "if constitutional rights are being violated, they are entitled to those rights as quickly as those rights can be made available" (p. 167). The respondents emphasized that desegregation was the legally correct and expedient response to inequities in black schools. Redding and Greenberg reiterated the legal goal of the LDF campaign by pointing out that the decision in Delaware should be applied to other regions of the country because separate facilities are not equal and segregation harms black students.

Petitioner Young was not part of a concerted legal campaign like his opponents were, and as a result he had to convince the Court that Delaware's pro-integration ruling should be overturned. Since the defense in the Belton and Bulah trials had presented few witnesses, Young lacked evidence from the trial record to support the separate but equal doctrine of *Plessy*. For example, he emphasized that some schools were equal and then went into detail about the ones that were unequal. He emphasized that black schools were equal in size and construction, but ignored the inequalities in programs, teachers, and learning opportunities. He stressed that Delaware was following the chancery court's injunction and that the schools would be equal in the future. Young asked the Court to deny the desegregation order and to allow the state more time to upgrade the black schools.

Justice Frankfurter asked Young why the injunction was a problem. Young responded that the judge in the Delaware court "said where there is an injury, as he found such to be here, then the injury should be redressed immediately . . . based on the equal protection provision of the Fourteenth Amendment." Since Frankfurter agreed with Young, he clarified rather than questioned this argument, "Automatically because there was a solution of the Fourteenth Amendment, and the Fourteenth Amendment requires automatic redress?" Young concluded, "That is right, precisely" (pp. 159–160). Justice Frankfurter dominated the questioning about the due process and equal protection provisions of the Fourteenth Amendment. At the time of the oral arguments, Frankfurter did not believe these provisions should apply to school segregation and he also felt that his expertise on this subject was superior to the other justices.

Just days after the oral arguments ended, the justices gathered in a conference to discuss what they thought of the briefs and the 1952 oral arguments. The records of the conferences cited in Dickson (2001) show the Court justices lacked consensus.

JUSTICES' REACTIONS TO THE ORAL ARGUMENTS

- Justice Hugo Black was convinced that the LDF attorneys had made their case. He said, "I have to vote that way, to end segregation" (p. 648).
- Justice Stanley Reed claimed that segregation was gradually disappearing on its own. He concluded that "In the Deep South, separate but equal schools must be allowed, I uphold segregation as constitutional" (p. 649).
- Justice Felix Frankfurter wrote, "I cannot say that it is unconstitutional to treat a Negro differently than a white, but I would put all of these cases down for reargument" (p. 651).
- Justice William O. Douglas emphasized that "The Fourteenth Amendment prohibits racial classifications, and so does the due process clause of the Fifth Amendment. Segregation is unconstitutional" (p. 652).
- Justice Harold Burton explained, "Education is more than buildings and facilities; it is a habit of mind. With the Fourteenth Amendment, states do not have the choice—segregation violates equal protection" (p. 653).
- Justice Tom Clark noted that "we have led states on to believe that separate but equal is O.K., and we should let them work it out" (p. 653).
- Justice Sherman Minton emphasized "segregation is unconstitutional, I am ready to vote now" (p. 653).

The justices decided to delay the decision until it was reargued the next year. By the time the attorneys reargued the consolidated cases called *Brown*, conservative Chief Justice Vincent had died, and Chief Justice Earl Warren replaced him. The 1952 argument was important to the final decision because the majority of the Court recognized that the graduate school precedents applied to elementary and secondary schools and that *Plessy* was not a sufficient precedent for upholding the legal rights of black students.

LESSONS

The legal campaign of the LDF originated in the NAACP's 1939 charter, gained momentum from the successful appeals in the graduate school cases in 1949–50, and intensified with the trials of Bolling, Brown, Briggs, Davis, and Belton and Bulah in 1950–52. The NAACP's legal campaign achieved a significant legal goal when the Supreme Court agreed to hear oral arguments in the consolidated *Brown* appeal in 1952. The oral arguments illuminate key appellate procedures and communication practices used by attorneys to bring their cases before the Supreme Court. In oral arguments, the reasoning and evidence are in the foreground, and the narratives are in the background. The narratives from the trial and the lower court decisions, however, create facts that support appellate attorneys' legal standpoints, themes, and rights arguments. Attorneys adopt a legal standpoint about how constitutional law should be applied in the case, stress the standpoint using a theme, condense and consolidate the arguments of the briefs, and connect their responses to the questions of justices to their legal standpoint and the themes. The legal campaign against segregation shows the difficult task that attorneys faced when they tried to develop law and change educational institutions.

The campaign of the NAACP was successful for several reasons. All of the LDF attorneys pursued the common goal of overturning *Plessy* and making segregation illegal; they also incorporated other LDF attorneys' arguments during their presentations. The progressive vision of the NAACP lawyers called for law development, and their coordinated team effort enabled them to concentrate on new precedents as justifications for overturning segregation.

The arguments of the attorneys supporting segregation were uncoordinated, and attorneys for one case made few references to the arguments made in the other cases. The conservative approach stressed historical and cultural narratives justifying segregation rather than the harm suffered by black children. As a result, prosegregation attorneys relied little on the facts developed from trial narratives or on the graduate school precedents. Instead, they tried to convince the Court that their states were making efforts to equalize schools.

After the Court made their decision, however, it became clear to the LDF attorneys that their legal campaign was not over. They would have to reargue their case, and it would take almost two more decades to fully integrate Southern schools. On the 50th anniversary of the decision, some scholars lamented that the decision was still not completely implemented (Cashin, 2004).

11

---◆---

Fictions in the
Roe v. Wade Arguments

Americans cannot avoid talking about the Supreme Court decision in *Roe v. Wade*. The subject comes up in family conversations, college classroom discussions, medical consultations, religious sermons, political campaign speeches, and Senate judiciary confirmation hearings. Calling abortion a hot-button issue is an understatement. The subject permeates religious discourse, energizes the pro-choice and pro-life factions of social movements, inspires political candidates, and confounds the judiciary. The public's profound emotional reactions to the subject of legal abortions inspire rhetorical excess; at the same time, they conceal the argumentation that led to the appellate decision.

In 1970, Sarah Weddington and Linda Coffee filed a five-page complaint on behalf of plaintiffs against District Attorney Henry Wade in the Northern Federal District Court of Texas. The plaintiffs' names were pseudonyms for Weddington and Coffee's clients: Jane Roe was an unmarried woman who was pregnant but could not get a legal abortion in Texas. Jane and John Doe were a married couple who had been told by doctors that if Jane conceived a child, the pregnancy would threaten her life. The third client was physician James Hallford who had been indicted for performing an abortion in Texas. Their complaint sought a legal judgment declaring that the Texas abortion law violated the plaintiffs' rights.

At the time, the Texas law made it a crime for anyone to administer or attempt to "administer drugs" or "use mechanical means" to cause a pregnant woman to abort a fetus. The law, however, did not make it a criminal act for a pregnant woman to induce her own abortion. John Tolle filed a response on behalf of Texas in support of the restrictive law, saying the law should be retained because the state had a right to create its own laws and because abortion violated religious principles. Attorneys presented their arguments to a three-judge panel composed of Sarah Hughes, William M. Taylor, and Irving Goldberg. The initial civil suit challenged Texas statutes that prohibited abortion in all cases except to save the life of the mother. The attorneys for the plaintiffs sought a declaratory judgment, that is, a judgment that would declare the Texas abortion law to be unconstitutional.

The unanimous decision of the judges was that Roe and Hallford had a constitutional right to sue but the Does had no legal standing. The judges issued an injunction, that is, "a court order to a party in the court's jurisdiction to do or refrain from doing something" (Hull & Hoffer, 2001, p. 121). The judges said specifically that:

> [T]he Texas Abortion laws must be declared unconstitutional because they deprive single women and married couples of their right, secured by the Ninth Amendment, to choose to have children. . . . Abortion falls within the sensitive area of privacy . . . one of the basic values of this privacy is birth control. . . . If an individual may prevent conception, why can he [she] not nullify that conception when prevention has failed? (*Roe v. Wade,* 1970)

The judges, however, did not grant injunctive relief to cease enforcement of the Texas law, and this issue became the grounds for appealing the case to the U.S. Supreme Court. The Court eventually overturned the Texas law and legalized abortion according to a detailed trimester system.

The major provisions of the majority opinion written by Justice Harry Blackmun stated that (1) women have a right to choose to have an abortion from the time of conception to the end of the first trimester (three months); (2) the state can regulate abortion in the second trimester (three to six months) based on risks to the mother; and (3) during the third trimester (six to nine months), the state will prohibit abortions except when medically necessary to preserve the life of the mother.

Those who debate abortion rights at times confound and confuse the legal provisions of abortion rights with religious, scientific, and economic issues. Whether the typical American knows a little or a great deal about the abortion decision, the subject never completely vanishes from the public radar. For more than 200 years abortion has been part of public debate, and there is no reason to believe the debate will end in the future. Hull and Hoffer (2001) explain, "The legal maneuvers and intellectual claims of abortion rights and anti-abortion rights litigants are not new. Instead, they are part of a dialogue over gender, law, medicine, politics, and religion going back to the beginning of the republic" (p. ix). Legally, the Court has decided that abortion relates directly to rights to privacy and to the due process provisions of the Fifth and Fourteenth Amendments, but the issues presented in social and political debates often conceal the legal issues. For example, the public debate focuses on issues about the humanness of the fetus at the time of conception, the ethics of doctors who perform abortions, the need for parental consent when young women seek an abortion, and the withdrawal of federal funds from institutions that provide abortions. After the *Brown* decision, the majority of people believed that desegregation was a sound legal decision. In contrast, many constitutional authorities and citizens continue to doubt the merits of the *Roe* decision.

The goal of this chapter is to bring to light some of the social and legal reasons for the continuing controversy over the Supreme Court decision rendered in *Roe v. Wade* (1973). This chapter (1) places the decision in a social and legal context, (2) summarizes the exigencies that prompted the Supreme Court to hear the case, (3) identifies how legal fictions influenced the civil proceeding prior to the appeal, (4) analyzes the fictions in appeal arguments, (5) evaluates the fictions in Justice Blackmun's majority opinion, and (6) emphasizes lessons learned about legal fictions and appellate argumentation.

SOCIAL AND LEGAL CONTEXT

All landmark Supreme Court decisions are about the constitutional rights of citizens. For example, *Brown* promoted the rights of black students and *Roe* promoted the rights of women. In 1973, the immediate constitutional questions were whether the states or the federal government held the authority to regulate abortion, whether medical providers had the right to perform abortions, and whether privacy and due process rights entitled women to have abortions. Justice Blackmun wrote that "This right of privacy . . . is broad enough to encompass a woman's decision whether or not to terminate her pregnancy." He emphasized this right was grounded in the Nineteenth Amendment's idea of personal liberty and the Ninth Amendment's reservation of rights to the people. Judges (1993) explains, "In *Roe*, the Court cast the abortion debate in terms of individual liberty" (p. 16). In doing so, the decision constitutionalized the abortion debate. *Roe* did not make the right to privacy for women absolute but left open the possibility that the government could limit privacy in three circumstances—for moral reasons, protection of a woman's health, and protection of potential life. The decision also limited the right of women to the option to have an abortion without physicians' consent during the early months of her pregnancy. The Court did not permit abortion on demand, although some media representations about the decision promoted this interpretation. The exceptions permitted in the *Roe* decision led to subsequent legal challenges from those opposing the decision.

The decision also ignited controversy about what the role of the judiciary should be. Should the judiciary make law? Should the justices rely on historical and medical evidence? Can a conservative president override *Roe* by appointing conservative justices to the Supreme Court? Historians disagree about the legacy of the *Roe* decision. For example, Hull and Hoffer (2001) conclude, "No legal historian or constitutional scholar can doubt that *Roe* is now a centerpiece of our constitutional history, in particular the constitutionalization of the rights of women and the rights of privacy" (p. 6). Colker (1992) claims that the decision "set the tone for how activist the

Court would be in our lives" (pp. 101–102). But other scholars (Dworkin, 1990) assert that "no judicial decision in our time has aroused as much sustained public outrage, emotion, and physical violence, or as much intemperate professional criticism" (p. 51).

Because U.S. presidents promote their political ideology through judicial appointments to the federal appellate courts and the Supreme Court, citizens often believe that a president has the power to overturn or uphold a controversial court decision such as *Roe*. This belief promotes the politicalization of the federal judiciary and turns abortion into an important presidential election issue. In fact, almost every governmental actor and every governmental power has figured prominently in this controversy (Devins, 1996). The passionate rhetoric that critics use to condemn the federal court's decisions about abortion is unprecedented. Political conservatives argue that "few Supreme Court decisions have come to be recognized as so faulty, and with such damaging social consequences that history has branded them not only as controversial or erroneous but also as watersheds of ignomity" (Horan & Balch, 1998, p. 73).

In the 1960s several states adopted the Model Penal Code of the American Law Institute. This code gave doctors and medical providers the right to make decisions about whether a woman could get an abortion, and it resulted in two cases that collided with some state abortion laws. The first involved Dr. Leon Belous, who in violation of California law, gave the name of an abortionist to one of his patients. In 1967, the state of California tried and convicted him for violating the state law (*People v. Belous*, 1969). His attorneys appealed the verdict to the California Supreme Court who overturned his conviction based on the fact that the wording of the California law was too vague. A second case involved Milan Vuitch, a full-time abortion doctor in Washington, D.C. The federal courts of the District indicted him for performing abortions in violation of the federal criminal law. The Supreme Court overturned Vuitch's conviction on the grounds that federal law was too vague (*United States v. Vuitch*, 1971). In both cases, the decisions affirmed the rights of the doctors to exercise their medical judgment, but neither decision dealt with the rights of pregnant women.

In controversial cases, a large number of *amicus curia* briefs usually are filed with the Court by parties with strong interests in the outcome of the appeal. When the petitioners for Roe and respondents for Texas submitted their written briefs to the Supreme Court in 1971, more friends of the court briefs were submitted on behalf of petitioners than for respondents. The *amicus curia* briefs are a kind of backdoor method for lobbying the Supreme Court justices to support a particular side of the case. Copies of these friends of the court briefs submitted in the *Roe* case can be found in Kurland and Casper (1990) along with the briefs of the appellate attorneys.

EXIGENCIES

The personal, social/political, and religious interests and values at a given time in history affect the way legal disputes are resolved. These factors create exigencies, urgent issues that demand a legal response, influence whether the Court will hear a case, affect the reasoning of the appellate briefs, and impact the arguments in the Court's decision.

Personal Exigencies

One exigency came from the threats of disease to the fetus. Early in the 1960s, when the only way that a woman could get an abortion in the U.S. was if a panel of medical providers decided that a pregnancy endangered a woman's life, two unforeseen medical emergencies altered the American abortion debate. The first was the discovery that the drug thalidomide caused severe birth defects for a pregnant woman. Sherri Finkbine, a Phoenix mother of four, discovered she had taken a drug containing thalidomide before doctors confirmed she was pregnant. Her doctors encouraged her to get an abortion because the fetus she was carrying likely would be deformed, but a judge denied her request; although many state laws permitted an abortion if the mother's life was endangered, the law did not address whether a woman could get an abortion if the fetus was deformed. Since she was unable to get a legal abortion in Arizona, Finkbine traveled to Sweden where abortions were legal. Other women who had taken thalidomide went to other countries to get abortions. These circumstances prompted legal and medical authorities to rethink state laws that prohibited abortions except to save the life of the mother (Faux, 1988; Hull & Hoffer, 2001; Tribe, 1990).

The second personal exigency resulted from an epidemic of rubella (measles) in 1965. Doctors knew that rubella caused severe deformities to the fetus, and many pregnant women had contracted the disease. Doctors in several states violated the abortion laws of that time and performed abortions, or they referred pregnant women who had contracted rubella to abortion providers. As a group, the rubella cases did not consider the impact of the deformity on the family, but emphasized doctors' rights to decide what the family could do under the law (Faux 1988).

Social/Political Exigencies

Activist groups created a second type of exigency. A deliberate campaign to change abortion laws was instrumental in the complaint filed on behalf of Jane Roe, and this campaign enabled the case to make its way to the Supreme Court. In 1966 a conference set up by Betty Friedan brought together people interested in women's rights from all over the United States. The conference created the National Organization for Women (NOW); the organization's goal was to liberate women from unfairness and injustice in their private lives. NOW lobbied Congress, promoted the Equal Rights

Amendment, participated in picketing and rallies, drafted legislation, and brought lawsuits on behalf of women seeking constitutional rights. In 1969, NOW collaborated with the National Association for the Repeal of Abortion Laws (NARAL; the group later changed its name to the National Abortion Rights Action League), and together these organizations promoted reproductive rights for women. Other women's rights groups joined forces with groups who favored legal abortions. Both Weddington and Coffee were members of these women's rights organizations, and these groups provided financial and legal assistance to them in their efforts to overturn Texas abortion laws (Hull & Hoffer, 2001).

By the time Weddington and Coffee presented the *Roe* case to the federal court in Texas, many women's rights organizations had already placed abortion rights high on their political agenda. For example, NARAL's goal was to "develop and sustain a constituency which effectively uses the political process at the state and national level to guarantee every woman in the United States the right to choose and obtain a legal abortion" (Wilder, 1998, p. 79). Weddington (1992) claims her participation in abortion referral services and her connections with clergy counseling services in Austin both motivated and supported her challenge to the Texas abortion statute. Other activist groups supported the *Roe* case, including "women's rights organizations, civil libertarians, and population control groups" (Yarnold, 1995, p. 7). Appellate case files show that the American Civil Liberties Union, Planned Parenthood, New Women Lawyers, Women's Health and Abortion Project, National Organization for Women, and the American Association of Planned Parenthood Physicians filed *amicus curia* briefs in support of *Roe*.

Religious Exigencies

Religious groups created a third source of exigency. Even before the decision, proabortion rights groups met formidable opposition from Roman Catholics, evangelical religious groups, and members of the conservative religious establishment. The National Right to Life Committee opposed abortion under any conditions. Other groups joined with the Right to Life organization and opposed any type of abortion. This coalition of antiabortion forces included the attorney generals of Arizona, Connecticut, Kentucky, and Utah; the Mothers for the Unborn; and the Association of Diocesan Attorneys. These groups also filed *amicus curia* briefs and offered legal support for attorneys representing the state of Texas. Some of these groups also demonstrated at family-planning clinics, boycotted doctors who provided abortions, and expressed their religious belief that abortion of any kind is murder.

Pro-choice forces predominated prior to the *Roe* appeal; however, after the decision pro-life activists mobilized their efforts to overturn *Roe* and to shut down abortion clinics. Pro-life activists succeeded to some extent when the Court decided *Webster v. Reproductive Health Services* (1989), a decision that restricted *Roe v. Wade* (1973) by prohibiting abortions from being performed in tax-supported hospitals, forbidding doctors from telling women about the availability of abortions, and allowing doctors to determine when a fetus was "viable." For this reason, the pro-life forces considered the *Webster* decision a victory.

The personal, social/political, and religious beliefs and values created exigencies that gained the attention of the legal establishment about how deeply divided society was about the issues of whether or not women had a right to get an abortion and whether medical providers had a right to perform one. In a legal sense, the *Roe* case was "ripe" for the Supreme Court; that is, the social conditions persuaded the Court to become involved with the state laws prohibiting abortions. With the availability of "the pill" in the late 1960s, many women practiced birth control and took advantage of government-funded birth control clinics. At the time of the test case and the appeal on behalf of Roe, the women's rights movement had elevated the rights of women to a prominent place on their national political agenda. Many physicians and nurses supported legal abortions. Moreover, the judges in the Texas court and at the U.S. Supreme Court shared a liberal ideology that favored women's rights. Various exigencies contributed to the importance of the abortion issue and encouraged the legal system to address the issue of abortion. The subsequent explanation of the legal argumentation illustrates how attorneys and judges argued about abortion rights.

LEGAL ARGUMENTS AND FICTIONS

Appellate argument is a specialized kind of reasoning that is constrained by principles of the common law systems, procedural rules, and the protocols of legal jurisdictions. Specifically, the appellate arguers' approach to facts, evidence, justification, and legitimation make appellate reasoning distinctive.

First, appellate courts do not create facts, but they regard the record of the lower courts as the facts. Trials find facts, and appellate courts deal with issues of law. If for some reason the appeal is based on an error in the finding of facts, then the appeal court redresses that error. In the appeal on behalf of Roe, the Court assumed the facts were as stated in the record of the Texas court (*Roe v. Wade,* 1970). Appellate attorneys and judges interpret the legal facts in relation to what they believe the law defines, proscribes, or permits.

Second, the kind of evidence used in appellate arguments is different from that used in the trial courts. The trial courts consider evidence from lay and expert testimony, real evidence (weapons, records, videotapes, etc.), affidavits, and/or depositions. The primary evidence in appellate argument consists of case facts decided in the trial courts as well as the texts of the documents being interpreted, such as a statute, the Constitution, or a treaty. Appeal arguments use secondary evidence, including sources that define the meaning of the words or the intent of primary legal documents, precedents, technical data, case specific data from disciplinary scholarship, and legal and constitutional theories. In the appeal from the court that decided *Roe,* the record consisted of facts derived from a couple of affidavits and the ruling of the three judges.

In a way that is typical of most appeals, the appellate briefs filed on behalf of Roe et al. presented evidence about the Texas state statutes, dozens of precedents, and a myriad of historical and medical evidence. The evidence was notable for its extensive use of medical definitions, cross-cultural data about abortions, definitions of rights, ancient history, explanations of pregnancy, pictures of the fetus at various stages of gestation, and definitions of marital and physicians' rights. Blackmun's majority opinion heavily relied on this secondary evidence, including the history of abortion in ancient society, the Hippocratic Oath, the right to an abortion in the American and English legal systems, and the American Medical Association's position on abortion.

Appellate attorneys and judges interpret the evidence to prove the particular legal standpoint that they support. Appellate attorneys justify their standpoints toward the disputed issues by giving reasons and evidence for the conclusions they draw. Justifications both explain how legal issues should be understood and validate attorneys' standpoints. The legal standpoint of the petitioners was that the Texas abortion statutes violated women's rights and should be overturned. They justified a woman's right to an abortion by explaining it as part of the right of privacy and within the tradition of modern medicine. The petitioners tried to convince the Supreme Court justices that the right to abortion is reasonable because the fetus is not a person until it is viable outside the womb. The legal standpoint adopted by respondents was that the Texas abortion statutes should be retained because these laws protect the rights of the fetus. Respondents justified their standpoint by claiming the fetus is a person from the moment of conception and the Texas law protects the rights of a person.

In appellate argumentation, legitimation differs from justification. Two senses of legitimation are relevant to this case. First, legitimation means that the arguments are drawn from legal principles and follow established standards for proof and legal reasoning. When judges conclude that an argument is legitimate, they mean that the content and method of reasoning fits with the principles and procedural rules of the Court. In a second sense, though, a legitimate appellate argument is one that makes sense to disparate legal and public audiences. In order for a judicial decision to be legitimate in this sense, other judges and the public must perceive the reasoning to be legally sound and within the bounds of the public sense of reasonableness given the particular details of a case and the salience of social and political issues of the era. Making reasonable arguments is the method justices use to persuade their various audiences that the decision they have made is legitimate. It is the only means the Supreme Court has to enforce their decisions because they "have neither force of arms nor the power of the purse" (Nelson, 1995, p. 13). Thus, the goal of appellate arguers is to build a persuasive legal case using facts, evidence, and fictions. The subsequent analysis concentrates on how appellate attorneys and judges use legal fictions to construct, justify, and legitimize their reasoning.

Appellate arguers do not produce truth; they advocate, defend, and refute a particular legal standpoint in regard to constitutional issues. To accomplish this goal, appellate advocates often have to search for missing parts from the argument and fill in the gaps with fictions that make their standpoints seem reasonable to the audiences they address (LaRue, 1995). Fictions permit attorneys and judges to support their legal standpoints by justifications and legitimizations based on facts and evidence. Concentrating on fictions offers both a descriptive and analytical framework for examining appellate arguments and judicial opinions. One way to define legal fictions is to identify common features of the various aspects of legal argumentation (LaRue, 1995).

FEATURES OF LEGAL FICTIONS

- Fictions come from the legal arguers' imagination, rather than from the facts. Fictions may be based on facts, but differ from them.

- Fictions extend evidence by supplying assumptions, imaginative inferences, and causal connections.

- Fictions allow arguers to construe the facts and interpret the evidence in line with a particular legal standpoint.

- Facts and evidence do not correspond to truth and fictions to falsehoods. By creating fictional assumptions and drawing fictional inferences from the facts and evidence, appellate arguers justify and legitimate their claims for their audiences.

- When attorneys and judges interpret facts and evidence, they fill in gaps with fictions, build bridges between facts and evidence and their legal standpoints, and assert causal connections that complete their arguments.

- Appellate arguments contain facts and evidence that are assertions rather than truths, and fictions persuade audiences that facts and evidence should be believed.

- Fictions in legal arguments persuade adjudicators because they show how judges' legal standpoints fit with their own knowledge, beliefs, and values.

- Fictions add persuasiveness to judicial decisions because they clarify constitutional issues that otherwise may be fuzzy or confusing.

Fictions surface in the argumentation when attorneys and judges make assertions so that they seem to be facts, treat assumptions as if they were legal principles, draw inferences from facts and evidence, and create tropes to add persuasive force to their arguments.

Test Cases as Fictions

Test cases, similar to that constructed on behalf of Jane Roe and the Does, promote controversy about the legitimacy of the decisions because they rely on fictions as the foundation for the legal actions. In test cases, attorneys solicit plaintiffs, present complaints, and seek relief or remedies from the court. Despite the fact that test cases are perfectly legal and relatively common, some of these types of cases create public suspicions because attorneys have solicited the clients and the clients never suffered actual harm from the existing laws.

In many situations, the public lacks knowledge about how a case originated until long after the case has been decided. For example, in 1925 attorneys recruited a young and inexperienced biology teacher, John T. Scopes, to test the Tennessee law that prohibited the teaching of evolution. The teacher did not complain that his rights had been violated nor did he say he had experienced any harmful repercussions when he taught evolution. Nonetheless, the famous attorney Clarence Darrow solicited Scopes to be a plaintiff in a lawsuit that complained the state had violated his legal rights. The legendary Scopes case, also known as the Monkey trial, was the result (Scopes & Presley, 1967).

When the real reasons for a test case are exposed, some citizens may be surprised to learn that some legal tests of the Constitution are based on fictions, but most legal practitioners realize that these kinds of cases are legitimate processes that test the constitutionality of a law. Many test cases, such as the graduate school segregation cases involving Sipuel, Sweatt, and McLaurin (chapter 10), and *Griswold v. Connecticut* (1965), involving birth control and women's reproductive rights, produced important precedents that helped the Court decide *Brown* and *Roe*.

The complaint in the Texas lawsuit filed on behalf of Roe, the Does, and James Hallford (who was subsequently included) started as a test case and ended up in the Supreme Court. Weddington and Coffee solicited clients to challenge what they considered to be an unjust and overly restrictive Texas abortion law. Using a test case to get a judicial ruling is neither illegal nor unethical; it enables attorneys to establish a factual record using fictions. In other words a test case establishes both facts and assumptions that ground the appeal in legitimate legal soil. After Weddington shared her research about legal precedents involving women's reproductive rights with friends from an abortion referral group, they encouraged her to file a civil lawsuit challenging the Texas law. The attorney then contacted a law school friend, Linda Coffee, who worked at a law firm in Dallas to help her with the case (Weddington, 1992).

Clients and Complaints as Fictions.   Clients and complaints have fictional attributes. Henry McCluskey referred a young woman who wanted an abortion but could not get one to Coffee. Since Norma McCorvey wanted to protect her identity, Coffee and Weddington called her Jane Roe in the lawsuit. They first met her at a coffee shop and explained how she could become a plaintiff in a lawsuit opposing the Texas abortion law and could represent other pregnant women who wanted but could not secure an abortion. The attorneys explained to their client why they thought the Texas law needed to be changed. McCorvey told them that she tried but could not obtain a legal abortion in Texas. Prior to her current pregnancy, this unmarried bartender and sometimes circus worker had given birth to two other children. One was being raised by her mother, and she gave up her other child for adoption on the day it was born. McCorvey told the attorneys that she was poor and unemployed, and she had become pregnant after being raped. She did not tell the attorneys that she had a long history of drug and alcohol abuse or that she had consensual sex with the man who impregnated her (McCorvey, 1994; Weddington, 1992). Other potential clients responded to Weddington and Coffee's request for plaintiffs, including a woman and her husband with the pseudonyms of John and Mary Doe. Mary Doe was not pregnant, but her medical condition was such that an abortion might be warranted in the future to save her life.

After securing their clients, Coffee and Weddington filed a lawsuit in a Texas federal court in March of 1970. The goal of the lawsuit was to win a declaratory judgment that the Texas abortion law was unconstitutional and gain an injunction that would stop the enforcement of the abortion law (Weddington, 1992). Weddington listed several reasons why Roe's and the Does' injuries justified overturning the Texas abortion statute. She argued that one reason for the lawsuit was that the Texas abortion law violated her clients' personal privacy and due process rights according to some provisions of the "First, Fourth, Fifth, Eighth, Ninth, and Fourteenth Amendments" to the Constitution. These plaintiffs' attorneys stipulated a number of facts in the Roe complaint: Roe was unmarried and pregnant, and she wished to have an abortion because of "economic hardships and social stigmas" (p. 55). Roe's life was not threatened, but she lacked the money needed to travel to another state to secure a legal abortion.

Additionally, Weddington and Coffee argued that an abortion performed in a hospital by a "licensed physician" is less dangerous than "childbirth" (p. 55). On March 19, two other Dallas lawyers petitioned to have their client James Hubert Hallford join the lawsuit. Hallford had been indicted for performing an illegal abortion. From the beginning, the defense attorneys contested the legal standing of Roe, the Does, and Hallford because they said that none of the plaintiffs could receive a concrete benefit from a decision overturning the Texas abortion law, they suffered no actual harm, and the court had no way of knowing the identity of Roe and the Does. Roe (McCorvey) had her baby before the Supreme Court decided the case, Mary Doe was not pregnant and in need of an abortion, and Hallford was already under indictment so nullification of the Texas law would have no effect on him (*Roe v. Wade*, 1970). The Supreme Court eventually dismissed the Does and Hallford as having no standing in the appeal, but they treated the case as a class action lawsuit in which Roe represented other similarly situated women.

Legal Principles as Fictions.   The term "standing" is a legal metaphor that the courts understand as a legal principle (Winter, 1989). Standing refers to the legal right of a party to bring a claim and to represent a class of people in similar situations. Appellate courts treat the fictions of legal standing and class actions as legal principles. Attorneys assert these legal fictions as part of the record of the trial court and thereby validate them as legal principles important to the reasoning of their case.

Realities behind the Legal Fictions.   After a case has been decided, the media or the participants themselves may reveal some of the fictional elements that permitted the case to go forward. John T. Scopes and his attorney Clarence Darrow eventually acknowledged the realities behind the fictions in the Scopes trial, and McCorvey and Weddington also revealed fictions when they wrote autobiographical accounts long after the *Roe* decision (McCorvey, 1994; Weddington, 1992). The posttrial autobiographical accounts affected how the public perceived the *Roe* decision. Both of these posttrial accounts disclosed secrets, admitted to errors in judgment, and added details about their motives. For example, McCorvey admitted that she had never been raped but had become pregnant through consensual sex with a drug dealer with whom she shared a house. After McCorvey became a consultant to NBC producers for a made-for-television movie about the *Roe* case in 1989 (McCorvey, 1994, pp. 178–185), the real details of her life became public. In her autobiography written years after the decision, Weddington admitted that she personally had used abortion as a method of birth control. She also disclosed that her husband and other attorneys from NARAL researched and developed the case and that NARAL funded the lawsuit and the appeal.

These disclosures encouraged oppositional rhetoric that claimed the decision was politically motivated. McCorvey's lies about being raped, secrets about her drug and alcohol abuse, and her lesbian lifestyle supported pro-life activists' rhetoric that abortion was not a legitimate right for McCorvey and by implication was not legitimate for other pregnant women either. Moreover, these disclosures persuaded those opposing *Roe* that they had been right all along and that the decision was based on fictions, not facts.

Fictions Created at the Trial

Instead of calling witnesses to testify in court, the Texas federal court conducted a civil proceeding in which plaintiffs' attorneys argued their case based on two signed affidavits, one from Roe about the facts of her pregnancy and her desire for an abortion, and another from Paul Trickett, a physician and director of the University of Texas Student Health Center, who explained the medical aspects of abortion. The defense called no witnesses, but they refuted the arguments made by the plaintiffs' attorneys. Weddington (1992) presented the affidavit from Roe as proof of the facts of her pregnant status; her age; and the effects the pregnancy had on her, such as her difficulty in gaining employment and her desire to terminate her pregnancy because of the economic hardship and social stigma an illegitimate child would create for her. Trickett stated that abortion involved "minimal risk to the patient" when performed during the first six to ten weeks of pregnancy and affirmed the safety of the medical procedure. He reported the "general circumstances of many Texas women" who had told him at the student health center that they wanted an abortion. He claimed that unwanted pregnancies resulted from the unavailability of birth control (p. 60).

Affidavits as Facts

Affidavits are a written declaration made under an oath before an authorized legal official, but attorneys construct affidavits by translating into legal terms what a client has told them, excluding information that jeopardizes a client's legal standing or credibility, and including statements that show legal legitimacy. An affidavit is a legal fiction, but it also establishes legal facts. The Texas court and the Supreme Court treated the Roe and Trickett affidavits as facts that proved legal standing and justified a class action suit.

Case Theories as Fictions

In the hearing, other fictions evolved through the case theories promoted by the attorneys. For example, Coffee argued that the plaintiffs had no remedy in state courts and that the Texas law violated provisions of the First, Fourth, Fifth, Eighth, Ninth, and Fourteenth Amendments. Weddington later noted that at the time of the appeal, she thought that the abortion law only violated the due process and equal protection clauses of the Fourteenth Amendment, but she still argued that the right to an abortion was implied in the rest of the amendments (Weddington, 1992). In the second part of the case, Weddington asserted that the law "has never treated the fetus as a person" (p. 64), and therefore the state should not prohibit licensed medical people from performing abortions.

In support of the Texas abortion statutes, Jay Floyd and John Tolle presented the defense in the Texas proceeding. Floyd claimed that plaintiffs had no legal standing, the right to an abortion did not exist in the U.S. Constitution, the state had a right to protect the unborn child during all stages of pregnancy, and the right of the unborn child to life was superior to the right of a woman to privacy. Floyd explained that "the state's interest . . . may be a consideration of whether or not murder occurs, that is, if this embryo is a human being" (Faux, 1988, p. 147). In response to an inquiry from Judge Goldberg, Floyd asserted that the right of privacy was the right to be left alone because it had nothing to do with abortion. Tolle claimed the state had a right "to protect life . . . at whatever stage it may be in . . . and if there is no absolute fact as to when life occurs, then it becomes, . . . a legislative problem as to when they're going to set an arbitrary time" (Faux, 1988, p. 148). The inferences drawn from the legal and historical evidence became part of the legal record that established facts on which the appeal depended.

PROCEDURES, PROTOCOLS, AND FICTIONS
IN THE APPELLATE ARGUMENTATION

Since the Roe civil suit was a test case, the goal of the attorneys was to move the case from the Texas court to the Supreme Court. No appeal is automatic; several stages of the appeal process determine whether the Supreme Court will hear the case. The official appeal of a lower court decision commences with the filing of a jurisdictional statement, a specialized brief, sent to the Court within 60 days of the lower court decision. The purpose of the jurisdictional statement is to persuade the Court that it should grant *certiorari*, that is, agree to hear the case. The jurisdictional statement is followed by the submission of appeal briefs. If the Court grants *certiorari*, the officials of the Court schedule the case for oral arguments. A judicial conference takes place after oral arguments. At the different stages in the appeal process, the justices and their clerks decide whether the appeal attorneys have addressed a compelling constitutional issue, understood the applicable legal principles, constructed reasonable arguments, and followed the protocols for the Court. At the judicial conferences, the justices usually poll each other to determine their impressions about how the case should be decided. At the conference a judge can volunteer or be assigned to write the majority opinion. If the decision is not unanimous, justices can write dissents.

The petitioners sought abortion rights for Roe and other pregnant women and the respondents defended the legality of the Texas abortion statutes according to the normative procedures for a legal appeal (Dickson, 2001; Stern, Gressman, & Shapiro, 1986). The petitioners filed a jurisdictional statement, and then the respondents representing the state of Texas had 30 days to respond. When the respondents expect that their reply will have no impact on the Court's consideration of the case, they usually decide not to file a response (Stern, Gressman, & Shapiro, 1986). The state of Texas respondents decided to file a short response.

Jurisdictional Statement

The petitioners claimed that the Supreme Court should hear the case because of "federal questions" that have not been resolved. They argued that the case involved "issues of profound national importance, affecting the lives of many thousands of American citizens each year"; the American Medical Association permits "licensed physicians to perform abortions in hospitals"; the issue has been debated by legislative bodies; and the courts are divided about whether or not abortion should be legal. The petitioners concluded that the Court should "accept jurisdiction and set the matter down for full briefing and argument" (Kurland & Casper, 1990, pp. 12–23). The respondents' short reply refuted some of the petitioners' arguments and introduced new ones. For example, the respondents claimed that injunctive relief is a moot point because: Roe has already delivered her baby and the Does do not have standing, federal courts should not interfere with state courts, and petitioners have failed to show that they are entitled to any type of injunctive relief.

Appellate Briefs

The appellate briefs present the key arguments for each side of the case. Although the attorneys for both sides argued the case before the Supreme Court twice, once in 1971 and again in 1972, the arguments presented in the initial briefs led to the decision. Roy Lucas, a key figure in NARAL, put his name at the top of the petitioners' brief, but the participants in the case agree that Sarah Weddington wrote the brief, with the assistance of her husband James R. Weddington, Linda Coffee, and Hallford's attorneys, Fred Bruner and Roy Merrill. Other attorneys for NARAL, Planned Parenthood, the American Civil Liberties Union, and the Association for the Study of Abortion contributed research and suggestions about the style and content, and they also submitted *amicus curia* briefs. Weddington worked on the brief at the office of the James Madison Law Institute in New York. After the appeal, Weddington (1992) recalled that she focused her arguments on the merits of the case and her husband concentrated on the other parts of the brief.

The formal brief consists of several parts that include statements of jurisdiction, lists of the statutes involved, the questions presented, a review of case facts, information about the relevant background, and a summary of arguments. The petitioners' brief established the case facts for the jurisdictional statement. As is typical of every appeal, the preponderance of evidence presented in the brief comes from legal precedents. This appeal dealt with precedents about the right to privacy, marital privacy, family rights, and health care access. Decisions in *United States v. Vuitch* (1971), *People v. Belous* (1969), and *Griswold v. Massachusetts* (1965) served as key precedents for the *Roe* appeal. Another source of evidence came from law review articles that provided legal interpretations about health, rights to privacy, due process, and reproductive legal issues. A third source consisted of explanations of legal terminology, such as the right to privacy, and the meaning of the language of other state abortion statutes. In general the evidence for the petitioners' brief paralleled what the Court generally expects. The content and structure of petitioners' arguments stressed legal principles.

PETITIONERS' ARGUMENTS

- Injunctive relief should be granted to Jane Roe, Mary and John Doe, and James Hallford, and others similarly situated.
- Roe, the Does, and Hallford have legal standing in the case.
- The Texas abortion statute abridges the personal rights of all appellants secured by the First, Fourth, Ninth, and Fourteenth Amendments.
- The right to medical care is a fundamental personal liberty.
- The right to marital and personal liberty is a national and international concern.

- The state of Texas has not shown a compelling interest to restrict medical, marital, and individual rights.
- Fetuses are not human beings and therefore not protected by federal law.
- The Texas abortion laws that criminalize abortion are unconstitutional.

Each argument followed a deductive chain of reasoning identified through the major heads in the outline of the brief. The petitioners tried to anticipate the respondents' arguments when they asserted that "an unborn fetus is not a 'human being,'" and killing a fetus is not murder or any other form of homicide. They then cited Texas's legal definitions of a human being, definitions from the common law, and a series of legal precedents to demonstrate that the law never grants rights to a fetus because the fetus has no legal standing. The brief then concluded that "science can offer no guidance on the question of when human life begins" (Kurland & Casper, 1990, p. 123).

Facts and Fictions in the Petitioners' Brief

Precedents are established legal principles that appellate attorneys use as evidence to show that a previous decision is applicable to the one being decided. Attorneys use precedents just like they use analogies. They infer that the circumstances in a previous decision were so similar to the case being argued that the reasoning and conclusions from the precedent should apply to the new decision. When attorneys make inferences about precedents, they often create fictions in order to explain how a given precedent applies to a new legal situation. One precedent that loomed large in the appeal brief submitted for *Roe* was a test case that the Supreme Court decided under the title of *Griswold v. Connecticut* (1965). In the case, the Court reversed the convictions of Estelle Griswold, a director of Planned Parenthood, and attending physician Lee Buxton. They had been convicted of giving contraceptives to a married couple. In Connecticut at the time of the decision, distributing contraceptives violated the laws of that state. The petitioners inferred that the *Griswold* precedent applied directly because it established a right to privacy between medical providers and patients and that it established a right of marital privacy that included couples having a right to decide whether or not to have a child. Providing contraceptives and having an abortion are two different actions, but the petitioners applied the precedent because it established the right of married couples to make a private decision about whether or not to have a child.

Fictions in the petitioners' briefs took several other forms—asserting premises and assumptions that permitted the attorneys to complete the argument, exaggerating the predictions about the consequences from the decision, using metaphors to embellish the arguments, and adopting refutation strategies that pointed to the weaknesses in the opposing attorneys' arguments.

Asserting Premises.   When they approached the Supreme Court, the petitioners asked the Court to grant standing to Roe, the Does, and Hallford because they recognized that several appellants and their different complaints would strengthen their arguments. Roe's unmarried status could make their case weak; although it showed she was unable to get a safe and legal abortion in Texas, it also could show that she was seeking an abortion as a method of birth control. Adding the Does' complaint allowed the petitioners to address another flaw of the Texas statute by showing that this law would not allow married couples to get an abortion even though they knew a pregnancy might jeopardize the life of the wife. Finally, Hallford's case showed that doctors could not provide a legal abortion to their patients even when the doctor decided that the abortion was necessary to protect the life of the patient. To address three different types of clients, the petitioners established three separate arguments.

First, they concluded that Americans have a right to good health care. They argued that Roe had a right to get an abortion in a medical clinic from a licensed provider, and this type of health care was not available for women seeking an abortion in Texas even when the women offered to pay for it themselves. Second, the petitioners further claimed that couples have a marital right to privacy that includes their decision about when or whether to have children and whether they need an abortion. The premise asserting marital rights showed that overturning the law would benefit married women with severe medical conditions and allow them to decide when they could safely engage in marital relations with their husbands. By including physicians, the petitioners established a third way of proving their legal standpoint that the Texas law should be overturned and an injunction should be issued to stop the enforcement of the law. They asserted that physicians have the right to protect the health of their patients.

Asserting premises in this way implies that granting standing to three different appellants is reasonable because it will help the Court to develop the law, establish abortion as a federal issue, understand the relevance of history, and conclude that the fetus is not a human until it is born. These premises asserted by the plaintiffs' attorneys are not facts, but they are assumptions established by fictions that support the legal standpoint that the petitioners have adopted.

Exaggerating Effects.   Another strategy that appellate attorneys use is to exaggerate the legal consequences of a lower court decision. The exaggeration is partially based on legal facts, but it predicts extreme consequences without providing evidence for those consequences. For example, the petitioners claimed the respondents never challenged Roe's affidavit in which she "presented a factual resume" showing that she was pregnant "out-of-wedlock," suffered from "a social stigma and economic hardship due to that pregnancy," wanted "to put an end to that condition," but lacked an ability to do so. "That there are many in her situation is uncontroverted" (Kurland & Casper, 1990, pp. 151–152). (All of the quotations from the appeal documents and the decision come from Kurland and Casper [1990] and are cited by the page number in that volume.) The petitioners concluded that Jane Roe and the class she represented suffered "economic, social, psychological and physiological effects of being forced to go through an unwanted pregnancy and deal with an unwanted child . . . could represent irreparable injuries" (p. 151). When the petitioners argued that severe and adverse consequences would follow, Roe had already given birth and put up her child for adoption. Moreover, no evidence existed in the trial record that women had ever been tried in the criminal courts in Texas for getting an abortion. The exaggeration of consequences is not a factual statement but is a fiction that appellate attorneys use to persuade judges about the undesirable legal consequences that could result if the case is not decided in their favor. An example of the petitioners' strategy of exaggeration follows:

> [T]he right to an abortion will reach the court as a criminal conviction, and that process might very well entail the convening of countless state courts, . . . the assembling of countless jurors, and the occupations of countless prosecutors, not to mention the untold anxiety, expenses and humiliation of those physicians willing to offer themselves as sacrificial lambs to test the statutes. (pp. 161–162)

Exaggerations of this type permeate the petitioners' brief; they are fictions that complete the argument. Another example was an exaggeration used to prove that the Texas statute is not rationally related to public health interests. Not only did the petitioners exaggerate the consequences, but they borrowed a medical metaphor of the pandemic to frame the exaggeration. They argued that statutes, like the Texas abortion law,

> create a public health problem of pandemic proportions by denying women the opportunity to seek safe medical treatment. Severe infections, permanent sterility, pelvic disease, and other serious complications accompany the illegal abortions to which women are driven by laws like this one. (pp. 115–116)

Using Metaphors.   Metaphors have the power to define (Bosmajian, 1992), and they help audiences understand the facts of a situation. Metaphors are not facts but interpretive language that evokes feeling and adds interest and thereby persuades audiences that facts exist. The petitioners added metaphors at different points in their brief to give persuasive force to their appeal. They stated that the Texas courts compelled Roe and other similarly situated women to "serve as an incubator for months and then as an ostensibly willing mother for up to 20 or more years. She must often forego further education or a career and often must endure economic and social hardships" (p. 186). This metaphor suggests that Texas law converts a woman into a life sustaining machine and mandates unwelcome motherhood.

The petitioners used other metaphors to establish the standing of the Does and Hallford. For example, they refer to the possibility of Jane Doe becoming pregnant as a "spectre [specter] of pregnancy" that would have "a divisive effect on her marriage" (p. 129); specter means that some event is terrifying and dreadful. This metaphor amplified the reasoning about why the Does belonged in the lawsuit. They hoped this would gain the attention of the Court as a legally substantive complaint even though the Texas court had claimed the Does had no legal standing. They used other metaphors as a plea to the Court to include Hallford in the appeal. They argued that doctors and their patients should not have to depend on "a cooperative martyr" like Hallford to defend their legal rights (p. 136). This metaphor suggested that Hallford sacrificed himself as a doctor in order to meet the needs of pregnant women.

The previous examples show that the petitioners used metaphors to characterize the appellants by showing they suffered violations of their rights and threats to their well-being because of the stringent Texas abortion law. These metaphors apparently did not persuade the Court that the Does and Hallford should be part of the appeal since the Court in the end failed to grant legal standing to either of the parties.

Adopting a Refutation Strategy.   The petitioners followed their metaphor strategy with a refutation strategy that reduced the claims of the opposition to absurdity, *reductio ad absurdum*. Near the end of their brief, they claimed that the Texas abortion law was absurd since the Court would never consider limiting other kinds of surgery except to save a life. For example, they would never prohibit "gall bladder surgery, kidney stone removal, the prescription of contraceptives, the use of antibiotics, vaccinations, or even the taking of aspirin" only if someone's life were in danger (p. 212). Appellate arguers often use refutation strategies of this kind to expose the fictions they believe exist in the arguments of the attorneys that oppose them.

Facts and Fictions in Respondents' Brief

The respondents' brief presented extensive biological information and pictures of the stages of the development of the fetus. Their primary goal was to prove that life begins at conception. This assumption allowed respondents to engage in consequential reasoning: if the law protects all life, then it must protect the fetus in the womb because it is human. Just as in all appellate briefs, the respondents provided extensive documentation for the evidence they presented.

Assistant Attorney General Robert Flowers took the responsibility for writing the respondents' brief with assistance from Crawford Martin and Jay Floyd, who represented the attorney general of Texas. Flowers credited a University of Texas law professor, Joseph Witherspoon, with the inspiration for his arguments about the humanity of the fetus. Although the professor's name did not appear on this brief, it did appear on the *amicus curia* brief from the Texas archdiocese (Faux, 1988).

The respondents' brief began in a standard way by stating the case; reporting the provisions of the Texas abortion statute; noting the questions presented; challenging the legal standing of Roe, the Does, and Hallford; and denying the vagueness of the Texas statute. The first 28 pages of the brief developed a clear deductive chain of reasoning, beginning with the respondents' claims that the Texas court erred in declaring the abortion law unconstitutional. The subsequent 27 pages deviated from legal reasoning and instead presented a detailed medical and historical explanation of "the human-ness of the fetus." This excerpt from the brief illustrates the consequential reasoning that the respondents used in this lengthy part of the brief:

> If we take the definition of life as being said to be present when an organism shows evidence of individual animate existence then from the blastocyst state, the fetus qualifies for respect. It is alive because it has the ability to reproduce dying cells. It is human because it can be distinguished from other nonhuman species, and once implanted in the uterine wall it requires only nutrition and time to develop into one of us. (p. 265)

The respondents' arguments addressed specific grounds of the appeal in short succinct statements of issues. Then the brief asserted that the fetus is a human being and therefore has constitutional rights from the moment of conception. The brief presented its central argument that shows "how clearly and conclusively modern science . . . establishes the humanity of the unborn child" (p. 265). The brief reported a chronology of the development of the fetus, giving evidence using pictures of the different stages of gestation. During respondents' oral argument, the questions asked by justices show that some of them paid close attention to the respondents' arguments about why the fetus is a human being. Although the number of arguments in the petitioners' and respondents' briefs was similar, the amount of space allotted to the respondents' argument that the fetus is a human being exceeded that of all the other arguments made by either side of the case.

RESPONDENTS' ARGUMENTS

- Roe, the Does, and Hallford lack standing because they have not suffered any harm from Texas laws.
- Texas abortion laws are not vague and overbroad.
- Petitioners improperly asked for class action relief.
- The Court should refuse relief for Hallford because he was under indictment in Texas prior to the filing of the case.
- Injunctive relief is not proper without demonstrating irreparable harm and inadequate legal remedies.
- The right of privacy is not absolute.
- The fetus is a human being from the earliest stages of development.
- The Due Process Clause of the Fifth Amendment accords equal protection to the unborn person.

The respondents emphasized that the Texas law was not vague or broad, but it provided the needed restriction and penalties to guarantee the rights of the unborn who are human beings. The respondents used fictions to convey facts when they asserted definitions and presented visual evidence.

Asserting Definitions.   Definitions are fictions that attorneys assert to establish or complete an argument. A definitional argument "isolates what might at the moment seem to be particularly important ideas or attributes" that are subject to refutation by others. Definitions are "continuously subject to revision" as the particulars of a legal case evolve and the political and social conditions change (McGee, 1999, p. 153). Legal scholars do not usually explain definitional arguments, although this kind of evidence supplies important "stipulations" for justifying a legal claim. Zarefsky (1998) explains that arguments by definition "are simply proclaimed as if they are indisputable facts" (p. 5). In appellate briefs, definitional arguments stipulate a material, social, or legal reality as if it were true and not subject to refutation.

Both the petitioners and respondents made use of the argument by definition. The petitioners defined rights to marital privacy, rights to health care, and physicians' rights as if they were truths. The respondents concentrated their argumentation on definitions of the fetus. They claimed that the fetus is an unborn child, and the fetus is a human being from the time of conception.

The respondents then used metaphors to reinforce their claim that the fetus is a human life from the time of conception. They implied that abortion is similar to "extermination" in the Nazi death camps by stating that "abortion is indiscriminate extermination" (p. 267). Later, the respondents seemed to qualify their definition that a fetus is a human being when they asserted that the "unborn child is a bridge between two stages of life" (p. 289), but then they stipulated that the time before birth is one stage of human life and after the birth is another stage of human life. If the law protects life after birth, it should also protect human life before birth. Because the respondents spent so much effort defining human life, they did not refute the reasoning of the petitioners as much as they should have. In ways similar to other definitional arguments used in legal discourse, the respondents' definitions were not truths but fictions. Definitions change according to the person who stipulates them, the language used in the definition, and the linguistic and legal contexts in which the definitions reside.

When the respondents defined human life, they legitimized their arguments with conservatives in the judiciary and the public by establishing a political standpoint. Respondents noted that

> the proponents of liberalization of abortion laws speak of the fetus as "a blob" of protoplasm and feel it has no right to life until it has reached a certain stage of development. On the other hand, the opponents of liberalization [the respondents] maintain the fetus is human from the time of conception. . . . It is alive because it has the ability to reproduce dying cells. It is human because it can be distinguished from nonhuman species. (pp. 264–265)

This definitional argument reinforced the respondents' moral and political standpoint and identified with audiences who agreed with their conservative standpoint on abortion. The stipulation that life begins at conception was a backdoor justification of the Texas abortion law. It supplied a premise that had never been stated in the statute, but one that helped make sense of the provisions of that statute.

Using Visual Imagery.   Not only did the respondents define life as beginning at conception, they used visual and verbal imagery to embellish the definition and make it appear to be a truth rather than a device for constructing and completing their appellate arguments. The brief contains several pages of pictures of the development of the fetus—a picture of the fetus at 40 days, at 6 weeks, at 12 weeks, at 16 weeks, and at 18 weeks. The visuals magnified the size of the hands and feet of a fetus during the second month of pregnancy so that these limbs appeared to be the size of the fingers and toes of a newborn child. These images functioned in ways similar to the figure of speech called "metonymy," that is, the pictures of the hands and feet of the fetus symbolically represented the existence of a human being.

In addition to these visuals, respondents emphasized the imagery by using emotional descriptions to identify the fetus using the same terminology that parents use to describe a newborn baby. Respondents noted:

> In the third month, the child becomes very active. By the end of the month he can kick his legs, turn his feet, curl and fan his toes, make a fist, move his thumb, bend his wrists, turn his head, squint, frown and open his mouth, [and] press his lips together. (p. 277)

The respondents justified their central argument using definitions, and they reified those definitions with visual and verbal imagery. The respondents did not justify their argument by connecting them directly to the legal principles and precedents that the petitioners had presented. They restated the finding of fact in the hearing, challenged the legal standing of the Does and Hallford, concluded that the Texas law was clear and explicit and not vague at all, and claimed that privacy did not apply to abortion laws.

The respondents' argument was unusual because it concentrated on the stipulation that life begins at conception. Additionally, the majority of the respondents' evidence came from textbooks on anatomy rather than legal sources. What the respondents left out of their appellate argument illuminated their standpoint as much as what they included. They made no distinctions between early- and late-term abortions. The thrust of their argumentation was that any state could define a fetus as a person if it chose to do so. The respondents' argument seemed out of line with the kind of reasoning that the Supreme Court usually expects, but some of the justices took seriously their explanations of fetal viability as a reasonable premise.

THE SUPREME COURT DECISION IN *ROE V. WADE*

Various scholars explain the contents of a judicial opinion. For example, Stevenson (1975) notes that:

> [T]he purpose of the written opinion is not for the judge to arrive at a conclusion. He has already done that. Rather, it is for him to project his conclusion and his reason for holding it to those audiences who need to know about it. . . . The written opinion is not a set of notes written by a judge for his own use. Rather, it is a persuasive essay directed outward to specific audiences. (p. 35)

One of the functions of written decisions is rhetorical because judges try to convince specific audiences that the opinion is legitimate. An enumeration of the functions of appellate court decisions provides some clues about the role of decisions.

FUNCTIONS OF APPELLATE COURT DECISIONS

- To provide evidence and rational procedures that convince the public that judges are making just decisions (Franklin, 1968)
- To persuade the losing party that the judgment resulted from a logical process rather than a process that was oppressive and arbitrary (Calamandrei, 1956)
- To clear up a judge's thinking: "The act of writing tells us what was wrong with the act of thinking" (Coffin, 1980, p. 57)
- To communicate with society: "Opinions are the principal vehicle for communication" with practicing lawyers, judges, law professors, and the public (Leflar, 1961, pp. 810–812)
- To translate "authoritative texts into the present moment, a kind of pushing forward of what was written in one context into another, where it has necessarily different meaning" (White, 1990, p. 246)
- To persuade audiences "that the result reached is right; these opinions contain fictions; the use of fiction is essential to persuasion" (LaRue, 1995, p. 3)

When he wrote for the majority, Justice Blackmun offered a variety of arguments as proof for his central theme that the Texas statute prohibiting abortion should be overturned because it violates federal law. Blackmun summarized his opinion in this way:

> This holding, we feel, is consistent with the relative weight of the respective interests involved, with the lessons and examples of medical and legal history, with lenity [linage] of the common law, and with the demands of the profound problems of the present day. The decision leaves the State free to place increasing restrictions on abortion as the period of pregnancy lengthens, so long as those restrictions are tailored to the recognized state interests. The decision vindicates the rights of the physician to administer medical treatment according to his professional judgment up to the points where important state interests provide compelling justification for intervention. Up to those points the abortion decision in all its aspects is inherently, and primarily, a medical decision, and basic responsibility for it must rest with the physician. If an individual practitioner abused the privilege of exercising proper medical judgment, the usual remedies, judicial and intraprofessional, are available. (*Roe v. Wade*, 1973, p. 887)

This summary does not stress the rights of women to have abortions as much as it emphasizes the rights of the state to regulate abortions and the rights of physicians to perform abortions.

In *Roe,* Justice Blackmun relied on fictions pertaining to the role and goal of the Court, physicians' and states' rights, motherhood, and personhood. To some extent, the acceptance of some fictions and the rejection of others originates with judicial visions about the role and power of the Court. Blackmun envisioned himself as a powerful and authoritative judge with specialized knowledge and information about medicine to develop the law. One of the judge-created fictions in the case was that the Court should define the rights of medical practitioners in relation to the rights of states and of women. This is a curious result since the Court dismissed Hallford, a physician, who had performed illegal abortions. This focus on physicians elevated the importance of medicine and health care in the decision and relegated the rights of women to a secondary place. Blackmun emphasized the rights of medical providers when he cited evidence about the history of medicine in relation to abortion, the Hippocratic oath, the notion of medical privacy, and the rights of medical providers. A relatively small portion of the decision addressed the rights of women to have abortions.

Blackmun's opinion provides legal guidelines to physicians about the time when abortions are legal and their responsibility to help women decide. This content suggests that physicians' rights and responsibilities exceed those of pregnant women. It is not surprising that Blackmun took this perspective because prior to his appointment to the Supreme Court he had been the legal counsel for Mayo Clinic in Minnesota, and prior to writing the decision, Blackmun spent the summer in Minnesota researching medical history and physicians' rights.

The key judge-constructed fiction was a trimester time frame that establishes the rights of medical practitioners to perform "legal" abortions during the last six months of a pregnancy. The opinion explains trimesters in this time sequence:

> (a) For the stage prior to approximately the end of the first trimester, the abortion decision and its effectuation must be left to the medical judgment of the pregnant woman's attending physician.

> (b) For the stage subsequent to approximately the end of the first trimester, the state, in promoting its interest in the health of the mother, may, if it chooses, regulate the abortion procedure in ways that are reasonably related to maternal health.

> (c) For the stage subsequent to viability the state, in promoting its interest in the potentiality of human life, may, if it chooses, regulate, and even proscribe, abortion except where it is necessary, in the appropriate medical judgment, for the preservation of the life and health of the mother. (*Roe v. Wade*, 1973, p. 886)

Through this content, Blackmun showed concern for legitimizing the opinion with the medical professionals, the judiciary, and the American public.

The opinion, however, did little to address the conflicting feelings of the public. The decision assumed that this fictional and diverse audience would rally around the decision because it provided a compromise that made abortions available for women in the first three months of pregnancy with the consent of physicians and at the discretion both of medical practitioners and the states during the remaining trimesters.

In ways typical of most other opinions, Blackmun never acknowledged his own standpoint, stated the extent to which his experience affected the standpoint, or acknowledged his judicial philosophy. The Constitution gives Supreme Court judges the power to create and assert their authority, seek the compliance of fictional audiences to their dictates, and conceal their own assumptions and biases. Subsequent analysis shows that Blackmun used several different kinds of fictions associated with legal conventions, causal inferences, and analogical reasoning.

Legal Conventions

Legal conventions helped Blackmun complete his written argument. He recognized that the appeal came from a test case and a class action suit contrived by the petitioners. The Court granted legal standing to Jane Roe (McCorvey) even though she had given birth and put her child up for adoption months before the lawsuit reached the Court. The Court dismissed the Does and Hallford. Blackmun reified the facts from the affidavit of the Texas court in the following excerpt:

> Jane Roe . . . instituted this federal action in March of 1970. . . . Roe alleged that she was unmarried and pregnant; that she wished to terminate her pregnancy by an abortion "performed by a competent, licensed physician, under safe, clinical conditions"; that she was unable to get a "legal" abortion in Texas because her life did not appear to be threatened by the continuation of her pregnancy; and that she could not afford to travel to another jurisdiction in order to secure a legal abortion under safe conditions. She claimed that Texas statutes were unconstitutionally vague and that they abridged her right of personal privacy, . . . She purported to sue "on behalf of herself and all other women" similarly situated. (*Roe v. Wade*, 1973, p. 842)

The justices of the Court treat lower court fictions as facts even though they know full well that the fictions are created by the attorneys as much as by the clients they represent.

Causal Inferences

A second kind of fiction surfaced in Blackmun's inferences from eight different sources of evidence: (1) negative attitudes of ancient philosophers toward abortion, (2) prohibitions of abortion as stated in the Hippocratic oath, (3) English common law definitions of the "quickening of the fetus" as the standard for restricting abortions, (4) English statutory laws limiting abortion to protect the life of the mother, (5) nineteenth-century American law prohibiting abortions, (6) the American Medical Association's position that abortion is a medical procedure that should be left to medical discretion, (7) the American Public Health Association's stand that abortions should be performed by licensed physicians, and (8) the American Bar Association's draft of the Uniform Abortion Act requiring licensed physicians to perform abortions within 20 weeks of conception. When presenting this evidence, Blackmun privileged the rights of heath care providers by choosing medical facts, excluding nonmedical facts, valorizing the ethics of medical practitioners, and paying little attention to the circumstances of pregnant women. The inferences that Justice Blackmun drew about medical evidence also permitted him to establish his credibility as a student of the history of abortion and as a judge with specialized medical knowledge. This approach legitimized his opinion with audiences in medical professions and with some members of the public because he could defend the opinion on medical grounds if it were criticized on moral or religious grounds.

Analogical Reasoning

Blackmun promoted a common legal fiction based on analogical reasoning; that is, a precedent from a previous time is sufficiently similar to a new case that the ruling from the old precedent should decide the exigency in a new case. Richard Posner (1990) explains that analogical reasoning from precedents can produce fictions that disguise the differences in situations, suggest conclusions not in dispute, and insert language that is irrelevant to a dispute. Some of Blackmun's arguments relied on analogies to create legal fictions that would help him to decide the dispute about whether or not a woman's decision to have an abortion was protected by a right of privacy (*Roe v. Wade*, 1973):

> The Constitution does not explicitly mention a right to privacy. (p. 873)

> Court precedents do recognize a right of personal privacy in the Fourteenth Amendment's concept of personal liberty . . . in the Ninth Amendment's reservation of rights to the people. (pp. 874–875)

> [These rights are] broad enough to encompass a woman's decision whether or not to terminate her pregnancy. (p. 875)

Blackmun admitted that the existence of a right to privacy depended on precedents that acknowledge a right to personal liberty. This analogy created a fictional claim because it disguised the ways in which the precedents differed from the issues of this abortion dispute. Many precedents used by Blackmun dealt with freedom of expression, racial discrimination, and rights to education. The precedents did not address women's rights as directly as they did physicians' rights and rights of minorities. These analogies distorted the facts of the cases and confused the right of privacy with the right of people to political liberty. My point is not that analogies produce nontruths. Instead these analogies make imaginative leaps using fictional constructions that permitted Blackmun to construct a right of privacy even though this right was never addressed directly in the Constitution.

Justice Blackmun justified the conclusions of his opinion by the balancing of rights. He claimed that competing rights were the crux of the decision—a right of the state to protect the potential personhood of the fetus after the first three months of pregnancy, the women's right to some privacy during the first three months, and the physicians' right to use medical knowledge to assist or make the decision during all stages of pregnancy. The metaphor of weighing rights has evolved into a legal principle that supplied a useful fiction for Blackmun's argument. The result of his assigning weight to the rights of these three groups seemed more arbitrary than objective. He concluded (*Roe v. Wade*, 1973):

> Appellants . . . argue that the woman's right is absolute and that she is entitled to terminate her pregnancy at whatever time, in whatever way, and for whatever reason. With this we do not agree. (p. 875)

> The right of privacy however based, is broad enough to cover the abortion decision; that the right, nonetheless, is not absolute and is subject to limitations. (p. 877)

> The State does have an important and legitimate interest in preserving the health of the pregnant woman. (p. 884)

> From and after this point [the end of the first trimester] the State may regulate the abortion procedure to the extent that regulation reasonably relates to the preservation and protection of maternal health. (pp. 884–885)

By using the metaphor of weighing, Blackmun established legal grounds for allocating the biggest portion of rights to the physicians, some rights to states, and some limited rights to pregnant women. The words did not expand women's rights very far: with the consent of a physician, a woman could obtain a legal abortion in the first three months of her pregnancy, but the physicians had no obligation to perform abortions if women requested them, and the states had no incentives to make abortions available.

LESSONS

Justice Blackmun wrote his opinion for legal, medical, and public audiences in the same way as other justices often do. He followed the legal mandates for writing an opinion. In following the procedures and protocols, he also made use of fictions that relied on legal conventions, imaginative inferences from evidence that supported his standpoint, and analogical reasoning that made his argument seem reasonable. The decision also offers some clues about why the opinion became so controversial.

If *Roe* "constitutionalized the rights of women and rights of privacy" as Hull and Hoffer claim (2001, p. 6), why are these rights so offensive to some people? One of the reasons may be that the public believed the Court went too far when they signaled that they can make new laws regarding a variety of issues (Colker, 1992). Others may be disgruntled that the Court did not make the decision in line with their own religious views. A religious viewpoint was the basis for Horan and Balch's (1988) hyperbole that the opinion is "so faulty" and has so many "damaging consequences" that it stands as a "watershed of ignomity" (p. 73). The angry response of some members of the public was driven more by the rhetoric of critics than by words or phrases in the decision that permitted abortion under specific circumstances with the consent of a physician. The reasoning of the decision itself granted more rights to medical professionals and the states than to pregnant women. The appellate attorneys and Blackmun's majority opinion followed many normative practices of appellate reasoning that permit them to use fictions to complete their arguments.

The fictions created in- and outside of the decision fueled the controversy about the decision. This was a test case and a class action lawsuit created by attorneys who opposed abortion restrictions. After the decision, groups supporting women's rights and abortion rights overstated the effects of *Roe* by claiming it was a major victory, when in fact it was a modest step toward those rights. Conservative religious and political groups blamed the judicial activism of Court justices for the opinion when in fact the Court had been activist and developed law since Warren had become the Chief Justice in 1954 when they decided the cases filed in *Brown v. Board of Education*. Legal scholars exaggerated the assertion that the right to privacy guarantees a woman's right to an abortion. The rhetoric about the decision has had a great influence on the minds of the social movement activists, legislators, and the judiciary—more than the actual arguments in the decision have. This public rhetoric in the past 20 years has encouraged state legislators to limit the provisions of *Roe*. The foes of abortion have succeeded in getting legislators to restrict the circumstances and situations in which women can seek an abortion during the first trimester of their pregnancies and when their life is threatened.

Bibliography

Abraham, H. J. (1980). *The judicial process: An introductory analysis of the courts of the United States, England, France.* Oxford: Oxford University Press. (Originally published 1962)

Abramson, J. (1996). *Postmortem: The O. J. Simpson case. Justice confronts race, domestic violence, lawyers, money, and the media.* New York: Basic Books.

A call to repentance. (2002, July 1). *National Review, 54,* 15–17.

Alexander, S. L. (1996, January/February). The impact of *California v. Simpson* on cameras in the courtroom. *Judicature, 79,* 169–172.

Alexy, R. (1989). *A theory of legal argumentation: The theory of rational discourse as theory of legal justification.* (R. Adler & N. MacCormick, Trans.). Oxford: Clarendon Press.

Alix, E. K. (1978). *Ransom kidnapping in America: 1877–1974.* Carbondale: Southern Illinois University Press.

Alter, J. (1997, February 17). The O. J. legacy. *Newsweek, 129,* 126–129.

Altman, A. (2001). *Arguing about law* (2nd ed.). Belmont, CA: Wadsworth/Thompson.

Altschuler, B. E., & Sgroi, C. A. (1992). *Understanding law in a changing society.* Englewood Cliffs, NJ: Prentice-Hall.

American criminal justice process: Selected rules, statutes and guidelines. (1989). St. Paul, MN: West Publishing.

Apodaca v. Oregon, 32 L.Ed. 184 (1972).

Arbetman, L., & Roe, R. L. (1985). Chicago Eight. In L. Arbetman & R. L. Roe (Eds.), *Great trials in American history* (pp. 145–161). St. Paul, MN: West Publishing Co.

Aristotle (1954). *The Rhetoric.* (Rhys. Roberts, Trans.). New York: Modern Library.

Auerbach, P. G. (1990). The effective opening statement. *Trial Diplomacy Journal, 13,* 27–39.

Bailey, F. L., & Rothblatt, H. B. (1971). *Successful techniques for criminal lawyers.* Rochester, NY: Lawyers Cooperative.

Balkin, J. M. (2002). *What* Brown v. Board of Education *should have said.* New York: New York University Press.

Ball, M. S. (1993). *The word and the law.* Chicago: University of Chicago Press.

Ball, D. (1997). *Theater tips and strategies for jury trials.* South Bend, IN: National Institute for Trial Advocacy. (Originally published 1994)

Balthrop, B. (1980). Argument as linguistic opportunity: A search for form and function. In J. Rhodes & S. Newell (Eds.), *Proceedings of the summer conference on argumentation* (pp. 184–213). Annandale, VA: Speech Communication Association.

Barber, S. (1987). *News cameras in the courtroom.* Norwood, NJ: Ablex

Barkan, S. E. (1985). *Protesters on trial.* New Brunswick, NJ: Rutgers University Press.

Barry, E. (2002, April 3). Priest treatment unfolds in costly, secretive world. *Boston Globe*, p. A1.

Baumann, P. (2002, September 13). Reforming the church. *Commonweal, 129*, 8–10.

Belton v. Gebhart & Bulah v. Gebhart, 91 A. 2d 864 (1952).

Behn, N. (1994). *Lindbergh the crime.* New York: Atlantic Monthly Press.

Bennett, W. L. (1978). Storytelling in criminal trials: A model of social judgment. *Quarterly Journal of Speech, 64*, 1–22.

———. (1979). Rhetorical transformations of evidence in criminal trials: Creating grounds for legal judgment. *Quarterly Journal of Speech, 65*, 311–324.

Bennett, W. L., & Feldman, M. S. (1981). *Reconstructing reality in the courtroom.* New Brunswick, NJ: Rutgers University Press.

Berger, A. A. (1997). *Narratives in popular culture, media, and everyday life.* Thousand Oaks, CA: Sage.

Bergman, L., & Docherty, N. (Writers), Docherty, N. (Producer). (1998). *FRONTLINE:* Inside the tobacco deal. PBS. Retrieved October 20, 2005, from http://www.pbs.org/wgbh/pages/frontline/shows/settlement/etc/script.html

Berry, J. (1994). *Lead us not into temptation.* New York: Image.

Birdsell, D. S. (1993). Kenneth Burke at the nexus of argument and trope. *Argumentation and Advocacy, 29*, 178–185.

Blaustein, A. P., & Ferguson, C. A. (1957). *Desegregation and the law: The meaning and effect of the school desegregation cases.* New Brunswick, NJ: Rutgers University Press.

Bobbitt, P. (1981). *Constitutional fate.* New York: Oxford University Press.

Bolling v. Sharpe, 347 U.S. 497 (1964).

Bosmajian, H. (1992). *Metaphor and reason in judicial opinions.* Carbondale: Southern Illinois University Press.

Bowers, J. W., Ochs, D. J., & Jensen, R. J. (1993). *The rhetoric of agitation and control* (2nd ed.). Long Grove, IL: Waveland Press.

Briggs et al. v. Elliott et al., 98 F. Supp. 529 (1951).

Brockriede, W. (1977). Characteristics of arguments and arguing. *Journal of the American Forensic Association, 13*, 129–132.

———. (1985). Constructs, experience, and argument. *Quarterly Journal of Speech, 71*, 151–163.

Brooks, P. (1996). The law as narrative and rhetoric. In P. Brooks & P. Gewirtz (Eds.), *Law's stories: Narrative and rhetoric in the law* (pp. 14–23). New Haven: Yale University Press.

Brooks, P., & Gewirtz, P. (Eds.). (1996). *Law's stories: Narrative and rhetoric in law.* New Haven: Yale University Press.

Brown, W. J., Duane, J. J., & Fraser, B. P. (1997). Media coverage and public opinion of the O. J. Simpson trial: Implications for the criminal justice system. *Communication Law and Policy, 2*, 261–287.

Brown v. Board of Education of Topeka, 98 F. Supp. 797 (1951).

Brown v. Board of Education of Topeka, 347 U.S. 483 (1954).

Brown v. Board of Education of Topeka, 349 U.S. 294(1955).

Bruschke, J. (1995). Deconstructive argument in the legal sphere: An analysis of the Fischl/Massey debate about critical legal studies. *Argumentation and Advocacy, 32*, 16–29.

Burge, K. (2002, January 17). Man testifies Geoghan fondled him. *Boston Globe*, p. B3.

———. (2002, January 19). Geoghan found guilty of sex abuse. *Boston Globe*, p. A1.

———. (2002, July 10). Geoghan judge's press ruling upheld. *Boston Globe*, p. B2.

———. (2002, July 13). Power of archdiocese with Law, judge says. *Boston Globe*, p. A1.

———. (2002, July 17). Archdiocese not party to deal, lawyers say. *Boston Globe*, p. B5.

———. (2002, July 27). Settlement arguments offered. *Boston Globe*, p. B6.

———. (2002, August 3). Law notes regret on wording. *Boston Globe*, p. A1.

———. (2002, August 6). Chancellor details money crunch. *Boston Globe*, p. B2.

———. (2002, August 7). Testimony turns to public statements. *Boston Globe*, p. A4.

———. (2002, August 17). Archdiocese not party to deal, lawyers say. *Boston Globe*, p. B5.

———. (2002, November 30). Judge's ruling frees documents in Geoghan case. *Boston Globe*, p. A1.

Burge, K., & Kurkjian S. (2002, August 1). Hearing weighs church-victim pact. *Boston Globe*, p. B2.

Burke, K. (1964). From poetic categories. In S. E. Hyman (Ed.), *Terms for order* (pp. 92–94). Bloomington: Indiana University Press.

———. (1966). *Language as symbolic action.* Berkeley: University of California Press.

———. (1968). Dramatism. In D. Sills (Ed.), *International encyclopedia of social sciences* (pp. 445–450). New York: Macmillan.

———. (1969a). *A grammar of motives.* Berkeley: University of California Press. (Originally published 1945)

———. (1969b). *A rhetoric of motives.* Berkeley: University of California Press. (Originally published 1950)

———. (1970). *A rhetoric of religion.* Berkeley: University of California Press. (Originally published 1961)

———. (1973). *Philosophy of literary form.* Berkeley: University of California Press. (Originally published 1941)

Burke, W. L., Poulson, R., & Brondino, M. J. (1992). Fact and fiction: The effect of opening statement. *Journal of Contemporary Law, 18,* 195–210.

Burkett, E., & Bruni, F. (1993). *A gospel of shame.* New York: Viking.

Burnett, A. (1999). Jury decision-making processes in the O. J. Simpson criminal and civil trials. In J. Schuetz & L. S. Lilley (Eds.), *The O. J. Simpson trials, Media, rhetoric, and the law* (pp. 122–138). Carbondale: Southern Illinois University.

Butler, P. (1996). Black jurors right to acquit. In J. Abramson (Ed.), *Postmortem: The O. J. Simpson case* (pp. 38–45). New York: HarperCollins.

California Penal Code, Cal. Code R. Of Cr. 98B (1994).

Cannon, C. M. (2002, May). The priest scandal. *American Journalism Review, 24,* 18–26.

Caplan, L. (1996). The failure and promise of legal journalism. In J. Abramson (Ed.), *Postmortem: The O. J. Simpson case* (pp. 188–210). New York: HarperCollins.

Calamandrei, P. (1956). *Procedure and democracy.* (J. C. Adams & H. Adams, Trans.). New York: New York University Press.

Cardozo, B. (1921). *The nature of the judicial process.* New Haven: Yale University Press.

Carrington, P., Meador, D., & Rosenberg, M. (1976). *Justice on appeal.* St. Paul, MN: West Publishing.

Carroll, M. (2002, January 6). A revered guest; a family in shreds. *Boston Globe*, p. A1.

———. (2002, January 8). Priests' victims victimized twice. *Boston Globe*, p. A1.

———. (2002, January 25). In letters, Geoghan showed self in denial. *Boston Globe*, p. A1.

Carroll, M., & Rosenwald, M. S. (2002, December 14). Priests see sadness, hope in Law's fall. *Boston Globe*, p. A16.

Carter, L. (1984). *Reason in law.* Boston: Little, Brown.

Carter v. Brown & Williamson Tobacco Corp., 723 So 2d 833 (1996).

———, 150 L Ed. 2d 751 (2001).

Cashin, S. (2004). *The failures of integration: How race and class are undermining the American dream.* New York: Public Affairs.

Castano v. American Tobacco Co., 84 F.3d 734 (1996).

Chafee, Z. (1941). The disorderly conduct of words. *Columbia Law Review, 41*, 381–389.

———. (1969). *Free speech in the United States.* New York: Antheneum.

Chicago trial: A loss for all. (1970, February 23). *Time, 127*, 38–39.

Cicero (1949). *De Inventione.* (H. M. Hubbell, Trans.). Cambridge, MA: Harvard University Press.

Cipollone v. Liggett Group Inc., 649 F. Supp. 664 (1986).

———, 505 U.S. 504 (1992).

Ciresi, M. V. (1999). An account of the legal strategies that ended an era of tobacco industry immunity. *William Mitchell Law Review, 25*, 439–446.

Ciresi, M. V., Walburn, R. B., & Sutton, T. D. (1999). Decades of deceit: Document discovery in the Minnesota tobacco litigation. *William Mitchell Law Review, 25*, 480–488.

Clark, M. (with T. Carpenter). (1997). *Without a doubt.* New York: Viking Penguin.

Clark, R. (Ed.). (1970). *Contempt: Transcripts of contempt citations, sentences, and responses* (pp. v–viii). Chicago: Swallow Press.

Clary, B. G., Paulson, S. R., & Vanselow, M. J. (2004). *Advocacy on appeal.* St. Paul, MN: West Publishing.

Clavir, J., & Spitzer, J. (Eds.). (1970). *The conspiracy trial*. New York: Bobbs-Merrill.

CNS Staff. (2002, December 16). Trust in priests and clergy falls 26 points in 12 months. *America, 187*, 5.

Cochran, J. (with J. Rutten). (1996). *Journey to justice.* New York: Ballantine Books.

Code of Canon Law and Commentary. (1990). Washington: Catholic University Press.

Code of Judicial Conduct. (1972). In *Selected statutes, rules and standards on the legal profession.* St. Paul, MN: West Publishing.

Coffin, F. (1980). *The ways of the judge.* Boston: Little, Brown.

Colker, R. (1992). *Abortion & dialogue: Pro-choice, pro-life, and American law.* Bloomington: Indiana University Press.

Colley, M. F. (1981). Friendly persuasion, comprehension, and acceptance in court. *Trial, 17*, 43.

Combs, J. E., & Mansfield, M. W. (Eds.). (1968). *Drama in life: The use of communication in society.* London: Oxford University Press.

Condon, J. F. (1936). *Jafsie tells all.* New York: Jonathan Lee.

Conley, J. M., & O'Barr, W. M. (1990). *Rules versus relationships: The ethnography of legal discourse.* Chicago: University of Chicago Press.

———. (1998). *Just words: Law, language, and power.* Chicago: University of Chicago Press.

Cooley, A., Bess, C., & Rubin-Jackson, M. (1995). *Madame foreman: A rush to judgment.* Beverly Hills, CA: Dove Books.

Cooley, J. W. (1989). *Appellate advocacy manual.* Deerfield, IL: Callaghan.

Cornelius, A. (1929). *The cross-examination of witnesses: Rules, principles, and illustrations.* Indianapolis: Bobbs-Merrill.

Court TV Web site (2006). Courttv.com.

Cozzens, D. (2002a, September 13). After the sex abuse scandal. *Commonweal, 129,* 17–19.

———. (2002b). *Sacred silence: Denial and the crisis in the church.* Collegeville, MN: Liturgical Press.

Craig v. Harney, 331 U.S. 368 (1974).

Crawford, R. J. (1990). Expanding the boundaries of the opening statement. *Trial Diplomacy Journal, 13,* 227–232.

Cullen, K. (2002, December 15). Seven people who made a difference. *Boston Globe,* p. A51.

Dann, B. M. (1993). "Learning lessons" and "speaking rights": Creating educated and democratic juries. *Indiana Law Journal, 68,* 1229–1268.

Darden, C. (with Walter, J.) (1996). *In contempt.* New York: Regan Books.

Davis, K. S. (1959). *The hero: Charles A. Lindbergh and the American dream.* Garden City, NY: Doubleday.

Davis, M. B. (1983). *Game theory: A nontechnical introduction.* Mineola, NY: Dover.

Davis v. County School Board of Prince Edward County, 103 F. Supp. 337 (1952).

de Certeau, M. (1988). *The practice of everyday life.* (S. Rendall, Trans.). Berkeley: University of California Press.

Dee, J. (1985, November). Selective perception in a non-vacuum: Thoughts on the Chicago Seven trial. Symposium on popularized trials, presented at the Speech Communication Association. Denver, CO.

Delaney, D. (1998). *Race, place, & the law 1836–1948.* Austin: University of Texas Press

Della Rocca, F., & Fitzgerald, J. D. (1980). *Canonical procedure.* Milwaukee: Bruce Publishing.

Denniston, L. W. (1980). *The reporter and the law: Techniques of covering the courts.* New York: Hastings House.

Dershowitz, A. M. (1996). *Reasonable doubts: The O. J. Simpson case and the criminal justice system.* New York: Simon & Schuster.

Derthick, M. A. (2002). *Up in smoke.* Washington, DC: Congressional Quarterly Press.

Dessem, R. L. (1998). *Pretrial litigation.* St. Paul, MN: West Publishing.

Devins, N. (1996). *Shaping Constitutional values: Elected government, the Supreme Court, and the abortion debate.* Baltimore: Johns Hopkins University Press.

Dicks, V. (1981). Courtroom rhetorical strategies: Forensic and deliberative perspectives. *Quarterly Journal of Speech, 67,* 178–188.

Dickson, D. (2001). *The Supreme Court in conference (1940–1985): The private discussion behind nearly 300 Supreme Court decisions.* Oxford: Oxford University Press.

Doe v. Bolton, 410 U.S. 179 (1973).

Dokecki, P. R. (2004). *The clergy sexual abuse crisis.* Washington, DC: Georgetown University Press.

Dred Scott v. Sandford, 60 U.S. 393 (1887).

Dreschel, R. E. (1983). *Newsmaking in the trial courts.* New York: Longmans.

Duncan, H. D. (1968). *Communication and social order.* London: Oxford University Press. (Originally published in 1962)

Dunne, D. (1995, February). L.A. in the age of O. J. *Vanity Fair, 58,* 46–56.

Dunston, R. (1980). Context for coercion: Analyzing properties of courtroom questions. *British Journal of Law and Social Psychology, 7,* 61–77.

Dworkin, R. (1990). The great abortion case. In R. M. Mersky & G. R. Hartman (Eds.), *Documentary history of abortion in the United States:* Webster v. Reproductive Health Services. Vol. 1. (pp. 54–61). Littleton, CO: Baseline.

Dyson, E. M. (1996). Obsessed with O. J. In J. Abramson (Ed.), *Postmortem: The O. J. Simpson case: Justice confronts race, domestic violence, lawyers, money, and the media* (pp. 46–56). New York: Basic Books.

Ehrlich, J. W. (1970). *The lost art of cross examination*. New York: G. P. Putnam's Sons.

Ehrmann, H. B. (1969). *The case that will not die:* The Commonwealth v. Sacco and Vanzetti. Boston: Little, Brown.

Ettema, J. S., & Glasser, T. L. (1998). *Custodians of conscience.* New York: Columbia University Press.

Farragher, T. (2002, June 14). U.S. leaders expect Vatican approval. *Boston Globe*, p. A41.

———. (2002, June 14). *Globe* denied access as punishment for story. *Boston Globe*, p. A40.

———. (2002, September 20). Settlement doesn't heal victims' hearts. *Boston Globe*, p. A1.

———. (2002, December 12). Lay group votes to seek cardinal's ouster. *Boston Globe*, p. A1.

Faux, M. (1988). Roe v. Wade: *The untold story of the landmark Supreme Court decision that made abortion legal*. New York: Penguin.

Federal Rules of Evidence. (1991). St. Paul, MN: West Publishing.

———. (1995). St. Paul, MN: West Publishing

Felsher, H., & Rosen, M. (1966). *The press and the jury box.* New York: Macmillan.

Feteris, E. T. (1990). Condition and rules for rational discussion in a legal process: A pragma-dialectical perspective. *Argumentation and Advocacy, 26*, 108–117.

———. (1999). *Fundamentals of legal argumentation.* Norwell, MA: Kluwer.

———. (2002). Pragmatic argumentation in a legal context. In. F. H. van Eemeren (Ed.), *Advances in pragma-dialectics* (pp. 302–309). Amsterdam: Sic Sat.

———. (2003). The rational reconstruction of pragmatic argumentation in a legal context: The analysis and evaluation of teleological argumentation. In T. Goodnight (Ed.), *Proceedings of the Fifth Conference of the International Society for the Study of Argumentation* (pp. 309–314). Amsterdam: Sic/Sat Publications.

Feuerlicht, R. S. (1977). *Justice crucified*. New York: McGraw-Hill.

Finkel, N. J. (1995). *Commonsense justice: Jurors' notions of the law.* Cambridge: Harvard University Press.

Fisher, W. R. (1984). Narrative as human communication paradigm: The case of public moral argumentation. *Communication Monographs, 51*, 1–22.

———. (1987). Technical logic, rhetoric logic, and narrative rationality. *Argumentation, 1*, 3–21.

———. (1989). *Human communication as Narration: Toward a philosophy of reason, value, and action.* Columbia: University of South Carolina Press.

Fontes, N. E., & Bunden, R. W. (1980). Persuasion during the trial process. In M. D. Roloff & G. R. Miller (Eds.), *Persuasion: New directions in research* (pp. 149–166). Beverly Hills, CA: Sage Publications.

Fontham, M. R. (1995). *Trial techniques and evidence.* Charlottesville, VA: Michie Butterworth.

Ford, A. (1995, October 9). The Simpson legacy. *Los Angeles Times,* p. S3.

Fortune, W. H., Underwood, R. H., & Imwinkelried, E. J. (1996). *Modern litigation and professional responsibility handbook.* Boston: Little, Brown.

Foss, S. K., Foss, K. A., & Trapp, R. (2002). *Contemporary perspectives on rhetoric* (3rd ed.). Long Grove, IL: Waveland Press.

Fraenkel, O. K. (1931). *The Sacco-Vanzetti case*. New York: Alfred A. Knopf.

Frankfurter, F. (1954). *The case of Sacco and Vanzetti.* Boston: Atlantic Monthly Press. (Originally published 1927)

Frankfurter, M. D., & Jackson, G. (1960). *The letters of Sacco and Vanzetti.* New York: Vanguard Press.

Franklin, M. A. (1968). *The dynamics of American law: Courts, the legal process, and freedom of expression.* Mineola, NY: Foundation Press.

Friedman, L. (Ed.). (1969). *Argument: The oral argument before the Supreme Court in Brown v. Board of Education of Topeka, 1952–1955.* New York: Chelsea House Publishers.

Friendly, A., & Goldfarb, R. L. (1967). *Crime and publicity.* New York: Twentieth Century Fund.

Fritch, J. E., & Leeper, K. K. (1993). Poetic logic: The metaphoric form as a foundation for a theory of tropological argument. *Argumentation and Advocacy, 29,* 186–194.

Furno-Lamude, D. (1999). The media spectacle and the O. J. Simpson trial. In J. Schuetz & L. Lilley (Eds.), *The O. J. Simpson trials: Rhetoric, media and the law* (pp. 19–35). Carbondale: Southern Illinois University Press.

Geller, L. H., & Hemenway, P. (1997). *Last chance for justice: The juror's lonely quest.* Dallas: NCDC Press.

Gewirtz, P. (1996). Narrative and rhetoric in law. In P. Brooks & P. Gewirtz (Eds.), *Law's stories* (pp. 2–13). New Haven: Yale University Press.

Ginsberg, F. (1998). Rescuing the nation: Operation Rescue and the rise of anti-abortion militance. In R. Solinger (Ed.), *Abortion wars: A half century of struggle, 1950–2000* (pp. 208–226). Berkeley: University of California Press.

Givens, R. A. (1980). *The art of pleading a case.* New York: McGraw-Hill.

Glantz, S. A. (1996). *The cigarette papers.* Berkeley: University of California Press.

Glantz, S. A., Barnes, D. E., Bero, L., Hanauer, P., & Slade, J. (1995). Looking through a keyhole at the tobacco industry: The Brown and Williamson documents. *Journal of the American Medical Association, 274,* 219–224.

Goffman, E. J. (1959). *The presentation of self in everyday life.* New York: Doubleday.

Goldberg, H. M. (1996). *The prosecution responds: An O. J. Simpson trial prosecutor reveals what really happened.* Secaucus, NJ: Birch Lane Press.

Goldfarb, R. L. (1998). *TV or not TV: Television justice, and the courts.* New York: New York University Press.

Goodman, E. (2002, February 5). Scandal in Boston archdiocese. Retrieved December 30, 2002, from www.Geocities.com/pheunghclick/Goodman.html.

Gong Lum v. Rice, 275 U.S. 78 (1927).

Graber, D. A. (1980). Evaluating crime-fighting policies. In R. Baker & F. Meyer (Eds.), *Evaluating alternative law enforcement policies* (pp. 179–200). Lexington, MA: Lexington Books.

Graham, F. (1995, October 9). The Simpson legacy. *Los Angeles Times,* p. S3.

———. (1998). Doing justice with cameras in the courts. *Media Studies Journal, 12,* 32–37.

Green, L. (1955–56). Jury trials and Mr. Justice Black. *Yale Law Journal, 65,* 482–499.

Greenberg, J. (1994). *Crusaders in the courts.* New York: Basic Books.

Grisham, J. (1996). *The runaway jury.* New York: Dell.

Griswold v. Connecticut, 381 U.S. 479 (1965).

Hanauer, P., Slade, J., Barnes, D. E., Bero, L., & Glantz, S. A. (1995). Lawyer control of internal scientific research to avoid products liability lawsuits: The Brown and Williamson documents. *Journal of the American Medical Association, 274,* 234–240.

Hannaford, P., Dann, L. M., & Munsterman, G. T. (1998). How judges view civil juries. *DePaul Law Review, 48*, 249–269.

Hans, V. P. (2000). *Business on trial: The civil jury and corporate responsibility.* New Haven: Yale University Press.

Harbinger, R. (1971). Trial by drama. *Judicature, 5*, 122–128.

Haring, J. V. (1937). *The hand of Hauptmann.* Plainfield, NJ: Hamer.

Hasain, M., Jr. (1994). Myth and ideology in legal discourse: Moving from critical legal studies toward rhetorical consciousness. *Legal Studies Forum, 4*, 347–365.

———.(1995). Remembering and forgetting: A postmodern interpretation of the origins of the "right of privacy." *Journal of Communication Inquiry, 19*, 33–49.

———. (1997). Freedom of expression, population "checks" and obscenity in nineteenth century England: A case analysis of the Besant-Bradlaugh trial. *The Communication Review, 2*, 349–380.

Hasain, M., Jr., Condit, C. M., & Lucaites, J. L. (1996). The rhetorical boundaries of "the law": A consideration of the rhetorical culture of legal practice and the case of the "separate but equal" doctrine. *Quarterly Journal of Speech, 82*, 323–342.

Hastie, R., Penrod, S. D., & Pennington, N. (1983). *Inside the jury.* Cambridge: Harvard University Press.

Hatfield, C. (1996). The privilege doctrines—Are they just another discovery tool utilized by the tobacco industry to conceal damaging information? *Pace Law Review, 16*, 525–558.

Haydock, R., & Sonsteng, J. (1991). *Trial theories, tactics, techniques.* St. Paul, MN: West Publishing.

———. (1994a). *Examining witnesses: Direct, cross, and expert examination.* St. Paul, MN: West Publishing.

———. (1994b). *Advocacy.* St. Paul, MN: West Publishing.

Hays, A. G. (1933). *Trial by prejudice*. New York: Covice-Friede.

Hazard, G. C., & Hodes, W. (1990). *The law of lawyering: A handbook of model rules of professional conduct.* Englewood Cliffs, NJ: Prentice-Hall.

Hazard, G. C., & Taruffo, M. (1993). *American civil procedure: An introduction.* New Haven: Yale University Press.

Heglund, K. F. (1978). *Trial and practice skills.* St. Paul, MN: West Publishing.

Herbeck, D. (1995). Critical legal studies and argumentation theory. *Argumentation, 5*, 719–729.

Heurer, L., & Penrod, S. D. (1989). Increasing jurors' participation in trials: A field experiment with jury notetaking and question asking. *Law and Human Behavior, 12*, 232–262.

———. (1990). Some suggestions for critical appraisal of a more active jury. *Northwestern University Law Review, 85*, 226–339.

Higgins, R. (2002, June 19). Catholics find voice. *Christian Century, 119*, 6–8.

Hoffman, D. (1998). *The Oklahoma City bombing and the politics of terror.* Venice, CA: Feral House.

Holman, C. (1972). *A handbook of literature* (3rd ed.). New York: Odyssey Press.

Horan, D. J., & Balch, T. J. (1998). *Roe v. Wade:* No basis in logic or history. In L. P. Pojman & F. J. Beckwith (Eds.), *The abortion controversy: 25 years after* Roe v. Wade (pp. 73–94). Belmont, CA: Wadsworth.

Houts, M., & Rogosheske, W. (1986). *The art of advocacy: Appeals.* New York: Matthew Bender.

Hovland, C. I., Janis, I. L., & Kelley, H. H. (1953). *Communication and persuasion.* New Haven: Yale University Press.

Hull, N. E. H., & Hoffer, P. C. (2001). Roe v. Wade: *The abortion rights controversy in American history*. Lawrence: University Press of Kansas.

Hunt, L. (May, 2003). Gaging legal literacy. Unpublished manuscript. Albuquerque: University of New Mexico.

Hutchens, R. M. (1927). Cross examination to impeach. *Yale Law Review, 36*, 384–390.

Hutcheon, L. (2000). *The politics of postmodernism*. London: Routledge.

Hutcheson, J. (1929). The judgment intuitive: The function of the "hunch" in judicial decision. *Cornell Law Quarterly, 14*, 274.

Iannuzzi, J. N. (1982). *Cross-examination: The mosaic art*. Englewood Cliffs, NJ: Prentice-Hall.

———. (1998). *Handbook of cross-examination: The mosaic art*. Paramus, NJ: Prentice-Hall.

Irons, P. (2004). *Jim Crow's children*. New York: Penguin.

Investigative Staff. (2002). *Betrayal: The crisis in the Catholic church*. Boston: Little, Brown.

Jeans, J. W. (1993). *Trial advocacy*. St. Paul, MN: West Publishing.

Jensen, J. V. (1981). *Argumentation: Reasoning in communication*. New York: D. Van Norstrand.

John Jay School of Criminal Justice, Sexual Abuse National Review Board. Retrieved June 4, 2005, from www.usccb.org.

Jonakait, R. N. (2003). *The American jury system*. New Haven: Yale University Press.

Jones, S., & Israel, P. (2001). *Others unknown*. New York: Public Affairs.

Joughin, G. L., & Morgan, E. M. (1948). *The legacy of Sacco and Vanzetti*. New York: Harcourt, Brace & Co.

Judges, D. P. (1993). *Hard choices, lost voices: How the abortion conflict has divided America, distorted Constitutional rights, and damaged the courts*. Chicago: Ivan R. Dee.

Judgment in Chicago. (1970, March 2). *Newsweek, 102*, 24–27.

Julien, A. S. (1980). *Opening statements*. Wilmette, IL: Gallighan.

Jurkowitz, M. (2002, July 28). When "two alien cultures" face off. *Boston Globe*, p. E1.

Kalven, H. (1970). Introduction: Confrontation and contempt. In *Contempt: Transcript of contempt citations, sentences, and responses* (pp. ix–xxiv). Chicago: Swallow Press.

Kalven, H., & Zeisel, H. (1971). *The American jury*. Chicago: The University of Chicago Press. (Originally published 1966)

Kane, M. K. (1996). *Civil procedure in a nutshell*. St. Paul, MN: West Publishing.

Karlen, D. (1971). Disorder in the courtroom. *Southern California University Law Review, 44*, 996–1035.

Kelner, J., & McGovern, F. E. (1981). *Successful litigation techniques*. New York: Mathew Bender.

Kennedy, G. A. (1994). *A new history of classical rhetoric*. Princeton, NJ: Princeton University Press.

Kennedy, L. (1985). *The airman and the carpenter*. New York: Viking Press.

Kirchheimer, O. (1961). *Political justice: The use of legal procedures for political ends*. Princeton, NJ: Princeton University Press.

Kluger, R. (1977). *Simple justice: The history of* Brown v. Board of Education. New York: Vintage Books.

———. (1996). *Ashes to ashes: America's hundred-year cigarette war, the public health, and the unabashed triumph of Philip Morris*. New York: Alfred A. Knopf.

Klumpp, J. F. (1993). A rapprochement between dramatism and argumentation. *Argumentation and Advocacy, 29*, 148–163.

Knapp, M. (1972). *Nonverbal communication in human interaction.* New York: Holt, Rinehart and Winston.

Kniskern, J. W. (1995). *Courting disaster: What runaway litigation is costing you and what can be done to stop the fallout.* Nashville: Broadman & Holman.

Kunstler, W. M. (1970). Introduction. In J. Clavir & J. Spitzer (Eds.), *The conspiracy trial* (pp. xiii–xvi). New York: Bobbs-Merrill.

———. (with Isenberg, S.). (1994). *My life as a radical lawyer.* New York: Birch Lane Press.

Kurkjian, S. (2002, February 24). Officials avoided confronting priest. *Boston Globe,* p. A23.

Kurkjian, S., & Burge, K. (2002, July 26). Lawyers, church say talks are at impasse. *Boston Globe,* p. A1.

Kurkjian, S., & Robinson, W. V. (2002, April 4). Law aides balking at Geoghan costs. *Boston Globe,* p. A1.

Kurland, P. B., & Casper, G. (Eds.). (1970). Brown v. Board of Education: *Landmark briefs and arguments of the Supreme Court of the United States (1954–55).* Arlington, VA: University Publications of America.

———. (1990). Roe v. Wade: *Landmark briefs and arguments of the Supreme Court of the United States (1973–1974).* Frederick, MD: University Publications of America.

Kuvin, H. A. (1965). *Trial handbook.* Englewood Cliffs, NJ: Prentice-Hall.

LaRue, L. H. (1995). *Constitutional law as fiction.* University Park: Pennsylvania State University Press.

Lavoie, D. (2002, January 18). Jury convicts defrocked priest. Retrieved December 28, 2002, from www.vachss.com/help_text/archive/geoghan.html.

Leflar, R. (1961). Some observations concerning judicial opinions. *Columbia Law Review, 84,* 810–813.

Levi, E. (1949). *An introduction to legal reasoning.* Chicago: University of Chicago Press.

Levin, J. (1992). *How judges reason.* New York: Peter Lang.

Levin, M. B. (1971). *Political hysteria in America.* New York: Basic Books.

Levine, M. L., McNamee, G. C., & Greenberg, D. (1970). *The tales of Hoffman.* New York: Bantam.

Lilley, L. (1999). Opening statements: Lasting impressions. In J. Schuetz & L. Lilley (Eds.), *The O. J. Simpson trials: Rhetoric, media, and the law* (pp. 36–57). Carbondale: Southern Illinois University Press.

Lindbergh, C. A. (1977). *Autobiography of values.* New York: Harcourt Brace Jovanovich.

Lofton, J. (1966). *Justice and the press.* Boston: Beacon Press.

Loftus, E. F. (1980). Language and memories in the judicial system. In R. W. Shy & A. Shunkal (Eds.), *Language use and the use of language* (pp. 257–268). Washington, DC: Georgetown University Press.

Loftus, E. F., & Ketchum, K. (1991). *Witness for the defense.* New York: St. Martin's Press.

Lotz, R. E. (1991). *Crime and the American press.* New York: Praeger.

Lubet, S. (1993). *Modern trial advocacy: Analysis and practice.* Chicago: National Institute for Trial Advocacy.

Luchins, A. S. (1957). Experimental attempts to minimize the impact of first impressions. In C. I. Hovland (Ed.), *The order of presentation in persuasion* (pp. 62–75). New Haven: Yale University Press.

Macdonald, D. (1970). Introduction. In M. L. Levine, G. C. McNamee, & D. Greenberg (Eds.), *The tales of Hoffman* (pp. xi–xxvi). New York: Bantam Books.

Madsen, A. J. (1993). The comic frame as a corrective to bureaucratization: A dramatistic perspective on argumentation. *Argumentation and Advocacy, 29*, 164–177.

Mann, M. (Producer). (1999). *The Insider* [Motion picture]. Burbank, CA: Touchstone Pictures.

Marable, M. (1986). *W. E. B. Dubois: Black radical democrat.* Boston: Twayne Publishers.

Marcus, P. (1982). The media in the courtroom: Attending, reporting, televising criminal cases. *Indiana Law Review, 57*, 235–287.

Martin, W. E., Jr. (1998). Brown v. Board of Education: *A brief history with documents.* Boston: Bedford/St. Martins.

Martineau, R. (1985). *Fundamentals of modern appellate advocacy.* Rochester, NY: Layers Co-Operative Publishing.

Matlon, R. (1988). *Communication and the legal process.* New York: Holt, Rinehart and Winston.

———. (1993). *Opening statements/closing arguments.* San Anselmo, CA: Stuart Allen Books.

Matsuda, M. (1989). Public responses to racist speech: Considering the victim's story, *Michigan Law Review, 87*, 2320–2381.

Mattingly, T. (2002, December 28). Catholic crises lead list of year's top 10 religious stories. *Albuquerque Tribune*, p. C5.

Mauet, T. A. (1992). *Fundamentals of trial techniques.* Boston: Little, Brown.

McCorvey, N. J. (with Meisler, A.). (1994). *I am Roe: My life,* Roe v. Wade. New York: HarperCollins.

McDonald's Settles Hot Coffee Law Suit. (1993, December 2). *Miami Herald,* p. C1.

McElhaney, J. W. (1979). Analogies in final argument. *Litigation, 6*, 37.

McGeary, J., & Winters, R. (2002). Can the church be saved? *Time, 159*, 28–38.

McGee, B. R. (1999). The argument from definition revisited: Race and definition in the progressive era. *Argumentation and Advocacy, 36*, 141–158.

McKerrow, R. (1989). Critical rhetoric: Theory and praxis. *Communication Monographs, 56*, 91–111.

———. (1991). Critical rhetoric in a postmodern world. *Quarterly Journal of Speech, 77*, 75–88.

McLaurin v. Oklahoma State Regents for Higher Education, 87 F. Supp. 528 (D.C.Okl.) (1950a).

McLaurin v. Oklahoma State Regents for Higher Education, 339 U.S. 637 (1950b).

Michel, L., & Herbeck, D. (2001). *American terrorist: Timothy McVeigh & the Oklahoma City bombing.* New York: Regan Books.

Miller, R. T., & Flowers, R. B. (1977). *Toward benevolent neutrality: Church, state, and the Supreme Court.* Waco: Markham Press Fund.

Miller, L., & France, D. (2002, March 4). Sins of the father. *Newsweek, 139*, 42–50.

Minnesota v. Philip Morris et al., Case Docket # C1-94-8565. St. Paul, MN: Court Records, (1998).

Minow, M. (1996). Stories in law. In P. Gewirtz & P. Brooks (Eds.), *Law's stories: Narrative and rhetoric in the law* (pp. 24–36). New Haven: Yale University Press.

———. (1997). *Not only for myself: Identity, politics & the law.* New York: The New Press.

Miranda v. Arizona, 384 U.S. 436 (1966).

Model Code of Professional Responsibility. (1980). Chicago: American Bar Association. Retrieved July 5, 2006, from www.abanet.org/cpr/ethics/mcpr.pdf.

Model Rules of Professional Conduct. (1983). Chicago: American Bar Association. 2002 version retrieved July 5, 2006, from www.abanet.org/cpr/mrpc_toc.htm.

Moldea, D. E. (as told by T. Lange & P. Vannatter). (1997). *Evidence dismissed: The true story of the police investigation of O. J. Simpson.* New York: Pocket Books.

Mollenkamp, C., Levy, A., Menn, J., & Rothfeder, J. (1998). *The people vs. Big Tobacco: How the states took on the cigarette giants.* Princeton, NJ: Bloomberg Press.

Montgomery, R. H. (1960). *Sacco-Vanzetti: The murder and the myth.* New York: Devin-Adair Co.

Morgan, E. M., & Joughin, G. L. (1948). *The legacy of Sacco and Vanzetti.* New York: Harcourt, Brace and Company

MSNBC news. (2002, May 3). Church rejects deal in abuse cases.

Murphy, C. (2002, May 5). Is Saint Pat's for sale? *Fortune, 145,* 32–34.

Murphy, J. J., & Katula, R. A. (with F. I. Hill, D. J. Ochs, & P. A Meador). (1994). *A synoptic history of classical rhetoric* (2nd ed.). Davis, CA: Hermagoras Press.

Murray, P. L. (1995). *Basic trial advocacy.* Boston: Little, Brown.

Murray, R. (1964). *Red scare: A study of national hysteria: 1919–1920.* New York: McGraw-Hill.

Musmanno, M. A. (1939). *After twelve years.* New York: Alfred A. Knopf.

Myers, R. D., & Griller, G. M. (1997). Educating jurors means better trials: Jury reform in Arizona. *The Judges' Journal, 36,* 13–17.

Nation. (1970, March 2). A commentary, *200,* 5.

Nelson, B. (1995). Rhetoric and law: Understanding the differences among Supreme Court decisions. Unpublished M.A. thesis. Minneapolis: University of Minnesota.

Nelson, D. (1988). A judge's reaction. In J. Schuetz & K. Snedaker (Eds.), *Communication and litigation: Case studies of famous trials* (pp. 213–216). Carbondale: Southern Illinois University Press.

Niehoff, K. (2004, January 21). The church tribunals and the pedophile cases. Speech. Albuquerque, NM: Aquinas Newman Center. (Notes of author).

Ny, S. H., & Bradac, J. J. (1993). *Power in language: Verbal communication and social influence.* Newbury Park: CA: Sage Publications.

O'Barr, W. M. (1982). *Linguistic evidence: Language, power, and strategy in the courtroom.* New York: Academic Press.

O'Connor, T. (1961). The origin of the Sacco-Vanzetti case. *Vanderbilt Law Review, 14,* 987–1006.

O. J. Verdict. (2005, October 4). *FRONTLINE.* New York: Public Broadcasting Company.

O'Keefe, D. J. (1977). Two concepts of argument. *Journal of the American Forensic Association, 13,* 121–128.

———. (2002). *Persuasion: Theory and research.* Newbury Park, CA: Sage Publications.

Okpaku, J., & Sadock, V. (1970). *Verdict! The exclusive picture story of the trial of the Chicago Eight.* New York: Third Press.

Online Newshour. (2002, December 13). Cardinal Law's resignation statement. Retrieved December 30, 2002, from pbs.org/newshour/updates/december02/law_resignations

———. (2002, March 13). Church in turmoil. Retrieved August 10, 2003, from pbs.org/newshour/bb/religion/jan-jun02/priests.

Orey, M. (1999). *The mavericks, the lawyers, and the whistle-blowers who beat big tobacco.* Boston: Little Brown.

Parker, J. (1950). Improving appellate methods. *New York University Law Review, 25,* 1–30.

Parrish, J. (Ed.) (1995). *Abortion law in the United States: From* Roe v. Wade *to the present.* Vol. 1. New York: Garland.

Patterson, J. T. (2001). Brown v. Board of Education: *A civil rights milestone and its troubled legacy.* Oxford: Oxford University Press.

Paulson, M. (2002, July 27). Law defends his response in clergy sex abuse case. *Boston Globe*, p. A1.

———. (2002, November 4). Cardinal begs abuse victims' forgiveness. *Boston Globe*, p. A1.

———. (2002, December 10). 58 priests send a letter urging cardinal to resign. *Boston Globe*, p. A1

———. (2002, December 11). More priests ask to sign letter to Law. *Boston Globe*, p. A39.

———. (2002, December 14). A church seeks healing. *Boston Globe*, p. A1.

———. (2002, December 16). New archdiocesan leader vows to work for healing. *Boston Globe*, p. A1.

Paulson, M., & Farragher, T. (2002, June 15). Bishops move to bar abusers. *Boston Globe*, p. A1.

Paulson, M., & Pfeiffer, S. (2002, June 14). Apologies sent; policy sought. *Boston Globe*, p. A1.

Peczenik, A. (1995). Formal aspects of legal reasoning. *Argumentation, 5*, 747–756.

Pennington, N., & Hastie, R. (1993). The story model of juror decision making. In R. Hastie (Ed.), *Inside the juror: The psychology of juror decision making* (pp. 192–218). Cambridge: Cambridge University Press.

People v. Belous, 71 Cal. 2d 954 (1969).

Perelman, Ch. (1963). *The idea of justice and the problem of argument.* London: Routledge and Kegan Paul.

———. (1967). *Justice.* New York: Random House.

———. (1980). *Justice, law, and argument: Essays on moral and leal reasoning.* Dordrect, Holland: D. Riedel.

Perelman, Ch., & Olbrechts-Tyteca, L. M. (1969). *The new rhetoric: A treatise on argument.* (J. Wilkinson & P. Weaver, Trans.). Notre Dame, IN: University of Notre Dame Press.

Pfeiffer, S. (2002, January 25). Letters exhibit gentle approach toward priest. *Boston Globe*, p. A21.

———. (2002, February 13). Woman says church ignored her outcries. *Boston Globe*, p. B1.

Pfeiffer, S., & Kurkjian, S. (2002, January 27). Law visits Geoghan parish. *Boston Globe*, p. A25.

———. (2002, January 28). Church settled 6 suits vs. priest. *Boston Globe*, p. A6.

Philadelphia & T.R. Co. v. Stimpson (1840).

Planned Parenthood v. Casey, 112 S. Ct. 2791 (1992).

Plessy v. Ferguson, 163 U.S. 537 (1896).

Pojman, L. P., & Beckwith, F. J. (1998). *The abortion controversy: 25 years after* Roe v. Wade. Belmont, CA: Wadsworth.

Pollard, A. W. (1904). *English miracle plays, moralities, and interludes: Specimens of pre-Elizabethan drama.* New York: Clarendon Press.

Posner, R. A. (1990). *The problems of jurisprudence.* Cambridge: Harvard University Press.

Powers, W. (2002, April 23). Sex, lies and journalists. *Atlantic.* Retrieved August 7, 2004, from www.theaatlantic.com.

Prentice, R. (1983). Supreme Court rhetoric. *Arizona Law Review, 25*, 85–95.

Pringle, P. (1999). The chronicles of tobacco: An account of the forces that brought the tobacco industry to the negotiating table. *William Mitchell Law Review, 25,* 387–395.

Rabin, R. (2001). The third wave of tobacco tort litigation. In R. Rabin & S. D. Sugarman (Eds.), *Regulating tobacco* (pp. 176–206). New York: Oxford University Press.

Race in America. (1995, July 25). Executive Producer, Dan Rather. *48 HOURS.* New York: CBS Television.

Ranalli, R. (2002, January 28). Cardinal tries to allay parishioners' fear, anger. *Boston Globe*, p. A1.

Rapoport, A. (1970). *Fights, games, and debates.* Ann Arbor: University of Michigan Press. (Originally published 1967)

———. (1999). *Two-person game theory.* New York: Dover.

———. (2001). *N-person game theory: Concepts and applications.* Ann Arbor: University of Michigan Press. (Originally published in 1970)

Regulation of tobacco products. (1994). Hearings before the Subcommittee on Health and the Environment of the Committee on Energy and Commerce. House Report. U.S. Congress, 103rd Congress. Sess. 104-149, Vol. 1 & 2. Washington, DC: U.S. Government Printing.

Rehnquist, W. H. (2001). *The Supreme Court.* New York: Knopf

Rezendes, M., & Carroll, M. (2002, January 1). Accusers' accounts tell of abuse and its scars. *Boston Globe*, p. A1.

———. (2002, January 16). Doctors who OK'd Geoghan lacked expertise, report shows. *Boston Globe*, p. A1.

———. (2002, January 26). Accusers' accounts tell of abuse and its scars. *Boston Globe*, p. A12.

———. (2002, February 8). 6 more priests removed on allegations of abuse. *Boston Globe*, p. A1.

———. (2002, August 8). $10m Geoghan deal is dwarfed by others. *Boston Globe*, p. A1.

———. (2002. October 4). 17 more allege abuse by Geoghan, file suit. *Boston Globe*, p. B1.

———. (2002, November 13). Advocates for victims release priest names. *Boston Globe*, p. B1.

Rezendes, M., & Pfeiffer, S. (2002, September 13). Diocese records show more cover-ups. *Boston Globe*, p. B1.

Richmond Newspaper Inc. v. Virginia, 448 U.S. 555 (1980).

Rieke, R. D. (1982). Argumentation in the legal process. In J. R. Cox & C. A. Willard (Eds.), *Advances in argumentation theory & research* (pp. 363–378). Carbondale: Southern Illinois Univ. Press.

———. (1986). The evolution of judicial justification: Perelman's concept of the rational and the reasonable. In J. L. Golden & J. J. Pilotta (Eds.), *Practical reasoning in human affairs* (pp. 227–244). Boston: D. Reidel.

Rieke, R. D., Sillars, M. O., & Petersen, T. R. (2005). *Argument and critical decision making* (6th ed.). Boston: Pearson.

Rieke, R. D., & Stutman, R. K. (1990). *Communication and legal advocacy.* Columbia: University of South Carolina Press.

Ripley, A. (2002, May 5). Inside the church's closet. *Time, 159*, 60–64.

Roberts v. City of Boston, 59 Mass. 198 (1850).

Robinson, W. V. (2002, February 24). Hundreds now claim priest abuse. *Boston Globe*, p. A1.

———. (2002, March 5). $20m accord seen in Geoghan cases. *Boston Globe*, p. A1.

———. (2002, March 12). Diocese, plaintiffs settle suit. *Boston Globe*, p. A1.

———. (2002, September 19). Geoghan victims agree to $10m settlement. *Boston Globe*, p. A1.

Robinson, W. V., & Pfeiffer, S. (2002, February 20). Allegations surface v. Abington pastor. *Boston Globe*, p. B8.

Robinson, W. V., & Rezendes, M. (2002, August 19). Geoghan victims agree to $10m settlement. *Boston Globe*, p. A1.

Roe v. Wade, 314 F. Supp. 1217 (1970).

Roe v. Wade, 410 U,S. 113 (1973).

Ross v. Philip Morris, 328 F 2d 3 (1962).

Ross v. Philip Morris, 164 F Supp 683 (1964).

Ross, W. S. (1976). *The last hero: Charles A. Lindbergh*. New York: Harper & Row.

Ruddy, C. (2002, June 6). The American church's sexual abuse crisis. *America, 186,* 19–26.

Russell, F. (1971). *Tragedy in Dedham*. New York: McGraw-Hill.

Rybak, D. C., & Phelps, D. (1998). *Smoked: The inside story of the Minnesota tobacco trial.* Minneapolis, MN: MSP Books.

Sacco case up today. (1921, October 22). *New York Times*, p. 6.

Sannito, T. (1981). Psychological courtroom strategies. *Trial Diplomacy Journal, 4,* 30–35.

Sannito, T., & McGovern, P. J. (1985). *Courtroom psychology for trial lawyers.* New York: John Wiley and Sons.

Sarat, A. (1987). *Race, law and culture: Reflections on* Brown v. Board of Education. New York: Oxford University Press.

Savellos, E. E., & Galvin, R. F. (2001). *Reasoning in law.* Belmont, CA: Wadsworth.

Scaduto, A. (1976). *Scapegoat: The lonesome death of Bruno Richard Hauptmann*. New York: G. P. Putnam's Sons.

Scallen, E. A. (1995). American legal argumentation: The law and literature/rhetoric movement. *Argumentation, 5,* 705–717.

Scandals won't mute church's political voice. (2002, November). *Church & State, 55,* 18–20.

Scelfo, J. (2002, June 24). Witness to shame. *Newsweek, 139,* 81–84.

Schelling, T. C. (1960). *The strategy of conflict.* Cambridge: Oxford University Press.

Schlumpf, H. (2002, October). Down but not out. *U.S. Catholic, 67,* 24–28.

Scholes, R., & Kellogg, R. (1966). *The nature of narrative.* London: Oxford University Press.

Schopenhauer, A. (1942). The art of controversy. In T. B. Saunders (Ed.), *Complete essays of Schopenhauer* (pp. 1–42). New York: John Wiley & Sons.

Schuetz, J. (1970). A Ciceronian analysis of the Coeur d' Alene Riot Trial of 1899. Unpublished M.A thesis. Pittsburg, KS: Pittsburg State University.

———. (1975). A contingent model of argumentation based on a game-theory paradigm. Dissertation Abstracts International, No. 76-394b. Ann Arbor: University of Michigan.

———. (1983). Staging the courtroom drama: An analysis of direct and cross-examination. In R. J. Matlon & R. J. Crawford (Eds.), *Communication and the practice of lawyering* (pp. 367–379). Annandale, VA: Speech Communication Association.

———. (1994). *The logic of women on trial.* Carbondale: Southern Illinois University Press.

————. (2001). Criminal trial process. In M. A. Dupont-Morales, M. K. Hooper, & J. H. Schmidt (Eds.), *Handbook of criminal justice administration* (pp. 205–221). New York: Marcel Dekker.

————. (2002). *Episodes in the rhetoric of government Indian relations.* New York: Praeger.

————. (2003). Assessing legal literacy. Unpublished manuscript, Albuquerque: University of New Mexico.

————. (2004). Argument of victims: A case study of the Timothy McVeigh trial. In F. H. Van Eemeren & P. Houtlosser (Eds.), *Argumentation in practice* (pp. 197–214). Philadelphia: John Benjamins.

————. (2005). Blogs, argument, and the Terry Schiavo case. Unpublished conference paper. Alta Conference on Argumentation. Alta, Utah.

Schuetz, J., & Lilley, L. S. (1999). *The O. J. Simpson trials: Rhetoric, media, and the law.* Carbondale: Southern Illinois University Press.

Schuetz, J., & Snedaker, K. H. (1988). *Communication and litigation: Case studies of famous trials.* Carbondale: Southern Illinois University Press.

Schwartz, B. (1996). *Decision: How the Supreme Court decides cases.* Oxford: Oxford University Press.

Scopes, J. T., & Presley, J. (1967). *The center of the storm: Memoirs of John T. Scopes.* New York: Holt, Rinehart and Winston.

Sennott, C. M. (2002, December 11). Law to confer with Pope, 2 officials say. *Boston Globe,* p. A1.

Serrano, R. A. (1998). *One of ours. Timothy McVeigh and the Oklahoma City Bombing.* New York: W. W. Norton.

Spark, D. (1999). *Investigative reporting.* Boston: Focal Press.

Spence, G. (1995, February). Let me tell you a story. *Trial, 31,* 72–79.

Shapiro, R. L. (with L. Warren). (1996). *The search for justice: A defense attorney's brief on the O. J. Simpson case.* New York: Warner Books.

Sheler, J. (2002, February 11). Unholy crisis. *U.S. News & World Report, 132,* 24–25.

Sheppard v. Maxwell, 384 U.S. 333 (1966).

Siedman, L. M. (1977). The trial and execution of Bruno Richard Hauptmann. *Georgetown Law Journal, 66,* 1–48.

Simmel, G. (1968). The dramatic actor and reality. In J. E. Combs & M. W. Mansfield (Eds.), *Drama in life: The uses of communication in society* (pp. 59–61). London: Oxford Univ. Press.

Simpson legacy. (1995, October 9). *Los Angeles Times,* pp. S1–10.

Sipuel v. Board of Regents of the University of Oklahoma, 332 U.S. 631 (1948).

Sinclair, U. (1928). *Boston.* New York: Boni Press.

Sipe, A. W. R. (1995). *Sex, priests, and power.* New York: Brunner/Mazel.

Slade, J., Bero, L., Hanauer, P., Barnes, D. E., & Glantz, S.A. (1995). Nicotine and addiction: The Brown and Williamson documents. *Journal of the American Medical Association, 274,* 225–233.

Smith, D. G. (1996). The historical and constitutional contexts of jury reform. *Hofstra Law Review, 25,* 377–506.

Smith, L. J. (1978). *Art of advocacy: Summation.* New York: Matthew Bender.

Smith, L. J., & Malandro, L. A. (1985). *Courtroom communication strategies.* New York: Kluwer Publishers.

Soetman, A. (1995). Formal aspects of legal reasoning. *Argumentation, 5,* 731–746.

Solinger, R. (1998). *Abortion wars: A half century of struggle, 1950–2000.* Berkeley: University of California Press.

Spangenberg, C. (1977). Basic values and techniques of persuasion. *Litigation, 3,* 13.

———. (1982). What I try to accomplish in an opening statement. In G. W. Holmes (Ed.), *Opening statements and closing arguments* (pp. 247–252). Ann Arbor, MI: Institute of Continuing Legal Education.

Spence, G. (1995, February). Let me tell you a story. *Trial, 31,* 72–79.

Spotlight Team. (2002, January 6). Church allowed abuse by priest for years. *Boston Globe*, p. A1.

———. (2002, January 7). Geoghan preferred preying on poorer children. *Boston Globe*, p. A1.

———. (2002, January 20). Text of Cardinal Bernard F. Law's open letter. *Boston Globe*, p. B4.

———. (2002, January 29). Documents show church long supported Geoghan. *Boston Globe*, p. A1.

———. (2002, January 31). Scores of priests involved in sex abuse cases. *Boston Globe*, p. A1.

———. (2002, December 18). Lennon to outline goals for archdiocese. *Boston Globe*, p. B4.

Staff report on free press-fair trial. (1976). U.S. Congress Senate Committee on the Judiciary, 94th Congress, 2d. Session, p. 8.

Starr, V. H. (1983). From the communication profession: Communication strategies and research needs on opening statements and closing arguments. In R. J. Matlon & R. J. Crawford (Eds.), *Communication strategies in the practice of lawyering* (pp. 424–448). Annandale, VA: Speech Communication Association of America.

Starr, H. V., & McCormick, M. (1993). *Jury selection: An attorney's guide to jury law and methods* (2nd ed.). Boston: Little, Brown.

Stein, J. A. (1985). *Closing argument*. Wilmette, IL: Callaghan.

Steinfels, P. (2002, April 19). The church's sex-abuse crisis. *Commonweal, 129,* 13–20.

Stern, R. L., Gressman, E., & Shapiro, S. M. (1986). *Supreme Court practice.* Washington, DC: Bureau of National Affairs.

Stevenson, D. W. (1975, October). Writing effective opinions. *Judicature, 59,* 134–139.

Stewart, C. J., Smith C. A., & Denton, R. E., Jr. (2001). *Persuasion and social movements.* Long Grove, IL: Waveland Press.

Stickney, B. M. (1996). *All American monster: The unauthorized biography of Timothy McVeigh.* Amsherst, NY: Prometheus Books.

Styan, J. L. (1973). *Drama, stage, and audience.* New York: Cambridge University Press.

Sullivan, A. (2002, June 6). Catholic church: Sexual misconduct by clergy. *Time, 159,* 63–65.

Sullivan, P. (1996). *Days of hope: Race and democracy in the New Deal era.* Chapel Hill: University of North Carolina Press.

Sunstein, C. R. (1996). *Legal reasoning and political conflict.* New York: Oxford University Press.

Surrette, R. (1989). Media trials. *Journal of Criminal Justice, 17,* 293–308.

———. (1992). *Media: Crime and criminal justice.* Menlo Park, CA: Brooks/Cole.

Swann, W. B., Giulano, T., & Wegner, D. M. (1982). Where questions can lead: The power of conjecture in social interaction. *Journal of Personality and Social Psychology, 42,* 1025–1035.

Swain v. Alabama, 380 U.S. 202 (1965).

Sweatt v. Painter, 339 U.S. 629 (1950).

Tanford, J. A. (1983). *The trial process: Law, tactics and ethics.* Charlottesville, VA: The Miche Company.

Taylor v. Louisiana, 419 U.S. 529 (1975).

Tobacco global settlement archives. (1999). Hearings before the Subcommittee on Commerce, Science and Transportation, 105th Cong. 1st Sess. Washington, DC: U.S. Government Printing.

Topp, M. M. (2005). *The Sacco-Vanzetti case: A brief history with documents.* New York: Palgrave Macmillan.

Toulmin, S. (1960). *The uses of argument.* London: Cambridge University Press.

———. (2001). *Return to reason.* Cambridge, MA: Harvard University Press.

Toulmin, S., Rieke, R., & Janik, A. (1979). *An introduction to reasoning.* New York: Macmillan.

Trapp, R., & Schuetz, J. (Eds.). (2006). *Perspectives on argumentation: Essays in honor of Wayne Brockriede.* New York: International Debate Educational Association. (Originally published 1990.)

Trial Record (Chicago Eight). (1969). *United States of America v. David T. Dellinger, Rennard C. Davis, Thomas E. Hayden, Abbott Hoffman, Jerry C. Rubin, Lee Weiner, John R. Froines, and Bobby G. Seale.* Reprinted & abridged. (1970). Judy Clavir & John Spitzer (Eds.). *The conspiracy trial.* New York: Bobbs-Merrill. Page citations in text are to the 1970 reprint.

Trial Record (Hauptmann). (1935). *State of New Jersey v. Bruno Richard Hauptmann.* Reprint, Chicago: University of Chicago Archives. Page citations in text are to the reprint published in 1937.

Trial Record (McVeigh). (1997). *U.S. v. Timothy James McVeigh.* Case No. 96-CR-68. Retrieved from http:\\205.181.114.35/casefiles/oklahoma/transcripts/0605om.html.

Trial Record (Minnesota Tobacco). Putnam Pit Trial Transcripts (1998). *State of Minnesota and Blue Cross and Blue Shield of Minnesota, Plaintiffs, v. Philip Morris, Inc., Et. Al.*, Defendants, Docket # C1-94-8565. Retrieved from http:\www.putnampit.com/tobacco/transcript.html

Trial Record (Sacco and Vanzetti). (1969). *State of Massachusetts v. Nicola Sacco and Bartolomeo Vanzetti.* New York: Paul A. Appel. (Originally published 1929)

Trial Record (Simpson). (1995). *California v. Orenthal James Simpson.* Retrieved from http://www.islandnet.com/-wlraven/simpson/html.

Tribe, L. H. (1990). *Abortion: The clash of opposites.* New York: W. W. Norton.

Turner, V. J. (1982). *From ritual to theatre.* New York: PAJ Publications.

———. (1988). *The anthropology of performance.* New York: PAJ Publications.

Tushnet, M. (1994). *Making civil rights law.* New York: Basic.

Tushnet, M., & Lezin, K. (1991, December). What really happened in *Brown v. Board of Education? Columbia Law Review, 91*, 1185–1250.

Uelman, G. F. (1996). *Lessons from the trial. O. J. Simpson.* Kansas City: Andrews and McMeel.

Underwood, R. H. (1997). The limits of cross-examination. *American Journal of Trial Advocacy, 21*, 113–128.

Uniform Jury Selection Act, 13 U.LA. 509 (1980).

United States v. Vuitch, 402 U.S. 62 (1971).

U.S. Conference of Catholic Bishops. (2002, June 14). *Charter for the protection of children and young people.* Retrieved July 5, 2006, from www.boston.com/globe/abuse.

U.S. Federal Code, 3 U.S.C. 5, 1990.

Vacek, E. (2002, December 16). Acting more humanely: Accepting gays in the priesthood. *America, 187*, 10–14.

Vandevelde, K. (1998). *Thinking like a lawyer: An introduction to legal reasoning.* Boulder, CO: Westview Press.

Voth, B. (1998). The wall separating church and state: A longitudinal analysis of metaphor as argument. *Argumentation and Advocacy, 34*, 127–139.

Walburn, R. B. (1999). Minnesota's document intensive strategy. *William Mitchell Law Review, 25*, 489–498.

Waller, G. (1961). *Kidnap: The story of the Lindbergh case.* New York: Dial Press.

Warner, A. (1921, September 28). Sacco and Vanzetti: A reasonable doubt. *Nation*, 343–345.

Weaver, R. M. (1953). *The ethics of rhetoric.* Chicago: Henry Regnery.

Weber, D. (2002, July 17). Law admits to receiving 1984 warning on Geoghan. *Boston Herald*, p. A12.

Webster v. Reproductive Health Services, 492 U.S. 490 (1989).

Wechsler, H. (1964). The nature of judicial reasoning. In S. Hook (Ed.), *Law and philosophy* (pp. 290–300). New York: New York University Press.

Weddington, S. (1992). *A question of choice.* New York: Penguin.

Weinberg, M. (1967). *Race and place: A legal history of the neighborhood school.* Washington, DC: GPO.

Weiner, F. B. (1967). *Briefing and arguing federal appeals.* Washington, DC: Bureau of National Affairs.

Weisberg, R. (1996). Proclaiming trials narratives: Premises and pretenses. In P. Brooks & P. Gewirtz (Eds.), *Law's stories: Narrative and rhetoric in law* (pp. 61–83). New Haven: Yale University Press.

Wellman, F. L. (1925). *The art of cross-examination.* New York: Macmillan.

Wenzel, J. W. (2006). Three perspectives on argument: Rhetoric, dialectic, logic. In R. Trapp & J. Schuetz (Eds.), *Perspectives on argumentation: Essays in honor of Wayne Brockriede* (pp. 9–26). New York: International Debate Educational Association.

Whipple, S. B. (1937). *The trial of Bruno Richard Hauptmann.* New York: Doubleday.

White, J. B. (1984). *When words lose their meaning.* Chicago: University of Chicago Press.

———. (1985). *Heracles' bow: Essays on the rhetoric and poetics of the law.* Madison: University of Wisconsin Press.

———. (1990). *Justice as translation.* Chicago: University of Chicago Press.

Whitman, M. (2004). Brown v. Board of Education. Princeton: Markus Wiener Publishing. (Originally published 1994)

Who killed the Lindbergh baby? (1985). Boston: Public Broadcasting System television.

Wigmore, J. H. (1940). *Evidence in trials in common law.* Boston: Little, Brown. (Originally published in 1905)

Wilder, M. J. (1998). The rule of law, the rise of violence, and the role of morality: Reframing Americas's abortion debate. In R. Solinger (Ed.), *Abortion wars: A half century of struggle, 1950–2000* (pp. 73–94). Berkeley: University of California Press.

Wilkie, C. (1981). The scapegoating of Bruno Richard Hauptmann: The rhetorical process in prejudicial publicity. *Central States Speech Journal, 32*, 102–110.

Wilkinson, J. H. Jr. (1979). *From Brown to Bakke: The Supreme Court and school integration 1954–78.* Oxford: Oxford University Press.

Williams, J. (1998). *Thurgood Marshall: American revolutionary.* New York: Times Books.

Wilson, P. (1995). *A time to lose: Representing Kansas in* Brown v. Board of Education. Lawrence: University of Kansas Press.

Winter, S. (1989, April). Transcendental nonsense: Metaphoric reasoning and cognitive states for law. *University of Pennsylvania Law Review, 137*, 1105–1237.

324   Bibliography

Wright, E. A. (1972). *Understanding today's theatre.* Englewood Cliffs, NJ: Prentice-Hall.
Yarnold, B. M. (1995). *Abortion politics in the federal courts: Right versus right.* West-port, CT: Praeger.
Young, W., & Kaiser, W. E. (1985). *Postmortem: New evidence in the case of Sacco-Vanzetti.* Amherst: University of Massachusetts Press.
Zarefsky, D. (1998). Definitions. In J. F. Klumpp (Ed.), *Argument in a time of change: Definitions, frameworks, and critiques* (pp. 1–11). Annandale, VA: National Communication Association.
Zegart, D. (2000). *Civil warriors.* New York: Bantam Dell.
Zoll, R. (2004, February 13). Panel faults bishops. *Albuquerque Tribune*, pp. A1–A9.

Index